MW00564040

THE BEAR RIVER MASSACRE
AND
THE MAKING OF HISTORY

THE BEAR RIVER
MASSACRE
AND
THE MAKING OF
HISTORY

KASS FLEISHER

*For Jenna,
a fellow
seeker,
Kass Fleisher*

State University of New York Press

This work contains materials reprinted with the permission of the University of Utah Press and the National Park Service.

Two sections from Chapter 10 were published in another form in the *American Book Review*.

Cover photo of Bear River Massacre roadside sign used by permission of the National Park Service.

Published by
State University of New York Press, Albany

© 2004 State University of New York

All rights reserved

Printed in the United States of America

No part of this book may be used or reproduced in any manner whatsoever without written permission. No part of this book may be stored in a retrieval system or transmitted in any form or by any means including electronic, electrostatic, magnetic tape, mechanical, photocopying, recording, or otherwise without the prior permission in writing of the publisher.

For information, address State University of New York Press, 90 State Street, Suite 700, Albany, NY 12207

Production by Marilyn P. Semerad
Marketing by Fran Keneston

Library of Congress Cataloging-in-Publication Data

Fleisher, Kass, 1959–
    The Bear River Massacre and the making of history / Kass Fleisher.
        p. cm.
    Includes bibliographical references and index.
    ISBN 0-7914-6063-0 (alk. paper) — ISBN 0-7914-6064-9 (pb : alk. paper)
        1. Bear River Massacre, Idaho, 1863. 2. Shoshoni Indians—Wars, 1863–1865. 3. Connor, P. E. (Patrick Edward), 1820–1891. I. Title.

E83.863.F54 2004
973.7—dc22

2003059617

10 9 8 7 6 5 4 3 2 1

For
Joe Amato,
yokefellow,
and all survivors

In Memoriam:
Helen Eyler Wolford, 1908–85

Fellow citizens, we can not escape history.
        —Abraham Lincoln, Message to Congress,
        December 1, 1862 (59 days before the
        Bear River Massacre)

CONTENTS

PREFACE

On January 29, 1863, Union-affiliated California militiamen, with the silent consent of Abraham Lincoln, attacked a band of 450 Northwestern Shoshoni sleeping along the Bear River in southeastern Idaho, slaughtering about 280 men, women, and children. After the fighting, the troops interrupted their pillaging to rape native women, some of whom were dying from their wounds.

On first encountering the story of the Bear River Massacre and Rape, most readers are left with one abiding question: Why didn't we know about this? The reasons for the cultural erasure of one of the worst acts of genocide in the history of the United States are complicated indeed.

I will posit that the fault lies with how we make, and how we read, history itself.

What you hold in your hands is not a work of "history." I am not a historian and will not claim to be. I must apologize in advance for the fact that I am (I'm so sorry) *a novelist*. A language worker. In the first one-third of this book, this novelist will try to lay out for you the story of the massacre and rape, along with the historical context of that event. To this end, I have interpreted, selected and arranged the results of research by people who are historians, anthropologists, and so forth.

The remaining two-thirds of the book will seek to understand how this story got away from "us" (I mean U.S. citizens), and what attempts are now being made to reclaim it at a grassroots, local level. I will ask, finally, whether those attempts do in fact have the potential to help us understand who we are, where we have been, and how we might avoid repeating our mistakes.

I will also ask for whom this story should be recuperated. For instance, I disagree with the European American women activists who say they have struggled to bring this event to national attention *"for them"*—that is, for the Shoshoni who were the first victims of this slaughter. I tell this story, and ask its inevitable questions, for all of "us." My primary purpose is not to contribute to the academic realm we call "historical scholarship." I hope academic historians appreciate my parsing of history as a text, but I cannot expect them en masse to embrace a critique of their industry. My primary concern is for "us," a nation of citizens, a world of humans. Are we mere consumers of the history that determines who "we" are?

I will argue that the way we write history has itself partly doomed us to repeat history. In the 1980s, Patricia Nelson Limerick and others ushered in a "New History" that now allows, they hope, for "multiple points of view"; but, while this was a good first step, our multiple perspectives continue to be structured in ways that encourage reader passivity. In particular, the insistence on the erasure of the makers of history—that is, the absence of historians in history—has made it difficult for us—we citizens and active readers—to participate in that two-step we call "accuracy." The rhetoric of "objectivity" similarly protects readers from a search for accuracy; as does history's addiction to the linear, rising narrative, which itself is organized around a false sense of beginning, rising action, climax, and denouement.

In summary, I demand from the beginning my reader's active attention to this assertion: I assume the presence of error in this document.

But perhaps it is the obsession with category that has allowed the Bear River Massacre and Rape to evaporate from U.S. political consciousness. Is it U.S. history, Utah history, Idaho history, western history, Native American history, women's history, Mormon history, Civil War history—or all of the above? Categories simplify things for academic departments and publishing markets, but often do so reductively; the Bear River Massacre is a most complex example of the collisions resulting from that complication our nation calls "Manifest Destiny."

By way of enacting that collision, this work—which, in marketing terms, I call a work of "creative nonfiction"—will cross disciplines, genres, and rhetorical modes. As Paul Metcalf noted regarding the 1996 edition of his collected works, "the method I was developing was both creative and scholarly, a fact that must be recognized" (1:vii).[1] While I cannot hope to equal the radical breadth of Metcalf's oeuvre, I will ask my readers to indulge a mash of scholarship, journalism, memoir, film review, travelogue—etc. In this way, a rather "creative" form will intersect a more "scholarly" content, and appropriately so, since it is my thinking, for instance, that the history of a domination, such as the one the United States effected upon nineteenth century Native Americans, traverses oppressions—that sexism, say, is necessary to implement racism. Hence, rape begets massacre. So yes, I will be asking my more scholarly readers to tolerate a bit of creativity, and for that matter, creativity of a (dare I say it?) *postmodern* sort (much more on this ever and anon).

Also, as you may be guessing by now, I will also force you to meet your maker of history, warts and all. I apologize in advance for what may seem to you a distraction, perhaps even a self-absorption. But in the end, this book will have argued that history tells us as much or more about the teller, the cultural context of that teller's biases, and the telling itself—than it tells us about What Happened. I begin with the assumption that beginnings, after all, contain the assumptions entailed in the selection of where to begin. In particular, thinkers begin with beginning assumptions, which is to say, we begin our "research" with our beginning questions, which then, thanks to the research, change. This process of asking, changing, and re-asking is perhaps one of the most important, and one of the more obscure, aspects of the process of making history. When and how we change determines the outcome of that changing. Which then determines who we are as a people.

Prepare to see me change my mind.

To clarify: I do not hope to provide you with History As It Should Be. How historians respond to the issues I raise (since I'm not the first to raise them) remains, literally, their business. Rather, again, my primary question is for my fellow citizens. How will history change if our expectations of history do not? Do we need to learn to read differently, to ask the sorts of questions that will bring about a more interrogative form of historical discourse? Even as we profit from the sins of our nation's past, do we not permit ourselves to ignore those sins by perpetuating a history that does not hold itself accountable for how it is made?

Perhaps what I'm after is the ultimate complication: redemption. We the people will never accept full responsibility for events such as the Bear River Massacre and Rape as long as we collude in the erasure of the making of that history. The goal of this work, then, is the collective, cultural reclamation of our accountability for those processes—so that we might reclaim accountability for that history.

NOTE

1. I regard my use in these proceedings of parenthetical citation as something of a compromise. Interested readers will no doubt wish to explore the "curious" history of superscript technology (see Grafton), ultimately to ponder its effect on the immediacy and presumed accuracy of one's presentation. In another context entirely, Bruno Latour has elicited the following from Michel Serres: "Don't you laugh at learned articles in which each word is flanked by a number, whose corresponding footnote attributes that word to an owner, as though proper names were soon going to replace common nouns? Common nouns belong to everyone, and in an honest book the ideas come from the author" (Serres 81). You will find, as well, that I harbor my own suspicions regarding those signs we call "quotation marks." While what follows is surely informed by (impeachable) fact and (tentative) conjecture, I trust readers will locate as well some quotient of honesty at work throughout, even as I quote extensively from and paraphrase the work of researchers more able than myself.

ACKNOWLEDGMENTS

This work would not exist without the kindly intervention of several forces and friends. I owe a debt to all of my teachers, but in this case am especially grateful to Hunter Gray (né John Salter, Jr.), my Indian Studies instructor at the University of North Dakota, who has always been available for electronic pep talks when most needed. For pushing the stroller of an emerging feminist, I am also eternally indebted to Sandra Donaldson, also of the University of North Dakota, and Marilynn Desmond of Binghamton University. And John Myers, Robert Winston, and Michael Conlon taught me the process of critical reading.

Because Idaho State University was kind enough to hire me in 1994, I was well placed to browse their library's materials on the Bear River Massacre. Faculty and staff members Eric Love, Chris Loether, Dennis Walsh, Janne Goldbeck, and Mary Ellen Walsh pointed me toward other sources there. I also thank Tamise Van Pelt for allowing me to kill her plants during that hot, humid summer of 1998.

During that summer, I was warmly received in the homes of the five people who are making this history happen, who spoke to me at great length, and with a frankness that humbled me. In particular, Curtis Warner was most generous in squiring me to the Shoshone-Bannock Tribal Council hearing, and in setting me straight when this white chick got quite the wrong idea about things racial. And Brigham Madsen was so kind as to consult on historical materials and forward articles and documents—in short, to treat me as a peer when I was not, and never will be, his equal. Mae Timbimboo Parry, too, kindly tolerated my shortcomings. Kathy Griffin and Allie Hansen were excessively nice to this stranger.

Further, National Park Service staffers Catherine Spude, Fred York, Keith Dunbar, Holly Bundock, Jannette Wesley, Michelle Schneider, and Samantha Richardson have all been endlessly generous over the years with time, material, and contacts. These people are model civil servants to whom all who care about Bear River should be grateful.

Appreciative acknowledgment is made to the editors of *American Book Review*, who published earlier versions of two sections of chapter 10.

In the spring of 1999, I presented a summary of the concerns addressed in this work to a roundtable of McNickle fellows at the D'Arcy McNickle Center of the Newberry Library. I thank all of them for pointing out areas of potential controversy, and to A. Lavonne Ruoff for arranging that meeting. For similar input, thanks also to the members of the Front Range Feminist Scholars, especially Oneida Meranto; and the members of WMST-L, the electronic discussion list for the National Women's Studies Association.

This publication would not be possible without the gracious shepherding of James Peltz and Marilyn Semerad, at the State University of New York Press. I am also indebted to Susan Ruether for her last-stand editing of the final draft.

My eight-year obsession with this topic has dominated many a dinner party, coffee date, e-mail exchange, etc. Apologies and thanks go out to Tony Noel, Janet Grant, Judy Smith, John Salter III, Barbara Schott, Anne Dawid, Ross Wheeler, Will Peterson, Yvette Johnson-Hegge, Alan Jackson (former head of the Idaho Museum of Natural History), Barbara Jackson, Ami Petersen, Merwin Swanson, Eleni Varsamidou, Paul Barrett, Cole Swensen, Anne Waldman, Laura Wright, Charles Alexander, Bhanu Kapil Rider, Patrick Pritchett, Barbara Wilder, Ben Lo Bue (former history archivist at the University of Colorado), the Fleishers (Norm, Gail, J.D., Alison Lewin, and Jolene, wherever she may be), and the Amatos (Dominick, Mike, Linda Mahfoud, and Anne Baker).

My dearest readers are those best of friends who suffered through early drafts of this manuscript, providing loving dissection and piercing sustenance: Jacquelyn Fox-Good, Steve Tomasula, Maria Tomasula, and Laura Mullen.

And on every page, please find the scrawl of that invisible scrivener, Joe Amato, inked in abiding affection.

PART I

THE BEAR RIVER MASSACRE

WHEN THE WHITE MAN
DISCOVERED THIS COUNTRY
INDIANS WERE RUNNING IT—
NO TAXES OR TELEPHONES.
WOMEN DID ALL THE WORK—
THE WHITE MAN THOUGHT
HE COULD IMPROVE UPON
A SYSTEM LIKE THAT.

—A sign in the Pierre, South Dakota, governor's
office put up by local natives, as reported by
Mary Crow Dog (to Richard Erdoes)
in *Lakota Woman*

WHAT (WE THINK) HAPPENED

To begin with, the Cache Valley would become a geological and climactic phenomenon.

It would be a valley to die for.

Back in Triassic times, about 250 million years ago, North America moved west, bumping up against the floor of the Pacific Ocean. The continental plate crumbled along its western edge, and the oceanic crust began to slide down into the hot mantle of the earth. The compressed western edge of the continent crammed into the fractures we call thrust faults, while the oceanic floor, jammed underneath, served to raise a welt, to elevate the continent further.

Meanwhile, heat was building. Steam and molten basalt rose from the sinking oceanic plate, melting granite magma. The raised welt was weakened, until it slid toward the east, creating the Rocky Mountains. Later, two microcontinents would join to form the Cascades and British Columbia. Millions of years of volcanic action followed, and volcanic activity continued to develop eastward as the continent drifted west over this new oceanic trench.

Lava blanketed the bed of the Columbia Plateau, in what we now call southeastern Oregon. Meanwhile, the basin and range areas of the Rockies began to develop southward. Seismic activity suggests that these north-pointing faults, these chips out of the mountains, are still expanding the valleys, pulling the mountains apart as the whole system moves east at the same rate as does the volcanic hotspot that formed Old Faithful in Yellowstone National Park. This hotspot, and the ongoing basin and range faulting processes, have created hot springs in the southeastern Idaho region, some of them carbonated.

The "basin" of this area formed when the Cascade Mountains rose to block the drainage of water west to the Pacific.

An oddly tropical climate may also have been caused by the Columbia Plateau's meteorite. The Ice Ages that followed that period brought still more precipitation to the region, with land near the ice sheets receiving generous moisture. Streams and rivers began to flow, and huge interior lakes formed in what is now Nevada and Utah, to drain these streams. Until about 15,000 years ago, near the end of what geologists call the Pleistocene Epoch, Lake Bonneville covered much of northwestern Utah and a good portion of southeastern Idaho. This inland sea, which in some places was nearly 1,000-feet deep, had no outlet, so the water backed up in pools and bays around the hills of the Wasatch Range.

What we now call the Cache Valley, in southeastern Idaho, was once the floor of the northernmost and easternmost bay, and the recipient of rich sediment.

When its walls could no longer hold these great waters, the Bonneville basin overflowed, sending a massive torrent of water crashing through the weak spot we now call Red Rock Pass. The spill water cascaded along Marsh Creek, into the Portneuf River, and then (north and west of present-day Pocatello) into the Snake River, scrubbing out the canyon walls we still see there, and dumping, among other items, several massive basalt boulders we now call Massacre Rocks. The floodwater crashed west, creating the Columbia River Gorge.

Once the Cache Valley had been drained empty, the Bear River found its oddly circuitous course: north from Utah into Wyoming; then west into Idaho's towns of Montpelier and Soda Springs (where it is damned at the Alexander Reservoir); passing Bear Lake; then south to Preston, Idaho; then back into Utah, passing Tremonton; ultimately spilling into the Great Salt Lake.

Salt Lake is what's left of Lake Bonneville, and two ancient water levels can be perceived in the "bathtub rings" on the mountains surrounding Salt Lake. The higher ring is the sea level at the time of the flood; the one 300 feet below that is the new sea level, created a few weeks later when water levels stabilized. About seven thousand years after the flood, a dry period reduced the water to contemporary levels, causing dozens of other less visible rings. The two major bathtub rings are actually benchlands, sandy deposits created by the ancient shores of Lake Bonneville, complete with still visible dunes and "beaches."

Stand on the benchlands east of Salt Lake City and look down into town, and you're looking at an empty ocean floor. A dead sea.

The Bonneville Flood occurred roughly simultaneously with the last Ice Age fifteen thousand years ago. Continental ice sheets enabled a migration, across the Bering Strait, of "Pleistocene mammals," and—some say—the northern Asians who hunted them. The giant elephants, mammoths, and bison, and their predators crossed from Siberia to Alaska; then, to avoid the encroaching ice fields, traveled east and south. The peoples of southern Idaho arrived about fourteen thousand years ago, fishing the abundant waters, and hunting the su-persized animals. Some scientists theorize that, because these peoples entered North America via the frigid north, the parasites and mi-crobes that cause disease may not have survived the journey. Conse-quently, millennia later, the immune systems of the descendants of these hyper-healthy voyagers may have been more vulnerable to dis-ease imported from Europe.

Eight thousand years ago, the climate began to dry, and the rivers and streams began to recede along with the great lake. Of the many valleys carved into southeastern Idaho and northeastern Utah by faults and water, the Cache Valley was the lushest. It was green and, compared to other regions, rainy; and it boasted hot springs that could warm people in winter. Ample buffalo and other large game grazed nearby.

The people who shared the bounties of this prized valley, while other valleys dried into desert, were lucky people indeed.

An immediate difficulty for European American anthropologists studying Native American history is the question of who was where when. It is not the only way to organize the history of this region, but we European Americans tend to see history that way, perhaps be-cause our society is organized around private property, and around the boundaries that must perforce exist in order to maintain private property. This presupposition makes for a cumbersome discussion of what was.

Actually, native groups were divided by geographical and climatic circumstances, which circumstances affected food supply. Geograph-ical overlap of habitat "boundaries" was inevitable. Two or more groups might utilize an area or a food supply, sometimes happily, sometimes not. And power shifts caused permeable boundaries, as well; according to Merle W. Wells, the mid-eighteenth century saw

Shoshone domination of a vast area of the Great Plains, this because the Shoshone's southwestern relatives helped them obtain and adapt to the horse more quickly. But a smallpox outbreak in 1781 curtailed this power just as their Plains neighbors, the Blackfeet, obtained firearms from the French. By the time Lewis and Clark visited Sakakawea, who was a Lemhi Shoshone, Shoshone boundaries had retreated west toward the Rockies.

Cultural anthropologists have found it easier, then, to locate on a map the placement of language stocks and families—distinct languages that could be mutually understood. The Shoshone language is part of the Numic family, which is part of the Utaztecan stock. Prior to European invasion, the Utaztecan language stock extended from (what we now call) western Wyoming to western Oregon; from western Kansas to eastern California; from northern Oregon and north-central Idaho to central Mexico. Not all of these inhabitants spoke in the exact same way; but, for instance, the Bannock Indians, who now share the Fort Hall Reservation with the Northern Shoshone, speak a dialect closely related to Northern Paiute. Bannock and Paiute are both of the Paviotso language, which is also part of the Numic family. Thus, the Bannock and the Northern Shoshone could communicate with one another, and often shared resources in southeastern Idaho— and shared the work of resisting the white emigrant invasion. On the other hand, the Nez Percé peoples of northern and western Idaho speak a language that is part of the Penutian stock. Anthropologist Deward E. Walker, Jr. points out that the difference between the Penutian and Utaztecan stocks can be roughly compared to the differences between the Sino-Tibetan and Indo-European stocks in the Old World. Which is to say, they were unable to communicate easily.

Such vast differences in linguistic practice are the result, Walker says, of thousands of years of separate developmental paths caused by geology, climate, and other factors. These linguistic differences might explain the fact that while the Shoshone and Nez Percé shared some lifeways and resources, they did not unite to resist the invasion by Europeans of "Idaho," but instead responded separately, and therefore, possibly, less effectively. But how did they share resources, given the language differences? Walker reports that native peoples were able to speak several languages. Children were sometimes exchanged so that they could learn various languages, and Chinook Jargon, a lingua franca, developed in the Northwest, so as to enable commerce. Further, and as popularly portrayed in old "Western" movies, an extensive sign language existed between nations. Natives responded to new European languages similarly. When the French arrived, native inhabitants of northern Idaho often learned French; French loan words appear in the Kutenai, Kalispel, Coeur d'Alene, and Nez Percé languages.

Spanish loan words are present in the languages spoken in southern Idaho because their shared Numic language family made for a cousinlike relationship between the Shoshone and the Ute, the Paiute, the Gosiute, and the Comanche. The Comanche gained access to Spanish resources after New Mexico was colonized in 1598; the horse, brought to the Western Hemisphere by the Spanish, quickly traveled north, on a trade route of shared languages.

And so, in the beginning, there was the shifting of tectonic plates. But there was also the word.

Since geology and climate defined food supply, they also affected tribal organization. The Shoshone, a Great Basin culture, organized itself into small bands led by the male members of the bands; the social practices of the bands differed depending on the resources to be found where they were located. Because the Great Basin is primarily a high-mountain desert area, bands frequently moved between various food and water sources, traveling to higher elevations in summer and lower elevations in winter, a nomadic practice that made the Shoshone one of the most ecologically efficient of the North American peoples, and perhaps, therefore, the most vulnerable to invasion, since they needed a vast habitat to sustain this efficiency. Staple foods included pine nuts and grass seeds; other foods included roots, cacti, insects, small game, and occasionally large game, including buffalo. Desert Shoshone interacted typically only with their closest neighbors, preferring, Walker says, a democratic, pacifist response, rather than war. Religious practice was also linked to the tenuousness of survival, with seasonal rituals intended to increase food supplies and individual vision quests intended to locate a tutelary spirit.

But northern Shoshone groups, living in the greener areas of southern Idaho, were, by Great Basin standards, rather wealthy. Those along the Snake River utilized the salmon runs and had access to game, birds, and edible plants. Northern bands were larger and several bands often united to consolidate power and resources. By the early eighteenth century the northern and eastern Shoshone were rich in horses, which sparked a cultural "efflorescence," as anthropologists call the explosion of cultural change and adaptation that occurs when two cultures meet. The horse, attained from the Spanish, did little for western Shoshone groups who lived on land too dry to sustain a horse's grazing needs. But in the north and the east, the migratory cycle could expand even farther on horseback, to as much as 1,200 miles per year; and band members did not have to move as often to obtain food, since food could be brought back to camp. Thus, meat became more frequent in the northern and eastern Shoshone diet.

The horse also meant that class differences began to develop according to horse ownership, and that the bison may have been hunted, as some academics believe, to near extinction in some areas. Some estimate that by the time of European American invasion, there were one or two horses per person, in a region whose population density was about one or two people per 100 square miles—a significant impact on that region's fragile, arid ecosystem.

Increasing game scarcity may have contributed to incursions farther and farther east into the Plains, in search of more bison, heightening contact—and hostilities—with the Plains peoples. Contact resulted in the adaptation of Plains war practices, such as counting coup—in which one warrior would claim conquest by touching (thus humiliating) an opponent, and both would ride off to fight another day—and the elevation of leaders based on successes at war. And, with the horse, the Spanish practice of scalping traveled from Mexico to the Basin and the Plains peoples. French trappers were with the Plains peoples in 1742 when they first encountered the Shoshone, known to the Plains peoples as the Snakes, possibly because the Shoshone painted snakes on sticks to frighten their Plains enemies. The Snake River was thus (mis)named for them in 1812. *Shoshone* is their word for themselves, and translates to "The People."

Most of southeastern Idaho received about 15 inches of rain per year, but the Cache Valley, shared by several groups, including the Northwestern Shoshoni, was the recipient of perhaps 8 more inches annually, making the area particularly valued for its rich game and vegetation. And those hot springs were especially appealing in winter.

(*Shoshoni* is the spelling the Northwestern band uses to refer specifically to themselves. *Shoshone* refers to the related groups sharing the Numic language.)

The foods of preinvasion Shoshone groups were diverse, with nutritional values often much higher than contemporary foods.

According to Walker, seeds may have come from over one hundred plants, including wild wheat and oats. Meat could be had from groundhog, jackrabbit, cottontail, porcupine, prairie dog, rodents, and badger. Merle W. Wells reports that communal rabbit and sage hen drives were often organized, as were antelope drives. Bird eggs were also used at times, as were grasshoppers, crickets, ants, and larvae. In southeastern Idaho, groups with horses relied less on small game and, using tools made of bone, dug camas root, wild carrot, and potato. These roots were vastly more nutritious than today's domesticated carrots and potatoes. Deer, mountain sheep, and bear were also hunted. Some Shoshone groups organized buffalo jumps, in which buffalo were herded toward cliffs over which they tumbled to their deaths.

Food gathering defined the work of seasons—and gender roles—but the research of anthropologist Martha C. Knack suggests that while labor was divided between men and women, the work of both was equally valued, minimizing sexism. Women labored through spring, summer, and early fall to gather berries, seeds, nuts, roots, and insects. Men assisted in the important pine nut harvest. Harvesting tools, such as seed beaters, were manufactured by women from basketry materials such as grasses; seeds were transported in conical baskets. Sagebrush was also woven to make containers for foods that were stone-boiled in baskets covered with rawhide. Seeds were pounded and roasted in basket trays; berries were mashed and sun dried in patties; roots were baked in earth ovens and formed into sun-dried loaves; meat was either broiled on an open fire or sun dried. For the men, spring brought the game hunt; boys tended the horse herds. Women assisted in hunting by setting traps for small game. Preparation for winter was of primary concern in late fall, when meat would be drained and cached, or stored, in dry, protected spots in areas—such as the Cache Valley—where the people intended to spend the winter. Winter was typically a time free from food gathering; occasionally bands would gather to share supplies and religious rituals. During this period, women manufactured food containers and harvest equipment.

Summer was the season of intertribal trading. According to Wells, the Shoshone played an important role in hosting one of three major summer festivals; others were at the Mandan villages on the Missouri River in North Dakota, and at the Cascades and the Dalles settlements on the Columbia River in Oregon. Available for barter were

Nez Percé and Walla Walla horses, Pacific coast seashells brought by Umatilla and Cayuse intermediaries, Shoshone buffalo hides and meat, and cedar tepee poles brought by Cheyenne and Arapaho bands. The Crow came seeking wives, Wells says, making the festival a marriage market as well as a commerce fair.

Groups tended to be identified by their dominant food source: for example, mountain sheep eaters, squirrel eaters, sagebrush eaters, camas eaters, and buffalo eaters. This practice may have contributed to the European American habit of denigrating some of the poorer Shoshone groups, who lived in the Nevada and California deserts, as "Diggers."

Northern Shoshone peoples lived in conical grass huts made of thatched grass or bark, until extensive contact with the Plains peoples resulted in a transition to lodges made of skins. Sunbreaks and windbreaks made of local vegetation, such as willow or sage, were common means of extending shelter beyond the lodge. Sweat lodges and menstrual huts were commonplace.

In prehorse times, women wore only sagebrush dresses and men wore only leggings and breechcloths. But Walker reports that the eighteenth century found the horse-rich Shoshone-Bannock groups outfitted in the buckskin dress common to the Plains groups. A long, fringed shirt was made for men from the skin of deer, antelope, or bighorn sheep; and fringed leggings were at times decorated with scalps. Men wore fur caps. Women decorated dresses made with deer, antelope, or bighorn hides, using porcupine quills for ornaments, and making a girdle of dressed leather; their leggings were shorter; and they wore basketry caps. Both wore robes from the skins of bison, antelope, deer, or bighorn sheep. Fur-lined moccasins were sometimes stuffed with sagebrush bark.

Before the horse, northern Shoshone groups were organized in patrilocal bands; that is, the bride moved in with her husband's family after marriage. Democratic leadership was provided by experienced male family heads. The horse resulted in larger bands and a more specialized leadership, Walker says, although most people continued to spend most of their lives with the three-generation grouping of their families. Leaders were elected from councils comprised of male family heads and prominent warriors, and retained their office only as long as they retained the favor of their people. Their leadership resulted in orderly social organization, but was not nearly as stable as the leadership of the Plains groups. Leadership was somewhat hereditary, but a leader's authority varied from band to band with the willingness of the people to be led by that leader; typically, Shoshone band leaders acted only as advised by their councils. People unhappy with their leaders often simply, and freely, switched bands.

But a leader's authority was not questioned during the hunt, and as bison hunts extended into Blackfeet and Crow territories, warrior societies developed in support of specific leaders. Membership was based on heredity and feats of bravery. Among the leaders, there was little hierarchy; each thought of the others as equal. But a caste system deepened primarily around the horse and around leadership: an upper class of leaders and horse owners, a middle class, and a small underclass of slaves obtained through trading or raids.

According to Wells, the notion of "chief" was one imposed by European invaders, who often identified, or even presumed to appoint, the chief with whom they preferred to deal. Followers were typically unimpressed by these appointments.

Walker reports that during pregnancy, a woman's diet was supervised by elder female relatives, limiting food primarily to roots, and beverages primarily to heated water. This kept the fetus from growing too large to deliver easily. She took care not to violate taboos. At the time of birth the mother was relocated to a special house where she was tended by midwives, who had special powers, as well as numerous female relatives who employed herbs, prayer, and manipulation to assist her. The baby's father sometimes bathed and fasted from the time of birth till the loss of the umbilical cord, which would be buried with a prayer for the child. A new mother would remain in isolation for several weeks.

A new baby spent the first year of its life in a cradle board, carried on its mother's back or attached to her saddle; after that year the mother carried the infant on her back in a fur for another year; at age two the child was weaned. Fathers were rarely involved in caring for the baby through infancy. Sometime during infancy, the child would be named, without ceremony, and might gain a nickname later. When the child began to walk, it was cared for by siblings, cousins who were addressed as Father and Mother, and especially the grandparents—all of whom rarely resorted to spanking the child for fear of breaking its spirit. In fact, Walker reports, if a boy child were to strike his father, it would be taken as a sign of his future bravery. Children were often questioned about their dreams, since dreams were thought to indicate what a child would become. Wells suggests that, because children were raised primarily by their grandparents, old ways remained intact, making Shoshone culture resistant to change.

Girls had a brief adolescence. At the first sign of puberty, they were ushered to a special house and instructed for days on matters of marriage and family life by elder women. During this period a girl was not to consume meat, but only roots, and preferably only water. Her behavior throughout this time was carefully controlled, since it was thought that that would determine her future personality. At the end of this period, she donned new clothes and emerged to confront her courtship period. She would be married soon after.

Boys had a more gradual period of adolescence, during which they would become increasingly involved in hunting with older men and with their peers. There might be a ceremony at the time of a boy's first game kill, and eventually he would join raids into the Great Plains. If he did well, he might join a warrior society, marrying at about age twenty.

A marriage might have been arranged in infancy, or later; but elopements were also common. Adult supervision of courtship was minimal at formal dances, and premarital sex was not forbidden. A boy might play a flute outside a girl's lodge, and she might come out to join him if she liked. He might announce his choice to his family, who would ask an older relative to negotiate a sort of dowry; or, less frequently, the girl's family might initiate the contract. The groom's family, Walker says, would present the bride's father with a gift of horses if both families were satisfied that the relative wealth of each was acceptable. At the time of the ceremony, the bride's family would reciprocate the gift.

Marriage was permitted between first cousins; the distinction between cousins and siblings was faint, with the name "brother" often used for both. Polyandry, the marriage of a woman to more than one man, was practiced at times by brothers. Both of these practices declined when the introduction of the horse made travel and search for other partners easier. Polygyny, the marriage of a man to several wives, may have increased after the introduction of the horse, perhaps due, Walker surmises, to the practice of slave trading. Mature men, rich in horses, used their wealth at times to gather several wives, forcing younger men to partner with very young girls, or women captured from other native groups. The caste system also motivated younger men to capture as many horses as possible from other peoples, by way of increasing wealth and marriage possibilities—and it also motivated younger men to abduct married women. The latter was less acceptable, but the couple faced the choice of living in exile, or making a settlement of horses sufficient to appease the insulted husband. Divorce, according to Walker, was easy to obtain, but he does not report whether women were permitted to initiate a separation. Levirate, or the practice of compelling a widow to marry her deceased husband's brother, was also practiced, since the life expectancy of men involved in hunts and war was short. A man might find himself, late in a long life, married to all of his brothers' wives.

But remarriage would occur only after the required yearlong mourning period that might involve the slashing of legs and the cutting of hair. It was not permissible to speak the name of the dead. Family and friends helped the spouse bathe and dress the deceased in his best, tying him in a robe. Usually the corpse was buried at a nearby spot, the head reaching to the west. Rituals were performed by shamans to protect the survivors from the ghost. Then a feast was shared and the deceased's property was distributed.

Walker explains that Shoshone religious practice is similar to that of other Native American groups, with myths designed to support the themes of "immanent justice, bravery, generosity, and repression of emotion. They also emphasize individual autonomy and resistance to centralized authority as well as dependence on supernatural power which was thought to determine one's fate" (158).

Members of the natural world had souls of their own, and people were thought to be part of a vast community of beings that included all of nature. Flora, fauna, birds, fish, stars—any of these could define a person's destiny, and often appeared in visions and in communication with shamans. Vision quests in isolated areas, such as mountaintops, were conducted by children after years of parental instruction. Children hoped to find the appropriate tutelary spirit and attendant personal power, which might also be located by observing a person's abilities and character. The quests involved fasting, exercise, cold baths, and vigil. If a vision did not appear, the quest would be made again. Results of visions were not shared with the band for fear of weakening the power of the vision. Symbols of the power might be carried in a bag, and rituals might later be performed to strengthen the power. If a person abused his power or spirit, bad things could happen, including death. But a soul was judged more by a person's observance of rituals than by how a person lived; an individual was punished on earth for their behavior, and for the offense of spirits or loss of supernatural power. At death, elaborate steps were taken to be sure that the soul reached the afterworld, which was construed as a continuation of the earthly world.

Walker notes that ritual and political authority were thought to be the same. A politically skilled person was considered to have strong supernatural powers. Hence, religious ritual was an affirmation of political authority, and reinforced loyalty to the band. Ceremonial dancing was a key expression of religious and social values. The most important dance was the circle dance, performed in the spring as a grass dance. Songs accompanied the drums and the dance, which inaugurated hunting season. A rabbit dance, when men dressed as rabbits and performed individually, excluded women; women of some Shoshone groups performed a scalp dance, dressing with eagle feathers or beaded costumes and dancing around a pole decorated most likely with the scalps of Nez Percé or Blackfeet. The ghost dance, designed to rid the country of whites, reached the Shoshone in 1889; and in the twentieth century, some groups of Shoshone adopted the Plains practice of war dancing, as well as sun dancing, another ritual that excluded women until the World War II era.

As Knack and others have observed, many natives of North America defined "individual" in the context of the community. Personal relationships were not defined hierarchically, although some people had more influence on the community than others did. Personhood was gender-free in many nations. The individual was not seen in opposition to society, but rather in the service of society, with full recognition of the necessity of interdependence for community— and thus individual—survival.

Further, natives of North America typically had two notions of racial category: us, and all others. "Us" can include anyone who is a friend. "All others" can include unfriendly natives of other nations, or Europeans. In encountering an unknown Other, the Shoshone typically responded as treated. Unless they or their resources were threatened, they would tolerate this new presence and share resources, often, as noted, adapting the more useful lifeways of the new presence.

Lewis and Clark met the Lemhi Shoshone in 1805; from 1810 on, northern bands of Shoshone consistently encountered Europeans,

beginning with fur trappers. For the most part, the populations of
Shoshone and Scots and French-Canadian trappers blended without
too much trouble, with many of the men taking wives and building
families and trade relationships. Some Shoshone groups joined the
hunt for beaver skins, which they traded for beads, blankets, needles,
iron tools, guns and ammunition, and perhaps alcohol; Brigham D.
Madsen in his book *The Shoshone Frontier and the Bear River Massacre* points out that this period can be described as a time of wealth
and friendship among the "us" (Shoshone) and the "others" (all
other native peoples, and the various European groups).

But mountain men held their rendezvous—trade festivals—in the
Cache Valley and many insisted on wintering there, which meant that
the Northwestern Shoshoni suffered the earliest and most sustained
cultural impact of the Europeans. Tensions ran high, and in 1832 a
fight broke out at the rendezvous at Pierre's Hole when an Iroquois
member of a white trapping party incited a fight between the Nez
Percé and the Gros Ventre. Beaver were almost trapped out by then
anyway, but nonetheless, Captain B. L. E. Bonneville built a post near
the Lemhi Shoshone in western Idaho that year; and in 1834
Nathaniel J. Wyeth started Fort Hall, just north of present-day
Pocatello, unwittingly providing a handy supply stop for future European emigration. By 1840 most mountain men could no longer
support themselves, and some began to work as guides for the earliest white emigration parties. The Shoshone returned to big-game
hunting to subsist and to trade with the slowly increasing numbers of
emigrants, who passed through the Fort Hall area each summer with
little thought of staying, accustomed as easterners were to pastures
greener than the mosquito-ridden desert of southeastern Idaho.

This mutual tolerance between the Shoshone and the immigrants
was not to last. George Stewart has estimated that in 1849, 22,500
people and 60,000 animals crossed the country on their way to California; by 1857, the total would climb to 165,000 people and 1 million animals. George Fuller's count for travel to Oregon between
1842 and 1852 is 18,287 people and 50,000 animals. Madsen adds
that the discovery of gold in Montana led to the opening of the Montana Trail, north from Salt Lake City, in 1862. Traffic on all three
trails would continue to be heavy throughout the century, even after
the transcontinental railroad was completed in 1869.

Almost all of this traffic ran north of Salt Lake City, around the
Great Salt Lake, directly through Northwestern Shoshoni and

Northern Shoshone territories. Madsen's conservative estimate has a final total of about 240,000 emigrants and 1.5 million animals traveling through the heart of the Shoshone–Bannock habitat, camping on the Portneuf or Snake Rivers, cutting Shoshone firewood, interrupting Shoshone forage, and grazing their stock on Shoshone pastureland. The Shoshone did not interfere at first, but particularly difficult for them was the annual return trip from hunting grounds in Wyoming and Montana, and the sight of their profoundly damaged winter grounds: clear-cut trees, blackened campfires, stunted grasses devoid of their precious seeds.

Madsen mentions a report made by the superintendent of the Fort Kearney, South Pass, and Honey Lake wagon road. F. W. Lander, on February 18, 1860, refers to a petition signed by emigrants who were perturbed to have been charged—by Mormon settlers—5 to 25 cents a head per night to graze livestock from Salt Lake City north to the Bear River. Based on those figures, Madsen calculates that if the Shoshone had charged for use of pasture, as their Mormon neighbors did, they could have been paid $222,750 for the 1.485 million animals who chewed up their lands.

The U.S. government neglected a compelling self-interest to adequately manage this increasingly conflicted region, this heart of red–white encounter. The Shoshone were perplexed by the forty-second parallel line drawn through this area, dividing the Utah Territory from the Oregon Territory, which resulted in some cousins—those south of that line—receiving much attention and "presents" from the Indian agent in Salt Lake City; and those north of the line receiving no attention whatsoever, since the nearest Indian agent resided many hundreds of miles away in what we now call Oregon. When Oregon was granted territory status in 1849, Northern Shoshone bands found themselves under the sudden, and uninvited, supervision of the federal government, although apparently few funds were ever appropriated to execute this supervision, perpetuating the north–south imbalance in subsidy.

Interest in rising to this responsibility was sparked only when the Shoshone began to resist emigrant incursion with violence. The Ward Massacre of nineteen emigrants by Boise-area Shoshone in 1854, for instance, resulted in a visit by agent Nathan Olney, who counted the Northern Shoshone as numbering about three thousand people. Beyond this, agents in Oregon knew almost nothing about the

Shoshone. Consequently, and as F. W. Lander wisely warned his superiors, the Shoshone remained uncompensated for the use of their lands even while their more warlike neighbors, the Lakota and the Cheyenne, had been paid annuities for many years. Pasturelands were slowly being ruined, driving big game from Shoshone reach. In 1861, matters worsened when the Washington Territory was cut out of Oregon, to include Idaho. The new territorial office, in Olympia, was even farther away. Madsen reports that the Washington superintendent's annual report for 1862 included a map displaying a vast nothing, which the superintendent had titled, "Unexplored."

At the time of the Civil War, fifteen hundred Northwestern Shoshoni lived in the Cache, Weber, and Malad Valleys. Bear Hunter's band totaled about 450 people, primarily in the Cache Valley.

While most U.S. citizens have heard countless stories about the Oregon Trail, most know far less about a busy route developed just before California's gold rush: the Mormon Trail. Mormonism, which now encompasses several denominations, was founded by an itinerant water diviner named Joseph Smith, Jr. in 1830 in upstate New York. That region was then rife with a religious fervor that birthed several similar sects, including Millerites, Campbellites, and other millennialist faiths. Smith, who was the recipient of several visitations, or "angelic visions," as a child began meeting with a "personage" named Moroni in 1823. ("While I was thus in the act of calling upon God . . . a personage appeared at my bedside. . . . He had on a loose robe of most exquisite whiteness. It was a whiteness beyond anything earthly I had ever seen; nor do I believe that any earthly thing could be made to appear so exceedingly white and brilliant. . . . Not only was his robe exceedingly white, but his whole person was glorious beyond description, and his countenance truly like lightning" sections 30–32). Moroni sent Smith to a hill near his home, where, according to Steven L. Shields, Smith found several artifacts, including plates that appeared to be of gold, and which bore an ancient, engraved narrative. Smith, who had been endowed by his god with a special ability to translate the plates, published his translation as The Book of Mormon in March 1830. It was Smith's belief that he had been called to effect a restoration of the real church established by Jesus Christ, which had been lost over the ages.

Interestingly, the vast majority of Smith's codified precepts addressed the necessity of accumulating wealth.

The gold plates, which later disappeared, tell the history of the Twelve Tribes of Israel, and the wars between the Lamanites and the Nephites, two "tribes" descended from Abraham. When Lehi and his sons—the worthy Nephi, and the wicked Laman and Lemuel—fled Jerusalem in 600 B.C., they journeyed to South America and there divided into two competing factions. God cursed the Lamanites with dark skin so that they could be distinguished from the righteous people, the Nephites, who had light skin. The Lamanites took Nephi land, wars ensued, and thousands were slaughtered on both sides; a feud drove both peoples through North America, culminating in the final battle in New York state, where Moroni became the last Nephite survivor. The plates Moroni left had the purpose of restoring the good Nephites to their rightful place, and to bring those blessings to the Lamanites. Indeed, a condition of Christ's second coming was the conversion of the Lamanites and their restoration as "white and delightsome people" (2 Nephi 30.6; recently revised to read "pure and delightsome").

Westward emigrating Mormons, then, understood the natives they encountered in their travels to be the Lamanites of prophecy. And the Lamanite–Nephite relation, as they knew it, was a complicated one. The dark-skinned Lamanites were brothers to the Nephites, but the prophet Micah also warned that these brothers should be feared, too: "ye shall be in the midst of them who shall be many; and ye shall be among them as a lion among the beasts of the forest, as a young lion among the flocks of sheep, who, if he goeth through both treadeth down and teareth in pieces, and none can deliver" (3 Nephi 20.16). This antithetical relation of legend—brothers to be feared—would be replicated in reality.

The Book of Mormon, as recited by Smith, also betrays an abiding concern with record keeping. My abridged concordance provides a list of forty-seven references to records, primarily urging a person to keep records (as in 3 Nephi 23.11: "And Jesus said unto them: How be it that ye have not written this thing"); but also urging the concealment of records from enemy outsiders, or the exposure of records to friends; and finally, insisting that a record be truthful. As historian Will Bagley has pointed out, Smith and Mormonism (unlike earlier forms of Christianity) came centuries after the arrival of the printing press, and "[t]he Lord's instruction to Latter-day Saints to keep personal journals sounded a call that even the semi-literate answered as best they could, creating a wealth of first-person accounts describing almost every aspect of the creed's trials and triumphs" (qtd. in Bigler 11). David S. Reynolds would point out further that early- and mid-nineteenth-century literacy rates among whites in the United States were as high as 90%, and that book production rates enjoyed vast increases from 1830 to 1850, signaling a general cultural affirmation of written culture; these factors doubtless contributed to this surfeit of documentation.

Smith's first church was founded in April 1830, and grew quickly when he moved to Kirtland, Ohio, in 1831. David L. Bigler writes that Smith's followers encountered resistance from their new neighbors when they formed "an illegal bank," and ultimately "flooded the area with worthless money" (26). Coincidentally, Smith's god decreed at that time that Independence, Missouri, was the real "Center Place," the "land of Zion," and the "New Jerusalem" (26). He ordered that a temple be constructed there, and subsequent colonies were established in Missouri in the 1830s.

It would be in the 1830s, in Missouri, that Smith would begin to consider the usefulness to the young church of a practice that would be called "polygamy." (Since women were not permitted multiple husbands, the correct term is *polygyny*.) The Mormon church had quickly become popular with women utopians, not least because social service, ghettoized in other religious organizations as "women's work" and often viewed as threatening to church hierarchies, was made part of the Latter-day Saints (LDS) church structure. Service by women was restricted to traditional divisions of labor, but was revered. Consequently, the sex ratio tilted in favor of women. Diaries and letters suggest that Mormon women were conflicted in their views of polygyny; some found it a cross to bear, while others were grateful for the companionship and the opportunity to share domestic duties. Mormon doctrine had it that a woman's greatest glory was to bear a large group of children; and that the place of a man in the hereafter was dependent on the number of children he sired.

Throughout most of its history as a "polygamous sect," only about 10% to 20% of Mormons consistently practiced polygyny; in particular, upper-class men were encouraged to marry multiple times. But neighboring "gentiles," as Mormons call non-Latter-day Saints, were hospitable neither to polygyny nor to the loss of economic power, and Mormon communities in Missouri were consequently disrupted. In 1838, Smith organized a paramilitary organization he called the "Danites," or "Avenging Angels," whose task it was to take vengeance on Missouri enemies.

In October of that same year, Governor Lilburn W. Boggs of Missouri sent in the militia to rid his state of Mormons, who, he ordered, "must be treated as enemies and must be exterminated or driven from the State if necessary for the public peace" (qtd. in Bigler 27). The militia ransacked the town of Far West, murdering eighteen Mormon settlers and stealing property. According to official Mormon history, "The chastity of a number of women was defiled by force; some of them were strapped to benches and repeatedly ravished by brutes in human form until they died from the effects of this treatment" (qtd. in Brownmiller 126). This brutality is known to contemporary Mormons as the Haun's Mill Massacre.

The rape helped convince many of the Latter-day Saints to abandon Missouri. Stephen C. LeSueur, in *The 1838 Mormon War in Missouri*, points out that the memory of Haun's Mill, and the desire to avenge it, would linger powerfully for decades among Mormons.

Smith clearly needed a place where his people could live unmolested by state leaders and their militias. He extracted from Illinois Governor Thomas Ford a promise of sovereignty for Nauvoo, a town Smith's people would build. Nauvoo would enjoy, in Ford's words, "a government within a government, a legislature with power to pass ordinances at war with the laws of the State; courts to execute them with but little dependence upon the constitutional judiciary; and a military force at their own command" (qtd. in Bigler 27). Bigler reports that, in return for sovereignty, Smith promised Ford that he could control the votes of his LDS followers in Ford's favor. North of Quincy, then, Smith and an apostle from Vermont, Brigham Young, set their people to draining a mosquito-infested swampland that would soon become one of the largest towns in Illinois. Smith's followers, according to Shields, "proceeded to build a magnificent city in which they merged government, business and religion in a unique blend of society. . . . There the Latter Day Saints prospered and grew numerically, with converts pouring in from all over the United States and England" (Shields 48). Given its city–state charter, Shields says, Nauvoo "became a political entity that ultimately could have controlled the state of Illinois" (48).

But Smith pushed his sovereignty a bit too far, and the city became a refuge for counterfeiters and thieves who attacked nearby towns with, Bigler reports, "little fear of arrest" (28). But "most alarming" to Nauvoo's neighbors was the Nauvoo Legion, which numbered four thousand men in an era, Bigler reminds us, when U.S. Army regulars totaled only eight thousand; thus Smith was, in effect, the "highest ranking military officer" in the country (28).

The short-lived Mormon prosperity of Nauvoo came to an end in 1844. Smith was staging his third-party run for the U.S. presidency when, in June, he shut down a dissenting newspaper, the *Nauvoo Expositor*, whose first issue advocated separation between church and state. Smith and his brother Hyrum, under arrest in the Carthage jail, were killed by a mob.

Smith had not planned for succession, and for the next twenty years, groups splintered and formed around various leaders. Ultimately, Brigham Young, who at the time of Smith's death was in Boston directing Smith's presidential campaign, would prove to be the most successful leader. He ignored advisers who suggested that the Mormons head for California, concluding rightly that California would become a popular destination. After consulting John C. Frémont's writings on routes to California, and after talking to Father De Smet, he convinced a large number of people to follow him to a third Zion, in a valley in the Rocky Mountains, beyond the control of U.S. government, owned by Mexico and so arid that non-Mormons would not want it. Today, the second largest surviving denomination, founded by Joseph Smith, Jr. and called the Reorganized Church of Jesus Christ of Latter Day Saints, is headquartered in Independence, Missouri, and has about 250,000 members worldwide; Young's group is currently one of the most rapidly growing religious organizations, with about 20 million members worldwide and far-reaching political, and particularly economic, influence, including a massive portfolio of corporate assets, and ownership of media outlets in all major American cities.

Federal officials preferred to avoid an outbreak of violence in a fourth Mormon state. President James Polk, in an apparent attempt to gain the loyalty of Mormon men to the United States, and thereby avoid the brewing conflict between the church and the government, enlisted five hundred Mormon men in 1846. The Mormon Battalion was deployed to the Mexican War. Brigham Young interpreted this alliance as a conspiracy to kill off Mormon men, but ultimately, these veterans would later serve as seasoned leaders of Young's own forces.

Brigham Young's exodus from Missouri was an impeccably organized, systematic emigration of hundreds, then thousands, of people.

Young organized the pioneers into pseudomilitary units of ten people each, providing unit leaders with the title of "captain." But his best-laid plans were thwarted by weather and disease, and on April 17, 1847, a smaller advance party leaving the Elkhorn River was sent ahead of the rest. This advance party comprised 141 white men; three slaves—Oscar Crosby, Green Flake, and Hark Lay; three women—Harriet Young, Clara Young, and Ellen Kimball; and two of Harriet Young's children. The party were of U.S., British, Canadian, Irish, and Scots nationality. Rather than follow entirely the Oregon Trail, Young opted for the north side of the Platte River to avoid competing with non-Mormon emigrants for pasture and other resources. From Hasting's Cutoff, his party followed a trail toward Salt Lake, cut the year before by the Donner–Reed party; it was the delay caused by cutting that trail which had resulted in some of that party perishing in the Sierra Nevadas. As it was, Young's own party was plagued by unpleasant encounters with Missouri citizens who also crowded the Oregon Trail.

The difficult journey was completed by July. Toward the end, most of the party suffered from an odd illness referred to as "mountain fever," though today's doctors speculate that it may have been caused by ticks. Young contracted it in the final two weeks of the trip, and sent ahead a final advance party on July 12, to continue on the Donner–Reed Trail and find the best route through Weber Canyon. The pioneers cut through Echo Canyon, rather than attempt what would become known as Donner Mountain. The advance party of thirty-nine men, including two of the slaves, entered Salt Lake Valley on July 22, 1847. Young would follow with a last group of eight carriages, led by Wilford Woodruff, on July 24.

Several free blacks, members of the Mormon church, emigrated to Utah with their white brethren; and many more slaves, held by a group of Mormon emigrants known as the Mississippi Saints, attended their owners on the second pioneer wave in 1848. By the end of 1848, there were about fifty African Americans, most of them slaves, residing in Utah.

The living conditions of both European masters and African servants were dire that first winter, which may have forced some whites to share humble quarters and scant food with blacks. While slaves and free blacks were at times considered helpmates to whites in these difficult emigration conditions, relations returned to that of apartheid after that first winter. Slaves still feared the corporal punishment uti-

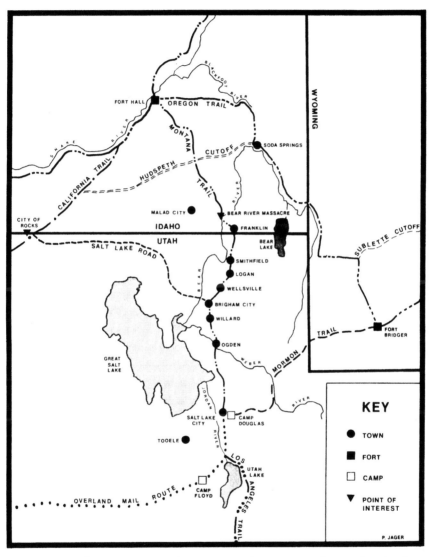

Figure 1.1. The emigrant trails. From Brigham D. Madsen, *The Shoshoni Frontier and the Bear River Massacre* (Salt Lake City: U of Utah P, 1985) 35. Reprinted courtesy of the University of Utah Press.

lized by some owners, and still feared being sold or separated from their friends and families. Utah historians document several instances of slave trading between Mormon owners. Meanwhile, slaveholders had their own fears regarding the behavior of their "property." According to Ronald G. Coleman, William Crosby wrote to Brigham Young in 1851, complaining that Green Flake was a "'boy' who was 'mean, dirty and saucy' to his owner, Mrs. Flake." Crosby worried that Flake would "leave his black wife and get him a white woman" if he were freed (99). Some slaves did try to run away, though the mountains surrounding the Salt Lake valley provided a formidable obstacle.

When Brigham Young's Latter-day Saints arrived in the Salt Lake valley in July 1847, they "discovered" the empty valley while the Shoshone were summering in higher elevations. Few natives were on hand to protest the plowing of new fields, which began within hours of the advance party's settlement, before Young himself descended from the canyon to gaze upon lands which, as his right-hand man Heber C. Kimball had it, was the property of "our Father in Heaven and we expect to plow and plant it" (qtd. in Madsen, *Shoshoni Frontier* 29; unless otherwise noted, Madsen citations are from this book).

For which privilege native inhabitants would pay a dear price; but meanwhile, Young established communitarian land use practices reminiscent of those of the natives he would displace. The church would retain ownership of the lands its followers used, while individuals (in good church standing) would serve as stewards of the small plots given them. "We have found a place," Thomas Bullock, Young's clerk, wrote, "where the land is acknowledged to belong to the Lord, and the Saints, being His people, are entitled to as much as they can plant, take care of, and will sustain their families with food" (qtd. in Bigler 39). The land could not be sold, Young decreed: "No man will be suffered to cut up his lot and sell a part to speculate out of his brethren" (qtd. in Bigler 38).

Young had come to a region he hoped would be beyond U.S. interference, but events were conspiring to disrupt his plans. In January 1848, John Augustus Sutter found gold at his mill in California, sparking a rush of travelers straight through Zion. (Ironically, it was a veteran of the Mormon Battalion, Henry Bigler, who built Sutter's mill.) In February, Mexico ceded the Pacific southwest to the United States in the Treaty of Guadalupe-Hidalgo. An immediate consequence of this latter would be the necessity of establishing a territorial government. Young was himself appointed governor of what he proposed, that March, be called the "State of Deseret." (*Deseret* is a word from The Book of Mormon signifying the beehive [still on Utah's present-day state seal] and connoting hardworking colonies.) When the United States approved territorial status, the name would be changed to Utah; and the job description of territorial governor would include the responsibilities of Indian superintendent.

But Young busied himself primarily with the work of establishing a community similar to the previous Mormon colonies, in which religion, commerce, and politics were closely combined in a theocratic organization. He also quickly moved to establish way stations, ferries, and other services for the gentile emigrants who were very soon to follow on the Oregon and California Trails, which roads would pass very near his new city. The crucial nationalist role of Mormon settlers and officials was that of providing supplies for sale to anyone who needed them in this volatile and intensely mobile time: Shoshone, emigrants, farmers, miners, federal troops. Thus, one foundation of the Mormon church's vast wealth was the exploitation of one country's Manifest Destiny.

The Mormon incursion into Utah had the profoundest impact on the Northwestern Shoshoni, who lived closest to Salt Lake City and whose lands straddled the forty-second parallel; Young also developed relationships with the nearby Northern Shoshone, and with the Eastern Shoshone, led firmly by the pacifist Washakie, who strove to be hospitable to the new settlers. Several high-ranking church counselors advised Young not to compensate the Shoshone for use of their resources, but Young replied famously that it was "manifestly more economical, and less expensive to feed and clothe, than to fight them" (qtd. in Madsen 29).

To assure his continued control of this new western territory, plagued by natives and gold seekers, Young sought to populate, again systematically, the regions north and south of the lake and city, by sending out young adults to spread farms and church wards across the vast region. Historians like Madsen congratulate Young on his requirement that his settlers share their meager resources with the Shoshone whose lands they were grazing and plowing under. Settlers struggled to do so; and the Shoshone struggled to be friendly; but there were inadequate appropriations of funds to meet the needs of the displaced Shoshone. By 1855 Young had populated an area larger than Texas. Ultimately, there would be no way to reconcile the mutually exclusive policies of pacifism and expansion—an exclusivity Young doubtless understood only too well, given his own history as a member of an organization that itself had been displaced.

Young's feed-don't-fight-them policy occasionally extended also to a "marry-them" policy. During a visit by Young to the Fort Lemhi settlement, Madsen reports, Young urged the young men there to partner with Shoshone women because "the marriage tie was the strongest tie of friendship that existed" (qtd. in Madsen 76)—a policy Young must have neglected to discuss with Shoshone leaders, since most Shoshone families rejected Mormon advances. Young would later claim to Shoshone leaders that the Mormons did not want to take Shoshone women. Nonetheless, in the short term, Young's expressed pronative policy—and the coincidence of such shared lifeways as polygyny and community land practices—won him the wary acceptance of Shoshone leaders, who preferred his policies to those of the federal government.

Young was equally contradictory in his positions regarding black slaves and freemen in Utah. He did not own slaves himself, preferring to hire free blacks to serve as coachmen; he felt, in practical terms, that slavery would prove unprofitable in the long term, and argued that his disciples should tend no more land than they could cultivate themselves. His official position on the matter was neutrality, which he hoped would offend neither side of this controversial question. He spoke publicly about despising the slaveholding Missourians who had driven the Mormons from that state, but he also needed the political support of the Mississippi Saints, who had brought their slaves with them to Utah—some of whom held leadership positions in the church and government.

Indeed, slavery had a complicated history within the Mormon church. Smith did not want to be identified with abolitionists, who in the 1830s and 1840s were a hated minority. Antislavery sentiments were particularly despised in Missouri, where Smith hoped to establish his community with at least minimal cooperation from his non-Mormon neighbors. So Mormon leaders publicly condemned abolitionists, and slavery, at the same time; in 1844, when Joseph Smith launched his third-party campaign for the U.S. presidency, he included an antislavery plank in his platform.

Young also thought slaves should be treated humanely, and believed, in accordance with Smith's The Book of Mormon, that his Nephites, the chosen people, should abhor slavery. But he also believed that African Americans descended from the seed of Caanan and had been designated by God to serve as "servant of servants" (qtd. in Coleman 101). According to Newell G. Bringhurst, this belief led to the church's refusal to permit blacks to ascend to Mormon priesthood, a decision formally in place by 1847, not to be overturned until the 1960s. Young would refer to this decision while arguing for the legalization of slavery: because blacks could not "bear any . . . priesthood," they could not "bear rule in any place until the curse is removed from them" (qtd. in Bringhurst 337). "[T]he seed of Caanan," Young concluded, "will inevitably carry the curse which was placed upon them until the same authority, which placed it there, shall see proper to have it removed. Service is necessary; it is honorable; it exists in all countries, and has existed in all ages; it probably will exist in some form in all time to come" (qtd. in Bringhurst 336). Still, Young suspected that institutionalized slavery contributed to miscegenation and other corruptions.

Young worked personally to mediate disputes between slaves and their owners, at times providing refuge for runaways, but did not immediately ask his legislature for a law legalizing slavery. When Utah first applied for statehood, soon after Young's emigration, the territory's apparent sanction of slavery was a factor in stalling congressional approval. In exchange for the admission of California as a free state, Henry Clay's Compromise of 1850 admitted Utah and New Mexico as territories without mention of slavery, which allowed residents of those states to decide for themselves whether to permit slavery. Still, Young did not rush to that judgment, and a law formalizing the slavery question in Utah Territory was not passed until 1852. This law made Utah the only state west of the Missouri River, and north of the Missouri Compromise line of 36° 30', to legalize slavery; but the law was more restrictive than those of southern states.

A slave market of natives, mostly children exchanged between Mexican traders and the Ute and the Paiute, had existed in the region long before the arrival of the Mississippi Saints. Many Mormon emigrants were distressed by this circumstance, and Utah's slavery regulations reveal a bias in favor of native slaves, caused not least by the Mormon belief that their brothers the Lamanites were superior to the people of Caanan. In examining this bias in favor of natives, however, it is also worth noting that a law limiting native slavery would entail none of the national political risk attendant to a law limiting African slavery.

Thus, two laws were passed in 1852: An Act in Relation to Service, and An Act for the Relief of Indian Slaves and Prisoners. The former permitted African slavery in Utah Territory, but discouraged the institution. Directed primarily at future emigrants to Utah from the south, the act placed on slaveholders the burden of proving that their property attended them "of their own free will and choice." Slaves could not be taken from the territory or sold without their consent, and their living conditions had to be "comfortable," with "clothing, bedding, sufficient food, and recreation." Owners were required to educate slaves who were six to twenty years old for at least eighteen months, and their punishment of slaves was restricted to that "guided by prudence and humanity" (qtd. in Bringhurst 334).

The law controlling native slavery was designed to "ameliorate their condition, preserve their lives, and their liberties, and redeem them from a worse than African bondage" (qtd. in Coleman 103). Owners were required to send native slaves of six to seventeen years of age to school for at least three months per year.

Historian Newell G. Bringhurst feels that the legalization of African slavery was the culmination of decades of Mormon restrictions on the rights of African Americans. In Nauvoo, only "free white males" could vote, hold office, or join the Nauvoo Legion. While mayor of Nauvoo, Joseph Smith himself fined two black men for violating his prohibition of intermarriage of blacks and whites; and in 1844, the year of Smith's presidential run, a free black man named Chism was charged with stealing in Nauvoo (that crime-tolerant city–state), and publicly whipped.

Young's slavery laws had mixed effects on race relations in Utah. The restrictions on slaveholders, formalized in the laws, did contribute to a decline in the number of African slaves held in Utah. By 1860, a dozen Mormons still held two dozen slaves. But the laws also had the effect of institutionalizing racism in Utah. In logical succession, the laws permitted the passage of codes restricting the civil rights of free blacks, including prohibitions against voting, holding office, and joining the militia.

And although section 4 of An Act in Relation to Service forbade sexual intercourse among whites and blacks, a few mixed marriages did exist in Utah at the time. But Mormons particularly condemned interracial contact between black men and white women. Tom Colburn was found dead in 1866, with his throat slashed and a note pinned to his body: "Notice to all Niggers! Warning!! Leave white women alone!!!" (qtd. in Coleman 105).

The question of why Utah Mormons legalized slavery, when the vast majority of church members opposed the institution, plagues African American historians, but some part of the answer may be found in women's history. In 1852, while the slavery laws were being enacted in Utah, Mormon officials finally made the first public admission—after twenty years of denial—that polygyny was encouraged by the church. Immediately following Brigham Young's public defense of this practice, the church was increasingly attacked in Washington. Polygynists and slaveholders forged an unholy alliance in their common assertions that popular sovereignty and states' rights were the legal justification for their "peculiar institutions," as they were denounced in debate. Young's adviser, Jedediah Morgan Grant, wrote in an 1852 letter to the *New York Herald* that Mormons were "with THE SOUTH" as "opponents of centralization" (qtd. in Bringhurst 333). The *Deseret News* announced its support for the South's attempts, in the early 1850s, to recommence the international slave trade, and crowed that "Congress has no power over the question of Slavery in the Territories and of course none over the question of polygamy. Those can now flourish wherever the people will it in any of the Territories of the United States and Uncle Sam can attend to his own business without troubling himself any further about them" (qtd. in Bringhurst 334). The 1857 Dred Scott decision, holding that slaveholders could not be prohibited by Congress from transporting their human property to any U.S. territories, was interpreted by Mormon leaders as favorable to the practice of polygyny.

In 1856, the Republican Party formally denounced both polygamy and slavery, deeming them "The Twin Relics of Barbarism" (qtd. in Bringhurst 334). The negative publicity resulted in a drop in LDS membership in Britain and Europe.

From the 1830s on, then, and at a geometrically increasing rate, European Americans poured west. The history of the development of the West has been largely a male history, with noted historians like Frederick Jackson Turner free to ignore the presence of women. In 1836, Narcissa Whitman became the first white woman to cross the Rocky Mountains with her missionary husband, and it is true that generally far fewer women than men would soon follow her. The sex ratio of emigrant men to women in the mountain and Pacific territories was nearly 3:1 in 1850, falling to 2:1 in 1860, and 1.5:1 in 1870.

Still, we may conclude that at least one of four emigrants in the 1840s and 1850s were women. The work of historians like Dee

Brown has contributed to the notion that most of these women were reluctant participants in western migration, and some letters and diaries collected by Lillian Schlissel and others confirm that this was the case for many. But it was not true for all, as Julie Roy Jeffrey's study *Frontier Women* argues. Some women like Whitman, and especially many Mormon women, emigrated willingly: to convert Native Americans to Christianity, to establish utopian communities, or to rejoin family members who had already emigrated. Most wagon parties consisted of groups of relatives, and women frequently served as heads of household in mining communities, which lost many men to transience and accidents.

Indeed, the cooperation of women was essential to the migration, since women bore much of the brutal workload required by emigration. In preparation for a half-year journey, women wove and sewed wagon covers and clothing; prepared necessities like bedding, soap and candles; and harvested, preserved and cured food. And as happened with slaves and their owners during emigration, divisions of labor were sometimes redistributed due to the difficulties of travel. Men usually drove oxen and maintained the wagons, while women cared for the children and washed, cooked, and gathered fuel. But some men cooked, some women drove oxen, and when the family settled, many women did the work of ranch hands and foremen. The "age of domesticity," as feminist historians have called this period which relegated middle-class women to the home, materialized differently in the West, where the contributions of women were crucial to survival—and where white women were likewise crucial to the invasion of the Shoshone country.

A good distance south and west of Salt Lake City, Mormon settlements established in the early 1850s were causing conflict between the Ute and Paiute peoples, and the Nauvoo Legion. One militaristic leader, Joseph Reddeford Walker, vacillated between attempts to repel the Mormons, and make peace with them. What finally angered Walker was Brigham Young's move to end the trading of young native slaves, captured by Walker's people and bought by non-Mormon whites from New Mexico. These gentiles initiated the tension by protesting the 1852 law limiting slaveholding to Mormons. Young announced to his followers that "a horde of Mexicans" were "stirring up the Indians" and arming natives in exchange for children (qtd. in Bigler 74). He ordered troops into the area to detain New Mexican traders.

Except as they illustrate the escalating tension between natives and Mormons, details of the resulting Walker's War are not pertinent to this study, and I refer you to Bigler's *Forgotten Kingdom* for a succinct account. But two points are salient to our discussion of the intersection of this gender- and culture-specific conflict.

First, the trigger for the conflict: the wife of James Ivie, at her cabin in Springville, gave flour to a wife of Shower-osho-a-kats, in exchange for fish. As Bigler has it, "When the male native disapproved the exchange and began beating his spouse in Ivie's dooryard, the settler intervened and a free-for-all ensued. With one blow, Ivie cracked the warrior's skull with the barrel of the man's own gun, then floored the Utah woman after she expressed her gratitude for his efforts on her behalf by hitting him in the face with a stock of wood" (75).

The warrior died some days later, and Ivie refused a town official's urgings to compensate Walker's band "to the tune of an ox," Bigler writes (75). Hostilities would not cease until Young and Walker made peace in the spring of 1854. Walker and his band were resettled near New Harmony, where he would live in some disharmony with local officials for a short time. He died of illness in 1864. Bigler reports the circumstances of his burial: "Two Indian women and as many as twenty horses were killed and placed beside the corpse in a burial pit at the base of a rock slide in the mountains to accompany his new spirit to its new home. Two Piede children were tied alive next to the body to act as guides. After the corpse began to stink, the youths pleaded piteously to be let go, but passing natives refused" (88).

For a thorough discussion of the escalating constitutional conflict between the U.S. federal government and the leaders of the Mormon state, I refer you again to Bigler. For our purposes, it is useful to note that the State of Deseret subverted such cherished U.S. notions as legal precedence and English common law. Mormons viewed the U.S. constitution, with its emphasis on religious freedom, as a divinely inspired document whose real intent was going unfulfilled; while, as Bigler puts it, federalists saw the document as "an end in itself" (36n). Regarding church control of the territory, Bigler writes, "A study of eighteen elections from 1852 to 1870 found that 96 percent of the 96,107 votes cast during this period went to the church ticket" (51). Also, at each new settlement Young's people founded, all men between the ages of eighteen and forty-five were "enrolled for compulsory training in the theocracy's military arm"—the Nauvoo Legion, also known as the

Militia of Utah Territory (53). By 1857, these men numbered 7,500. Their leaders were seasoned veterans of earlier militias and the Mormon Battalion.

Between 1851 and 1862, Bigler reports, at least sixteen U.S. officials abandoned their posts, some of them in great haste, often citing polygyny, physical threat, and blatant disregard as reasons for their inability to serve. One early office of contention was the position of Indian Superintendent. Garland Hurt arrived in the spring of 1855 to replace Young, and found the latter celebrating the twenty-fifth anniversary of the church. On this occasion Young reminded his followers that the conversion of the Lamanites was a prerequisite of Christ's second coming—an occurrence church leaders had predicted would happen some time around 1891. Young announced a new effort to convert the region's Lamanites. Hurt, his authority already threatened, determined that he should attempt to remove natives from the charity of the LDS church, and of the U.S. government, by teaching natives to farm; which would have the further benefit of reorienting the loyalty of natives away from the theocracy and toward the U.S. government.

Hurt allied himself with David Burr, the government surveyor sent by the federal government to thwart Young's conviction that the Mormon god owned the region known as the Utah Territory. Burr and Hurt understood that quickly surveyed lands, which could then be all but given away to non-Mormon settlers—as well as surveyed reservations to house the natives suspected as allied to Young—would bring an end to Young's grip on the region. In 1855 and 1856 Burr reported back to Washington that his surveying teams were being harassed by Mormon locals.

Young's move to convert natives in his region may also have been connected to the sharp drop in church membership abroad, a result of his defense of polygyny. By way of increasing rolls, in 1855 he also encouraged girls to marry at fourteen, and boys at sixteen to take as many wives as they could. Finally, late in 1855 he announced an aggressive recruitment plan to bring more followers from Europe. The church had established a Perpetual Emigration Fund to subsidize westward journeys for members, the coffers of which had been in decline; nonetheless, he asked the "honest poor" to come anyway: "let them come on foot, with handcarts or wheelbarrows; let them gird up their loins and walk through, and nothing shall hinder or stay them" (qtd. in Bigler 104). For a full accounting of the worst disaster in the history of U.S. westward settlement, I refer readers to Rebecca Bartholomew and Leonard J. Arrington's *Rescue of the 1856 Handcart Companies*. About four hundred Mormon travelers died in the emigration of 1856, daunted by bad leadership, delays, and weather.

Besides "Indian Problems," the Handcart Disaster, and attempts by the federal government to subvert Young's control, another storm was sweeping the settlements in 1856. Church leaders sensed a coming fight for sovereignty with the United States, and began to believe they could win it. To silence complainers, achieve total unity among the populace, and cleanse the community in preparation for independence from the United States, a call went out for mass atonement. The 1856 Reformation was led by Jedediah Morgan Grant, who sent church leaders to the homes of members to quiz them on their sins. Confessions had to be complete, and atonement might entail, depending on the severity of the sin, some level of blood sacrifice as decreed by leaders. This last caused some members to defect from the church, and confirmed the feelings of non-Mormons that the church was barbaric.

Among the complainers about church policy were women who were unhappy with the recent institutionalization of polygyny. During the reformation, Young offered these women a one-time opportunity to divorce their polygynous husbands at the upcoming general conference of the church. "How many took him up on this offer is not known," Bigler writes (126), but perhaps a goodly number, since Young later felt compelled to add a condition: that they afterward "marry men that will not have but one wife" (qtd. in Bigler 126).

Meanwhile, reformation burned feverishly through the settlements, partially contributing, historians believe, to the exodus of federal officials, as well as to the Mountain Meadows Massacre (of which more later), and to what is now known as the Utah War.

In 1856, Washington officials feared that Mormon "barbarians" were forming alliances with both southern dissidents and western native groups, and that a Utah secession was brewing. Shoshone leaders were so irritated by federal betrayals that, when President James Buchanan sent federal troops to Utah to squelch the secession threat, they offered to unite with Young to defeat the federals. Shoshone support of Mormons during the Utah War would escalate suspicion in Washington that Mormons were encouraging the hostile actions of nearby Shoshone.

The Utah War began in 1857 when Young was removed as governor and replaced by Alfred Cumming. Later, in July 1862, the Mormon church would formalize the secret "State of Deseret," a "ghost government," installing Young as governor and meeting one day per year, the day after the closing of a legislative session, to affirm the laws passed by the "actual" government and apply them beyond Utah, to the entire "Mormon Empire." The members of the Deseret legislature were exactly identical to the Utah legislature; and all were Mormons; and so one might conclude that the ghost government was unnecessary. The same could be said for the Deseret alphabet, invented in the 1850s by Mormon linguists. This phonetic alphabet was learned by Mormon schoolchildren and by non-English-speaking Mormon emigrants, and would fall out of use by the 1870s. But in 1862 the Deseret government and the Deseret alphabet would achieve a simulation, at least, of theocratic self-determination.

But in 1857, with reformation fever burning, President Buchanan sent General William S. Harney with an army to Utah to assure a peaceful transition of power from Young to Cumming. Command was later transferred to Colonel Albert Sidney Johnston. Until Johnston could arrive, the troops were led by Colonel Edmund Alexander, an indecisive man who, rather than fight under his own authority, chose to await his new commander.

The troops, impeded by deep snows and "the old woman," as his men called Alexander (see Bigler 154), camped near Fort Bridger (in present-day Wyoming), allowing Young the opportunity to claim that he had not yet been legally replaced as governor. He sent the territorial militia—including his legendary secret police force, the Danites—to Echo Canyon, where they destroyed Johnston's supply trains and stole one thousand head of cattle. The U.S. government's concerns are reflected in a reprimand Young received in November 1857: he was scolded for going over his territorial budget, for traveling to Oregon "to give presents to Indians not under your control," and for "studiously endeavor[ing] to impress on the minds of the Indians that there was a difference between your own sect, . . . and the Government . . . [and] that the former were their friends and the latter their enemies" (qtd. in Madsen 78).

Young's journal, recording his thoughts on the skirmish, was written in the Deseret alphabet.

Meanwhile, trouble had been brewing on the Humboldt Road, trouble Young feared would be exacerbated by the presence of

Buchanan's troops. The Humboldt Road ran west of the Mormon settlements through an area Young had called the most difficult part of his territory to control, an area where the Shoshone had been forcibly demanding ammunition from travelers and stagecoach operators. That summer, much of the Holloway party had been killed: the two-year-old daughter was held by the feet and smacked into a wagon wheel, her mother scalped while feigning death. That same month, Wood, an Englishman, lost his wife and baby, later identifying a white man as one of the attackers; James Tooly was killed trying to escape angry emigrants who convicted him in an impromptu trial. Frequently, then, "depredations" along the emigrant roads were committed not by Shoshone but by white desperadoes exploiting a delicate situation. A band of highwaymen composed of natives, Spaniards, and Americans was reported operating out of the Truckee Valley. An editor of the *Sacramento Union* asserted that the majority of attacks on emigrants had been perpetrated by whites who viewed natives as subhuman, and by wagon masters who punished the Shoshone for even the smallest losses in stock, most of them unexplained. In one of the editor's examples, a "depredation" consisting of three missing cattle was the excuse for the deaths of eighteen Shoshone.

Young blamed most of the incidents on a band of four hundred Californians who had a policy of shooting any native they saw—which policy provoked attacks by the Shoshone. And Buchanan's troops made things worse. Understanding that the Utah War was coming, the Shoshone north of Salt Lake were raiding Mormon farms, to lay in a food supply; in the Fort Lemhi area, Shoshone and Bannock groups felt emboldened to attack Mormon settlers, killing two in February 1858 and driving off cattle and horses. Young was right to sense that the introduction of federal troops into this unstable atmosphere would aggravate his impossibly balanced relationship with the Shoshone.

It wasn't only the Shoshone who were alarmed by the news of approaching troops. Mormon settlers viewed this as a new and familiar threat to their livelihoods and religion. Settlers had already been whipped into a furor by reformation fever and, Madsen says, by leaders such as Heber C. Kimball, who wrote, "Send 2500 troops, our brethren, to make a desolation of this people! God Almighty helping me, I will fight until there is not a drop of blood in my veins. Good God! I have enough wives to whip the United States, for they will whip themselves" (qtd. in Madsen 81).

Just then, the Fancher party was journeying through southern Utah on its way from Missouri to Los Angeles. On a recent visit, the party had made themselves unwelcome with their anti-Mormon rhetoric and their failure to prevent livestock from grazing on lands held by church stewardship. When asked to rein in their animals, they retorted that the grass belonged to the U.S. government. Frenzied Mormon settlers were led by the influential John D. Lee, an adopted son of Brigham Young's. (Many of the LDS leadership had adopted each other in an attempt to establish one dominant family of Israel, with Joseph Smith as its origin.) Lee and his people refused to sell supplies to the party, who threatened that, once in California, they would raise a militia, return, and punish the Mormons. Local leaders, trying to decide whether to wipe out the party rather than risk the threatened return, appealed to Young for advice.

Young replied that the party should be permitted to move on, but (supposedly) his message did not arrive in time. Lee and his followers, hoping that blame might be diverted onto the few Shoshone present, had already attacked the Fancher party in their camp at Mountain Meadows. The emigrants circled their wagons and fired back; the fight continued over four days, during which time emigrant volunteers attempted to slip away for help. (The Shoshone slipped away with Fancher cattle.) The escapees were apprehended; to protect themselves from what they feared would be inevitable exposure should anyone survive, the Mormon leadership determined to wipe out the rest of the company. (I refer you to the works by Juanita Brooks, Will Bagley, and Sally Denton for the details of this event.)

In short, Lee drove into the camp under a white flag and requested the surrender of the party, purportedly so they could be escorted from the area by the Mormon militia. Women and children led the way, followed by the men in single file, each accompanied by a member of a force of about fifty armed Mormon men. Most were shot, their throats cut—men, women, and children over the age of seven (those younger were considered by Mormon doctrine to be "innocent blood").

This tragedy in the history of western emigration (second worst only to the Handcart Disaster) took the lives of approximately 140 emigrants. Only seventeen (some say eighteen) children survived. The dead were thrown into ravines, where they were sprinkled with a layer of dirt too thin to thwart coyotes; and the cover-up was on.

Local Mormons assumed a cloak of silence, disabling federal attempts to prosecute guilty leaders. Brigham Young helped keep it
quiet, then blamed the Shoshone, then indirectly blamed the United
States, asserting that tension between the Mormons and the U.S.
Army had incited natives to violence. John D. Lee went so far as to
bill the federal government for cattle he gave to the Shoshone (cattle he stole from the Fancher party); Young rewarded Lee with a
seventeenth wife. But ultimately, pressure to investigate the church's
responsibility came from church members themselves, and Lee was
the LDS scapegoat. In the early 1870s, in a different political clime,
Lee was first excommunicated (though appointed to a distant post
on behalf of the church), then tried for the crime. He was executed
on March 23, 1877. His tombstone, in Panguitch, Utah, bears the
verse from St. John: "Know the truth, and the truth shall make
you free."

(In 1961, Lee was reinstated to LDS church membership by the
Quorum of the Twelve Apostles. In 1990, descendants of John D. Lee,
and relatives of his victims in the Mountain Meadows Massacre, gathered to dedicate a monument to those lost in that attack. A marker put
up on Utah Highway 18, about ten miles south of Enterprise, does not
include information about who perpetrated the killings.)

In 1857, the Mountain Meadows Massacre provided still more
evidence to persuade U.S. citizens back east that the Utah Saints were
fanatic savages—who had a bad habit of uniting with those other
savages—against harmless, gentile emigrants.

Indeed, Brigham Young continued to exploit vague similarities in
lifeways between his and the Shoshone peoples. In November 1857,
Young wrote to a nervous Washakie, whose Eastern Shoshone band,
near Fort Bridger, was closest to the oncoming troops:

> Some of the whites in the United States are very angry at the Mor-
> mons because we wish to worship the Great Spirit in the way in
> which we believe he wants us to and have more than one wife, and
> they have sent some soldiers to this country to try to make us get
> drunk, to abuse women, and to swear and dispute and quarrel as
> many of them do.
>
> Now we don't want to fight them, if they will only go away and
> not try to abuse and kill us when we are trying to do right. But if
> they try to kill us we shall defend ourselves but we do not want you
> to fight on the side of those wicked men. . . . You know that when

the Americans come to you they want to lie with your squaws, but the Mormons do not. . . . And if they lie and swear, you may know they are not Mormons. . . .

I do not want you to fight the Americans nor to fight us for them, for we can take care of ourselves. I am your brother. B.Y. (qtd. in Madsen 83)

But it was the Northwestern Shoshoni, closest to the Mormon center of Salt Lake City, who were most shaken by the threat of Mormon/federal crossfire. According to Madsen, Little Soldier, camped at Weber River, discussed his concern with settler Dimick B. Huntington, who encouraged him to learn to farm and "to be Baptized and then he could tel [*sic*] when the Gentiles told him a lie" (84). Little Soldier then traveled to Camp Scott, where, as Madsen puts it, he "assured the Indian agent [Jacob Forney] that he had always kept aloof from Mormon delusions and was friendly toward the government" (84).

Up in the Cache Valley, where new settlers in Wellsville had harvested their first crop, elder Peter Maughan began reporting to Young about native activity. In June 1857, fifty Shoshone had come to his home "all stripped naked and roade around and yelled like as many fiends against you and Arrapean [*sic*; a Mormon friendly Ute leader], and made a demand for Shirts, Flour, Powder & two Oxen, then ground their knives and charged their guns." They performed a war dance around the house and complained that they were hungry, had received no presents, "and that we were liveing on their Land, etc etc" (qtd. in Madsen 84). Maughan gave them a cow, and after they had gone, 250 Shoshone camped for the night a half mile from Wellsville, leaving the next morning. Young complained, Madsen says, about the federal government's failure to appropriate adequate funds for Shoshone subsistence—funds, it could be argued, that were necessary primarily to permit Young's own expansion program to continue unmolested. Because the Cache Valley Shoshone had received "but little" from Washington, they became "a Sore tax upon the people" (qtd. in Madsen 86). By October, concern over the potential conflict between the Mormons and the federal troops had driven most Northwestern Shoshoni north.

Hearing that Mormon fighters were determined to take more than supplies from their federal opponents, an embarrassed President Buchanan worked all winter to effect a conciliation. A mediator agreed to travel to Camp Scott, near Fort Bridger, to meet Governor Cumming. Young still did not trust Colonel Johnston, and ordered the abandonment of the northern settlements. In June Buchanan sent two peace commissioners, who offered Young amnesty in return for the establishment of a military post in the territory. On June 26, Salt Lake City was evacuated, and the army trooped through town and headed for Cedar Valley, forty miles south, where Johnston established Camp Floyd at a respectable distance. "Buchanan's Blunder" was over.

Forty miles was still a bit too close for Young's people, but the Mormons were not entirely unhappy with Camp Floyd's proximity. It was hoped that a military presence would offer protection for white settlers plagued by Shoshone raids, but Johnston wrote that "the Mormon people enjoy an immunity from their outrages. For the protection of these people against Indians there is no necessity for the presence of a single soldier" (qtd. in Madsen 89). Still, Mormon settlers felt an increasing threat from Shoshone groups, who, despite the obviously conflicted peace, were still caught between two sides and unsure who deserved their fealty. In October, near Spanish Fork, a white woman and child were captured—and the woman was reportedly raped—by a small band of Ute. Johnston sent several companies to find the guilty men, but the Ute, forewarned, fled to the hills. A small group of stragglers resisted being arrested for the deed, and their leader Pinteets was killed when he broke away. Three Ute promised to bring back the responsible party, and did so; the men were jailed in Salt Lake City. As it happened, Madsen reports, it was this brutality of the federal troops that motivated Arrapeen, the Ute leader, to ally with the Mormons. He offered to unite sixteen Indian nations with the Mormons to defeat the United States; Young respectfully declined.

Federal troops quickly found a better purpose when the Overland Weekly Mail Route, opened in 1858 and 1859 by Captain James Simpson of the Corps of Topographical Engineers, suffered the attacks of renegade Shoshone bands in August. Johnston's minor attempts to patrol the route were ineffective, not least because most of the Shoshone encountered were friendly. New Indian Superintendent Jacob Forney traveled the same region offering presents and promising more to come, finding the natives to be hungry and "poor, miserably poor" (qtd. in Madsen 91). Pine nuts were exhausted and the chief source of food was now stolen cattle; the Ute were also driven to stealing horses from their cousins, the Eastern Shoshone, who had been less dramatically affected by European presence.

Settlers returning to northern settlements after the Utah War found their homes vandalized by Northwestern Shoshoni. The band had also been stealing cattle from California emigrants. Cache Valley settlers were the last to return, under heavy guard, in April 1959, where they found fifteen hundred bushels of stored grain missing.

Despite the continuing conflict in the Cache Valley, a month later another settlement, Mendon, was established in this emerald oasis. Two more settlements were founded by the end of the summer, and by the end of the year, 150 Mormon families lived there. Peter Maughan organized a militia, the "Minute Men," to chase stolen horses and cattle, usually to no avail. Neighboring Shoshone had become "saucy." According to Matthew Fifield, they made a habit of taunting white women. When their husbands objected to this harassment, the Shoshone warriors "spatted their bare behinds toward them and asked them what they could do about it" (qtd. in Madsen 98). Northwestern Shoshoni were also performing war dances around Mormon invaders and, "well armed," were demanding "Beef flower tea and sugar Tea and sugar was out of the question and we had but little flower But every body divided what they had and Peter Maughan Sent a man after a Beef So the Indians killed the Beef and took what flower they could get and finely went of" (qtd. in Madsen 99).

By 1860, because of overcrowding in some Mormon settlements to the south, and especially thanks to Maughan's announcement that the Cache Valley was the most habitable spot in the region, the federal census of 1860 would count 2,605 people in 510 households in the valley—nearly 7% of the total population of the region, Madsen calculates. The Northwestern Shoshoni accelerated their response to this incursion, pulling knives on housewives and threatening livestock, making the Cache Valley, by 1860, a major center for red–white conflict in the west. Meanwhile, pillaging of the California Trail, the Pony Express, and the Overland Mail Route intensified. This year also saw such legendary "depredations" as the Otter Party Tragedy and the Pyramid Lake War.

By 1861, then, a tense atmosphere of profoundly complicated loyalties was complicated further by profound divisions on both sides. In June 1861, one hundred soldiers resigned from duty at Camp Floyd (renamed Fort Crittendon for the senator from Kentucky who was attempting a reconciliation between the North and the South), and joined Confederate forces. In July, Washakie announced his intention to make war on the Cheyenne, who had killed his son and three leaders. By then, the remaining Fort Crittendon troops were decamping and moving east, leaving no military force to protect the trails, the mail routes, and the settlers who now feared they would be caught in the crossfire of Washakie's intertribal war. Telegraph wires were connected to Salt Lake City in October, eliminating the need for the briefly successful Pony Express, but overland mail service was expanding. Natives living near the mail lines were almost completely deprived of their supply of grass seed by the Overland firm's monopoly of grasslands, necessary to fuel company stock. The pine nut harvest had also failed. Mormon settlers met that year with Northwestern Shoshoni leaders Bear Hunter and Sagwitch, among others, to make food presents in return for the leaders' agreement to leave the Cache Valley, once and for all.

Patrick Edward Connor (né O'Connor) was born in Ireland in 1820, on Saint Patrick's Day; he moved to New York City as a child, and enlisted in the regular army at the age of nineteen. He served for five years on the Iowa frontier, returned to New York to learn the mercantile business, and moved to Texas in 1846. There he joined with volunteers in July to fight in the Mexican War, reenlisting in the regular army when his regiment was discharged in September. Promoted to captain in February 1847, he fought at the Battle of Buena Vista, receiving a hand wound early in the going but continuing to lead his troops all day. He resigned his commission in May and left for California when gold was discovered, arriving in January 1850.

Nearly killed in a boating accident, and financially strapped, Connor had many adventures in his attempts to make his fortune. Eventually he prospered, as Madsen details, establishing a surveying company, a gravel company, and the Stockton waterworks; and he was awarded the contract to build the foundation of the new state capitol building in Sacramento. He left this project when he reentered the military in 1861—as a staunch Unionist despite the Confederate sympathies predominant in Stockton. He married and had three sons, only one of whom survived. Madsen avers that Connor was "obviously a man of courage and adventurous spirit—shrewd, energetic, feisty, and independent and with natural talents for leadership and soldiering" (145).

Meanwhile, back east, President Abraham Lincoln had become worried about the depth of California's loyalty to the Union; about the possibility of Confederate attack from the west; and about the possibility that the Pacific coast—and its gold—could be severed from the rest of the country. He requested of California one regiment of infantry and five companies of cavalry to guard the Overland Mail Route from Carson Valley to Salt Lake City and Fort Laramie—Shoshone country. Colonel George Wright, an Indian fighter in eastern Oregon and Washington, was appointed commander of the Pacific Coast Division and promoted to brigadier general. California's governor appointed Colonel Connor to command the California Volunteers.

Madsen argues that these two appointments in themselves signify an unsubtle sea change in federal Indian policy. The appointment of an experienced veteran like Connor, a proven "man of action and resolution" (153) to patrol duty, to protect a mail line harassed by poorly armed natives; coupled with the selection of Wright, an Indian fighter, to head the Pacific division: taken together, these appointments are remarkable. Union officials knew well that Connor would not be content with occasional scrapes.

Recruitment of volunteers began in September 1861; the new troops settled at Camp McDougall in October. Much of Connor's recruiting that fall and in the following spring was done in mining camps; his men were frequently arrested for drunken brawling. General Wright, Connor's commanding officer, held the troops in Benicia Barracks for the winter; meanwhile, he declared the Shoshone along the mail route to be "in a starving condition," and parceled out provisions just sufficient to keep them from attacking while Connor's troops were being trained and transferred.

Still, Indian agents continued to report mass starvation along the Humboldt; the Paiute and the Shoshone continued to steal cattle; and attacks on the eastern end of the route actually intensified. Indeed, in April 1862 things were so bad that the postmaster general ordered all mail delivered by sea until the Overland Mail Route could be secured, a decision that stranded stagecoach passengers in Utah. Madsen points out that Shoshone destitution had reached a breaking point that can hardly be described in words, and is perhaps best measured by the intensity of the attacks, a clear result of deprivation: "The [mail] stations were well stocked with food and horses and served as convenient corner grocery stores inviting starving natives to plunder them" (154).

Meanwhile, Utah's latest governor, John W. Dawson—whose appointment a distracted President Lincoln apparently forgot making—prepared to abandon his post in frustration with the recalcitrance of the Mormon theocracy. He reported to Washington in early 1862 that an army should be sent at once.

In June 1862 Wright reviewed the California troops and praised the "industry and untiring zeal and energy of Colonel Connor. . . . He has a regiment that the State may well be proud of" (qtd. in Madsen 146). Marching orders were sent down for Connor's troops for July 5, even as most of his troops and many Californians hoped that Connor's "Utah Column" would be sent to a greater duty much farther east than Salt Lake City—a hope so great that the soldiers would eventually volunteer to deduct $30,000 from their pay to finance travel to Virginia. The news was not received well in Utah either, as Brigham Young insisted that Dawson's replacement, Governor Frank Fuller, was neglecting Young's Utah militia as an obvious source of protection. Indeed, Governor Fuller himself had been neglected in April, when President Lincoln and Secretary of War Edwin Stanton ordered a telegraph sent to Young, rather than Fuller, asking that cavalry be mustered for ninety days to protect the area around Independence Rock on the Oregon Trail. Thanks to Young's patrols, the mail began to move again in June.

President Lincoln's gratitude was only partial. On July 1, 1862, he signed the Morrill Act, which criminalized polygyny. As usual in this history of resistance not just to polygyny but also to theocracy, the bill also limited the amount of real estate a church could hold to $50,000. However, content to "let sleeping dogs lie," as he put it (qtd. in Bigler 218), Lincoln did not attempt to enforce the bill.

Also in July 1862, the discovery of gold in Montana brought a rush of miners from all over the West. Since Salt Lake City was the closest supply point, the east–west overlanding would now be intersected by a north–south route—again, through the heart of Northwestern Shoshoni lands. Washington's commissioner of Indian affairs quickly saw that "depredations" by the Shoshone and the Bannock along this northerly route would be inevitable. He ordered new Indian Superintendent James Doty on July 22 to treat with area natives. He also ordered Doty not to pay compensation for the affected lands, but to arrange provisions and annuities in exchange for the safety of emigrants on what would now be three major trails. Up to this point, the federal government had permitted a sore neglect of the Northern and Northwestern Shoshoni groups, the same groups who were experiencing the heaviest European American imposition, even while other natives—as the Northern and Northwestern Shoshoni well knew—had won treaties promising them annual presents of food and clothing. Madsen observes that these bands recognized that attacking Europeans was the quickest means to a treaty of their own.

Late 1862 was a time of bloodshed. Six white men were killed in isolated incidents in July; on August 9 and 10, 150 warriors attacked the Smart train near what would later be called Massacre Rocks, in Idaho; and then these warriors attacked Captain George Adams's company, killing five white men. Four more white men were killed attempting to retrieve property stolen from the two parties; Adams's daughter died of wounds later. It was reported that the natives had been led by white men and armed with rifles. Raids continued throughout August, with the area around the Snake River widely considered the most dangerous. On September 19 the commissioner issued a proclamation warning travelers of the great risk of journeying across western trails. Newspapers warned also of renegade whites who, with the natives, had stolen thousands of dollars from travelers in the Fort Hall area. Doty was told by Little Soldier, leader of the Northwestern Shoshoni in the Weber region, that the Shoshone and the Bannock were turning away from Washakie's pacifism and banding together to fight the increasing traffic on the trails.

Given the diversion of military resources from this region to the Civil War, it is likely that desperate natives exploited an opportunity to forage violently, and with impunity. Although Mormon leaders were unhappy about the return of federal troops, many settlers were anxious for the arrival of Connor's Volunteers.

Although academics tend to compartmentalize the past into "Native American history," "African American history," "Western history," "Mormon history," and "Civil War history," all were inextricably entwined during the 1860s. Indeed, the pressures of these merging histories may have accelerated a process social psychologists call "cognitive dissonance." Although the United States had been founded on idealistic principles of equality, in the early nineteenth century leaders had little choice but to change their minds, so to speak, regarding the relative value of whites and peoples of color. To

permit westward expansion and economic development, native genocide and black slavery had to be acceptable.

Lincoln's administration would be plagued in many ways by this
dissonance.

In the earliest days of secession, the Confederate government
moved quickly to annex the Indian Territory (roughly, the future state
of Oklahoma, where southeastern native nations had been relocated),
and make natives pawns in the coming war. Shrewd southern leaders
coerced alliances with the Cherokee, Choctaw, Chickasee, Creek, and
Seminole by exploiting divisions between antislavery full-bloods and
slave-owning mixed-bloods. The Confederates raised regiments of
native soldiers. Lincoln, ever distracted and slow to perceive the value
of an alliance with the Indian Territory, withdrew his personnel from
the region and abandoned the trust responsibility outlined in early
treaties, which had promised to protect the natives from domestic
strife and foreign invaders. The Confederates saw an opportunity in
this abandonment, and in order to deprive the Union of any available
resources in the Indian Territory, torched those areas of the territory
that remained resistant to the Confederate alliance. This scorched-
earth action resulted in a massive flood of refugees into Kansas.

When Kansas protested the presence in their state of more than
ten thousand destitute natives, and begged repeatedly for the small
fortune in federal funds that would be necessary to feed them, Lincoln was forced finally to pay attention. He accepted proposals to return the natives to their homes, and to provide them with funds until
they could reestablish their former settlements. These proposals failed
primarily because a military escort could not be organized. White soldiers refused to serve on behalf of natives, and state leaders would
not tolerate arming native warriors. The refugee disaster would linger
for years.

The Civil War period, with its emphasis on militarism, ushered in
a dramatic—but unacknowledged and undebated—change in federal
Indian policy. If possibly the first hint of this policy shift came with
the appointments of Wright and Connor in the Pacific region, the first
implementation of the new policy occurred in early 1862 in remote
regions of Arizona and New Mexico. There General James Carleton
had been sent to skirmish with Confederate troops, and there he
found tense relations between whites and natives—and gold on native land. Carleton had been given a free hand to respond as he chose.
He sent Kit Carson against the Apache with orders to kill every

native man he encountered, anywhere, and to destroy the prairie habitat. Later, the military would turn against the Navajo as well.

Indeed, the late summer of 1862 was a difficult one for natives in several regions, including the Dakota, who after years of having their territory reduced by the Ojibwe (who themselves were crushed into Dakota territory by westward creeping white emigration) now were forced to share resources with the settlers of the new state of Minnesota. For huge tracts of land, the U.S. government had agreed in 1851 to pay $1,665,000 in cash and annuities to the Wahpeton and the Sisseton bands of what were then known as the "Upper Sioux"; likewise, $1,410,000 was to go to the Mdewakanton and the Wahpekute bands of the "Lower Sioux." The treaties left these groups with thin strips of reservations straddling both banks of the Minnesota River. The Lower Sioux were never happy with their lands, which were prairie rather than their preferred woodlands. They also felt that traders conspiring with mixed-blood natives had cheated them out of $400,000 of their money. A second treaty made in 1858 chopped away the land on the north bank of the river, squeezing the Dakota further still.

These and other circumstances combined to reduce Dakota respect for the Great White Father. The winter of 1861–62 was one of near starvation, caused by a crop failure; and, most important historians say, by midyear 1862, the Dakota were further incited by the failure of their annual goods and monies to arrive. Strained by the costs of war, the U.S. government was hard-pressed to send the $71,000 in gold coin finally presented to the Dakota on August 16, several months late. And in actuality, it was white traders, such as Andrew J. Myrick, who were the real beneficiaries of annuity payments to natives, since they "sold" provisions at exorbitant prices to the temporarily cash-rich natives. While the natives waited for their long overdue annuities, Myrick and others refused credit to the hungry Dakota. Finally, in 1862, the exasperated Dakota noticed that many of the white male settlers had left the region to fight in the Civil War. Indeed, Lincoln was repeatedly begging western governors to draft more and more troops.

On August 17, four Dakota who were, even by the standards of their own people, troublemakers, stopped for food at a farm near Acton. There they killed five settlers, including two women. It was said that the murders were committed in sport, but certainly they were also committed out of anger at the declining situation of the Dakota.

Two of the four shooters would be killed by their own people. A council of Dakota leaders was quickly convened. Several leaders expected that since retaliation by the settlers was inevitable, they might as well take the opportunity to clear the land of some of these encroaching settlers, and take back Dakota territory. Wabasha was then the primary leader of the Dakota, and he opposed the war on the grounds that the Dakota could not fight off the better-armed settlers, but Little Crow was persuaded to lead the uprising. Leaders who opposed the war felt they had little choice but to follow the will of their people.

From August 18 until September 26, Little Crow's Dakota warriors attacked Minnesota agencies and villages. Several hundreds would die on both sides of the conflict; and the Dakota captured hundred of women and children, including Sarah Wakefield, who would later publish a narrative describing her "Six Weeks in the Sioux Tepees." Governor Alexander Ramsey sent frequent panicked telegrams to Secretary of War Stanton, and also wired President Lincoln, requesting that the most recent draft of men for the Virginia campaign be deferred. Lincoln answered, "Attend to the Indians. If the draft *cannot* proceed of course it *will not* proceed. Necessity knows no law" (qtd. in Carley 55). Lincoln was receiving similar panicked telegrams from several western governors who faced a "red menace," but still a response from Washington was delayed. Lincoln seemed stymied by every difficulty presented by natives. Little Crow fought on for several weeks with little resistance.

On September 6, Ramsey wired Lincoln: "This is not our war; it is a national war. . . . Answer me at once. More than 500 whites have been murdered by the Indians" (qtd. in Carley 55). At last convinced, Stanton ordered Major General John Pope, recently defeated at Bull Run, to take command of the troops fighting the Dakota. Pope delegated field command to Colonel Henry H. Sibley, who until then had been leading a small group of Minnesota volunteers through several losses to the Dakota. Ammunition arrived on September 11, and on September 13, 270 infantrymen of the Third Minnesota Regiment returned from Virginia. On September 23, the Battle of Wood Lake resulted in a decisive victory for the Minnesota troops; on September 26, 269 white and mixed-blood captives were freed at Camp Release. Sibley took twelve hundred Indians into custody; several hundred more would enter the camp voluntarily.

On September 29, President Lincoln promoted Sibley to the rank of brigadier general.

A five-man military commission was established to prosecute those Dakota who had participated in the uprising, which had resulted in the deaths of almost five hundred whites and the removal of European Americans from twenty-three counties. If the commission was not entirely just, it certainly was swift, trying 392 men from September 28 to November 5, sentencing 307 to death for rape and murder and 16 to prison. Episcopal Bishop Henry B. Whipple, who had warned President Lincoln of the coming troubles back in March 1862, visited the president and requested intervention. Lincoln sent a staff of men, including John G. Nicolay, his private secretary, to examine the sentences.

Minnesota's congressional representatives were outraged by Lincoln's interference, claiming that the Dakota had "seized and carried into captivity nearly one hundred women and young girls, and in nearly every instance treated them with the most fiendish brutality. . . . [A]lthough they sometimes spared the lives of the mothers and daughters, they did so only to take them into a captivity which was *infinitely worse than death.*" In his order to reduce the number of death sentences, Lincoln wrote, in reference to the prisoners "proved guilty of violating females," that, "[c]ontrary to my expectations, only two of this class were found" (qtd. in Wakefield 5).

On December 6, Lincoln approved death sentences for "only" (as the Minnesotans would have it) thirty-nine of the prisoners (the Dakota doubtless thought this thirty-nine too many). It was a wildly unpopular but politically pragmatic decision that fully satisfied, and fully disappointed, no one. It outraged—but not too much—the bloodthirsty Minnesota populace while appeasing—almost—the eastern liberals on whom Lincoln relied for support. Another conviction was later overturned on new testimony. At ten o'clock on the morning of December 26, thirty-eight prisoners were hung in Mankato, where martial law had been declared for the day, on a scaffolding surrounded by fourteen hundred soldiers and untold numbers of settlers. Despite Lincoln's perceived leniency, the hangings remain, for U.S. history, the largest state-sponsored mass execution of people whose guilt was not fully determined. The bodies of the executed were placed in a shallow grave along a nearby river, but were dug up the next day by area physicians anxious for an opportunity to study anatomy.

Among those executed was Chaska, a protector of Sarah Wakefield's, in defense of whom she had risked her family and social standing to testify. Chaska had served as Wakefield's protector during her captivity, and she was able to account for his whereabouts during the uprising. Purportedly, his execution was an accident, due to mistaken identity; but it is possible that the "error" was attributable to the popular resentment of Lincoln's interference; and especially to an angry suspicion among Minnesotans that Wakefield and Chaska had enjoyed an inappropriate friendship. Chaska's mother was furious that Wakefield could do nothing to help her son, when her son had done so much to help Wakefield.

Connor left Stockton, California, on July 12 with 850 men, fifty wagons of equipment and provisions, a large herd of cattle, three ambulances, and carriages for officers' families. Almost immediately he experienced discipline problems with his Volunteers: thirty men deserted during the march. Ultimately, 21% would desert in the four years of service ahead. Also on the march, Major Edward McGarry, although frequently drunk, emerged as a reckless leader of men, and as the officer on whom Connor would primarily rely.

On his way through the Humboldt region, Connor was early afforded an opportunity to gather accolades as a great Indian fighter, when in mid-September reports arrived of an attack on emigrants near Gravelly Ford. Shoshone bands may have been helped by white men to kill twelve (originally reported as twenty-three) whites. Connor sent McGarry with Companies H and K to investigate, ordering the major to "destroy every male Indian whom you may encounter in the vicinity of the late massacres. This course may seem harsh and severe, but I desire that the order may be rigidly enforced, as I am satisfied that in the end it will prove the most merciful." He added, "In no instance will you molest women and children" (qtd. in Madsen 167). McGarry's troops shot and killed twenty-four natives in various incidents that occurred while ferreting out the guilty.

In Salt Lake City, the *Deseret News* denounced the practice of indiscriminate killing and worried that it might incite more violence. Connor, visiting Salt Lake City to select a place for his camp, was no more happy with the Mormon population than they were with him, writing to his superiors that Mormons were a "community of traitors, murderers, fanatics, and whores" led by a despot the federal government would be unable to control (qtd. in Madsen 169). His superiors likely concurred: although Brigham Young had expressed his support for the Union, the secretary of war reportedly feared a loss of Mormon loyalty following the signing of the Morrill Act; and there were perpetual reports of Mormons selling guns to natives—purportedly so they could hunt.

The late-October arrival of the Volunteers was thus fraught on both sides. A detailed diary kept by the Volunteers' chaplain John A. Anderson recorded a rumor that flew among the troops, that the Mormons intended to send the Danites to fight the troops at the Jordan River. Anderson reports that Connor distributed ammunition and led his troops right through the center of town: up East Temple (now Main) and east on First South, directly past the home of yet another new governor, Stephen Harding. "Every crossing was occupied by spectators, and windows, doors and roofs had their gazers. Not a cheer nor a jeer greeted us." The Mormons would be partly happy to have the soldiers, Anderson speculated, not least because "it would bring many a dollar into city circulation" (qtd. in Madsen, *Glory Hunter* 70).

Connor ignored distant Fort Crittendon, and established Camp Douglas instead, on the eastern benchlands overlooking the city; this, Madsen says, so as "to keep a close watch on the Mormons as well as to police the mail lines. From this point on he waged a cold war with Mormon authorities. Warning his commander that he fully expected Brigham Young's militia to attack him at any time, he made repeated requests for more troops" (169). He would also accuse Mormons of supplying natives, and of purchasing stolen emigrant goods from them.

One of Connor's earliest encounters with local natives occurred in November. During the massacre of the Otter party on the Snake River in 1860, Alexis Van Orman, his wife, and one son had been murdered. Three daughters were captured, only to die of starvation. Another captured son, Reuben Van Orman, was the only survivor. In late 1862, Zachias Van Orman, the boy's uncle, heard that a white boy had been seen in the Cache Valley with Bear Hunter's band. Connor ordered McGarry to Providence, in Cache Valley, where McGarry attempted to surprise a small band in the early morning. The Shoshone took a better position in a canyon and McGarry was able to capture only one warrior; Bear Hunter and his men paraded high along the benchlands and "made a war-like display, such as shouting, riding in a circle, and all sorts of antics known only to their race" (qtd. in Madsen 172). The major proved early that he was easily baited by such behavior. He ordered the soldiers "to kill every Indian they could see" (qtd. in Madsen 173) and sent them in three divisions to fight for two hours. When Bear Hunter appeared showing a flag of truce, a spectator, Lee Dees, was sent to negotiate with Bear Hunter. Dees reported that the leader "did not want to fight anymore," due to his "long friendship with the whites and always desiring peace" (qtd. in Madsen 173). McGarry ceased fire and accepted the surrender of Bear Hunter and twenty warriors.

On hearing that the white boy had left the camp days before, McGarry held Bear Hunter and four other men hostage until the boy was brought in by band members, when McGarry released the hostages. But the blond-haired, blue-eyed boy probably was not Reuben Van Orman. After only two years in captivity he spoke no English, and several Shoshone reported that he was the son of Washakie's sister and a French mountaineer.

Bear Hunter and his band went to Providence the day after the boy was turned over to McGarry, angry with the Mormon "cowards" there, who had failed to help the Shoshone keep their cousin (qtd. in Madsen 173). According to a witness, Bear Hunter threatened to attack the soldiers, and dared them to come north and meet him in battle. In response to this demonstration, seventy Minute Men were sent from Logan.

The Northwestern Shoshoni were to be even more enraged when a pattern of indiscriminate army retaliation began to develop. In early December, Connor ordered McGarry to take one hundred cavalrymen to Bear River Ferry, west of Brigham City, where a large native encampment was reportedly in possession of emigrant stock. The troops left Camp Douglas secretly and marched all through the next night. But the natives heard about the approach and cut the ferry rope. McGarry left behind the horses and crossed the river in a scow, captured four Shoshone, and sent a message that the four would be shot if the stock was not released. The Shoshone packed up their camp and headed for the Cache Valley, while McGarry tied the hands of the four captives to the ferry rope, and executed them, dumping their bodies into the river. The execution required fifty-one shots, prompting the *Deseret News* to criticize the troops' marksmanship, to wonder about this missed opportunity to attack a larger group of Shoshone, and to ask again whether these four killings would only incite more violence.

Back east, the winter of 1862–63 was one of supreme discontent, as The War Between the States slogged on. Mid-December, just as Dakota warriors were being hung for their participation in Little

Crow's war against the Minnesotans, the great Union "disaster" occurred at Fredericksburg. Afterward, both armies wintered on opposite sides of the Rappahannock River, the Confederates operating a series of tormenting raids behind federal lines.

On January 1, 1863, President Lincoln signed the Emancipation Proclamation. In the occupied South, newly freed slaves celebrated their freedom. Lincoln, who had volunteered to fight in the Black Hawk War of 1832 (he saw no combat), but who had a reputation for generosity toward those individual natives he had personally encountered, never considered extending any similar emancipation to indigenous peoples. Indeed, we may easily conclude that in January 1863, Lincoln was exhausted by the persistently nagging and distracting problems natives were causing him all over the West. He may have been willing to do anything that would spare him having again to divert personnel, ammunition, and attention, west. And his abiding concern with maintaining mail routes to California resulted in his silent consent to this policy of genocide—a policy of removal, of easement, by murder. We can also conclude that he knew as much, though historians like Madsen have uncovered no documents substantiating Lincoln's knowledge of these operations. Indeed, the absence of documentation speaks volumes, suggesting that Lincoln may well have understood the political ramifications of his scrupulously unrecorded policy shift.

This new policy was largely unrecognized by citizens of the eastern United States, whose newspapers were crowded with the details of the January 21 "Mud March," a move by federal troops to flank General Robert E. Lee on the Rappahannock. Cold rain deterred the deployment of men and materiel, and Major General Ambrose Burnside resigned as head of Lincoln's army.

Burnside's departure marked a controversial turning point for the Union, giving citizens much to debate. On January 25 Lincoln appointed General Joseph "Fighting Joe" Hooker to succeed him. Hooker would begin a process of reorganizing the army, separating the cavalry into its own corps, and resupplying it with rations and arms. He would begin the process of gearing up for Chancellorsville, and ultimately, Gettysburg.

January 1863 in the Cache Valley was a bad season. On January 5, word went out that native raiders had killed ten white men headed south on the road from the mines. The next day a party of eight men missed the main ford near Franklin and ended up near Richmond. When three went for help, the other five were robbed of their stock. Some of the stock was returned and the men moved to the east side of the river; on the west side natives fired across, killing John Henry Smith. Four men were sent by Mormon Bishop Marriner W. Merrill to rescue Smith's body for burial. On January 14, the operator of an express service between Salt Lake City and Montana reported that two expressmen, George Clayton and Henry Bean, had been killed on the Cache Valley Road, and that the Shoshone were set on avenging the executions at Bear River Ferry.

A warrant to arrest leaders Bear Hunter, Sanpitch, and Sagwitch for the murder of John Henry Smith was issued by Chief Justice John F. Kinney. Territorial Marshal Isaac L. Gibbs was told to engage Connor's troops to assist in the arrests. Connor had already decided to move against the Shoshone: "Being satisfied that they [the Indians] were part of the same band who had been murdering emigrants on the overland mail route for the past fifteen years and [were] the principal actors and leaders in the horrid massacre of the past summer, I determined, although the weather was unfavorable to an expedition, to chastise them if possible" (qtd. in Madsen 179). Connor's intentions were affirmed by an April 7, 1862, order he had received from the Department of the Pacific: "Every Indian captured in this district during the present war who has been engaged in hostilities against whites, present or absent, will be hanged on the spot, women and children in all cases being spared" (qtd. in Madsen 179).

A newly violent tide was turning toward the Shoshone, unbeknownst to them. Even Brigham Young may have been backing off his feed-don't-fight policy. It was reported in the *Sacramento Union* that when Northwestern Shoshoni leader Sanpitch asked Young to help reestablish peace with natives to the north, Young replied that Mormon settlers had had enough of the Northwestern Shoshoni, and that if more Mormons were killed, Young might even "pitch in" to support federal troops against the natives (qtd. in Madsen 179).

Connor began to prepare his troops, purportedly in secret, for an extraordinary winter engagement. His was a new strategy, breaking from the traditional practice of drawing warriors away from the camp to fight on a battlefield in summer. Heretofore unattempted, a winter attack would give him the best advantage because the comfortably settled warriors would be burdened by the presence of their families, and less likely to respond effectively, especially in the cold.

Connor's secret preparations were obvious to locals, who had also heard his recent promise to "exterminate" the natives who were killing overlanders.

On January 22, 1863, in a heavy snowstorm, Captain Samuel W. Hoyt left Camp Douglas with seventy-two men from K Company, Third Infantry Regiment; a detachment of twelve cavalry; fifteen baggage wagons carrying a twenty-day supply of rations; and two howitzers with one hundred shells. It was said that they were marching to escort a wagon train moving grain in Cache Valley. On January 24, Connor moved out with 220 men from Companies A, H, K, and M, Second Cavalry. His ration orders for the cavalry alone totaled an astounding sixteen thousand rounds of ammunition for rifles and pistols. The plan was to march through the night to a rendezvous with the infantry, to attack the Shoshone at Bear River.

The exit from Salt Lake City must have been impressive, if quiet. On January 28, the *Deseret News* crowed that the Union-affiliated troops would "wipe them out" (qtd. in Madsen 180).

Hoyt's march was slow: 13 miles the first day, then 25, then 18, then 14, then 25. Their route was to the Weber River, then to Willard, and then Mendon, where they awaited the cavalry. On January 28, Corporal Hiram G. Tuttle's diary records that they "left camp 12 at night, went 34 miles to Franklin and camped," arriving at 5 P.M. (qtd. in Madsen 180).

The march took place during what must have been, had records been kept, a record-making cold snap in the region. It was so bitterly cold that the whiskey rations froze in canteens. The cavalry, who rode 68 miles their first night out, arrived in Brigham City with their feet frozen in stirrups, and (as reported in the *San Francisco Bulletin*) "whiskers and moustache . . . so chained together by ice that opening the mouth became most difficult" (qtd. in Madsen 182). There was a foot of snow in the Salt Lake valley, and four feet on the divide between Brigham City and Cache Valley. Moving the howitzers was a daunting challenge, and seventy-five cavalrymen were abandoned at Mormon settlements with frozen feet. As Madsen notes, "Fighting Indians in midwinter at below zero temperatures was an unusual experience in United States military history, but Connor never wavered" (182).

Famed Mormon guide Orrin Porter Rockwell had been engaged by Connor for $5 a day; Rockwell warned Connor that the Shoshone were ready and waiting and had built entrenchments at the camp.

Connor expected six hundred warriors manning rifle pits behind breastworks to defend what he knew to be seventy-five lodges. Thus Madsen disputes Connor's calculation of his opposition as a vast overestimation—one of which Connor was probably conscious. At an average of six persons per lodge, seventy-five lodges could typically hold only 450 people altogether; therefore, Madsen estimates that there were fewer than 200 warriors present. And Rockwell's assessment of Shoshone intentions was also not credible. A miner on the road to Salt Lake City reported talking to some Cache Valley Shoshone who told him they would not harass the settlers further but intended only to continue to exact revenge from white travelers for McGarry's actions.

In Franklin, just before the troops arrived, Bishop Preston Thomas ordered nine bushels of wheat be given to three Shoshone sent by Bear Hunter. William Hull complied, taking the opportunity to taunt the Shoshone about the approach of soldiers, whom the Shoshone called "Toquash." "We had two of the three horses loaded, having put three bushels on each horse . . . when I looked up and saw the Soldiers approaching from the south. I said to the Indian boys, 'Here comes the Toquashes maybe, you will all be killed.' They answered 'maybe Toquashes be killed too,' but not waiting for the third horse to be loaded, they quickly jumped upon their horses and led the three horses away, disappearing in the distance" (qtd. in Madsen 183). Bear Hunter may also have visited town that day to trade. Thus it is clear that the Northwestern Shoshoni were warned about the presence of the infantry. But Madsen points out that they probably did not know about the cavalry, and could have known neither the full extent of the party sent to march against them, nor of their new intentions.

Connor ordered Hoyt to move out with the infantry, the howitzers, and the wagon train at 1:00 A.M. But he was at first unable to find a local guide to lead him to the Shoshone camp. Mormon leaders finally "counseled" Edmond and Joseph S. Nelson of Franklin to accompany Hoyt (such is the term used by the *Franklin County Citizen*; qtd. in Madsen 183).

They set out after 3:00 A.M., two hours late.

The infantry was also delayed by the equipment, and, as Madsen says, "wished they could have traded their wagons for the sleighs knowledgeable Mormon settlers used for winter transportation in Cache Valley" (183).

Mercifully, the howitzers were abandoned six miles from the river. Connor left with the cavalry at 4:00 A.M., catching up with Hoyt four miles from the river.

Madsen believes that Major McGarry and the first cavalry troops reached the bluffs overlooking Bear River "at 6:00 a.m., just as dawn was breaking" (183); local historians in Preston believe the time to have been closer to 7:00 A.M. They are all in agreement, however, that the soldiers were able to see smoke rising from early fires at the camp across the stream. Madsen describes the scene as discovered by the soldiers:

> As the Volunteers surveyed the scene before them, they realized the "miniature Sebastopol" they faced in the Indian position. At this point, Bear River meanders through a flood plain about a mile wide, bounded by sagebrush-covered bluffs about 200 feet high. The river runs roughly in a north–south direction but turns to the west where it receives Battle Creek [then Beaver Creek], which courses southwest before also turning west to enter Bear River [providing an excellent defensive position behind the steep river, on a flat tableland of about three-tenths of a mile wide]. During the winter season, the latter [swift-flowing] stream is about 175 feet wide and 3 to 4 feet deep and was, on January 29, filled with floating ice. The Indian camp was located on the west side of Battle Creek in a narrow valley filled with willows up to 10 feet high and bounded on the east by a steep embankment from 6 to 12 feet high. There were three narrow passageways cut through the bank to allow horsemen access, and some children's "foxholes" were dug out of the side of the embankment. About seventy-five comfortable lodges were spread alongside the stream and connected by narrow footpaths through the dense willows. . . . The Indian horse herd was a mile or so below the camp near some hot springs [today called Wayland Hot Springs]. The village seemed a strong, defensible position to Indian and trooper alike. (*Glory Hunter* 80–82)

Madsen has also written, "The bluffs on the south side are so steep that it would be almost impossible to get a wagon down them; they would even be difficult for men on horseback to negotiate. . . . Cedar Point, a sharp headland, juts out close to Battle Creek where the stream enters the main valley" (184).

The Shoshone, then, had woven long branches of willows along the creekbed to provide shelter. Around the bend, it was on the north side of Cedar Point that the horses were pastured. Most of the lodges were between the horse pasture and the creek's entry into the river, directly east of Cedar Point; lodges were elevated by stones and earth gathered underneath to warm the interior.

The Northwestern Shoshoni bands of Bear Hunter and Sagwitch had camped in the area for the winter, and had recently hosted a gathering attended by Pocatello's band—the warm dance. Pocatello and his people had just left the region; Madsen and Mae Timbimboo Parry, a keeper of the Shoshone oral history, both dismiss contemporary reports that some Bannock were present.

At six or seven o'clock, then, on the morning of January 29, a tide of events had carried Major McGarry to the bluffs overlooking the Shoshone settlement. The two bands camped there slept peacefully, secure in their position behind Beaver Creek and unaware of a significant change in U.S. Indian policy. In response to the recent developments leading to this day, Sagwitch and Bear Hunter (as well as Pocatello, who had just left the area) had no reason to expect anything but the usual rounding up of those who had perpetrated the recent killings.

But at 6:00 or 7:00, then, on the morning of January 29, Sagwitch, an early riser, emerged from his lodge that morning and saw an alarming sight.

There were two hundred soldiers on the other side of the river.

Sagwitch began shouting. He rousted the warriors and their leader, Bear Hunter, out of bed.

Connor had ordered McGarry to cross the river and surround before engaging the enemy. Cavalry Companies K and M began to ford. Private John R. Lee later wrote, "That was a bad looking river, half frozen over and swift. The horses did not want to go in it. Two old boys got throwed by their horses" (qtd. in Madsen 186). Most of the men got wet. On the other side, the men landed on a plain some 500 yards from the ravine.

In his report, Connor wrote that Bear Hunter and his men "sallied out [from the ravine] . . . and with fiendish malignity waived the scalps of white women and challenged the troops to battle" (qtd. in Madsen 186). The *San Francisco Bulletin* correspondent, the only newspaper correspondent on the scene (some Mormon neighbors were also present, watching from the bluffs), reported that "[o]ne of

the chiefs was galloping up and down the bench in front of his warriors, haranguing them and dangling his spear on which was hung a
female scalp in the face of the troops, while many of the warriors
sang out, 'Fours right, fours left, Come on, you California sons of
b——s'" (qtd. in Madsen 186).

McGarry proved consistent in his inability to resist being baited
in this way. He decided to disobey orders and engage Bear Hunter's
men before the camp had been surrounded. Connor would report
that McGarry did so due to the challenges of the terrain. Regardless
of the reason, his decision would cause two-thirds of the casualties on
the soldiers' side.

From another perspective, this decision was the only Volunteer
act that day which gave the Shoshone half a chance to stage a fair
fight.

Regarding what happened next, Shoshone and European American histories diverge. White history has the Shoshone firing first.

McGarry advanced his troops slightly and, facing a barrage of bullets from Shoshone entrenched in the east bank of the creek, dis-
mounted, forming a line, with every fourth man taking horses to the
rear. One trooper was wounded in this early volley. The soldiers sought
what cover they could find to avoid the fury of bullets. Companies A
and H joined the line shortly. In the first half hour of engagement, fourteen of McGarry's men were killed and twenty wounded; five horses
were lost. McGarry finally retreated out of range at about the same
time Connor arrived from the rear and took command.

Connor ordered McGarry to flank the Shoshone to their left, up
and around the bluffs that led down to the south of the Beaver Creek
ravine; Lieutenant Cyrus Clark was ordered to bottle in the Shoshone
on the south end of the creek, where Beaver Creek met Bear River.
Company K, Third Infantry, had arrived but was unable to ford the
river; the infantrymen were victims of the cold, their uniforms freez-
ing to their bodies. Connor ordered the horse holders to ferry the infantry across the river, then sent half with McGarry and half with
Clark, who was ordered to contain escapes at the mouth of the creek.
Lieutenant John Quinn was sent around the south end of the creek to
prevent escape over the west bluffs; Lieutenant George Conrad was
sent to block passage into Bear River near the mouth of the creek.

Thus was the entire camp to be hemmed in.

All units were to attack when they heard McGarry's fire. The
Shoshone had not nearly as many arms and ammunition as had the

soldiers; old men and women molded bullets during the fight, and at least one soldier was wounded with an arrow. From a strict military perspective, the abandoned howitzers would have been most useful to the California Volunteers: likely most of the federal casualties would have been avoided and the Shoshone would have suffered far more greatly.

The struggle went on for two more hours in the form of hand-to-hand combat. The soldiers moved among the lodges, facing what Madsen terms the "dogged obstinacy" of the Shoshone (188). The federals suffered another center of casualties directly opposite the camp, where Captain George F. Price lost eight men. But generally, the advantage in arms would favor the U.S. troops. When counting bodies, soldiers would find a pile of forty-eight Shoshone where Price had been leading his troops.

The women and children in camp, Madsen says, "apparently sought shelter" (189), although Shoshone oral history, and Mormon witnesses quoted by Newell Hart, have some women engaging the soldiers as warriors.

Eventually the warriors were forced, by fire from both north and south of the ravine, to break out of their hold there and run for Bear River. Lieutenant Conrad was sent to cut them off just north of where the soldiers had forded. The warriors were chased into the willow thickets along the riverbank, and more hand-to-hand combat ensued. Madsen says that although no official orders were given, the soldiers "fought to the finish" (189). Riflemen shot at those Shoshone who leaped into the river. Of these, some drowned, and some escaped by hiding under foliage. Some managed to run up the west bluffs and escape into the plains.

The "fighting" ended at around 10 A.M.

Which is when the raping began.

Madsen dedicates to the rape only one paragraph in his 1985 book, *The Shoshoni Frontier and the Bear River Massacre*:

> In addition to taking nearly all Indian property, after the battle some soldiers spent the rest of the day in more reprehensible activities. Soldiers reported to Alexander Stalker [a local Mormon resident] that wounded Indians who were so incapacitated they could not move "were killed by being hit in the head with an axe." James Martineau wrote of one instance in which a soldier found a dead woman clutching a little infant still alive. The soldier "in mercy to

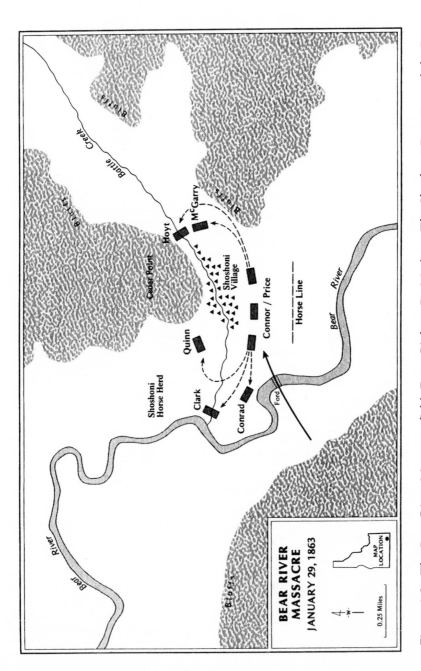

Figure 1.2. The Bear River Massacre field. From Bigham D. Madsen, *The Shoshoni Frontier and the Bear River Massacre* (Salt Lake City: U of Utah P, 1985) 185. Reprinted courtesy of the University of Utah Press.

the babe, killed it." Martineau also recorded more barbarity: "Several squaws were killed because they would not submit quietly to be ravished, and other squaws were ravished in the agony of death." "Matigund" [a native] told Samuel Roskelly "the way the Soldiers used the Squaws after the battle was shameful. . . ." In confirmation of these atrocities, Peter Maughan reported to Brigham Young that about twenty strange Indians had come into Franklin and that "all are familiar with the conduct of the troops toward the Squaws etc. . . ." In another letter, Maughan wrote: "Bro Israel J Clark has just returned from visiting the Battlefield and give the most sickening accounts of the inhuman acts of the Soldiers, as related to him by the squaws that still remain on the ground. . . . They killed the wounded by Knocking them in the head with an axe and then commenced to ravish the Squaws which was done to the very height of brutality they affirm that some were used in the act of dying from their wounds. The above reports are substantiated by others that were present at the time." Maughan stated that the Indian women were afraid to come into the settlements because the soldiers might return. Most of the survivors traveled to the head of Marsh Creek several miles north where Chief Sagwitch had set up a temporary camp after his escape from the conflict. (193)

David L. Bigler disagrees with Madsen's assessment. In his book, published in 1998, he writes:

> Connor was also accused of indiscriminately killing non-combatants and allowing his men to rape native women, but such charges are difficult to verify and even harder to square with his character. According to one participant [John Kelly, whose statement is published in the *Daily Bulletin*, Blackfoot, Idaho, January 19, 1929], when the women saw the soldiers did not wish to kill them, they left the ravine and walked to the rear where they sat in the snow "like a lot of sage hens." (231)

I have no idea why Bigler would privilege these memories, published sixty-six years in retrospect, over the contemporary observations of residents recorded within days and weeks of the event. As for the rapes not squaring with Connor's character, it may be useful to note that, according to Madsen, no orders had been given to "fight to the finish" either. Connor was not in control of his men, as evidenced also in his unfortunate selection of McGarry as his favored officer.

Bigler's own biases must be considered, as well. He dedicates less than five pages of his otherwise informative book to the Bear River

Massacre—fair enough in a book focused on the Mormon theocracy. But in a book published eight years after the name of the event was officially changed (more on this later), he still calls it the Battle of Bear River. Generally, the Shoshone are barely mentioned in the work at all, and when they are, they are usually called "Utes." The phrase *Northwestern Shoshoni* does not appear in the work at all.

I cannot share Bigler's dismissal of Madsen's research.

On January 29, 1863, the day of the massacre, Brigham Young married another wife. Before his death in 1877, he would have married, or at minimum "sealed to" himself, more than twenty wives.

And now for the numbers game.

The *San Francisco Bulletin* reporter filed this story: "The carnage presented in the ravine was horrible. Warrior piled on warrior, horses mangled and wounded in every conceivable form, with here and there a squaw and papoose, who had been accidentally killed" (qtd. in Madsen 189). Observers agree that about twenty of the estimated two hundred warriors escaped; Madsen notes that at least some of the warriors fighting had to have been elderly or disabled (190).

Sagwitch miraculously escaped, with no more than a wound to his hand. Contemporary reports had it that he "tumbled into the River and floated down under some brush and lay there till night, and after dark he and some more warriors . . . took off two of the soldiers horses and some of their own ponies and went north" (qtd. in Madsen 190). His twelve-year-old son, Da boo zee (Yeager) Timbimboo, playing dead on the battlefield, was discovered by a soldier who several times raised his rifle against him, but for some reason did not pull the trigger. His two-year-old son, later known as Frank Timbimboo Warner, also survived, adopted by a Mormon family.

For white history, the death of Bear Hunter is a mystery. Newell Hart tells us that after the fighting a rumor flew that Bear Hunter was killed while molding bullets by a campfire. But Madsen thinks it unlikely that a war leader would have been so trivially distracted during a fight. Madsen states also that only seven members of Bear Hunter's band survived.

Varying reports after the battle recounted fatalities among women and children as being anywhere between 3 and 265; Madsen settles on the estimate of 90, from Franklin settlers. Given the confined area in which hand-to-hand combat occurred, Madsen believes that significant casualties would inevitably have been incurred by the women and children hiding in the lodges. Connor's report states that 160 women and children survived the incident, and that he arrested these and then let them go the next day with provisions. In assessing the veracity of his report, it may be useful to recall that, although shifting federal Indian policy had encouraged the slaughter of combatants, Connor's superiors had expressly and repeatedly ordered him to spare women and children.

As has happened with most conflicts that occurred between Native Americans and European Americans, much energy has gone into attempting to establish the number of native dead. Although we have a precise record of casualties on the military side—*twenty-three*—down to name, how wounded, when died, where buried, and with what eulogy—the record on the Shoshone side is, at best, an estimate. Connor counted bodies till he reached 224, and then quit counting. Madsen points out that he did not differentiate in his count between warriors and women, children, or the elderly, probably because, again, he did not want to be known as a "squaw killer." Most observers placed the number between 250 and 300. In 1985, Madsen settled on the number 250. More recently, he revised that figure closer to 280.

A dispute in numbers is not limited to European American history. Madsen reports that Moroni Timbimboo, Sagwitch's grandson (and Yeager's son), spoke for Shoshone tradition when he asserted that "there ain't no 200 Indians killed. There were less than that" (qtd. in Madsen 190).

After the fight, the Mormon people of the town of Franklin were asked by Porter Rockwell and others to minister to wounded soldiers. Men brought sleighs to collect wounded soldiers, and women nursed them, turning the meetinghouse into a hospital. "The suffering was terrible," Mary Ann Hull wrote. "We could hear nothing but moans all night" (qtd. in Madsen 195). Those of Connor's troops who were still ambulatory gathered many trophies, which, a *Union Vedette* reporter said "more than paid all the expenses of the expedition" (qtd. in Madsen 192). Wagon covers taken from the Shoshone bore the names of emigrants, and it was clear that many materials had not originated with the Shoshone, including blankets, mirrors, cooking tools, and hair ornaments. The soldiers also found more than one thousand bushels of wheat, as well as flour, potatoes, beef, chickens, and horses. "A portion of the food was left for the women and children," the *Vedette* reported (qtd. in Madsen 192); but the soldiers "appropriated to themselves as trophies of the war buffalo robes, gewgaws, beads, pipes, tomahawks, arrows, and all such things" (qtd. in Madsen 193).

Settlers also reported that they were profoundly disturbed by the kai-yai of Shoshone women, who mourned loudly for their dead.

Mormon settlers may have been sickened by the brutality of Connor's troops, particularly in the matter of the rape; but they were to be the primary beneficiaries of the massacre. Their official record expressed relief. "*We, the people of Cache Valley, looked upon the movement of Colonel Connor as an intervention of the Almighty*, as the Indians had been a source of great annoyance to us for a long time, causing us to stand guard over our stock and other property the most of the time since our first settlement" (qtd. in Madsen, *Glory Hunter* 85). Peter Maughan wrote to Brigham Young,

> I feel my skirts clear of their blood. They rejected the way of life and salvation which have been pointed out to them from time to time (especially for the last two years) and thus have perished relying on their own strength and wisdom.
>
> We have pretty good reason to believe that if they had gained the Victory over the soldiers their intention was to take our Herd and drive it right to the Salmon River Country for their own special benefit. (qtd. in Madsen 194)

Madsen notes that the division between Mormons and the federal troops eased when the troops turned their attention to the Shoshone; since the army and the Shoshone were both "removed from the Saints' preoccupation with establishing the Kingdom of God on earth and surviving in their desert environment," settlers "tended merely to look on as bystanders." Consequently, he writes, "Tacitly, if not overtly, the Mormons were accomplices in the encounter with Chief Bear Hunter's people . . ." (176).

In his report, Connor praised Major McGarry, along with Major Patrick Gallagher and the camp's surgeon, R. K. Reid, for their "skill, gallantry and bravery" (qtd. in Madsen 197). Connor's commanding officer, Brigadier General Wright, trumpeted the "signal victory" and "heroic conduct . . . in that terrible combat" of Connor's troops (qtd. in Madsen 197), as did California Governor Leland Stanford.

Connor refused to acknowledge, in his report, the aid provided by area Mormon residents.

From Washington, General-in-Chief H. W. Halleck declared it a "splendid victory" (qtd. in Madsen 197), and promoted Connor to the rank of brigadier general, a reward of which his superiors—Stanton and Lincoln—had to be aware.

The only criticism Connor received was for having lost so many men.

Had Sagwitch not lived to reorganize what was left of his band at Marsh Creek, it is doubtful that the Northwestern Shoshoni would have survived at all.

The Shoshone dead lay on the field, their flesh to be picked over by predators.

Captain James L. Fisk visited the site in the fall of 1863. "Many of the skeletons of the Indians yet remained on the ground," he wrote, "their bones scattered by the wolves" (qtd. in Madsen 194). Five years later, a *Deseret News* reporter saw that "bleached skeletons of scores of noble red men still ornament the grounds." The reporter went on to say that it was too bad that the soldiers had lost an opportunity to do the same to Pocatello and his "gang" (qtd. in Madsen 194).

The massacre at Bear River did not have the immediate effect of ending Shoshone raids on Cache Valley settlers, or attacks on the trails west of South Pass. For six months, raids intensified, although Pocatello's band and other groups took pains to avoid Connor's troops. Rumor had it that Connor had issued orders to shoot all natives on sight. He would continue to attack other bands, particularly the Ute, hoping to repeat his success at Bear River; and would continue to antagonize his Mormon neighbors, whom he still viewed as being allied with his native enemies. To protect the Montana Trail, he planned to establish a new camp near Soda Springs, and to found at the same time a gentile, or as he put it, "an anti-Mormon," settlement (qtd. in Madsen, *Glory Hunter* 97).

Sagwitch, from his end of this political triangle, suspected the Mormons of collaborating with the federals, and staged a brief rebellion, reportedly pledging to kill all white men on sight. Two settlers loading wood were attacked by Cache Valley Shoshone on May 1, though neither fatally, and a herd of horses was stolen. Minute Men captured Sagwitch, his two sons, and a few others, but the horses were by then unrecoverable, and the men were released. On May 9, members of Sagwitch's band drove off a few horses in Box Elder Canyon and tried to steal another herd. A relief party found the naked and mutilated body of William Thorp, a father of ten children, who had been mining coal nearby.

Soon, however, the Bear River Massacre did achieve its intended effect. Indian Superintendent Doty (soon to be governor of Utah) was able to negotiate five treaties that year, bringing to a close one of the longest periods of European American–Native American warfare in American history: the conflict in the Great Basin and the Snake River areas that had been twenty-five years in the running. On July 30, 1863, he concluded the Treaty of Box Elder with leaders from nine bands of Northwestern Shoshoni. Those signing included Pocatello and Sanpitch. Sagwitch was not present because he had been arrested again, this time by Connor's troops. Doty had asked for his release so he could attend the treaty negotiations, but the next night Sagwitch was shot in the chest while in custody (somehow the perpetrator could never be located); he recovered from the wound.

The Treaty of Box Elder promised a signing bonus of $2,000 in presents, and an annuity of $5,000 thereafter, and established the land for Pocatello's followers as being between the Portneuf Mountains and the Raft River. Congress later added an article stating that the Shoshone could not have more land than they had formerly occupied under Mexican law. On July 3, 1868, the Treaty of Fort Bridger "awarded" government recognition, annuities, and a home to the Fort Hall and Lemhi Shoshone and Bannock. Hostilities between the miners and the Boise Shoshone and the Bruneau Shoshone continued into 1869, when these latter natives became the first to settle on the new Fort Hall reservation.

"There is no doubt," Madsen concludes, "that Connor's 'victory' at Bear River and subsequent expeditions to Soda Springs and elsewhere helped convince the tribes that treaties were the best course, but such agreements had been sought for years and the Indians were pleased finally to get some assurance of protection and annuities from the government." Such agreements, Madsen suggests, could have been established without the "unnecessary and extremely cruel action" of the massacre at Bear River, had the government provided assurances of protection earlier (223).

Several months after the massacre, a survey error was discovered, and the line dividing Utah and Idaho was shifted southward, south of

Franklin and Preston. This error exacerbates the time–space warp that is the history of the Bear River Massacre, and provides an excuse for excluding the incident from both state history texts. Idaho may truthfully say, It was there then. Utah may truthfully say, It is there now. Both may say, It is theirs now.

In 1864, as the Civil War finally turned in favor of the Union, and in the face of "depredations" committed by native neighbors in Colorado, Colonel John Chivington discussed with General Patrick Connor the best way to deal with a band of Cheyenne and Arapaho natives who had been settled—by invitation of Colorado Governor John Evans—on Sand Creek, near what is now known as Chivington, Colorado. In agreeing to be "protected" from the coming Indian war by the government, the natives had surrendered many of their arms. It is not clear the extent to which Connor and Chivington, who were political rivals, consulted on the situation at Sand Creek. But Chivington wrote that Connor said, "I think from the temper of the men that you have and all I can learn that you will give these Indians a most terrible thrashing if you catch them, and if it was in the mountains, and you had them in a canon [sic], and your troops at one end of it and the Bear river at the other, as I had the Pi-Utes [Northwestern Shoshoni], you would catch them, but I am afraid on the plains you won't do it" (qtd. in Madsen, *Glory Hunter* 121). And whether Chivington followed Connor's strategies precisely or not, it is clear that Chivington borrowed Connor's invention of the winter attack. Thus was another predawn, chilly surprise planned—this time for Black Kettle's Cheyenne and White Antelope's Arapaho—and executed on November 29 by the Colorado Volunteers. And the murder of about 130 Cheyenne and Arapaho men, women, and children was followed by the sexual mutilation of bodies left on the massacre field.

David Svaldi writes of Sand Creek that "based upon evidence drawn from both military and Congressional hearings, the encounter is described as a 'merciless slaughter' of men, women and children of a proven friendly demeanor" (5). As Lieutenant James Connor reported:

> In going over the battleground the next day I did not see a body of man, woman or child but was scalped, and in many instances their bodies were mutilated in the most horrible manner—men, women and children's privates cut out, etc. I heard one man say that he had cut out a woman's private parts and had them for exhibition on a stick. . . . I also heard of numerous instances in which men had cut

out the private parts of females and stretched them over the saddle-
bows and wore them over their hats while riding in the ranks. (qtd.
in Brownmiller, 152)

This time, U.S. citizens noticed—even though the Civil War was
still running at full throttle. Five government investigations followed
the massacre, although no official sanction ever came of them. Chivington, Evans, and their greatest defender, *Rocky Mountain News*
founder William N. Byers, suffered some loss of national reputation,
but all three continued to prosper in Colorado.

Why the U.S. public, and their officials, attended to Sand Creek
but not Bear River, and why contemporary history perpetuates this
choice, is one of the primary questions facing practitioners of what
European American academics call "Native American" history.

Most academic histories of Native Americans end with whatever
destruction befell a particular people, neglecting the survival story
that followed that destruction. What follows here is, in strict narrative terms, anticlimactic indeed. But it is also the most important part
of the story, since herein lies our contemporary responsibility to one
another.

The Northwestern Shoshoni were decreased in number, but they
were not annihilated. This despite some wishful thinking by their European American neighbors.

For the next several years, survivors of the Northwestern bands
traveled to the Brigham City area to pick up their annuity of food,
clothing, and other supplies. Fort Hall Indian Reservation, as noted,
was established in 1869, and by 1875 many resided there. But in
1874 and 1875, several hundred Shoshone, including Sagwitch, had
been baptized by Mormon missionary George Hill, who conducted
evangelical meetings near Corinne, at the mouth of the Bear River
where the Shoshone gathered. Hill, who spoke the Shoshone language, was part of an 1870s effort by the church to convert Lamanites, which, as noted earlier, was required before Christ could return
in 1891. Hill helped the natives start farms in the summer of 1875.

But Corinne was a gentile settlement existing in conflict with the
dominant Mormon culture. Mormons were again accused of inciting
riots among the increasingly large number of Shoshone gathered
there, and troops were called in, on the second day of harvest, to dis-
patch the Shoshone back to Fort Hall. Thus the harvest was lost; and

Sagwitch was heard to cry, "What have I stolen? Who have I killed?" Most of the Shoshone, angry with the Mormon church for failing to protect them at Corinne, determined to reside at Fort Hall. But three hundred loyal Mormon converts, led by Sagwitch, remained in northern Utah, seeking yet again to rebuild their community.

Brigham Young had discouraged mining as a means of making a living, preferring agriculture, which would settle a vaster region of empire, and avoid the rush of non-Mormons that would surely follow a mineral strike. After the Civil War, Patrick Connor turned down a military commission and elected to remain in Utah. "The Father of Utah Mining" was a member of the first mining corporation formed in Utah; an early developer of steamship transportation on the Salt Lake; helped found the *Union Vedette*, an anti-Mormon newspaper; and served generally as Chief Utah Gentile, encouraging non-Mormon emigration and settlement. He helped found Corinne, on the Union Pacific Railroad line, hoping his new, non-Mormon city would eventually rival Salt Lake City as the center of commerce in the region.

Since the Bear River Massacre would immediately be forgotten by the American public, Connor would not be rewarded, as he had hoped, with a reputation as a great Indian fighter. Madsen believes that he would have been much remembered had the massacre occurred during the 1870s—during General George Armstrong Custer's era.

After the Civil War, Utah's African slaves were free. Some remained near their homes, and some gathered in Corinne, that "gentile capital," making for a substantial presence in that unusual Utah community.

In 1869, the frontier closed, as some historians would have it, when the transcontinental railroads were joined at Promontory Point.

In the late 1860s, as the Central Pacific Railroad lines arrived in Utah, thousands of Chinese railroad workers also entered the territory. Admired for their ability to blast tunnels with nitroglycerin, at times working from baskets lowered over cliffs hundreds of feet high, most of the Chinese were not immigrants in the European sense, since most did not intend to remain in the United States. Most hoped to return to their homeland when the work was finished and the railroad wages dried up.

But many did remain. After the final spike had been driven at Promontory Point in 1869, most of the Chinese who stayed in Utah settled in Box Elder County, working as section hands for the railroads. Corinne boasted a population of nearly three hundred Chinese in its bustling heyday, around the time that Sagwitch's people were driven from the region.

When the railroad rerouted away from Corinne, and its economy crumbled, some Chinese Americans headed for newly established mining camps like Park City, where a Chinatown of 131 Asian residents was counted in the 1890 census. That same year, 271 Chinese Americans were counted in Salt Lake City. Many of these entrepreneurs established thriving laundries, groceries, and restaurants, despite the anti-Asian sentiment pervasive among their European American customers. In Park City in 1902 and 1903, mining unions boycotted Chinese American merchants, hoping to end Asian presence in the region.

The *Utah History Encyclopedia* records the presence, in the Uinta Basin, of a man named Wong Sing, a prosperous businessman who owned a merchandise store with an inventory, in the 1920s, of more than $60,000. He spoke the Shoshone language, and pursued an interest in Native American society. On the event of his death in 1934 from an automobile accident, sixty Ute men gathered at the Indian agency to mourn him.

In 1869, sparsely populated Wyoming Territory became the first territory to give women the right to vote, possibly to encourage women to emigrate to the region. In 1870, Utah followed, but for more complicated reasons. Gentile emigrants were flooding the territory, and Mormon officials wanted to strengthen the LDS voting base. The church also wished to demonstrate, by the support of women, that polygyny was not an oppressive institution. Further, influential Mormon women such as Emmeline Blanche Woodward Wells, editor of the *Women's Exponent*, were active suffragists. Meanwhile, some in Washington hoped women voters would help defeat theocracy. As a result of this temporary alliance, the first legal vote cast by a woman in U.S. history was that of Seraph Young, a niece of Brigham's.

As it turned out, the Mormons were right. Six thousand women gathered to protest the Cullom Bill, another attempt to end polygyny and theocracy in 1870. Speakers pronounced polygyny "the only reliable safeguard of female virtue and innocence" (qtd. in Bigler 282).

In 1887, a defeated congress passed the Edmunds–Tucker Act, tightening controls on the church, increasing penalties for polygyny, and repealing women's right to vote in Utah.

In 1871, as federal officials began aggressive attempts to control both polygyny and theocracy in Utah, Young was placed under house arrest for "lewd and lascivious cohabitation"; in 1872 he was arrested again for murder. He would not stand trial due to complicated political maneuvers regarding Utah's repeated bids for statehood; but also due to advocacy on his behalf by the esteemed Utah Gentile, Patrick Connor.

After Sagwitch and his fellow Mormon converts were driven from Corinne, the church endeavored to settle the Northwestern Shoshoni elsewhere, and established, in 1880, a farming colony in Malad Valley. It was named Washakie, for the pacifist Eastern Shoshone leader who, because of his location, had never presented much of a problem for Brigham Young, and was revered by Mormons as a noble man. But Washakie himself was said, by some who claimed to have overheard him, to despise Sagwitch's people. "You are not Shoshone," he reportedly told a massacre survivor. "The Shoshone are not defeated. You are defeated" (qtd. in Hart 67).

As it happened, the 1870s inaugurated an era of federal Indian policy known as "Mission Policy." The government was easily persuaded to allow the Mormon church to lead this settlement with little federal interference, and the church purchased 1,700 acres for the Shoshone colony. The other parties in question were equally easily persuadable. In the context of their final effort to prepare for the second coming of Christ, Mormons were happy to return Lamanites to the faith. Finally, Wovoka gained notoriety as the Shoshone cousin who had had a revelation about the removal of the deadly white man; possibly influenced by contact with Mormons, he also taught that Christ would return in 1891. He traveled the West encouraging native nations to take up the ghost dance.

Thus enabled by the climate of the times, and as Madsen relates, the church launched a far-reaching program to make the Washakie Shoshone self-reliant, supplying farming equipment and training. The Shoshone attended school, worshiped in the Mormon church, farmed, and were thought by their white Mormon neighbors to be devout and moral. The church invested greatly in this effort: eventually the holdings would grow to 18,000 acres.

The early days were tough going, though. In 1882, more than thirty children died of whooping cough, measles, and other diseases. A few Shoshone built houses, while most continued to live in lodges, but by the turn of the century most lived in houses and wore Western clothing. Some more fundamental cultural habits were harder to break. Property was still owned in common; and disaffected members of the community often went to Fort Hall to live. Meanwhile, Washington paid little attention to the settlement, since it seemed to be an exemplary demonstration of assimilation and prosperity, necessitating no intervention by the strained Office of Indian Affairs.

In 1884, Sagwitch died. It is said that he died on the very spot where he was buried in Washakie.

In 1890, Lakota ghost dancers wore the ghost shirt, a garment first popularized by the Shoshone and the Bannock peoples who had seen Mormons wearing their temple garments. They got the idea that the one-piece, cloth undergarment could stop a bullet. Any hope for the powers of the ghost shirt were destroyed in December, when many wearing them were killed at Wounded Knee.

By the 1930s, census figures had the population of Washakie as 133. In 1939, Madsen says, church authorities commenced a new era for the Shoshone with the ordination of Moroni Timbimboo (Sagwitch's grandson) as the first Native American bishop in the history of the church. His local church officials were also Shoshone. A new chapel was dedicated at Washakie. But six years later the authorities named a white man as bishop, and whites held the position thereafter.

In 1966 the Mormon church closed down the Washakie Ward, transferring the few remaining church members to the ward in nearby Portage. Madsen explains that the Washakie Shoshone had found defense work in towns north of Salt Lake City, and the congregation had scattered. But the question of exactly how these vast Shoshone lands, once owned in common and held in trust by the Church of Jesus Christ of Latter-day Saints, came gradually to disappear, is a matter buried in paperwork.

For most Native North American groups, Knack tells us, colonization resulted in the invasion of sex-based hierarchies into native societies. Until European-gender constructs arrived, most native men and women had enjoyed a complementary reciprocity. If women in some groups, like the Shoshone, had less political control than their male leaders, their contributions to the community's livelihood were nonetheless valued equally. But the loss of habitat meant that men immediately lost their "jobs": hunting became impossible. Gathering was impossible, too, but native women just as immediately found a market among emigrants for their basketry and other goods, as well as their labor. Native women were hired by white families to clean, cook, mind children, sew, and help store food during harvest. The fact that white communities defined "women's work" as lesser than men's was not lost on disenfranchised native men, who were often ridiculed by white men for their inability to manage their money-earning women. Meanwhile, "chiefs"—who in Shoshone communities were always men—were awarded a social control they had never before enjoyed. And some of what had been "women's work" in a mobile community—food processing and storing, tanning hides for shelter—became unnecessary when the Shoshone gathered in villages, while hunting remained useful. So the loss of the value of that women's work resulted in the loss of status for women, even as increasing limits on sexual behavior (for instance, decreasing tolerance of premarital sexual relations) reduced women's autonomy. Gender hierarchies, and their attendant oppressions, had arrived in Shoshone country.

The Territory of Utah would be denied statehood status five times between 1857 and 1896, when it was finally granted under certain conditions. It is interesting to note that, while slavery became a moot concern in the debate following the end of the Civil War, polygyny was not the federal government's only misgiving in repeatedly denying statehood to Utah. Theocracy and monopoly became major obstacles. But both theocracy and polygyny faded from popularity among Mormon citizens along with their hopes of Christ's return. As 1891 came and went without a reappearance, Utah's leaders finally agreed to end their theocracy, and to effect at least a nominal separation of church and state, by ceasing official church involvement in state politics. Leaders also agreed to rescind the official policy of doing business only with other Mormons. And they agreed, of course, to end the official sanction of polygyny.

Brigham Young, who died in 1877, would not live to see the 1896 criminalization of polygyny in Utah. In 1882, Congress, seeking to enforce the 1862 Morrill Act, passed the Edmunds Act, which disenfranchised convicted bigamists and provided for fines and prison time.

The criminalization of polygyny caused the first real rift in Young's Zion. In 1890, Mormon President Wilford Woodruff issued a manifesto against plural marriage. But although many Mormons agreed that the formal divide was politically necessary, many remained sympathetic to their polygynous cousins. Some were active in a systematic resistance of the federal agents sent to round up fugitive "polygs." Secret communication codes and warning signals were established, with hiding places along an escape route through southern Utah, and on across the Mexico border, known as the "underground railroad."

According to Richard Patterson, the family of Maximillian and Ann Gillies Parker, of Circleville, Utah, were among those who were active in the work of hiding fugitives. In the 1850s, the Mormon church had staged a vast recruitment campaign in Europe, looking for craftsmen to join the church and emigrate to Utah. Maximillian and Ann were the children of two such converted British families, and both had spent the latter parts of their childhoods in Utah. They met and married there in the 1860s. Ann was a devout Mormon who tried to raise her six children to follow the church covenants; but Maximillian eschewed church services, took up smoking, and resented the Mormon officials who had decided a lands claim dispute unfavorably to him. The oldest of their six children, Robert Leroy, was sixteen when the Edmunds Act passed, and although he shared his father's suspicions of Mormon authority, and his mother had given up trying to get him to attend church services, he became his family's leader in the resistance to federal polyg hunters.

In 1884, at the age of eighteen, Bob Parker decided to leave Circleville, purportedly to try his hand in the mines of Telluride, Colorado, but more likely to deliver a herd of stolen horses for a rustler working from the Robbers' Roost area in eastern Utah. Bob had little affection for the notion of mimicking his father's life, scratching out a living with 160 acres and second jobs on the side. Eventually, he would formally take up the outlaw career, living under the name of Butch Cassidy. It is said that, at Robbers' Roost, the hideout he shared with the Wild Bunch, he continued to provide hospitality for fugitive polygs on the run from federals.

In 1885, monogamous Mormons, the vast majority, split from polygynous Mormons.

The area around the Bear River massacre site has been agricultural grazing land since shortly after the atrocity.

In 1911, a flood came to Bear River and Battle Creek, wiping out the recently completed West Cache Canal, which had been dug along the massacre field. The region continued to be plagued by landslides over the years, and landslides, together with the flood, have effected a natural burial of the Shoshone dead there. Local legend held that enraged natives had cursed the earth, causing the slides. A disappointed descendant of settlers in the Battle Creek area told Newell Hart that, indeed, tons of earth had poured down from the cliffs and onto the "battlefield," making relic hunting a much more challenging hobby.

Another descendant, born on the massacre field in 1885, told Hart in a 1980 interview that in his younger days he often found arrowheads and knives in the soil. Once, he said, while digging, he found a body. As of this writing, and despite recent federal laws prohibiting the collecting of native remains and effects by non-native U.S. citizens, no bodies or "relics" have ever been transferred from Cache Valley whites to the Shoshone.

Shifts in federal policy toward Native Americans would affect the Northwestern Shoshoni less directly than most native groups. As the Mission era came to a close, an elite white group of "Indian reformers" convinced the U.S. Congress that native peoples would not survive if they did not assimilate into the U.S. economy. The best way to do this, they argued, would be to take back the community-owned reservation lands, and allocate 160-acre parcels to individual—which is to say, male—natives. Individual men would then be free to do with this asset as they chose: farm it, sell it, lease it. Reservation land not allocated would be bought (cheaply) by the government, to be turned over to white settlers. The Dawes Severalty Act of 1887 (the same year Utah women lost suffrage) would ultimately result in the diminishing of native land holdings by more than half; it would also compromise efforts to maintain traditional lifeways, such as communal sharing of resources.

In 1924, Native Americans were made citizens of the United States, purportedly in gratitude to the ten thousand native U.S. soldiers who died in World War I. But citizenship would permit further subversion of native control of lands. In 1928, the "Meriam Report" decried the state of Indian country and blamed allotment for poor reservation conditions, and the Bureau of Indian Affairs (BIA) for destroying traditional lifeways. A concerned Indian commissioner, John Collier, responded by proposing the Indian Reorganization Act. Passed in 1934, this legislation dealt yet another well-meaning blow to native culture. Although natives would now be permitted to practice the religion of their choice, and to live as they pleased; and although the act included the founding of schools and the restoration of some lost lands; nonetheless, a self-governance program mandated by the act would replace traditional forms of governance. Indeed, the funding that came with the act would be withheld if tribes did not replace their governance with "democratic" election processes. Some native groups declined the offer. For the rest, the BIA established chartered corporations to run each reservation; constitutions would provide for representatives to be elected by enrolled members of each band. But the traditional response to political difference, for most native nations, had been to simply go away when natives disagreed with their leaders; therefore, many tribal officials would be "elected" primarily by assimilated natives (those who did not protest via abstention). Governments would have the assistance of the BIA only as long as they were willing to keep the BIA happy. Puppet governments—often known as "BIA progressives"—frequently clashed with traditionals.

By the 1950s, federal policy had shifted once more, toward "termination" of federal meddling in reservation matters. What may have sounded, again, like the emergence of a new era of butting-out was really an attempt to reduce U.S. government responsibility—which is to say, expenditures—to native nations. The Indian Claims Commission was in the process of squelching most native land claims, and now the government wanted to eliminate treaty obligations as well. "Relocation programs" removed to cities those natives who had resided on lands previously disputed before the commission. "Termination" ushered in a new era of poverty for increasing numbers of urban natives, as well as those who remained on the reservation.

In later decades, native groups would turn to the Supreme Court to seek remedy for stolen lands, treaty violations, and neglect. Quite frequently, they would win.

The Church of Jesus Christ of Latter-day Saints has been, and remains, the fastest growing religion in U.S. history. It has grown by 220% since 1970 alone; during that same period, the second-fastest growth has been seen by Southern Baptists, at 33%; Episcopals have lost 28% of their membership; and Presbyterians have lost 36%. Growth among overall religions in the United States was 34%. Birth rates among Mormons are above the national average, but the church reports that two-thirds of their new members each year are converts. An aggressive recruiting operation has been particularly successful in

South America. More than fifty thousand missionaries, primarily young men, are dispatched each year across the United States and to 120 other countries.

Amassed wealth has supported that operation. In a November 13, 2000, article, the *U.S. News and World Report* quotes analysts who estimate an annual revenue of almost $6 billion, most of which comes from tithing. Church assets are estimated at between $25 billion and $30 billion, primarily in real estate, stocks, and media outlets. Recently the church has divested itself of more churchlike commercial assets such as hospitals, as well as banks and manufacturing plants, and members are encouraged to involve themselves in national politics. As Harold Bloom observed in 1992, "We have not yet had a Mormon President of the United States, and perhaps never will, but our Presidents are increasingly responsive to Mormon sensibilities, rather more than might be expected for a religious movement representing just two percent of our population" (89). That political access is primarily Republican in affiliation.

The 1970s saw the beginning of a wave of LDS church excommunications of feminists. A case of particular renown was that of Sonia Johnson, an Equal Rights Amendment supporter who went public with what she construed to be a secret LDS effort, organized at the national level, to defeat the amendment's ratification. She was excommunicated in 1979. More recently, Karen Chase, a founder of the Mormon Women's Forum, which advocates priesthood for women, was "disfellowshipped," or stripped of her rights to participate in sacraments.

In 1995, the church hired a public relations firm to improve its image in the United States and beyond—on their own terms. Although recent church materials have attempted to emphasize a centrality of Jesus Christ to its theology, and to define Mormonism as a restoration faith that corrects the misguided path of Christianity *since* Christ, other Christian organizations have expressed reluctance to accept Mormonism as Christianity. In 2000, The United Methodist Church held that LDS doctrine is not in step with the apostolic tradition of Christianity.

Meanwhile, the prolific record keeping of LDS church leaders and members has proven a mixed blessing for officials of the religious empire Mark Twain once called an "awful mystery." On the one hand, as Will Bagley has pointed out, every nuance of church history is thoroughly recorded and so perhaps excessively unmysterious; on the other hand, descriptions of "secret ceremonies," as lapsed-Mormon Deborah Laake titles her 1993 book, are also contained in these documents. Church officials walk a fine line between maintaining church privacy, and inviting suspicion of cover-ups. In November 2001, the church settled a dispute with Utah State University, which had made the papers of Leonard J. Arrington available to researchers. Arrington, a church historian from 1972 to 1982, had researched the nineteenth-century ceremonial practices of the church, and had a copy of The Book of the Anointings, which describes some of the most sacred rituals of the church. Before his death in 1999, Arrington deliberately chose Utah State over Brigham Young University as depositors of his papers, because he suspected the church would attempt to suppress his findings. The settlement terms allowed for the return to the church of the most sensitive documents; Utah State will control the rest.

Polygyny also persists as a concern in the Mormon intermountain west. Estimates have 20,000 to 50,000 people living in polygynous families faithful to six Mormon sects, in towns like the border communities of Hildale, Utah, and Colorado City, Arizona. Although polygyny is illegal in both Arizona and Utah (indeed, across the United States), officials of these two towns have generally been unable to prosecute. Rulon Jeffs, aged "Mouthpiece of God" and leader of the local sect called the Fundamentalist Church of Jesus Christ of Latter-day Saints, is said to have between nineteen and sixty wives. Pressure on Jeffs to end polygyny resulted in his followers' withdrawal, in September 2000, of one thousand children from the schools of those communities, thus removing the ability of school officials to intervene in those children's lives. Farther north, Salt Lake City officials have prosecuted one or two high-profile abuse and/or polygyny cases each year through the late 1990s.

In the 1920s, a land claims case was filed on behalf of the Northwestern Shoshoni who had not been compensated for lands appropriated by the Box Elder Treaty of 1868. By 1931 the case had expanded to include lands lost by other Shoshone at the Fort Hall and Wind River reservations, and the Northwestern bands added a claim that they had not been paid the $5,000 annuity promised.

In 1934 Superintendent F. A. Gross asked the Office of Indian Affairs to provide enough farmland for the Washakie Shoshone to make them independent of the Mormon church. He noted that of the forty homesteads filed by the Shoshone, only eleven remained, and "some of the allotments were acquired by white men through fraud or other irregular means" (qtd. in Madsen, *Northern Shoshoni* 104). Another suit confirmed the ownership of six of eleven other tracts. By 1935, 500 acres of the original 18,000 were held by twenty-seven Shoshone families. Sixteen hundred acres "white people took from them for nontaxpayment," according to Indian Agent J. E. White (qtd. in Madsen, *Northern Shoshoni* 104). The LDS church owned another 1,870 acres. Gross's request for more land was ultimately denied. In 1961, Madsen reports, only five of the six tracts were still being held in trust by the government for individual Shoshone families.

It was not until 1971 that a report was filed as part of the lands claim case brought by the Shoshone; Madsen was himself retained to research the claims on behalf of the Shoshone. According to this report, the Northwestern band totaled 205 members at that time. Only two families remained at Washakie farming 560 acres:

> . . . about one-half of the remainder lived in the cities of northern Utah, 65 or one-third lived on the Fort Hall reservation, and the remaining 37 resided in other western states and Florida. . . . Of the 64 households interviewed, nearly all the able-bodied adults were gainfully employed. Ten percent were in college or were college graduates, and about 50 percent had graduated from high school. Of the 64 families, 46 percent owned their own homes. The final approval bestowed by the very precise government report noted: "This comparatively small group of Northwestern or Washakie Band of Shoshoni Indians is generally well integrated, well educated, and relatively independent through employment in fairly good jobs. The 30 percent who live on Fort Hall Reservation are reservation-oriented and depend upon the Bureau of Indian Affairs for various services, but the other 70 percent have had very little attention from the Bureau and have assumed their role in society on the same basis as their non-Indian neighbors. It would appear that there are few major problems among the Northwestern Band of Shoshoni Indians." (*Northern Shoshoni* 105)

In 1972 the Northwestern Shoshoni were awarded, as Madsen details it, "$1,375,000 plus earned interest, less a $181,732 offset," to be distributed on a per capita basis. "With the apportionment of the land claims case, the history of the Washakie Northwestern Shoshoni, as a tribal entity, came to an end" (105).

Well, not quite. After Madsen's *The Northern Shoshoni* was published, the Northwestern band finally, in 1980, won federal recognition as a separate tribe, and were allotted 180 acres in the Washakie area to protect graves, including that of Sagwitch.

And so the people who were "rubbed out"—actually weren't.

"The Mormon effort," Madsen concludes, "had demonstrated that, with patience and much help, an Indian group could learn to 'live like white men,' although there were some regrets, finally, for the loss of a culture" (106).

Like most historical events, the Bear River Massacre never ends. For instance, a document was uncovered at an estate sale in the 1990s by Jack Irvine, a dealer from Eureka, California. Penned by a Sergeant William L. Beach, Company K, Second Cavalry Regiment, apparently at the end of his life, it told the tale of a vicious battle. Irvine offered to trade the University of Utah Marriott Library for a California-related document, but it was the late historian Harold Schindler who stepped forward with a document to trade with Irvine. The Beach papers are now owned by the Schindler family.

The narrative contributes new information to our understanding of the event of January 29, 1863. While Madsen had thought that the Shoshoni warriors had been unable to get to their horses, Beach's narrative asserts that several fighters broke on horseback from the ravine. It also reveals the attitudes of individual California Volunteers. Here are a few tidbits, from the *Utah Historical Quarterly*, which in 1999 published a typescript of the papers:

> The Boys were fighting Indians and intended to whip them. It was a free fight every man on his own hook. . . . Midst the roar of guns and sharp report of Pistols could be heard the cry for quarters but their was no quarters that day. . . . The fight lasted four hours and appeared more like a frollick than a fight the wounded cracking jokes with the frozen some frozen so bad that they could not load their guns used them as clubs. . . . Our loss—fourteen killed and forty two wounded Indian Loss two hundred and eighty Kiled. . . . I received six very severe wounds in my coat. (Schindler 307, 308)

He concludes: "In the language of an old sport I weaken" (308).

Beginnings, endings. We "Americans" seem to have a need for these. Framework. Situation.

Historian John Unruh has attempted to count the fatalities suffered on the trails from 1840 to 1860. According to his calculations, natives killed 362 emigrants, and emigrants killed 426 natives. Of the

European American fatalities, 90% occurred on the roads west of South Pass, especially along the Snake and the Humboldt Rivers—the heart of Shoshone country.

And yet, in popular mythology as well as academic history, the Shoshone remain neglected. They are often absent in pictures of western development, while the Cheyenne, the Lakota, and the Nez Percé, for example, replace them in history.

Beginning to remember.

In July, 1973, *The American West* published an article by historian Don Russell, "How Many Indians Were Killed? White Man Versus Red Man: The Facts and the Legend." Russell lists the five Far West massacres that resulted in the highest number of fatalities—and to which historians have devoted the greatest resources.

The Bear River Massacre is not listed.

Beginning to count.

In 1996, the U.S. Department of Interior's National Park Service proposed that a National Historic Site be established on the field of the Bear River Massacre. Their supporting document, *Final Special Resource Study and Environmental Assessment: Bear River Massacre Site*, provides a chart reciting for us the most important massacres in U.S. history. "None of the estimates of people killed in these massacres are incontrovertible numbers. For the purposes of comparison, the lowest estimates have been used in every case."

Bear River Massacre, January 29, 1863, 240 Northwest Shoshone
Sand Creek Massacre, November 19 [*sic*—29], 1864, 130 Cheyenne
    [*sic*—and Arapaho]
Washita Massacre in Oklahoma, November 27, 1868, 103 Cheyenne
Marias River Massacre in Montana, January 30, 1870, 173 Piegans
Wounded Knee, December 29, 1890, 146 Oglala Lakota (*Final
    Resource Study* 9)

But these lists are never finally complete. In the "middle," for instance, one could add:

Camp Grant Attack, April 30, 1871, 150 Aravapai Apache

Beginnings and endings—which so concern us.

Bear River is not even quite the beginning, since the first hint of a federal policy shift away from treaty and toward genocide occurred with Kit Carson's assault on the Apache.

Most of us have forgotten about that almost entirely.

Then there was Bear River.

Then there was Sand Creek, which some of us are beginning to remember.

But wait. Before the United States was the United States, four hundred—or maybe five hundred?—Pequot were slaughtered at the Mystic Massacre in Connecticut in 1637 by colonists led by Major John Mason. (Two English were killed and twenty wounded.)

Few remember that our religiously upright Puritan forefathers sold the survivors of the Pequot War into slavery, in Bermuda. Which was a beginning of another sort.

Then, too, the end did not come with Wounded Knee. The struggle to subjugate Hawaiian peoples went on into 1892. Perhaps one-third of Hawaiian natives, by the way, had been converted to Mormonism beginning in the 1850s by a renegade Mormon potentate named Walter Murray Gibson.

Perhaps the lesson here is that beginnings and endings are what we make them. As we frame the picture, situate the sightings, citations. As we do the counting, without becoming more accountable.

The broader picture?

Patricia Nelson Limerick writes, in *Sweet Medicine: Sites of Indian Massacres, Battlefields, and Treaties*, in 1995: "Americans ought to know what acts of violence bought them their right to own land, build homes, use resources and travel freely in North America. Americans ought to know what happened on the ground they stand on; they surely have some obligation to know where they are" (125).

From beginning to not-yet end.

PART II

THE MAKING OF HISTORY

Unless there is a frank understanding between the two people, red and white, so that the relationship between them is honest, sincere, and equal, talk about culture will not really matter. The white man will continue to take Indian land because he will feel he is HELP-ING to bring civilization to the poor savages.
—Vine Deloria, Jr., Custer Died for Your Sins:
An Indian Manifesto

2

HOW IT CAME TO ME

And now we begin again.

It's a dark and stormy December night (really, it is) when I finally get in my pickup and head down to Preston, Idaho, for the second of four public hearings. It's 1995. The hearings will gather the opinions of locals regarding the National Park Service proposal to build a National Historic Site at the location of the Bear River Massacre. I don't feel like going. At Idaho State University, where I teach English, it's the last week of classes. I've broken my contract with the University—I'm packing to move to Chicago midyear, about to abandon my entire life to join my partner Joe, who teaches there—I'm more than worn out. Plus, it's raining. I don't like driving my truck around here in the rain. Rain in Idaho means a vague, spritzing thing, just enough to mix with the oil on the roads, whisking a lethal salad dressing on the streets. My truck, with no weight in the back, skids on braking, spins on accelerating. Then too, I have no idea where I'm going. In early December, the sun goes down before supper—in the rain, I won't be able to see a damned thing.

But something pulls me. It's a piece of history I should have known about long ago, and didn't.

Why didn't I know?

Is it the story that pulls? Or my dismay at not having heard it before?

I should have known.

Certain instincts kick in. Journalists get farther in life than do academics and artists—and I can safely say this, because at different

85

points in my thirty-six-year life, I have been all three. In an attempt to look more like press than brain, I yank an old blazer on over my more typical sweater and jeans, and dig my job-interview portfolio out of the box I just packed it in. I find my favorite pen, the one that flows well so I can write a mile a minute and not miss (much of) anything—and get in the truck an hour and a half before the hearing is scheduled to start.

Like I told you, it's a dark and stormy night—really—so I can't see the mountains looming over the Portneuf Gap as I hang that long curve on I-15 out of Pocatello and through the spot where all that ancient floodwater, that huge Lake Bonneville, once escaped to form the Columbia River Gorge, a whole nother time zone away. I can't see Malad Summit looming at the other end of the valley, can't see Scout Mountain, which Joe and I had finally managed to climb this summer. I can't see a damned thing except an occasional light from a distant ranch in the valley.

I take US-91, which cuts east and south around the side of Malad, rather than climbing the mountain to the pass, as the interstate does. I've never taken this road before. It's a winding valley road, a good one, wide, clear. There's the occasional farm light, the occasional hefty, serious pickup—not a toy truck like mine—passing me doing 70. I'm losing the country music station out of Pocatello, so I pop in a Trisha Yearwood tape, sing badly at the top of my lungs, refuse to think about all the papers that need grading, the friends that need good-byeing. When I've driven another half hour, I know I should start looking for the turnoff to Preston, on the right. Shouldn't be hard to find. The road's still wet but the rain's quit finally. Clouds low, still can't see a damn thing.

I'm singing loud as hell when suddenly the road dips down. It's been flat for thirty miles, but now I'm on a sharp grade, headed steeply, surprisingly, *down,* with that roller-coaster sense that the ground has fallen out from under me, and my soul hangs in the balance of gravity. There's a farmhouse on my right, one ahead on my left, at a level lower than the road I'm on now. I'm headed into some sort of deep hollow.

Then something happens to me. It's a quick grip in my stomach. A sense of presence. Of not-aloneness in this dark, empty hole. It's a—sudden wrench of the gut. A sharp tingle in the spine.

This is it!
I can feel it.

I look to the left—nothing. Look to the right—nothing. There is nothing visible to justify this feeling *I'm here! This is it!* My skin crawls, a chill spreads under my blazer, dance spirits tap icily across my spine.

I must be here!

But where is here? I don't know where the hell I am.

I'm here!

The intellectual, practical me kicks into gear as I downshift the truck. I try to soothe myself, warm the chilled-spine me. No, I tell myself, it can't be. I'm in the middle of nowhere.

Or—not quite. Here's a street sign, the first street sign I've passed in many miles. It's posted at an intersection to my right—Hot Springs Rd.—so I must be near Preston. Right after, a long eastward bend in the highway; then the town sign; then a lit intersection, a wide boulevard heading into gathered lights made fuzzy orange by the low-hanging clouds.

I'm disoriented—by driving in pitch darkness, by the ominous dancers on my spine. Preston looks like every small town I've ever seen, aggressively dolled up for Christmas—irritating to this atheist out of the foxhole. It's a town too small to get lost in. I have to drive around for all of four minutes before I find the Senior Citizen Center, which is supposed to be at 64 West First South, a typically bizarre western address, so confusing to us easterners, modeled on Brigham Young's method for laying out Salt Lake City.

I drive past the center, pull into a residential area, and park in front of someone's Christmas-screaming house.

But I was trying to tell you how this story came to me.

It's a few months ago, September; classes have just started. I'm thirty thousand feet up, shooting forward at 500 miles per hour, breathing recycled air, already missing the man I've left behind.

When I see it, of all places, in an in-flight magazine:

The little-known, single largest act of genocide in America's history as a country, the Bear River Massacre of 400 Northwestern Shoshoni occurred in southeastern Idaho in 1863.

The words shock me and I stare hard at them until they have burned onto my retina. *Single largest act of genocide . . . southeast Idaho.*

Bear River.

I am stunned primarily for this reason: *Why don't I know about this?*

After all, I live in Pocatello, in—*duh!*—southeastern Idaho, where my apartment is near the border of the Fort Hall Shoshone–Bannock reservation. Plus, as an academic my primary area of "expertise," as they call it, is women's writing, but for odd reasons of which I've recently become suspicious, I've long harbored a secondary interest in Native American studies. I fancy I know a little something about Native American history, literature, policy. Occasionally I write about it—gingerly, because I am a white person of German descent, and it's my thinking that race matters.

Single largest act.

All those Indian Studies classes I took in grad school.

How could I not know about this?

Back on terra firma, the Salt Lake City airport, I duck under the huge, then-hopeful "Olympics 2002" banners, get my small pickup out of parking hock, and head north on I-15. *Single largest act of genocide.* My eyes are not on the snow-tipped Wasatch range to my right or the vast salt flats to my left. My eyes burn across those five words. I barely see the Salt Lake drivers careening past me, flying through their evening rush hour. *Single largest. Bear River.* Where is that?

December again. In the three months since the story came to me, I've been on one of those obsessive reading kicks. In my university's library, there's a thorough collection of all that's been written about Bear River. But it has many names, and sometimes you have to look it up under "The Battle of Bear River" or "The Battle Creek Massacre" where older materials hide. I'm surprised to discover that there *is* an academic historian who's published on the incident: Brigham D. Madsen, at the University of Utah. My library also has an odd, self-published, 8 1/2 × 11 bound volume of about 350 sheets: The *Bear River Massacre: Being a complete Source Book and Story Book of the Genocidal Action Against the Shoshones in 1863—and of General P. E. Connor and how he related to and dealt with Indians and Mormons on the Western Frontier.* By Newell Hart. Copyright 1982, by the Cache Valley Newsletter Publishing Company, Preston Idaho, Newell Hart, Editor.

Obsessed, I'm reading everything I can find.

On my first reading of Madsen's book, I can't help but notice internal contradictions in his logic, which occur every time he addresses the question of the involvement, in this event, of leaders of the Church of Jesus Christ of Latter-day Saints. On the one hand, he faithfully reports that local Mormon leaders couldn't have been happier when the Shoshone were "rubbed out." But he continually admires and excuses the empire-building strategies practiced by Brigham Young. I think back to how little I knew about Mormon history before coming to Idaho a year before, and I wonder whether the church has been happy to play a role in the forgetting of this story—and whether Madsen and others have unconsciously played along with that forgetting.

Well. What else can I expect. After all, he may be an excellent historian, but his first name's Brigham!

One day during the reading kick, I have lunch with the English Department's authority on Native American literature. He's lived here for twenty years, helped start the Indian Studies program. Sixty miles from the site.

I ask him if he's ever heard of the massacre.

He says it rings a bell.

One day during the reading kick, I'm sitting on my couch, sifting through my afternoon newspaper, the *Idaho State Journal*, and a small article on a back page leaps out at me: "National Park Service to Commemorate Bear River," the small font reads. Dates and times of the public hearings are listed in boldface.

Inside the Senior Citizen Center, the white light is head splitting on pupils that have been straining to see through darkness for the past hour. The place is lit like no tomorrow, fluorescent installations ablaze. I'm dizzy and can't really remember how to talk to people, but a woman stands behind a table inside the door. She's dressed in a business suit, couldn't smile any wider if you paid her. I walk to the table and squint at her nametag: Catherine Spude, Ph.D., Team Captain/Archeologist.

Thanks for coming! she says brightly. I look down at a stack of copies of the official Park Service proposal. Please take a copy! she says, and pushes one toward me as I shake my head. Are you a neighbor?

Press, I say, and lift the portfolio I'm carrying as if it's a badge of some kind. It's damn near a lie I'm telling her, but, like I told you, it's an old instinct from when I actually was press, twenty years ago. People leave you alone when you flash a notebook.

Great, she says, her smile relaxing a bit. We really appreciate the coverage. Who are you with?

I shrug. Depends on who buys, I say. I'm freelance.

And I'm making this up as I go along.

Well, thanks, she says. Let me know if you have any questions. She points into the adjacent room. We'll start in about twenty minutes. There are refreshments around the corner there. Help yourself.

I look. Another table is covered with white linen and stocked with trays of pale cookies. A pitcher of red liquid stands next to a leaning tower of Dixie cups.

My atheist self is starting to itch. The room she's pointed me to has a podium in the front, a slide screen hanging behind the podium, and rows of folding chairs arranged to face front. A slide projector is set up in the back. The walls are decorated with seals and banners and pictures of honorees. What with the paper cups and chocolate chips, it's feeling like a church social to me, a church social lit by fluorescent doomsday light, a church social where an error in behavior could be lethal.

But hey, that's just my atheist's terror of church socials talking.

Some of what's hung up in the front of the room are photos and maps that read Bear River Historical Site Alternative I, and II, and III and IV. There are paintings of the site, of a chief in feathered headgear. I stand and study the maps while people file in.

Since I drove in under total darkness, I can't find a single landmark on the maps to orient myself. Apparently there's a ridge that hangs behind a river flowing through some meadowed flatland. The site seems to be slightly north and west of the town. To figure out where I am, I look for US-91. I follow the highway with my eyes, down past Downey—

Hey! Here's where the road sloped down, down from the ridge, where I got that chill—aw geez—right across from the site.

Right across from the site.

I'm getting a chill again.

Yep, there's the street sign I saw—Hot Springs Rd.—directly, it turns out, across the road from The Current Monument.

Wow. I really was *right there*. That *was* it.

In fact, that slope I dropped down is just to the west of the bluffs where the infantry gathered before riding down on the village.

The icy dancers tear-ass down my spine again—me, a nonbeliever in regimented spiritualities.

People who live in high-altitude desert drink a lot of water, and after an hour's drive I have to pee. When I come back I take a seat in the back row, breathe deep, focus on the chatter of people as they take off their coats and settle in. Most of the attendees are middle-aged. The men wear boots, cowboy hats; one sports a BYU jacket.

All are white.

Right there. I was right there. And somehow I knew it.

I sense that everyone seems to have noticed an older woman, who walks in with an unwieldy armload of stuff—folders, papers—and greets Spude, who shuts the door behind her. Isn't the town pretty? she says loudly. Too loudly, I suspect, though I don't know these people. Too cheerfully.

I eavesdrop as people settle into chairs around me. I drove past the site, a woman says, on the way home to dinner this afternoon. It's just gorgeous. You can see why they camped there.

Another woman nods. I know things were tough for everybody, she says, but I can't help feeling sorry for a whole tribe of Indians, being massacred like that.

Vision Statement: "The Bear River massacre site should be a place that is protected from any development that would harm its significant historical and sacred qualities. The site should commemorate not only the soldiers that participated in the massacre, but also acknowledge the lives of the Shoshone people that were lost on its soil. It should be a place where visitors can learn the various viewpoints of what happened, as well as the historical and social context of the times, and the consequences of its occurrence. It should be a place that retains its rural character without unduly affecting the lives of people who now own and use the land."

Before summarizing the four proposed alternatives, the draft reports that, currently, "an existing road-side monument erected by the Daughters of the Utah Pioneers and an interpretive sign placed by the Idaho Department of Transportation near the site commemorate the massacre by emphasizing the roles of the nineteenth century settlers and the military. The surrounding 1691 acres are designated a national historical landmark. With the exception of a highway right-of-way, all land is privately owned," by twenty-eight landowners. In 1986, a group of white women residents, one of whom was Allie Hansen, supported a joint resolution of the legislatures of Idaho and Utah creating a "Battle of Bear River Monument." The persistence of this misnomer finally irritated Shoshone descendants enough to act. Mae Timbimboo Parry threatened to file her own legislation. To

resolve this dispute, the draft says, then-Senator James McClure of
Idaho requested that the National Park Service (NPS) undertake a
national historical landmark study.

In 1990 the chief historian of the NPS, Edwin C. Bearss, finished
the study and officially renamed the event as the Bear River Massacre. The site was declared a national landmark.

(Geez. There's actually an office in Washington, DC, where a man
sits and decides what to call national historical events?

(History in the making.)

The Park Service then conducted a study to decide whether this
new National Historic Landmark should be upgraded to a National
Historic Site. The draft proposal I hold in my hands is the result of
that study, and proposes five options. The first, and most obvious, of
these is: No Action. Everything remains as is.

The first alternative to No Action would require the most minimal of actions. It would designate a County Historic Site, operated by
local officials: "It would provide for local protection of resources, interpretation of the massacre with a more balanced story of what happened the day of the massacre, and provide some suggested guidelines
to local government to protect the scenic qualities of a cultural landscape. Most current private landowner use would be preserved by
minimizing visitor access to the site and providing the majority of interpretation in the town of Preston"—which is to say, a visitor center
or museum located a few miles away from the site.

Alternative 2 would result in a State Historic Site, providing for
"combined state and landowner protection of resources while preserving most landowner use. Landowners would relinquish the land
on a voluntary basis and would be compensated through the state acquisition of scenic or conservation easements." From one of the
nearby ridges, a visitor center would provide for "a more detailed
contextual story . . . overlooking the massacre site." Further, "a
Shoshone memorial would commemorate the Shoshone dead."

Alternative 3 would create a National Historic Reserve "that
places greater emphasis on the national significance of the site by extending federal protection to the significant cultural resources. . . .
Provisions maximize visitor experience within constraints placed by
landowners, but still preserves most landowner use."

Alternative 4 "proposes a traditional National Park Service area
with NPS ownership of the massacre field and a cultural landscape protection area defined by the views from all overlooks within the [current

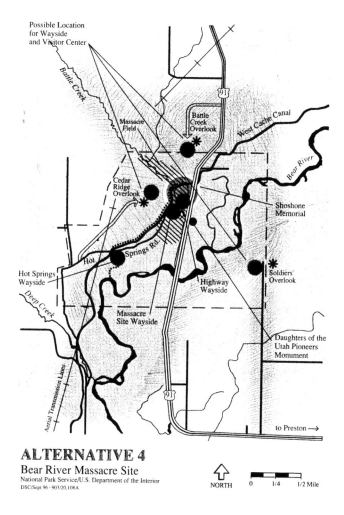

ALTERNATIVE 4
Bear River Massacre Site
National Park Service/U.S. Department of the Interior
DSC/Sept 96 · 903/20,108A

NORTH   0   1/4   1/2 Mile

Figure 2.1. Map of proposed improvements as per Alternative 4. Used by permission of the National Park Service.

national historic] landmark boundaries." This alternative "maximizes the visitor experience by telling the individual stories of the day of the massacre in the places where they occurred. This experience is enhanced by re-creating, to the extent possible, the landscape at the time of the massacre, and by providing a trail system that circles the massacre field." In this case, "most of the current landowners would retain existing use of their land within guidelines established by the National Park Service. NPS management would be enhanced through strong cooperative agreements with Shoshone tribes and landowners."

Costs:

Alternative 1, $1.3 to $1.5 million
Alternative 2, $7.3 to $9.3 million
Alternative 3, $9.5 to $12.0 million
Alternative 4, $12.3 to $14.9 million

The study draft also recites the selection criteria the Park Service has been directed to utilize: they are to find sites that are nationally significant; that are suitable and feasible additions to the system; and that require protection.

Regarding significance: "The event was the first of several conflicts between the United States Army and American Indians in the late nineteenth century that ended as massacres. Even the lowest estimates of the Shoshone dead at Bear River exceed the number of people killed at later massacres." The draft sets the casualties at 240 Shoshone dead. Further, "Military historians cite the Bear River event as the first time that the U.S. Army deliberately attacked a winter village at a time of year when American Indians were known to gather together, instead of drawing the warriors out to another location to do battle. The cold weather assisted the army's undetected approach and hindered the escape of wounded people." And finally, "The massacre eventually led to the creation of several reservations in the region, opening prime agricultural land to settlement by farmers and mineral wealth to miners. The massacre and its aftermath permanently changed the way of life for Shoshone and other American Indian peoples in Idaho, Nevada, Wyoming and Utah."

As to the present shape of the land, because much of it has been used primarily for grazing, "it retains a high degree of integrity as a true, accurate, and relatively unspoiled example of the resource." At the same time, "no site of the massacre of American Indians is cur-

rently represented by a unit of the national park system." The
Wounded Knee site is "on the Oglala Sioux reservation of Pine Ridge,
and is held in public trust for the members of that tribe." (I find out
later that a study similar to the one conducted for Bear River had
been completed for the Sand Creek Massacre site; it would be enacted
by Congress in 2001.)

Regarding feasibility, "it is important to note that interest in the
creation of a park unit to commemorate the massacre site originated
with grass-roots organizations at the local level." Most important,
this site is different from other possible sites because "very little land
needs to be removed from private ownership and private control. In
all alternatives, every effort has been made to ensure that the rights,
privileges, and privacy of land-owners and residents would be respected, and that, in most cases, their current use of the land would
continue. . . . As stipulated throughout this study, any land acquired
by public entities would be recommended only when a willing seller
situation exists."

Therefore:

> On the basis of this analysis, it has been determined that the Bear
> River massacre site . . . offers an excellent opportunity to tell the
> story of the conflict between American Indians and the United
> States Army in a single, well-defined location that is easily accessi-
> ble to travelers. . . .
>
> All Americans, both Indian and non-Indian, should be given the
> opportunity to learn about this uncomfortable aspect of the nation's
> history—the massacres of whole villages of American Indians. The
> knowledge of the violence that bought all Americans the right to
> own land, build homes, use resources, and travel freely throughout
> the country will increase their understanding and appreciation for
> those rights. At the very least, the price the Shoshone paid should be
> acknowledged.

When I finish perusing the Park Service study draft, something
troubles me. Something is missing.

Ah, yes.

Nowhere in the Park Service document is there any mention of the
rape that followed the slaughter, as documented by Brigham Madsen.

Dr. Spude calls the meeting to order just a few minutes after 7:00;
two other NPS staffers are also there, Fred York and Keith Dunbar.

About forty people have gathered; only one other person seems to be press, scribbling notes crazily like me. Spude begins by explaining the laborious process entailed in establishing a National Historic Site: the research, the public hearings, the writing of the study, more hearings, the writing of the legislation. She emphasizes that the Park Service is only in the early stages.

Yesterday, she says, we met with residents of Brigham City, the headquarters of the Northwestern band of the Shoshoni Nation, where 250 Shoshone live, most of them descendants of massacre survivors. She asks for the lights to be lowered, and shows a few slides of the massacre field. Cows graze a pasture near a meandering creek, wheat stretches in rows toward stark bluffs that reach for blue sky— your basic agricultural utopia. The crowd seems a bit restless, unimpressed. This is their town: they know this. The lights come back up.

In the front row, the woman who came in with the armload of papers raises her hand. Spude keeps talking:

We strongly encourage you to send your comments in writing to our Denver address. Everything we receive will be considered in our final report, which will be submitted in February. By summer we will submit our cost estimates, based on land values.

Down in front, the woman's hand still hovers high over the proceedings, more urgently now. Spude holds her eyes on the room at large and keeps talking, explaining the first of the three proposals. People living on the land, she says, can continue to live there and use the land. We anticipate minimal disruption of privacy and land use.

At this, people shift in their seats impatiently, and the front-row woman's hand begins to wave insistently. Spude surrenders. She nods at the woman, takes a step back, lowers her head. She seems to know what's coming.

The woman stands, clutching her many papers to her chest, and turns to face the room. I'm seeing that there are no Indians here tonight, she says. Where are the Shoshone tonight? Why didn't they come here to tell us what they think? I want to hear the Shoshone point of view, so we know why, after a hundred years, why they want to disrupt our lifestyle. We'd like to know from them personally why they're now taking our land.

From her face, reactionless, I can tell that Spude is ready for this. Her voice is level. We did have the opportunity, she replies, to hear some of the Shoshone point of view yesterday at the Brigham City meeting. It's important to realize that this massacre is considered a

holocaust event for them. The population of that tribe has never recovered from this event.

The woman is still standing. You can't trust the NPS, she says to
the audience. They say this now, they say there'll be no impact, but
later they'll take our land.

Nearby, a man is nodding his head angrily. Promises have been
broken, he says, turning his head to face the room. In other cases they
took the land. He shifts forward again and glares at Spude. You better be careful, he admonishes her. You are liable for any misinforma-
tion you give out to these people.

Hands are shooting up all over the room. Front-row woman sits
down, looking victorious—she has derailed Spude's presentation, gotten the meeting away from her. Spude acknowledges the hand of the
woman near me who had called the site gorgeous. There's already a
monument at the site, she says. Isn't that monument sufficient?

Another woman, pointing a finger at Spude: You're taking my retirement. That land is twenty-five years of my work. Let's put up a
bond on your home, and see how you like it.

Spude puts her hands up to ward off more comments. The issues
here are complex, she says. It's not that simple. What about the matter of graves protection? In 1910, a newspaper reported that during
the building of the West Cache Canal, remains were found. The
Shoshone don't want to excavate for further remains—they want
their ancestors to rest there in peace. There's an illegal market for
bones, as most of you know—and here Spude carefully stops short of
accusing locals of having trafficked in same—and this matter deserves
some attention.

More hands are up but Spude presses on. She takes a new tack,
playing this time to a prevalent complaint among Idahoans who are
being Californicated: Another thing, she says. This proposal protects you against equity-rich urbanites buying land and running up
your taxes.

It doesn't work. But we'll be forced to sell, a man argues. We
can't graze or plow or dig the land if you take it over.

Spude is still calm—shifts into yet another argument: And this is
something Congress is going to decide—not the NPS. We hold field
hearings, and depending on what we find, then legislation is introduced. At least one of your own representatives would have to spon-
sor this legislation—Kempthorne, Crapo, or Craig—you can call
them with your views. But before you do, you might want to talk to

the landowners around City of Rocks, which has been a historic reserve for five years now. That site has been very beneficial to the
economy of Cassia City.

Yes, a man says, but when we're ready to sell at retirement, who's
going to buy it?

The National Park Service will, Spude replies.

A melee breaks out—everyone talking at once.

But for how much? When there's only one buyer you get just a
fraction of your value—

Let's put up *your* house with one buyer and see what *you* get
for it—

The Shoshone never showed any concern till you started all this
hoopla. I've never seen one Indian on that site—

We used to be safe here. We moved here because we wanted to be
able to look out the window and say, There go the Talbots. Our kids
aren't going to be safe here anymore—

Since you started this mess I got junior-high Native American
kids telling my son, "We're taking your land back!" They'll be in
fights about this—

Spude raises her own voice in an attempt to stem the tide. It
would be a lot easier, she says loudly, for me to answer questions if
three or four people weren't shouting at the same time. Let me clarify. We do not propose giving this land to the Indians.

A man toward the back raises his hand and Spude calls on him.
He speaks carefully. I have children too, he says. We take them to the
site fairly often, because we want to teach our kids the history of
that place, and our own history as a people, which is closely tied to
the site—

OK, history, another man says. But is history important enough
to give up land? We already have yearly coverage of the thing in our
newspapers, an annual ceremony. How important is this really? I'd
like to have a few acres left to pass on to my kids—

And what about this part of the proposal where the site will be
opened up to Indians who want to hold rituals there—what kinds of
things will they want to do?

Spude is still unflappable. After all, the meeting may be noisy, but
most of the noise is being made by perhaps ten people. Everyone else
listens respectfully. Those are benign ceremonial activities, Spude answers. Putting sage in the air, prayers, that sort of thing.

But our work on the land is restricted while they do this—

Figure 2.2. Bear River Valley as seen in 1995. Used by permission of the National Park Service.

And we don't know these people. We don't know what they'll do there. How activist are these people?

Spude tries to sound reassuring—a difficult task, since the conversation hasn't focused on a discussion of the different alternatives, and it's not clear which alternative threatens the speakers most. We would not countenance fire building, she replies, or anything threatening to landowners.

Front-row woman is at it again: Why aren't they here so we can ask these questions? This is where the place is. Why aren't they here?

That does it. Spude's had it. I'm not sure that's relevant, Mrs. Griffin, she snaps. Do you intend to go to the Fort Hall meeting on Wednesday to hear *their* views?

That shuts everybody up for, well, only a split second. But still. Score one for Spude.

I think it's around this time that I notice that a policeman is now standing uncomfortably against the front door. He hadn't been there before and I'm wondering what the hell he's doing there. He has a slight, public-looking smile on his face and I suspect he'd rather be in a dentist's chair right about now.

The noise begins again. You don't care what the landowners think anyway, someone says. You have no intention of taking a vote of the locals.

As Spude has no choice but to repeat herself, she's looking more annoyed. This is a public process, she says. You have elected officials to speak on your behalf—

Don't kid us, a man growls. You, the Shoshone, and the Congress will decide. People who've never been here, who don't know a thing about us.

Mrs. Griffin stands up again. My brother, David Hansen, has something he wants to say.

The man next to her stands as she sits. He addresses himself to Spude. It's history, he says. The battle is over. It's gone. It's not there on the land anymore. This isn't the Grand Canyon. It's not Yellowstone. It's just nondescript farmland with nothing on it. You can't turn the clock back. You don't preserve history by trying to reconstruct the world.

He stops for a moment and takes a breath. What happened there is a tragedy. The settlers stole the land and the Indians stole livestock and food from the settlers. Now you want to steal the land again. If we learned anything from history it's that we shouldn't steal land.

He sits.

A woman near me speaks. The Shoshone should have come here tonight and told us to our face they were taking our land—

Only the Shoshone benefit from this proposal, says a man down front, shaking his head hard. His voice contains the sarcasm of the defeated. They're not out nothing if it goes through. You know what they're going to say without them coming to a meeting.

I want to be careful not to misrepresent the Shoshone position, Spude says. There were some who were opposed to this project because it's a painful and very personal memory some would prefer not to expose to public scrutiny. And to tell you the truth, there were some who opposed the project because they don't want Preston to benefit financially from the resulting tourism.

If there's a buck to be made, they want in on it, Mrs. Griffin barks. Their lawyer was at your meetings, paid by the government— *we* don't have a lawyer paid by the government—

The locals have been totally left out of this—

The man who spoke of taking his children to the site speaks again: Brad Smith is here, our city commissioner. Maybe he can tell us whether we've really been left out, and what he thinks of the proposal.

All heads turn toward a clean-cut man who is dressed like an executive on his off hours: slacks, button-down shirt, blazer. He's been leaning back in his chair and listening intently, with no outward response, for the entire session. He sits forward now and stares at his loafers for a moment. Then he speaks.

Generally, he says, the city council agrees on the importance of the historical event. Look, he says, and throws up his hands as he lifts his eyes to face the room. The word is out. It's been written up in that tour book, *Idaho for the Curious*. People are coming and looking now. They know how to get there now, from Hot Springs Road. We have to do something to protect our interests. We have to do something to mitigate the effects of the knowledge of the site. We have to understand: *it's gone national*. We're going to be affected one way or the other.

And we need to understand also, Spude says, jumping in while people are still listening, that this is a slow, uncertain process. The report will be submitted to Congress in a year. Then we have field hearings, then the legislation has to be written. Even if it's passed, appropriations take years. Five to seven years is the earliest we would start buying land. About $150,000 will have been spent over three years on the study. The NPS has a flat budget, so the money has to come from our own priorities. We'll be taking money from Yellowstone to pay for this. All of that still has to be discussed.

But the landowners are in the minority, Mrs. Griffin says. Many people want this to happen. We stand to lose the most for the good of everything else.

I think, Brad Smith says, that Senator Craig, who has been approached about sponsoring the legislation, is a proponent only of the willing-seller plan, for the protection of landowners.

Yeah, David Hansen growls, willing seller with a gun to his head. Willing seller whose rights are restricted.

We're going to be protected to death, Mrs. Griffin snaps. I've got articles here, she says, waving her stacks of papers so everyone can see, for anyone who wants one. It's happened other places, like down there in West Virginia, in Arkansas, in Ohio. It's happening all over, and this tells all about it. The NPS is not to be trusted!

The Park Service has made mistakes in the past, Spude says, as Mrs. Griffin passes around photocopies. It's not our intention to do so again.

We'll be overrun, Mrs. Griffin says. We have a sign up at our place: Private Property, Keep Out. And they drive right down to our barn. Right down to it! I tell you, when people hear about this nationally, the majority of people will side with the Shoshone.

Yeah, a man says. It'll be just like the easterners and the wolves. Easterners don't know a darn thing about wolves, but they think they know that predators should be dropped into managed land to feed off our cattle. That's what easterners know.

Easterners. Funny he should complain about easterners, of which I are one—hailing as I do from the distant suburbs of Philadelphia. And I'm accumulating several antiwestern biases.

As a novelist and academic gypsy, I've been teaching literature and writing at Idaho State for over a year now, but things are not going well. Mormons hold a strong majority in town and in the student body, a fact that was not communicated to me during my job interview, during new-faculty orientation, or even in casual hallway conversations with my new senior colleagues.

Why didn't I know this? I ask myself over and over. But in the year since I moved to Idaho, I've learned that there are broad segments of

American history involving the Latter-day Saints that remain wholly removed from our country's historical consciousness.

Why don't we know this?

And the more I see of Mormon Idaho, the less I like either Mormons or Idaho. My department chair, it seems, is a Mormon bishop, and by the end of my sixth week on campus, I've noticed a complicated series of programmatic practices he's using to suppress my work in radical literature. First he begins a paper trail to establish I am not fit for my job, so he can fire me. This is when a kind colleague, whose girlfriend was fired last year, sits me down to tell me I'll be the sixth woman in six years to be either run out of town or fired by this man—a fact of which no one else in the department, not even the senior women, are aware. When I ask the women to organize to resist this, and they do, they manage to keep my job for me.

But the chair, otherwise unimpeded by the department, still has other means. First, he declines to allow me to repeat my course Literature of Revolution, despite its popularity. Then, when I retitle the course but offer the same book list he approved the semester prior, he informs me that I have exceeded the department's expense limit for books. When I ask the senior women if they've ever heard of a policy limiting book expenses, they say no. At the next department meeting, he announces a new book expense policy on behalf of our fee-taxed, struggling students. Meanwhile, I arrange to have the rest of my books secretly sold by a nearby bookstore. Ultimately, the dean would step in and remove this man from office—but not before I am exhausted beyond salvage. When I quit midyear, the new chair doesn't so much as ask why I'm resigning.

It's not just the administration. My Idaho students seem to be excessively uncomfortable with discussions of—in ascending order of discomfort—race, class, gender, and sexuality. Discussions of religion are entirely out of bounds for many: when I lay out my critical orientation, so they know where I'm coming from, and tell them I'm a feminist, warmed-over-marxist, and atheist thinker, they're not happy with the first two, but the last makes them skitch in their seats, and they refuse to respond except to shake their heads. At Christmas, a student presents me with a copy of The Book of Mormon. Others beat a deep path to the chair's office to complain about my transgressions.

And they have a bad habit of refusing to read certain assignments. My pastor, an older woman student announces cheerfully, told me just not to read the chapter on Marxist literary criticism. One woman student seems particularly disturbed; discussions of feminism seem to leave her close to nervous collapse. She calls me at home, almost hysterical, to explain why she's missing classes, paper deadlines, readings. Well, says a colleague, you've heard that she's the product of a polygamous family, right? A few radical sects of the LDS church, she tells me, have gathered in remote communities of southern Idaho and northern Utah, practicing polygyny with full knowledge of most public officials.

Why didn't I know this?

And more. Because our assigned composition textbook provides a review of *Thelma and Louise*, I arrange to have the class view the film. It requires two class periods to see it, meeting an hour each time. During the second meeting, I'm startled when several young women walk out huffily during the Geena Davis–Brad Pitt sex scene. Subsequent office hours find women in tears who concede that they can't so much as peek at an image of (gasp) liberated female sexuality— also startling. But I'm even more startled when I realize:

No one walked out during the rape scene, in the first part.

Then too, there are the students born and raised around here who are not LDS, and are sick to death of persecution. I'll spare you their stories about growing up in a place where 70% of your schoolmates participate in a restrictive religious community, and refer you to a succinct study of the question, the film *SLC Punk!* Apparently, when everyone around you is conservative as hell, kids have to rebel to some desperate nth degree.

At the bottom of one of my course evaluations, under the institutional prompt to suggest changes that would improve this course, a young man writes, in caps:

GO BACK TO YOUR RADICAL-INFESTED CITY AND STAY THERE.

So as I say, I'm developing a fairly nasty bias, and now have no choice but to tell you that two of my very, *very* closest most intimate friends and favorite people on earth are Mormon—

Etc., etc.

In that fall 1995 class—Literature of Revolution without the title—all of the students are, as usual, light-skinned, and most are light-eyed and light-haired. I find that their responses to poems and stories by African Americans are predictably reflective of the dominant national media coverage of blacks. There is no specific hatred of blacks in the commentary, even though our classroom is 16 miles away from the national headquarters of the U.S. Militia Association in Blackfoot. Hailing predominantly from rural areas, these students have little experiential reason for more than a bemused irritation with the black community's apparent inability to overcome (institutionalized) poverty. Those people, one student proclaims, mostly run in gangs and destroy themselves with their own rage. They should grow up and knock it off, grab hold of their bootstraps. Forget the slavery of the past—it's history.

Hmm, I think. Not so much racism here as classism. If African Americans weren't endlessly portrayed in the media as poor, the conversation might be different.

It's when we do the section on Native American literature that the colors fly. Resentment is thick: several students grew up in farm families who lease cropland from the nearby Shoshone. Their landlords are inordinately unreasonable, often piddling away the lease money on booze. Most students seem to know someone off the reservation who's only part-Shoshone but who nonetheless receives free medical care on the rez, plus free money from tribal settlements for land treaties—and all of these folks seem to be boozers undeserving of an endless stream of taxpayer support. *We* don't get free tax money to do whatever *we* want, one student complains. The government builds houses for *them*—not for *us*—and look what they do to the houses. They trash them. It's a trash heap, the whole place.

After we read Mary Crow Dog's (and Richard Erdoes's) *Lakota Woman*, we view Michael Apted's documentary *Incident at Oglala*, which is about the 1975 Pine Ridge killing of two FBI agents and the subsequent federal conspiracy that, as many of us believe, continues to perpetuate Leonard Peltier's political imprisonment. It's my intention to expand a discussion of truth, to ask whether there's a difference between FBI truth and Lakota truth, whether our cultural differences make it impossible to understand Peltier's refusal to expose the man who really killed the agents. Peltier's Ojibwe–Lakota idea of justice differs from *wasichu* justice—why is this? And how true is Apted's film, which uses a number of fictional devices to persuade the viewer of Peltier's persecution? Is objectivity possible?

But we never get to this discussion. The students argue back and forth about who was right. Why won't Peltier just tell who did it? asks one. Why won't Mr. X come forward to save his friend, to tell the truth? Peltier's guilty of other charges anyway, he was there that day, he probably did *something*, maybe he really did do it—after all a jury *did* convict him.

A few students try. Don't you understand, one says, it was a war zone in Pine Ridge back then, the FBI was in cahoots with the non-traditional tribal council, innocent people were dying, mining rights were being stolen. Why should Peltier confess anything when justice is always on the side of the whites, when justice isn't about fairness but about *sides*.

I try to limit my role to that of interlocutor. What makes *us* think we have the right to an unwavering opinion about what the truth was? I ask. Since all of *us* are *whites*?

The discussion heats up. It's a class of fifty-five students, arranged in a huge circle in a large room that is not quite large enough, so when they get to debating each other from 50 feet away, it's noisy. I listen, make myself busy scribbling notes so they'll speak to each other and ignore me. Truth! a male student yells. It's their word against the government's. They tell all these *"stories"* about what happened, while the government has *real* documentation, on *paper*. They have all the evidence they need in those files.

But those stories they tell, that *is* truth in an oral culture, a woman says. An *oral* culture is just as true as a *written* culture, right? she asks. I mean, *paper* isn't infallible, *right*?

Look, the male student responds angrily, something happened, we know it did, so we have to find the truth! People have to be held accountable when murder happens, and we can't do that if we won't look for the real truth!

Finally a young man in the back of the room bellows, *All* of those Indians should have *died* that day! Where do they get off shooting at FBI agents, at law enforcers, no matter what the reason? They should *all* have been wiped out as accomplices to murder. Those agents had families! What those Indians did was wrong—they should have obeyed the law like the rest of us have to!

The class is stunned to silence by the violence of the outburst. I stop scribbling.

All the Indians should have died that day?

As I look around the room, I see a significant number of young men nodding vehemently.

But I've been struggling to tell you the story of how this story found me.

I wait for a week after the all-the-Indians-should-have-died-that-day debacle before trying again.

Beginning with my colleague who teaches Native American lit, I've been conducting an unscientific survey.

Has anyone ever heard of the Bear River Massacre? I ask the class.

Nearly all fifty-five students are shaking their heads. I'm shaking mine too—all fifty-five of these young people have spent their entire lives within 5, 20, 60, and 100 miles of the site.

But wait.

There's a hand.

A light-haired, green-eyed young man in trousers and dress shirt has his hand up. Timidly.

His jaw is dropped as far as mine. His smile is bemused.

You've heard of this? I say.

He nods.

How did you hear about it? I say.

How did *you* hear about it? he says.

Three months of work with this group of students, and I've never heard this young man's voice. He comes to class early, sits in the back of the room by the door, is among the first students out the door when class is over. I've noticed him talking quietly when I've asked the students to speak together in small groups, but he's never spoken to this large, unwieldy group before. And he's never spoken to me.

We should talk, I say.

After class, I make a beeline for the back of the room. He's still in his seat—it's unusual for him not to have bolted out of class. So you know about this? I say. I have to speak loudly over the noise of fifty students collecting their things and chatting as they swarm out the door.

He nods again. He takes a breath, as if he's deciding how much to tell.

I descend from the Northwestern Shoshoni, he says.

No shit, I say. I'm thinking he looks about as Shoshone as I do.

My great-great-grandfather was Chief Sagwitch. You know him?

No *shit*, I say. You're *kiddin'* me.

The icy dancers trip a pas de deux down my spine.

We stare at each other for a long moment. Most of the students have shuffled past us and the room is quieting down.

Well, I say, realizing that it's up to me, the teacher, to keep a conversation going. You've probably heard about the thing the Park Service wants to build on the site.

I'm the cultural resource specialist for the tribe, he says calmly. Mostly I deal with hunting and fishing rights, but since NAGPRA (the Native American Graves Protection and Repatriation Act) was passed I'm also in charge of recovery of remains. So I'm the liaison to the Park Service on the historical site, which is also a graves site.

No *SHIT,* I say. Now you're *really* kiddin' me.

He shakes his head.

The spinal spirits are out of control.

At our next class meeting, Curtis Warner comes in with a flyer he's been posting around town, announcing public meetings to be held by the Park Service to solicit citizen commentary on future protection of the Bear River Massacre site. The hearings are scheduled for our last week of classes; the first one, December 11, will be held in Brigham City, Utah. The second one is scheduled in Preston, the town closest to the site, on the 12th. On December 13 they'll hold one in the Shoshone–Bannock Council Chambers in Fort Hall; the last one will be two days later, in Fort Washakie, Wyoming. Curt's number is at the bottom of the flyer, for additional information.

I can get you a copy of their proposal if you want, he says.

Do I! I say.

He leaves it in my campus mailbox the next day.

December 13, 1995. I'm taking a break from grading and packing and meeting people who stop over to examine my furniture, decide whether to buy it. I have to get to school soon, to meet my afternoon lit class—Curt's agreed to give me an interview, too—but I flip through the material from last night's hearing in Preston and study the photocopies Mrs. Griffin gave me when I approached her after the meeting. She says she'll be more than happy to give me an interview, to explain her family's position on the matter.

The handout is an 11 × 14 copy of what looks to be a newspaper. *Land Use Review,* she tells me. May 1995 issue. I've underlined the important parts, she adds.

Indeed she has. A section header reads "Property Rights"; a 60-point headline warns, "In the beginning, they told us we would never lose our land. . . ."

She's underlined the lead: "Cannan Valley, West Virginia: In the beginning- these 'trusting mountain people' were told the refuge would not interfere with their fragile economy and way of life."

The second paragraph she has not underlined: "A memo written by the Fish and Wildlife Refuge manager admitted their spokespersons 'provided erroneous information . . . deliberately misleading . . . have avoided discussing issues . . . (telling them) whatever they wanted to hear to build support for the proposal.'" The article explains that the study, on which the proposal was based, stated clearly that the refuge's impact on locals would be devastating, probably even total: "Audubon Society believed it was important for local people to be informed and voice objections, but the ultimate decision is not theirs alone - state and national significance must be considered."

Underlined: "Park Service secretly designated large areas as 'nationally significant.' They became 'National Landmarks' without consent of the landowners. The Landmark program is recognized as a 'feeder' for Park designation, but people were led to believe this was an 'honor' with no negative consequences."

Asterisked: "**Note:** Don't let anyone tell you these studies aren't important. This 'Study' was done 20 years ago, and is now being used to take the land from these people."

The article details "massive scale land grabs" at Buffalo National River in Arkansas ("Families forced from homes at gunpoint"); at the Boundary Waters in Minnesota ("In the beginning they said we would always have access. Now. . . . A once-popular vacation area is being closed to the public: 75 resorts out of business . . ."); at Bridal Veil in Oregon ("Historic lumber town along the Columbia River, leveled. All trace of human habitation removed, so it could be made into a park . . ."); at Cuyahoga Valley in Ohio ("Nearly all of the 500 homes and businesses were removed 'For the Good of All.' They were considered 'an intrusion' on the scenic beauty. . . . The few remaining buildings were boarded up, patrolled by armed rangers . . .").

Not underlined: "In the beginning they told us it was just a study . . . Do you really believe it will be different from the rest? It's up to you to help Stop the Recommendation. For more information contact the Citizens for Responsible Zoning and Landowner Rights. . . ."

Mrs. Griffin had made no marks on a second article on the same page, but I found it to be most revealing of the publication's bias: "Property rightists flex muscle": "There's a political movement afoot in America not unlike the one that founded it. More and more landowners bearing economic battle scars from environmental regulation believe government no longer represents their interest."

This second article details the work of the Alliance for America, a cross-country computer and fax network with a membership sufficient to generate as many as 25,000 letters to congressional representatives when they wish to be heard: "All Alliance members have anecdotes about environmental excess or tales of economic woes. Beneath the stories lie a growing anger and desperation at the effects of confiscatory regulation on property."

Indeed. In fact, property issues are at the heart of that thing that happens when the liberals of the East part company with the libertarians of the West.

After class Curt and I sit in my university office. He's pissed off at me because I've asked him what percentage Shoshone he is. That's got nothing to do with anything, he says. It all depends on what matters to you. He's married a white girl. Still a complete jerk, I awkwardly express a muted surprise at this. It doesn't matter, he says irritably. My kids will still know, he says. They'll still be part of that.

He tells me his father spent twenty-five years in the service trying to pass as Mexican. He'd drop hints, Curt says, that he'd come up from the south, let them think he once worked the fields—let them think whatever they wanted. People called him Spic, Greaser. That bugged him, but he knew he'd get called worse if he told them the truth. He wouldn't get the promotion or the job he wanted. As a kid I never really understood this.

Is that why you pursue this project with the Park Service? I ask. I mean, it's an interesting choice you're making, given the fact that you could actually pass for white.

Curt looks irritated with me again. The Park Service started this because of that law that said they have to research historically significant sites, he says. Then he looks away from me. But I think my father's kind of proud of me for standing up for who I am, since he didn't think he could. Curt's staring at the floor now, as if he doesn't want to be saying any of this—so I know he's doing me a favor. I want to dedicate my life, he says, to my family members who were lost there, to protect their remains. It's my way of saying thanks for my Indian heritage, of paying back my ancestors for the massacre.

We sit with this for a moment, until he speaks again.

People asked me in class, he says, how I felt when you'd say things like, All of us are white here, what right do we have—and all that. He lifts his head to look at me directly again. It really didn't bother me, though.

Liar, I say.

You didn't know.

It's interesting that you didn't tell us, I say, but then you'd be the only person in that whole huge class to situate yourself as a person of color. Plus, you know, All the Indians should have died that day.

Doesn't bother me.

Uh-huh.

He's looking at his shoes again.

So you learned about the massacre by reading Madsen's book? I ask.

He nods. But it was Mae Parry, he says, who tells the tale for our people. I first heard about it from people who told what she told. My family talked often about Frank Timbimboo Warner, my great-grandfather, Chief Sagwitch's son, who escaped into the hills the day it happened. He was adopted by the Warner family. Wayne Warner was his son, my father's father. As a kid I heard about the Treaty of Fort Bridger, from 1863, about how our people lost the Washakie Reservation. We recently got 184 acres back, you know, because there are graves there. Near Malad.

How did this Park Service scheme end up in your lap? I ask.

NAGPRA, mostly, he says. Kind of a problem, that law that says that all Indian remains have to be returned to their native nations. We didn't have any warning that they were going to pass the law and we weren't really ready for it. No money came with it to help us do anything. There's a lot of confusion about which remains go where and what to do with them when we get them back. As far as the Bear River site goes, we've been looking at that for a long time. Somehow the local whites have managed to find no remains there, even though they've been plowing and digging wells and foundations for one hundred years now. There's no question that they're selling the bones.

No kidding, I say. That nice old lady I talked to last night, selling bones?

You never know about people, he says, even when they have good intentions. Not everybody likes this plan because of that. There are about four hundred bands of Shoshone, and the Northwestern band wasn't even recognized as a band until 1980—everything rides on the opinion of these anthropologists, and I can't say anyone trusts them much. They pretended that we'd all been wiped out by this massacre, decided we didn't even exist. Nothing against Fred York, the anthropologist who worked on the proposal—he's a good guy, really trying hard—but it's not a good relationship.

So how'd the first meeting go?

Brigham Madsen was there! he says, his eyes brightening. I wanted to get him to sign my book but a million people lined up to talk to him.

I can't believe you like that guy, I say. I mean, don't you think his perspective is a bit biased in favor of the Mormon church?

Curt shrugs. He told the story, he says. That's what matters.

We swap notes. He gives me a copy of the report he typed up for the Tribal Council. I give him a photocopy of the notes I took last night. You shoulda been there, I say. Amazing.

I'll bet, he says.

We sit reading. It's immediately clear that the concerns expressed at the Brigham City hearing were vastly different from those of the Preston hearing. In his report, Curt has summarized the different alternatives covered by the draft study, and then has listed Questions Asked (and here I've edited his creative spelling):

1. Which alternative provides for on-site staff to protect site?
2. What's the response of the landowners?
3. What interest, if any, does the state of Utah have in the massacre site?
4. Has there been any resistance to using the term massacre instead of battle?
5. Is there any consideration being given to the proposal to change back the name of Battle Creek to Beaver Creek?
6. Is there any possibility the site could be called by a Shoshone name?

The rest has to do with costs and time frame, the same logistics covered in Preston. But I'm struck hard by the second question. The Shoshone seem primarily concerned with protecting the site and its remains; yet it's clear they also feel a pressing worry for the welfare of the whites currently residing in the area.

Curt finishes reading my notes of the Preston meeting. Wow, he says, though neither his face nor his voice demonstrates any real reaction to what he's read. Nothing I haven't heard before, he says.

We sit shaking our heads.

I'll pick you up at 6:30, he says.

I really appreciate your driving me to the council hearing, I say. Really helps me a lot.

No sweat, he says. Anything that helps get the word out.

I really *do* appreciate Curt's driving me to the hearing to be held with the Tribal Council. I suffer an intense discomfort on reservations that goes back to my days in grad school at the University of North Dakota, when I was auditing Indian Studies courses on the off hours between my courses in linguistics, literary theory, American literature, creative writing. The English Department there was housed on the first floor of a distinguished old building at the edge of the quad. The Indian Studies Department, touted then as one of the largest such programs in the country (it's since fallen on hard times), was located on the second floor of the same building. People—that is, whites—called that floor "The Reservation." English folks did not wander up there casually. To walk up the steps to the second floor was to experience a distinct change in atmosphere. Twenty-four steps, and suddenly you're in a place where there are far fewer women, and no white folks to speak of. Suddenly you've got clumps of men with long, dark hair staring at you suspiciously. It seemed there were always these clumps of men—doing what?—hanging out. Just hanging in a space they felt entitled to. They stared at me and I looked away. Only the people you knew, your Intro to Indian Studies teacher, maybe, were welcoming. Mine, John Salter (now Hunter Gray), the civil rights activist and author of *Jackson, Mississippi*, hosted me for hours in his office, regaling me at length with the stories of his Micmac/St. Francis Abenaki/St. Regis Mohawk ancestors. He was (is) a gentle man, always patient with stupid questions. More patient than I. But after I left his office, I had to negotiate the band of men hanging in the hallway.

Or maybe my discomfort goes back further than that. Born in the closing years of the Eisenhower administration, I'm an impressionable middle-schooler when the hippies are appropriating Native American rhetoric—and sometimes their land. In 1970, when I'm eleven, Dee Brown publishes *Bury My Heart at Wounded Knee*, though I don't read it cover to cover until I'm fifteen. *Billy Jack* comes out in 1971; when I see it at a cheap, second-run theater a few years later, it makes a profound, and profoundly unfortunate, impression on me. I publish my first short story in a student journal in

1975, just as I'm turning sixteen. It's a silly tearjerker about Indians, inspired by an exercise my tenth-grade creative writing teacher gives us. He hangs up a picture of Iron Eyes Cody, that one where the tear runs down his face because the environment is being destroyed (by whites). I have a pretty bad, heart-bleeding case of middle-class liberalism by then. My big dream in life is to end suffering everywhere and clean up pollution while I'm at it. I'm president of my school's Environmental Action Club, and I take my peers on jaunts to nearby suburban parks, where we bag the empty beer cans, crushed candy wrappers, and used condoms that litter the parking lots. I figure Iron Eyes Cody and I are united in this antilitter concern. But he's suffered a lot more than I have, I figure.

Or maybe my self-consciousness goes back even further. My grandmother, maybe. The poor Indians, she would say. We stole all their land and left them with nothing. She'd say stuff like this often. She and my grandfather owned a trailer on a remote slope of Tuscarora Mountain, in central Pennsylvania, a few miles from the Mason–Dixon line. What's Tuscarora mean? I asked when I was about ten. It means we stole some land from the Tuscarora Indians and then named the darn place after them, she said.

These comments are remarkable not least because my grandmother was not a woman given to political speeches. She wasn't an early feminist. I have no idea who she voted for, or what she thought of whoever was president, though I assume she was a devoted Roosevelt Democrat, like my grandfather. No one ever pursued these comments she made, discussed these matters with her. I never asked her what she meant. The comments settled like dust in the room, and life went on. It seemed OK to *say* that Tuscarora Mountain had been stolen from the Tuscarora, but it didn't occur to any of us to do anything about that.

When I visited Taos, New Mexico, I couldn't follow the other white tourists out to the Pueblo. But they *want* your admission money, my companion argued. Tough, I said. I'll send a check. I won't make a spectacle of their everyday lives. But you'd learn so much about this very different culture, he argued. I'll read about it in books, I replied. I go to pow wows, although they aren't much easier. But it's an educational tool, my friends say, they *want* you to come and learn. Come and try the frybread. See the fancydancing. I don't enjoy making a spectacle of a history that's hanging by a thread. But it doesn't hang by a thread, they say, it survives this way.

So you can see: my walking into a Tribal Council meeting alone: *No fucking way.* But with an escort? With sponsorship?
I'm there.

December 13, 1995. Fort Hall's tribal headquarters are formidable—a surprise to me. Through-traffic on the reservation, using I-15 or US-91 between Pocatello and Blackfoot, sees only a couple of rundown trailers, a truck stop called The Trading Post, a scattered town in the distance. Travelers frequently stop, but only to view the old ruts of the Oregon Trail. Not hard to guess that the real scene is somewhere off these roads, but you know me, I hadn't wanted to pry.

Curt's car, a shiny-new midsize, white with gray interior—Nice ride, I tell him—is the only car in the lot when we climb out and look around. I look at my watch, but we're not early. Ah yes, I think: Indian time. Expect this one to stretch on a bit, I tell myself. Good thing I peed before we left, I tell myself.

The weather's still a bit misty, but the real rain's holding off for later. Headquarters is a large, dark structure with that sort of contemporary architecture in which the front door is not apparent. There aren't many windows. Curt guides me into a large, tiled lobby. Really nice, I say.

This has been open a few years now, he says. It's much nicer than the old place we had. Offices are nicer.

We head down a dark, cobblestoned hallway and he pulls open the doors of what looks to be a medium-sized auditorium. It's a beautiful room, oval in shape. Upholstered theater seats nestle in plush carpet, slope down in rows toward the front, where a long table curves toward the audience. The table is elevated significantly, and towers a bit over the front rows of seating. A dozen executive chairs sit waiting behind the table; microphones dot each station. A huge buffalo head growls down on the table; a bighorn sheep ogles the seats from a side wall; a banner reading "Shoshone–Bannock Tribal Council" hangs behind the center chair. Yellow-toned recessed lighting illuminates the room gently; on the walls, paintings: Snake River scenes, ceremonies.

Beautiful, I breathe toward Curt. I feel the need for a hushed, reverential tone.

He nods.

The meeting is scheduled for ten minutes ago, but no one is there except the two people from the Park Service, seated in that lowly front row. I'm brought up short by their appearance. Fred York looks the same, but Cathy Spude is an entirely new woman. The business suit is gone in favor of a denim blazer, a long tan skirt, casual shoes, silver and turquoise jewelry. She waves and looks relaxed. York sits next to her this time, instead of covering the back of the room.

Curt and I take seats toward the back and off to the side and chat idly about school stuff, about a rare Idaho State history professor who does include Bear River in his western history course.

A few minutes later a man enters the room and heads for Curt's chair, sits down behind us. He and Curt shake hands solemnly. Curt turns to me. This is my father, he says by way of introduction, nodding his head toward the dark-complected man. This is my English teacher at the university.

Mr. Warner shakes my hand and lowers his head. He's smiling broadly. Hope he's not giving you any trouble, he says.

None at all, I say. If anything it's the other way around.

Curt and his father bear little physical resemblance that I can perceive, but they seem to share the same careful manner.

The two men talk together in low tones for some time. It's now over a half hour since the meeting was scheduled to start. A few more people have filed in and are talking quietly, including a few men who've gathered in front of the table.

I pull my watch off and stuff it in my purse.

It's probably 8:00 P.M. before the council, with two members sitting at the table, is called to order. About twenty-five people have scattered throughout the auditorium. Spude begins as before, though her tone is more congenial. She explains the process of park designation, has York hit the lights and turn on the slide projector.

If we are able to build Alternative 4, the full ownership of the entire site, with visitor center and full staff, she says, showing the slide with the cows grazing peacefully in the meadow, approximately seventy-two landowners and their family members would be affected.

She stands with the projector remote in her hand. We realize, she says, that for some of you, this is sacred ground. We feel strongly that this ground needs to be protected. Unfortunately, it has not always been respected by the people living nearby.

She presses a button, and on the screen appears a picture of what amounts to a trash dump on the bluffs above the meadow.

I can't say whether others in the audience are snapped back in their chairs as hard as I am. This is not a slide she showed to the

Figure 2.3. View of the bluffs overlooking the Bear River Massacre site. Used by permission of the National Park Service.

whites in Preston. She remains quiet for a moment and allows us to take it in. The grasses on the hilltop are scattered with rusting car parts, a set of bedsprings, a refrigerator.

This is why we find it imperative that something be done to protect this site, she says. The good news is that Idaho has one of the strongest laws in the country regarding protection of native remains. But, she continues, Alternative 4 is, of course, our least likely option. "Takings" are almost impossible in the current political climate. The Park Service has no eminent domain or condemnation authority. But we want to protect the site as much as is feasible given today's situation.

York turns the lights on and Spude asks for questions. The council members begin first. Their questions are complex property issues: Who owns the river? What's the difference between private land and Indian land? If Congress bought the land could they sell it back later? And constituency issues: Would it be possible to have preferential hiring of Shoshone at the site?

It strikes me as profoundly ironic that these people, whose ancestors two hundred years ago rarely so much as encountered the notion of private property, now possess a shrewd knowledge of its procedural manipulations.

When the council members have finished, a man in the audience stands. We all wait while he takes a moment to gather his thoughts. He seems agitated, fusses with his fingers as he talks. I disagree with the ownership of that land, he begins. He speaks slowly, to Spude. In 1834 that land was Shoshone reservation. The Shoshone were operating there. You people have no respect. You trespass over our bones. You farm. You build homes on it.

Spude takes no offense, nods in agreement. And there's no guarantee we'll succeed here, she says. Twenty years ago a study was done on the Washita site, and Congress chose not to act. The law is now being reconsidered, but I don't know that the political climate has evolved along with the recent laws passed regarding historical sites and remains.

The man continues. Which laws are you referring to? he asks. White man's law, or God's law? Why do you swear on the Bible? You shot us like rabbits.

A woman raises her hand. Diane, Spude says, calling on her.

The woman stands as the man sits down. Do the people of Preston support these plans? she asks.

Spude shrugs. Some do, believe it or not. Several have approached us to offer help. The landowners, however, are understandably threatened by the notion of losing their livelihoods.

I ask, Diane says, because we have our own differences within the Shoshone tribes. How can we facilitate all of these differences? How can the legislation address that?

The first man stands again. Once again, he says, this legislation is something that gets done *to* the Shoshones, like NAGPRA, and we're neither consulted nor prepared. How can we prepare for this? We've been waiting since March 7, 1864, for the Treaty of Box Elder to be honored, the treaty with the Northwestern Shoshoni. Was that treaty meaningless?

York stands and turns toward the audience, shaking his head. It's not meaningless in the historical sense, he says, but the intent of Box Elder has been changed by the treaties that followed.

Maybe the tribes should get together and make their own park, the man responds. Our ancestors' bones are still there. We have our aboriginal rights. The remains law is not being enforced.

York nods. Federal law, he says, is specific regarding Native American remains, and it provides an extensive repatriation process. Designating a protected site would further support that process.

Diane stands again. (And I can't help but draw your attention to the speech rituals enacted here: waiting for someone to finish speaking, then standing in order to be heard, rather than standing as a means of controlling the discussion.) Diane speaks: There's already a monument on the site, right? But I'm told it commemorates the soldiers? The American soldiers who died there?

Why would they commemorate the *soldiers*? the man asks irritably.

They were expressing affection for their grandparents, York says. Now that time has passed we can see the event more dispassionately.

We are grateful to the Park Service for trying to correct that history, Diane says. We know the oral history. There are few descendants here at Fort Hall, but many relatives. We as Indian people know it was a massacre. The history books claim it was a massacre of *whites*. The Park Service documents make that responsibility clear.

Alternative 4, Spude says, would bring out the true story.

A man toward the back stands. But we don't have much clout, he says. One percent. Our voting power in this country is one percent. If we put our support behind Alternative 4, that would probably kill it.

What would be wonderful, Spude says—what would be wonderful at this site would be for people to come together, finally, after all this time, all this history—for people to come together and finally do something right.

Yes, the man says. I understand you. It was Indians who were subjected to the terrors and torments of European immigration. Our people have experienced pain and suffering, and we need to put politics aside so we can pay our respects to our people. Because this thing happened during the Civil War, little attention was paid to it, and it was not noticed until recently. We need to understand why it happened so we can avoid it happening again. Enculturation, he continues, as the audience listens quietly. Ethnocide. That's what has happened, and we contribute to that if we don't do something to set the record straight.

Around the room, many nod their agreement.

Thank you, Spude says. She waits for a moment to see if anyone else will speak. No one does. Thank you all for coming and for speaking so frankly. If anyone has further questions I'd be glad to talk to you individually, she says.

The audience begins to talk quietly together; some people cross the room to speak with others. It's clear that a good part of the business here is conducted in these smaller groups, afterward. Spude and York talk with the council members and then head for the back of the room. I head for Spude.

You must be exhausted, I say.

She laughs. Well, it's almost over, she says. Just Washakie tomorrow, on the Wyoming side, which will be more of this. A little more supportive.

Diane approaches the two of us and she and Spude talk about how the whites responded in Preston.

As I listen to them, I see that it's just us three girls here, and decide to risk the question that's been eating at me.

Very carefully.

It's wonderful what you're doing here, I begin, so I hope you'll forgive this question. You say you want to provide "the true story," but there's no mention in the Park Service study of the rape that occurred after the massacre. You've decided not to include that in the site's historical material. Why is that?

It may be my imagination, but Spude looks a bit stunned by this question.

Am I the first to ask? Maybe so.

Well, she says, I've read the material on the rapes. She and I both glance quickly at Diane to see how she's handling this talk. She seems OK. Spude takes a breath that comes back out sounding like a sigh. You know, she says, the number one constituency of National Historic Sites, the group that visits parks in the largest numbers, are busloads of schoolkids. She shakes her head. I have kids, she says, and I don't mind talking with them about such things. But I just don't know how any of that would fly with the general public.

Diane and I are both shaking our heads sympathetically. I decide to let loose my academic self a bit here. It's too bad, I say, especially given the War Crimes Tribunal in Bosnia this year—now that it's accepted that rape has been an effective military tool. A means of population control in wartime. That rape gets civilians to move away from areas where rapes have occurred, ceding territory to the rapists. To the enemy.

Spude nods. And also, Spude says, so *many* horrible things happened to women that day. There are so *many* stories, maybe too many to tell. Federal troops reported that Shoshone women fought that day, you know. Like soldiers. Some died like soldiers. She shakes her head hard, looks away. In the early parts of the research, she says, we met with descendants. And there was this one woman. She got up at the meeting and told a story that her mother told her, and her mother heard it from her own mother, and her mother learned it from her mother. This woman's great-great-grandmother was a survivor. And that day, as the killing of the warriors was ending, this woman saw what was happening to the survivors, to the women and children. She was hiding with her child in the willows near the hot springs, along the riverbank, and she saw what was going on. How the children were being killed and how the women were being—Spude looks at Diane and me and stops herself. She saw it, and she thought it was over for them. Spude's voice breaks, and when she draws a breath it catches. She continues: She saw it and her child started to scream, and she was afraid that all those who were hiding would be discovered. So she made a choice. She took her own child and went out into the river. She took that child and pushed it out into the water, watched it float away till it stopped struggling, drowned that child in that river her own self so none of what was happening would befall that child, and so the people hiding would not be caught. Then the soldiers stopped—the soldiers were suffering themselves from the cold—and they started to retreat, and she managed to escape in the grasses in the river.

Spude's cheeks are wet as she looks at Diane and me again. In all my research of this event, she says, I had never encountered that story. But that woman got up at that meeting and she told it, and everyone nodded their heads like they'd heard that story all their lives, like it was gospel, like it was truer than true, and we all cried. It was the most amazing thing.

Diane and I are still shaking our heads at what Spude is saying. It's just us women here, talking about what women face. Awkwardly, I put my hand out and touch Spude's arm. She's rubbing her face, shoving away the tears, lifting her head. Too much suffering, she says. Too much. Too much to tell it all.

3

THE TRUTH TOUR

Dr. Spude's comment at the hearing, about stories—too many stories—follows me for two and a half years.

How are the stories being told, anyway?

Because really, I'm not sure this whole notion of building a historic
site in order to protect history—is a realistic thing. History seems like
something that keeps changing. And place—place is so static.

Sure. Let's build a historic site to commemorate a mass murder,
and refuse to commemorate the rape.

Is this good?

How *are* the stories being told, anyway?

It's 1998. Chicago's OK. It's a radical-infested city indeed, busy,
crowded, lots of people to meet. I've been teaching and writing—
finished a novel, a nonfiction project, lots of articles and reviews. I
need a new writing project. And that whole Bear River thing is still
bothering me. Off and on, I've tried to sell a few magazine editors on
the idea of an article about it, but they've all turned me down flat.

Which I find hard to figure. Why aren't they interested?

Maybe it's too big a story for an article, I think. Maybe it takes a
whole book just to convince an editor why it's an important story.

I don't know. I can't afford the research I need to do anyhow, not
without the support of an editor somewhere, or a university somewhere. I have neither. The money thing with writers: always a rock and
a hard place. You need time, you need resources, and both cost money.

But then another one of those coincidences occurs, the sorts of accidents that have peppered the history of my involvement with this story.

123

One of my former colleagues at Idaho State University, Tamise Van Pelt, offers me the use of her apartment for six weeks while she's off to a National Endowment for the Humanities seminar, expanding her intellectual horizons. I'll make some small effort to keep her plants alive in the summer heat, and meantime, research this book.

This is how it is with writers. Without any funding of my own, Tamise's apartment is the only way. Without it, there would be no book.

So I pack my moisturizer and sunscreen, abandon my partner once again—to 1998's brutal heat of a Chicago third-floor walkup— and head my little pickup west, back to Pocatello.

Here's something we know about history: it's through tertiary documents that an academic study becomes Historical Truth. As Society Knows And Consumes It.

Which is to say, academic historians deal with primary documents—records made at the time of the event. Brigham Madsen, for instance, examined the actual letters and church archives to draw his conclusions. He selected materials from those primary documents, and organized his conclusions, in his book—a secondary document. From his examination of those documents, and from information supplied by other documenters of primary materials, I provide for you a summary of those conclusions, with questions of my own—a tertiary document.

Historical evidentiary procedure stops there. If I take my summary and fictionalize it in a novel, or write a screenplay, or compose a narrative to be displayed on a wall in a National Park Service visitor center, these are also tertiary documents.

Primary documents are not an active part of our cultural makeup, since very few of us see them. Secondary documents are on their way to becoming cultural truth because a few more of us see them— mostly academics and lay intellectuals. Tertiary documents, including the blockbuster history genre Stephen Ambrose has popularized, *are* cultural truth—because this is what the vast majority of us see.

How are the stories being told?

First thing I do when I get into town is stop by the Walrus and Carpenter Bookstore, center of the leftist universe in Pocatello, gathering place of the Birkenstock gang. Will Peterson is still there, combing through his overstuffed shelves. He has a decent section on Native

American history, an even better section on western history, and the usual wacky collection of used books. You never know what you'll find at the Walrus.

We're standing at the register chatting about how all the bad things that happen in life have a New-Agey positive meaning—when my eye snags a dog-eared paperback perched on his "Special Interest" shelf.

Idaho!

I recognize the cover design from my late teens—the late seventies. "Wagons West—Thirteenth in a Series," the cover announces. A bald eagle carries these words on a banner in his beak. Red, white, and blue bunting stretches across a standard romance-novel picture, circa early eighties, of a man intently clutching a resisting woman. His face is shown in intense profile, while hers, all lusty despair, faces the artist/reader/consumer/lover. Typical. These books always place the woman in unattainable communication with the reader, to be the seducer of those who might consume her—female buyers who want to be her, male passersby who want to have her—even as she herself is being near raped. *The Towering Saga of Rugged Men and Tempestuous Women Carving out America's Future from a Savage and Perilous Land.* By Dana Fuller Ross.

Damn—my mother bought all these books. I'd read them when I was—sixteen?

A book about the history of this "Savage and Perilous Land"?

Hmm. Exactly what I came to Pocatello to research!

How are the stories being told?

I snatch up the volume. On the back cover, things get even better. "Only the most daring crossed the River of No Return to enter this wild, lawless region. Mountains laden with riches lured prospectors burning with gold fever. Easy money brought ruthless young men with guns for hire. And hidden amid the vast forests of white pine were the war ponies of Shoshoni and Nez Perce—bloodthirsty Indian warriors who gathered to drive the white man from the red man's ancestral home."

Will's got a price of $2 scribbled on the inside cover—half the price the damn thing sold for in 1984, its copyright date. I've got to have this, I tell Will. It's not the sort of research material I was hoping to find at the Walrus, but since pulp novels such as this one are, for good or ill, a major source of historical information for mass-market American citizens, I'm curious.

How are the stories being told?

Stretched out on Tamise's couch, I thumb through the well-nubbed first pages. The promotional material is endless. Page one: "IDAHO! The thirteenth thrilling novel in the saga of *WAGONS WEST*—true-to-life stories of high-spirited Americans who dared to leave safety behind as they pressed onward into the danger and excitement of vast, unexplored lands."

True-to-life? Excellent!

Opposite the copyright page, I'm further assured of the "truth" of this work: "This is a work of fiction. While the general outlines of history have been faithfully followed, certain details involving setting, characters, and events may have been simplified."

Faithfully followed. (If simplified.) Good to know.

But a list of (stock) characters alerts me to a possible problem, a problem perhaps caused by this faithful simplification of history. You've got your white military hero ("true son of the west . . . determined to stem the tide of lawlessness"); your eccentric old white miner, who, Will-Geer-like, has no friends save a "talking crow and a patient burro," and whose desire for the gold he's discovered may prove "deadly"; your white, upper-class Madonna who can't possibly be permitted happiness in her privilege ("her dreams of happiness coming true at last . . . until an old nightmare returns"); your somewhat sluttier Amazonian—but happier—and British—white female ("good with a gun"); your sluttiest white "courtesan" Whore with a "lurid past" that makes her very unhappy; and your young white lovers "separated . . . tested by sweet, forbidden temptations."

But you've also got your nod toward affirmative action. It's nice to see the Chinese contributions to western migration made present, but "Wang" is a "huge, powerful hatchet man for a San Francisco tong" who "yearns to avenge his honor by drenching the streets of Boise in the blood of the man who crossed him." Ah, yes. I've heard how those Asian hatchet men drenched Boise back then.

And—of course—you've got your Indians. You've got, in fact, the two kinds of Indians you've grown to love: the noble and the savage. "Stalking Horse" is the "loyal companion" of the aforementioned white military hero—he's the white-approved Native—you've met him elsewhere as Tonto. Finally, meet "Running Bear: Hot-headed young rebel of the Nez Perce Indians, his words urge his people to war; his hate demands death for his greatest enemy" (the white military hero, natch).

A quick look at the "Wagons West Family Tree" reveals that it should have been named the Wagons West *White* Family Tree. None of the people of color noted above are present in this genealogy.

The novel is set, we know from the first sentence, in 1869, a year most important to western and Mormon historians: the year the frontier ended, as Utah historians have it, with the connection in Utah of coast-to-coast rail service. Of course, 1869 is also that most important year in which most Idaho natives finally gathered on reservations. So the book begins when all that muss and fuss is done and gone. There will be no discussion of historical causation here. We can also see from the promotional materials that the novel's Idaho setting is actually western and northern Idaho—and that the Boise area has been transformed (*mirabile fictu*) into a country of "vast forests of white pine." That is, the huge, high-altitude desert, which comprises most of southern Idaho (including Boise), and which many people find not particularly pretty, will not exist in this "true-to-life" novel. We can also see that the Shoshone, who suffered the larger part of the white-red interaction—primarily in southern Idaho, where several trails passed—will not exist. They've been replaced in this novel by the Nez Percé, a group European Americans have managed to romanticize in a vaguely positive way. (Recall Joseph's vow, "I will fight no more forever." Now attempt to recall one quote you have heard uttered by a Shoshone leader.)

Again: *Hmm.*

Also immediately interesting in this novel: The first scenes are set in and near Salt Lake City, on the newly connected train lines. But nowhere are Mormons mentioned in these pages.

I settle in with the novel, thinking that surely it will have no choice but to attempt in some way to explain how, in 1869, southern Idaho had been cleared of the "savage . . . peril" that once would have prohibited easy passage for those "rugged men and tempestuous women." How will the Bear River Massacre and Rape be reported? Thankfully, I don't have to read for long.

Page 43: "Something had just been done, however, to curb the excesses created by young warriors of the Shoshone and Nez Perce, who had been raiding and robbing the homes of ranchers and other settlers in the area. Both tribes had signed treaties with the United States and were living on reservations. Even so, there were many hotheaded young braves who continued to go out on raids, and the peace was disturbed nightly by violent incidents."

I keep reading; surely there's more. But the main subject on page 43 is the trouble local lawmen are having trying to keep peace with the hotheaded, and the next paragraph mentions the recent arrival of the new lieutenant governor, who may be counted upon to restore order.

So that's it.

One paragraph.

One paragraph.

"Something had just been done. . . ."

Indeed.

Now that's what I call faithful, simplified history.

Besides pulp historical novels, another common source of historical education for our citizenry is—sightseeing. Adventures in the American August. Surely our government-sponsored Historic Sites do a far better job of clarifying history for tourists than do pulp novels. Right?

How are the stories being told? Is it possible to build a place for the protection of history?

Well, let's see. If you were planning to learn about the Bear River Massacre, you might start in Utah, where it all started. And if you were planning to visit Utah, you might order a copy of the official *Utah! Travel Guide.* Signed by Governor Michael O. Leavitt and produced by the state-sponsored Utah Travel Council, the glossy magazine lists information on "accommodations and resources," but also provides a brief history lesson. "This is Utah" is a general overview of the state with explanations of points of interest, and it begins with a short section titled "People and Culture": "Utah's original Pueblo Culture inhabitants are represented today by several Indian tribes with strong cultural legacies which continue to flourish in the state. Visitors and residents alike are reminded of Utah's link to these important civilizations of the past by the state's web of sacred natural places, dwelling sites, and intriguing rock art messages."

And thus are the Shoshone annihilated—symbolically—more completely than any massacre could ever have done—replaced once again by another, more positively constructed nation, the Pueblo. Historically, then, the only Indian "civilizations" that "link" contemporary Utah to the past are the ones that are still there, and the ones with whom sustained, violent conflict did not occur. Shoshone

contributions to the original settlement of Utah are forgotten—
indeed, the very existence of the Shoshone is forgotten.

> Utah also retains a bit of the frontier spirit which is evocative of the
> mountain men who found in Utah's landscape the fodder for their
> legendary stories and deeds.
> The Mormon pioneers, who began settling the Salt Lake Valley
> in 1847, left behind an example of religious devotion and hard
> work which remains a vital part of modern-day Utah. Today about
> 70 percent of the state's population is Mormon, which is a simpli-
> fied reference to the Church of Jesus Christ of Latter-Day Saints,
> sometimes referred to as the LDS Church.
> During the last century, people of many ethnic, cultural and re-
> ligious backgrounds have made great contributions to Utah's qual-
> ity of life. Together, the values of Utah's citizens make the state an
> industrious, clean and safe place in which to live and work.

Things do not improve in the section titled "Utah's Historical
Background":

> Ancient Pueblo People, also known as the Anasazi Indians, or An-
> cient Ones, raised corn in southern Utah from about 1 A.D. to
> 1300. Ute and Navajo Indians roamed the region for centuries be-
> fore the arrival of outsiders, and the state takes its name from the
> Ute Tribe. In the mid-1700s Catholic Spanish explorers and Mex-
> ican traders began to arrive. In the 1820s fur trappers including
> Jedediah Smith, William Ashley and Jim Bridger discovered [sic]
> the area and its abundant trapping opportunities; they made
> northern Utah a popular site for mountain man rendezvous. Per-
> manent pioneer settlement began on July 24, 1847, when Mor-
> mon leader Brigham Young looked across the Salt Lake Valley and
> said, "This is the right place." During 1847, 1,637 Mormons mi-
> grated to the Salt Lake Valley. By the time the first transcontinen-
> tal railroad was completed at Promontory, Utah in May of 1869,
> more than 60,000 Mormons had come to Utah by covered wagon
> or handcart. Utah became America's 45th state on January 4,
> 1896. Since settlement days, Utahs [sic] history has been shaped
> by people from diverse cultural, ethnic and religious backgrounds.
> Today, Utah is a unique balance of modern sophistication and nat-
> ural wonder.

Again with the Pueblo—not that there's anything wrong with remembering them. And this brief history skips from the 1820s, when

the Shoshone (including the Ute) supported the very mountain men named here; to 1847, the year of the Mormon invasion; to 1869, the year the Shoshone were finally gathered on reserve land in Idaho. This as if the conflict with the Shoshone, during the intervening years, were irrelevant to an understanding of how Utah developed.

Clearly the Utah Travel Council's primary concern is to persuade visitors of the vast cultural "diversity" and "sophistication" enjoyed by Utah residents. I found not one use of the word *Zion*—the Mormon church's naming of Utah as the promised land—in the Travel Council copy.

So. So far it's not looking good. But just in case the promotional material does not reflect the work actually done at the historical sites, whatsay we take a little roadtrip—a little truth tour—and check out the information available to an average citizen with an average level of curiosity about U.S. history?

A stop at Salt Lake City's Pioneer Memorial Museum confirms the historical evaporation of the Shoshone. The museum is operated by the Daughters of Utah Pioneers (DUP), who state their organizational objective as being "to perpetuate the names and achievements of the men, women and children who were the pioneers in founding this commonwealth . . . thus teaching their descendants and the citizens of our country lessons of faith, courage, fortitude, and patriotism." Any woman may join who is "over the age of eighteen years, of good character, and a lineal or legally adopted descendant of an ancestor who came to Utah Territory before the completion of the railroad, May 10, 1869"—always that magic date, an obsession in these parts—meaning, any ancestor who was present *before* the Shoshone were on reservations. Meaning, any ancestor who would surely have encountered the Shoshone at some point and in some way. "As you enter the Pioneer Memorial Museum," reads the brochure, "you literally walk back into history."

Literally.

Excellent. Exactly what I was hoping.

The Pioneer Museum lists "Native American Relics" as one of many displays in its collection. But a hunt through the basement where this display supposedly resides results in the discovery of a single display case. In this, six items are protected under glass. The largest item is a vase dated as "1100 AD" (not identified as such, but clearly southwestern—Pueblo?—in origin). The remaining items are all designated "Sioux": a pair of leggings, moccasins, a tobacco pouch, a leg ornament.

And that is all.

Is it possible these are mislabeled? By the nineteenth century, the Lakota and the Shoshone shared similar clothing practices.

But either way, and once again, the Shoshone are evaporated, replaced here by the Lakota, who, again, in this region at least had posed no threat to white invaders.

The Pioneer Memorial Museum, which was originally financed both by the state and by members of the DUP, and which is now operated by the DUP but maintained by the state, is immediately remarkable for another reason. Any U.S. citizen who's been steeped in standard pioneer mythology (recall the Wagons West series, for instance) emphasizing the poverty, hardship, and deprivation suffered by the invaders—will be surprised by the contents of the displays. Instead of plain work dresses and bonnets and domestic tools, one finds rows and rows of collections of lace. Dress gloves. Perfume bottles. Parasols. Slippers. Silverware, jewelry, opera glasses, hat pins. Pianos, chairs from the box seat in the opera house where Brigham Young once sat. One is tempted to suggest that the museum would be more aptly named, Upper-Class Mormon Pioneer Memorial Museum. Perhaps inadvertently, the museum revels in the wealth that some of the Latter-day Saints brought with them to this region, and many would amass later.

Copies of published emigrant guides are on hand, including such titles as the *Latter Day Saints' Emigrants' Guide, Being a Table of Distances Showing all the Springs, Creeks, Rivers, Hills, Mountains, Camping Places and all other notable Places, From Council Bluffs, to the Valley of the Great Salt Lake. By W. Clayton, St. Louis, 1848.*

On the other side of town, up on the benchlands, at the mouth of Emigration Canyon, we find This Is the Place State Park. The most frequently visited state park in Utah, This Is the Place boasts a "living historic village" as well as a massive monument purporting to honor the settlement of Salt Lake Valley. This site is also supported financially by the state. Old Deseret Village, according to its brochure, provides "the opportunity to see everyday life as it was lived in pioneer Utah. You will see Utah as it was from the time when the Mormon pioneers arrived in 1847 to the time when the railroads arrived in 1869." Which is to say, the twelve years encompassing the whole of the Mormon–Shoshone conflict. At Old Deseret Village, "we breathe life into history by portraying the lifestyles, activities and values of its people." Here, "imagination meets experience." So this is the right history: "The Old Deseret Village experience has been carefully researched and recreated to provide you with a glimpse into yesterday and the opportunity to experience the past."

And as you are coming to expect, the Northwestern Shoshoni, who lived nearby and with whom there was so much local conflict *and* interdependence, are entirely missing in action. The "strong, independent [white Mormon] people" actively portrayed here by costumed workers are not shown protecting themselves from Shoshone raids, or sharing food with Shoshone, or gathering local information from Shoshone. And at the monument, which consists of a series of sculptures of important people, including a section titled "Those Who Came Before," no Northern or Northwestern Shoshoni are present. Not even Sagwitch, who converted to Mormonism. Instead, we have another replacement—the friendly Eastern Shoshone chief is here. "Chief Washakie," the brochure reads, was "an intelligent and highly respected leader of the Eastern Shoshone. . . . Although most of his activities took place in Wyoming's Wind River Range, Washakie was reportedly a close friend of Brigham Young and the Mormons and was well-known throughout much of the Great Basin region."

Reportedly.

The geographical commentary is itself indication of the curiously glaring omission, as it immediately begs an obvious question: If Washakie operated in western Wyoming, who operated in northern Utah? What happened to them? Clearly the state feels no necessity to answer this question—from which we can gather that few people are asking.

The monument contains no statues of women.

This Is the Place State Park does clarify one powerful piece of historical mythology: Brigham Young's "This is the right place" comment. Now Utah's tourism motto (Still the right place), the statement exists only thanks to quite belated hearsay; thirty-three years *after* leading Young's carriage through the canyons, Wilford Woodruff recalled Young saying something similar. The quote is apparently *not* the result of a divine intervention that led Young to discover the Great Salt Lake Valley and establish it as a new safe haven for persecuted Mormons. A plaque reminds us that Young was detained by mountain fever and was thus one of the last of the original wagon train to reach the valley. Apparently he reached the mouth of Emigration Canyon, saw the settlement below, and said, "It is enough. This is the right place. Drive on."

As you continue with your sightseeing in Salt Lake City you may begin to wonder whether the Shoshone ever lived near here, whether Bear River ever happened—whether the whole damn thing was made up. Consequently, The Fort Douglas Military Museum comes as something of a relief. Located on Connor's original camp, not far from This Is the Place State Park in Emigration Canyon, Fort Douglas is now a small army base. Its museum is the only site where the "Battle of Bear River," as it there remains known, is indeed central to the displays regarding Connor and the California Volunteers.

But the story is still flawed. At this "battle," deemed an "impressive victory" by one of the displays, the Volunteers "inflicted a decisive defeat on a band of 600 Shoshones, effectively ending further Indian resistance in that area." Of course the number was closer to 450, not that numbers matter overly much. According to the museum's brochure, "the regiment won military supremacy over the garrison and began successful prospecting for mineral wealth in the surrounding mountains."

Garrison?

In this museum, "administered under the auspices of the U.S. Army Center of Military History" (i.e., one of the few government-sponsored historical museums in Salt Lake City relatively uninfluenced by church or state), the reason for the Volunteers's presence in the city is given primarily as the necessary protection of the Overland Mail Route. But also, "The Volunteers manned the camp because Mormon loyalty to the Union during the Civil War was questioned by some northern states." The brochure states vaguely, "In the early years, the Army presence in Utah was unpopular with Mormon settlers, but the Fort ultimately became an integral part of the community and a treasured landmark."

Connor, a display notes, has been called "the first gentile of Utah," as well as (and more famously to contemporary Utah schoolchildren) "the father of Utah mining." The display notes Connor's significant contributions to Utah history after he mustered out of the military in 1866: founder of the first daily newspaper (also the first secular newspaper); first to use electric light in the state; first to operate a steamer, his *Kate Connor*, on the lake; and founder of Stockton, Utah.

In a small park outside the museum, a monument to Connor stands. But his burial place is at the Fort Douglas cemetery, now located outside of the base, a half mile away in—rather oddly—the center of an industrial park. In the middle of this small military cemetery stands a tall monument to the (white) casualties of Bear River. The names are listed by company. Individual graves are nearby.

I'm struck by something troubling in the arrangement of the gravestones. The men killed at Bear River, and their markers, face the monument from the west—just as the Shoshone would have buried their dead, given the chance. The arrangement is startling because the monument itself faces slightly west and north, and the men thus lie with their backs (so to speak) to the dramatic view of the Great Salt Lake Valley—and their Mormon neighbors. The arrangement is not, then, the intuitive choice; consequently, and whatever the reason, it seems a strikingly purposeful architecture. Tall junipers shade Connor's grave; he too faces the monument, his back to the valley that once resented his presence. A bronze tablet sports a bald eagle and a bust of Connor in relief, along with these words:

Patrick Edward Connor
Brigadier General and Brevet Major General
U.S. Volunteers
Born March 1820. Died December 17, 1891.
Camped in This Vicinity With His California Volunteers
October 20, 1862. Established Camp Douglas, Utah,
October 26, 1862. Participated in the Battles
of Buena Vista, Bear River and Tongue River.
The Father of Utah Mining
Erected 1930 by the Garrison of Fort Douglas, Utah,
Assisted by the Utah Historical Landmarks
Association and Patriotic Citizens of the West.

Perhaps in Idaho, things will be better. After all, while the history of the encounter at Bear River may have begun in Utah, you must turn north, cross that magic line, to pursue its eventuality.

Headed north on US-89, you pass through Logan, home of the public university nearest to the site of the Bear River Massacre and Rape, Utah State University. After that, Franklin, and after that, Preston. The wide, pretty streets of these quiet towns do not hint that *"something had just been done here. . . ."*

Following US-91 out of Preston and toward Pocatello, you reach the massacre site in a matter of minutes. The land drops sharply down into this hollow few people have heard about.

If *you've* heard about it, the sharp, sudden, unexpected drop in the road may be enough to start the spirits dancing on your tingling spine. Here, the landscape is a crucial part of the emotional experience of knowing What Happened.

U.S. citizens who haven't heard may speed through this area at 65 miles per hour (at least) and note nothing except perhaps an odd sign that hangs midway along the valley's pastureland—a sign that marks the entrance to a small trailer park. "Site of the Bear River Massacre," it reads.

This sign is inexact, since the trailer park is several hundred feet away from the actual massacre field, but folks tearing by at 65 miles per hour might not notice it anyway.

If you were out for a leisurely Sunday drive, or if you had promised yourself, perhaps in a New Year's resolution, to stop at every historical marker you see, you would notice the monument and marker on the right-hand side of the highway, a quarter mile beyond the trailer park.

But if you pulled over and read all three of the signs that stand there, you might return to your vehicle as confused as ever.

A large sign prepared by the Idaho Historical Society and placed by the Idaho State Highways Department reads: "BEAR RIVER BATTLE. Very few Indians survived an attack here when the California Volunteers trapped and wiped out the Cache Valley Shoshoni." In smaller print: "Friction between the whites and these Indians, who had suffered from too many years of close contact with fur hunters [!], led P.E. Connor to set out from Salt Lake on a cold winter campaign. The Shoshoni had a strong position along Battle Creek canyon just north of here. But with a loss of over 400 [!], they met the greatest Indian disaster in the entire West, January 29, 1863."

On the Battle Creek Marker, dedicated 1932:

> The Battle of Bear River was fought in this vicinity January 29, 1863. Col. P.E. Connor, leading 300 California Volunteers from Camp Douglas, Utah against Bannock and Shoshone Indians guilty of hostile attacks on emigrants and settlers, engaged about 500 Indians of whom 250 to 300 were killed or incapacitated, including about 90 combatant women and children. 14 soldiers were killed, 4 officers and 49 men wounded, of whom 1 officer and 7 men died later. 79 were severely frozen. Chiefs Bear Hunter, Sagwitch, and

Lehi were reported killed [!]. 175 horses and much stolen property were recovered. 70 lodges were burned.

At the bottom: "Franklin County Chapter, Daughters of the Utah Pioneers, Cache Valley Council, Boy Scouts of America, and Utah Pioneer Trails and Landmarks Association."

A second plaque on the marker was placed by the Daughters of Utah Pioneers during a 1953 "rededication":

Pioneer Women. Attacks by the Indians on the peaceful inhabitants in this vicinity led to the final battle here January 29, 1863. The conflict occurred in deep snow and bitter cold. Scores of the wounded and frozen soldiers were taken from the battlefield to the Latter Day Saint community of Franklin. Here pioneer women, trained through trials and necessity of frontier living, accepted the responsibility of caring for the wounded until they could be removed to Camp Douglas, Utah. Two Indian women and three children, found alive after the encounter, were given homes in Franklin.

Continuing north, ever hopeful. Around mile marker 30 on US-91, just south of Downey, right in the middle of a dramatic rock outcropping, an Idaho highway sign marks a "geological site." That sign reads,

RED ROCK PASS. You are standing in the outlet of ancient Lake Bonneville. A vast prehistoric inland sea of which Salt Lake is a modern remnant. Covering over 20,000 square miles when it overflowed here about 14,500 years ago, its winding shoreline would have stretched from here to New Orleans if it were straightened out. This pass was deepened considerably when Lake Bonneville began to flow into Snake River. For a time a torrent several times larger than the Amazon was discharged here. Finally with a hotter, drier climate that slowly emerged about 8000 years ago, Lake Bonneville gradually disappeared.

Pocatello, the second-largest city in Idaho, with plenty of chain hotels, would be a logical place for the average American Auguster to overnight while seeking historical veracity.

Some descendants of massacre survivors live in the Fort Hall–Pocatello area (some live in Brigham City, Utah, and Fort Washakie, Wyoming—others are scattered across the country). But a visit to historical sites in Pocatello yields little information about the Bannock and the Northern and Northwestern Shoshoni, who preceded whites here. The Fort Hall Replica—which sits in town, about 10 miles from the actual site, which is now reservation land—sports a billboard that reads, "Fort Hall, Keystone on the Oregon Trail/ America's road to destiney [*sic*] . . . the Fort site has been designated as a registered historical landmark by the National Park Service." Displays inside the fort replica provide a sketch of the history of the "mountain men" who trapped (primarily beaver) in the region and traded with natives in the early nineteenth century (those mountain men of mythology who later made their livings as emigrant guides when the furs began to run out). Their histories as entrepreneurs who sold goods to such institutions as the Hudson Bay Company does include occasional obscure mention of their contact with Shoshone and Bannock peoples. "The present Fort Hall 'bottoms' had been for years a favorite gathering and camping place for the Shoshoni." When Nathaniel Wyeth built the original Fort Hall, a nearby camp of Bannock was considered a "good omen." He traded widely with the Shoshone and Bannock: blankets, beads, and pelts were the main currencies. Two photos of natives are here, both unnamed: one titled "Bannock Brave" and one titled "Shoshoni Warrior, 1859." The latter is by famed photographer Alfred Bierstadt.

That is the unnamed extent of the presence of natives in this history. A summarizing list of important dates in Fort Hall's history, titled "Fort Hall's Final Years," skips from 1855, when the Hudson Bay Company abandoned Fort Hall, to 1868, when the Fort Hall Indian Reservation was created. As usual, no mention is made of the intervening conflicts, or the massacre that led to the treaty that led to the reservation.

Across the lot in the Bannock County Historical Museum, we fare slightly better. Although dominated by a massive mural wall "dedicated to the Mormon pioneers who settled Bannock County," the museum does display a small collection of Shoshone–Bannock artifacts (unaccompanied by any historical explanation). The museum also includes a slim and poorly lit collection of reproductions of photos taken by Benedicte Wrensted. This Dutch woman's portraits of local natives, made between 1885 and 1912 in her Pocatello studio, are stunning artworks of light and reverence for subject. (Another display can be found in the February 1996 issue of the *Smithsonian*.

I refer you to an article by Diane M. Bolz, which is accompanied by well-reproduced samples of Wrensted's work.)

Perhaps you will not be surprised to hear that the most specific and detailed discussion of Shoshone development and lifeways—limited though that discussion is—can be found, ironically, at the Idaho Museum of *Natural* History, on the campus of my former employer, Idaho State University. This irony is the result of vestiges of institutionalized academic racism: mainstream "history" museums contain the stories of white peoples; while "science" museums contain the stories of earth, animals—and nonwhite indigenous *human* animals. The Museum of Natural History contains displays explaining plate tectonics; Ice Ages; the Bonneville flood; and the evolution and extinction, ten thousand years ago of the massive Pleistocene mammals, including the horse, the bison, and the bear. Huge skulls and skeletons are the museum's biggest draw.

In this context, then, the collection also provides evidence of what is offered as the "human presence," dating back to twelve thousand years ago. The display divides this indigenous history into two periods: the Paleoindian period (12,000 to 9,000 years Before Present), and the Archaic Period, which has three subperiods. "Ancestors of the Shoshone–Bannock are documented in the archaeological record" of the Late Archaic Period, 3000–150 B.P. The "Historic, or Contact, Period" begins in 1804 with Lewis and Clark (which nationalistic designation ignores Shoshone contact with Spanish and French explorers in the 1600s and the 1700s). "The traditional aboriginal lifeway was to be brushed away in less than 50 years," the museum announces, but there is no discussion of how or why this would happen—no recollection of, for instance, the Bear River Massacre. Again, "*Something had just been done here. . . .*" But in this museum, photos of Shoshone individuals identify their subjects by name. One display explains how sagebrush bark was (is?) softened to make fabric and clothing. Baskets and beadwork are displayed, as is a collection of parfleche containers of painted rawhide.

Still seeking historical truth, and the process by which truth is made, you might plot a course west of Pocatello, on I-86, and visit Massacre Rocks State Park.

Massacre Rocks is a thin strip of state park along I-86 west of American Falls. The interstate, the park, and the Snake River all squeeze between dramatic rock formations dropped there like pebbles by the powerful Bonneville Flood. The 900-acre park offers hiking, picnic areas, horseshoe pits, camping, fishing, and access to Oregon Trail ruts.

Massacre Rocks? Must have been a massacre there. Probably a massacre of natives, right? Since there was a lot of that going on. Let's check the brochure.

> "Gate of Death" and "Devil's Gate" were names given to this area during the Oregon Trail period. These names referred to a narrow break in the rocks through which the Oregon Trail passed. Pioneers apparently feared that Indians might be waiting in ambush. Diaries record a series of skirmishes between the Shoshone Indians and Pioneers on August 9 and 10, 1862. Ten pioneers died in the fight, which involved five wagon trains.

Hmm.

Not that keeping body counts is a culturally productive activity, but yes, you heard right. When white folks are killed "in a fight," *ten deaths constitute a massacre.*

But wait. It turns out that Massacre Rocks State Park is not even the precise location of the event in question. The state park brochure admits sheepishly that the actual skirmishes "took place east of the park, not at Devil's Gate, as commonly believed. Some attacks may have occurred there, but they remain unverified."

So. To clarify: Probably, no massacre ever took place at Massacre Rocks.

Even though many felt one probably did, given the intimidating nature of the landscape.

So we've built a monument to a killing that felt like it could have happened there.

It gets worse. Something else that probably happened, some thought, and some still think: the Almo Massacre. We turn our truth tour south, headed for the California Trail, which cut through the even more striking, and eerily frightening, landscape now known as the "City of Rocks," recently made a National Historic Site. Here we pass through the small town of Almo. The wide, quiet streets remind you a great deal of Preston, Franklin, and Downey—but less green.

In the center of town, a plaque is mounted on a stone slab similar to the one near Preston, the one marking the Bear River Massacre. The title of this plaque: "The Almo Massacre."

You might obey the impulses of your New Year's resolution, pull your car over, get out to read the description on the plaque, and learn about the greatest emigrant disaster in history. For four days, their wagons circled, three hundred European American settlers fought off Indians (Shoshone?), who kept them from going for the water that was one short mile away. They attempted to dig wells, to no avail. Five people escaped and managed to get to Brigham City, whence a party was sent to rescue the train. But when they arrived, all (295) had been murdered by the Indians. The rescuers buried the victims in the freshly dug, dry wells.

It's a horrible, shocking story.

Reading the monument erected by interested citizens in 1937, you think to yourself that it's a truly tragic thing you're reading here, this monument to the memory of so many people who died so terribly.

But you would be wrong.

What's truly tragic about this monument is that the Almo Massacre never happened.

Not one researcher has been able to turn up a shred of evidence.

The Idaho Historical Society has officially declared the event to be a myth.

All we really have today is some vague speculation about what might have caused such a rumor to start.

A few encounters with Shoshone did result in casualties in 1852. But not *that*.

In this case, *something did NOT happen here. Not even probably.*

And yet there is this monument to an old, racialized fear.

By now, you may be ready to give up the search for roadside historical truth. But there's one last place to try.

A stop at Pocatello's visitor's center produces a brochure distributed by the Fort Hall Shoshone–Bannock Reservation. It advertises the Annual Indian Festival (second weekend in August), and the Trading Post Complex, with its Oregon Trail Restaurant, Gaming Facility ("High Stakes Bingo"), Tribal Museum, grocery store, post office, gas station.

The brochure also presents some history:

Ruts of the historic Oregon Trail lead past an obscure monument at the site of the original Fort Hall on the Fort Hall Indian Reservation. Founded in 1834 as a trading post by Nathaniel Wyeth, Fort

Hall later became an important supply and rest stop for the seemingly unending flow of settlers to the west. . . .

The Shoshone and Bannock people originally roamed parts of Idaho, Wyoming, Nevada and Utah in extended family groups. They were hunters and gatherers, and fished for salmon. When horses were introduced to the tribes in the early 1700's, they began to travel great distances to pursue buffalo across the Plains.

Lewis and Clark were the first whites to arrive in the Lemhi Shoshone area in 1805. This was home to Sacajawea, a member of the expedition. Next trappers, then pioneers traveling the Oregon and California Trails and, finally, settlers emerged upon the scene.

Tensions began to mount with each new encroachment. Presidential Executive Order established the 1.8 million acre Fort Hall Indian Reservation in 1867. The Fort Bridger Treaty of 1868 confirmed the arrangement, but a survey error reduced it to 1.2 million acres in 1872. The Bannock Wars of 1878 led the final attempt of some independent hunters to fight for their traditional existence.

In the late 1880's the tribes felt the effects of the allotment process when 160-acre parcels were allotted to each adult and 80 acres to each child. The "surplus" was turned back to the government to sell to non-Indians within the reservation.

Today the reservation consists of 544,000 acres, with 3593 enrolled members. The tribe is organized as a sovereign government and provides many services to tribal members and non-Indians with tribally driven revenues from mining, agriculture, business enterprises, taxes and other operations.

A few minutes' drive north from Pocatello on US-91 or I-15 will deliver you to the reservation. The Shoshone–Bannock Tribal Museum in Fort Hall is in a roundhouse right off the reservation's exit from I-15. This museum is much more interdisciplinary than our European American history or science museums, but it too does not always fill in all of the historical blanks, and occasionally mimics the white-academic approach to history. A display titled "Agaidu'umlau'ka, the Ancient Fishermen," provides first the Coyote legend of why salmon swim upstream to spawn; then repeats the same information about the "Paleo-Indian" period presented at the Idaho Museum of Natural History. The self-congratulatory suggestion is that the Agaiduka of ancient oral legend are indeed the archaeologists' "human presence" of Paleo-Indian times. Thus we should conclude that this (white) scientific confirmation proves that oral traditions—even oral traditions twelve thousand years old—are "true." In European American terms, that is.

Evidence of human presence in Fort Hall dates back 3,500 years, another display announces. A case showing relics from the Old Fort Hall, and another displaying tools of the early-nineteenth-century trappers, are reminiscent of the items in the Fort Hall Replica in Pocatello. Here too is a collection, much larger and more prominently displayed, of reproductions of the Wrensted photos.

But there is a great deal of new material here, including a display of present-day/traditional artwork. Here we see that sagebrush bark *is* still softened that way, and the old lifeways *do* persist, despite the Natural History Museum's use of the past tense. The artists are young people. Also: a showcase of Indian cowboy relics and a discussion of "Sacajawea" (that white-approved female native) and of her people, the Lemhi Shoshone, who have their own reservation at Fort Lemhi in north-central Idaho. The Lemhi presence here is notable because this is *not* their reservation, and so one suspects that, again, the replacement thing is happening, where the Northern and the Northwestern Shoshoni replace themselves with their more famed cousins.

One wall provides an explanation of religious practices, including the sun dance, the warm dance, and the grass dance. (Here I learn that women are now permitted to participate in the sun dance because women staged sun dances during World War II, while many of the men were away in service to their country.) Also here are explanations of how foods were collected and prepared, a long list of the things that were made from buffalo, and a description of various sorts of shelters built by the old ones.

Among other unchallenged mythologies, tales of horses predominate. As with European American history, there is little here about the quite recent prehorse culture (seventeenth century and back).

And there is almost nothing here about the Bear River Massacre. *Almost.* Under a photo of a "chief," we find this caption:

> Chief Pocatello, an elusive Shoshone who gave the white settlers second thoughts when they rode into his territory. Chief Pocatello's actions against the white settlers made him an outlaw in the eyes of the United States government. History shows that his reasons were justified.
>
> Pocatello's band was a segment of the Northwestern Shoshone, who were almost totally exterminated by Col. Connor and his California Volunteers on January 29, 1863. Only seven members of this band of over 450 survived.

Only seven members.
Wow.
I struggle to figure out where they got this number, and all I can come up with is this: Bear Hunter's band was reduced to seven. If my speculation is correct, then this museum has erased the survival of Sagwitch's band—from which we may infer the depth of resentment against Sagwitch's people, who converted to Mormonism and to agricultural lifeways. Or, we may find in this gross underestimation of the band's survival rate an internalization of the European American habit of vanishing Native Americans by saying they are gone.

But also, this caption is the only political resistance (*"his reasons were justified"*) expressed in the museum; it's also one of very few mentions of the toll taken on this native nation by the invasion of European Americans. This erasure, or internalization, makes for an odd contradiction to the museum's putatively primary purpose: celebration of survival, recuperation of presence, erasure of erasure. But this museum houses a *nationalist* survival celebration—that is, it celebrates those cousins who helped along the birth of a great country (Sakakawea guiding Lewis and Clark, for instance), and it celebrates contributions made to that new culture, of art, spirituality, and of land use. To revere the good cousins, the museum is willing to help erase the bad cousins. *We're still here*, and *We helped you*, are the themes—not *You were wrong*.

A tough line, admittedly, to walk.

As it happens, the tribal museum's small shop has several interesting books on Shoshone history, including Madsen's *The Shoshoni Frontier and the Bear River Massacre*. I decide to quit relying on the library, buy a copy of my own, and head back out into the heat, my magical mystery tour concluded.

Across the road from the museum, at the Trading Post, I'm holding my new book, standing in front of a billboard looking at announcements of forthcoming events, wishing I could go to the sun dance this weekend—but deciding I can't, as I'll be menstruating by then. The sign specifically forbids the presence of menstruating or pregnant women—an act of exclusion that really irritates me. I'm thinking maybe I'll rebel against the exclusion, maybe I'll just go anyway—what are they going to do, check for tampons at the door??—and isn't this just another silly way to keep women from sites of power and information? When he was working on *The Spirit of Crazy Horse,* Peter Matthiessen didn't have this problem! I'm feeling a bit huffy about it, going back and forth on it.

Ultimately I decide that going would be a flagrant act of cultural disrespect. Still, it bugs me to be excluded because of a shedding endometrial lining.

I'm standing there pondering the poster when an elderly gentleman approaches the billboard too, nods at me, and then sees the book I'm holding. He lifts his finger to speak to me. That was, he says, poking his finger toward the book, the worst massacre of any group of Indians in the history of the west. He shakes his head. The worst, worse than Custer, worse than the Knee, worse than anybody. And it's never been publicized. No one knows.

Why do you think that is? I ask him.

He tilts his head back to consider this question. He seems very comfortable taking the position of lecturer to the younger—white or red. Well, he says carefully, it was the Civil War. The reporters were distracted with other things. They had a lot on their mind that was closer to home.

I tell him that I was surprised not to find much about it in the museum. He nods. A good number of the survivors converted to Mormonism afterward, he explains. They were active in the church down there near Salt Lake, and they had their own land in Washakie. The church took that away after the war, just took it back just like that.

I'd been wondering about how the Shoshone lost Washakie, and wasn't sure which war he meant. After the Civil War? I ask.

No no, he says, shaking his head and smiling patiently. After World War II. In the forties some time. Just marched in there and took it all back. Left them all with nothing. Some of them blame the church for that and some of them don't. But they've had their own thing going, made their own deals, separate from ours.

I ask him what he thinks about the Park Service's proposal to create a historic site on the massacre field. I don't think it'll happen, he says. They can't get all those people out of there. I'd really like to see it happen, because I think it needs to be remembered, but you have to consider all those people. You can't just push them off that land. It wouldn't be right.

I tell him that I'm a writer working on the story of this site, and ask if I can quote him. Immediately his manner changes; he shakes his head hard. He says that he works for a tribal agency and wouldn't want people thinking his opinion reflected that of the agency. It's important, he says, that the agency appear neutral. It's just one person's opinion. We can't take sides, can't have one side thinking we're on the other side. You can tell people what this one person thought, but don't tell them who I am or where I work.

Done.

And so I'm discovering, *how the stories are being told*.

4

MADSEN

Pocatello's summer of 1998 is as hot as Chicago's. And almost as humid, too, weird for this part of the country.

Perfect weather for talking to the people who've worked so hard to commemorate what happened on that cold, cold day, so long ago.

The first day of July. I've driven down from Pocatello to a pleasant neighborhood on the south side of Salt Lake City, to visit Professor Brigham Madsen in his small, impeccably neat apartment. I'm here to consult the definitive historian of the Bear River Massacre, and to ask about the origin of his interest in the Northwestern Shoshoni. And as you know, I've been a bit concerned about visiting someone whose first name is Brigham, and whose books have expressed some ambiguity about the role of the LDS church in the massacre. I'm worried that we're going to tussle a bit over this church thing.

But he's a friendly man, tall, with sharp, blue eyes. When he tells humorous stories about his family or his career, he doesn't laugh. He isn't a man who laughs easily. Instead, he gets a glint in his eyes. A sparkle. And he has a funny habit of rising abruptly—right in the middle of a sentence—to grab a book he wants to consult—all the better to be precisely accurate as he answers my questions.

In fact, I discover quickly that accuracy is a major concern of his. An abiding concern.

Madsen offers me a seat and says he's lived in this apartment since just before the passing in 1997 of his wife Betty, a linguist and former thesis editor at the University of Utah, where Madsen himself eventually won tenure toward the end of a turbulent academic career. The turbulence, he says, stalled his research; after his dissertation, written in the 1940s and published as *The Bannock of Idaho*, he did not write again until 1979—not least because he could not get another academic job after resigning his first position at Brigham Young University.

This news cheers me up considerably.

It seems that Madsen suffered "intellectual differences" with BYU. (As a spokesperson for Madsen's publisher later said to me, "Brig left BYU before it was the cool thing to do.") But eventually, his career proceeded triumphantly at UU. Madsen received the university's Distinguished Teaching Award, an achievement he calls "the greatest honor of my life"; and was recently awarded an honorary doctorate—his second Ph.D.—again by the University of Utah. He also speaks proudly of his wife, with whom he coauthored *North to Montana* (recently reissued by the University of Utah Press), a book about the Montana Trail; and talks affectionately of all four of his children, including his son David, who is now a renowned Great Basin archaeologist.

He says the origin of his interest in Native American history goes back to his beginnings. Born October 21, 1914, Madsen grew up on the western edge of Pocatello, the son of a carpenter and builder, working on neighboring farms in the summers. He attended Idaho State for two years, finishing his degree at the University of Utah. "So I'd been around Shoshone–Bannock all my life as a youngster, used to buy hay from them. They were in town every Saturday night. I was intrigued by them."

When the Japanese bombed Pearl Harbor, Madsen had completed his master's and only the first part of his doctorate at Berkeley. He dropped his studies to work first in a draft-deferred job in the shipyards, in the welding section. But as a skilled carpenter, he thought building would be a better use of his talents. Carpentry was not a draft-deferred job, so to be a carpenter he would have to be drafted. "I wanted to go in—I was healthy and I thought it was not right for me not to go in." He spent three years in the infantry. In the summer of 1946 he mustered out after several months in occupied Germany.

When we talked, Signature Books in Salt Lake City was about to publish his autobiography, appropriately titled *Against the Grain: Memoirs of a Western Historian*. "I've been very independent my whole life, scholarly and in every other way," he says, by way of explaining his title. The first major rebellion of his life occurred when, home from the war, it was time to select a dissertation topic at Berkeley. Madsen proposed the project that would eventually become *The

Bannock of Idaho. "My chairman said, 'Brig, if you do it we'll never be able to get you a good job. Indian history has no significance—it's on the periphery of everything. We won't be able to place you at a good university.' But I was an ex-GI by then, and nobody could tell me anything.

"Now as I look back at it," he continues, "now with the plethora of Indian history—and it's been going on for twenty-five or thirty years now—what a change. I was way ahead of my time. Especially when I was told you shouldn't do it—then I was determined to do it. No one had done a study of the Bannock, so I was attracted by that."

But he was uncomfortable with his racial status relative to the people about whom he was writing. In the late 1960s, Madsen was asked to serve as the official historian of the Shoshone-Bannock tribe at Fort Hall. At the time, lawyers were arguing the lands claim against the federal government, and historical evidence was necessary to support the case. White attorneys, rather than tribal leaders, approached him and asked him to take the job. "My first reaction was, 'I'm the wrong person to do it. You find an Indian historian—he'll do a better job than I could ever do.' They said, 'We can't find one.' This was in 1968 or so. 'There just aren't any who know the Shoshone and Bannock people. You've written a book on it, you know something about it, and if you don't do it, what are we going to do?' And that's the way I took the contract. I didn't want to take it."

The Shoshone–Bannock won the case, got a $1.5 million settlement. "Not very much, really," Madsen says, and certainly not in the ballpark of the $32 million case won for the Ute some years prior, by the same Washington law firm founded by Ernest Wilkinson (later, president of Brigham Young University). But during his research, Madsen discovered a problem with the 1868 Treaty of Fort Bridger. The military men and the Indian agents who signed it were "mostly from the East," Madsen says. "They didn't know anything about irrigation," since back East, most agriculture thrived on rains alone. "They provided for a farmer, for farm equipment, for everything except an irrigation system. It was a simple thing, but they didn't do it. So I did a lot of research, wrote a long paper, and the attorneys said this is more important than any claims case they've got." The attorneys added to the land claim the fact that the Indians suffered at the reservation for more than forty years without any sort of irrigation system. "They just couldn't farm," Madsen says. "As a result, they won $5.5 million, based on the fact that the government didn't provide an irrigation system for them. I feel good about that, because the attorneys said, 'Without you we wouldn't have had a case.'"

But this success did not resolve the tension that existed when a white man presumed to write the history of the Shoshone. Madsen's contract with the council provided for permission to write books of history with the evidence he developed on behalf of the tribe. *The Northern Shoshoni* was the first result of this arrangement, a study of that band's history and culture, along with the history of how the city of Pocatello was parceled out of the original reservation. *The Lemhi Shoshone: Sacajawea's People* followed, as did a short biography of Pocatello. Eventually he wrote the only academic study of the massacre, *The Shoshoni Frontier and The Bear River Massacre.*

"I got to know the tribal leaders very well," he says. "They used to hold their annual meeting, an all-day meeting, at a buffalo lodge on the edge of the Snake River—at which they didn't have any whites—maybe one or two, a white lawyer from the Wilkinson firm, and a white secretary. It was their meeting. Two different times they invited me to come. They invited me to give a speech, to tell them about their wonderful history. It gave me a chance to tell them that they were a great people." Here he adds a side note: "It was interesting to me that the tribal men took charge of the meeting, but the women did all the work. They made the proposals, and they voted on them, and they ran the meeting. It was great—these were younger women who had some training. It was interesting to see that change."

But he had gotten word that the Shoshone didn't want him to publish his book. *The Northern Shoshoni* was in manuscript then, and was promised to Caxton Printers in Caldwell, Idaho, but the people didn't want him to publish it after all. "My contract said I could, so I asked for a meeting with the business council, the tribal council, and they allowed me to come talk about this book." Madsen recalls the layout of the council chambers—similar to the one I visited, with an elevated table for the leaders. "They're up on this and you're way down here," he says, that glint in his eyes flashing as he moves his hand above his head, then below his knees. "They did it deliberately," he says about the room's design. "Oh, absolutely. They'd had enough of whites telling them what to do, so they wanted to be up there looking down.

"So I stood up and said, 'What's the matter? It's in the contract. This is for your benefit, really, and might even help with other lawsuits in the future.'"

Finally, he recalls, "a great big Indian, a plain-spoken, shoot-from-the-hip kind of person, said, 'Well, nobody else will tell you, so I'll tell you. We don't want you to write this book because you're a Mormon. You'll write a pro-Mormon history of our tribe. We do not want you writing any pro-Mormon history of the tribes. Your first name's Brigham!'"

Madsen assured the Shoshone leaders that he was not, and is not, an active Mormon. "In fact I'm an agnostic," he says. "They haven't thrown me out yet, but they should," he tells me. "If I were in their shoes, I'd throw me out."

Madsen's problems with the Mormon church are professional—academic, even: "I don't believe The Book of Mormon is history. If you don't believe that, you don't believe anything." Madsen has written about his concerns, and once stepped forward to edit church historian B. H. Roberts's exposé of the church when several Mormon historians had refused to be associated with the work. "I don't consider myself a Mormon historian," Madsen says. "I'm a western historian. But I volunteered."

It was a risky move because Roberts is a legendary church figure. He was a member of the Council of Seventy, high in the church hierarchy, and had earlier written the officially sanctioned, six-volume history of the church. Originally, Roberts had been lauded as "the defender of the faith," and had spent a lifetime rebutting attacks on The Book of Mormon. But later in his career he addressed some nagging questions, and his *Studies of The Book of Mormon* states flatly that Joseph Smith did not receive divine words, but wrote the book himself.

Ever since Madsen edited the work, he says, "I've been on the list." Like Madsen, Roberts has not been excommunicated. "It's difficult for them to do so because all it would do is highlight the fact that the great B. H. Roberts came to the same conclusion, that The Book of Mormon is not history." In the past ten years, Madsen agrees, most excommunications have been levied against more vulnerable segments of the church, primarily women—including a recent case of an English professor who was excommunicated because she told students that she prays to a *Mother* in Heaven, as well as a Father in Heaven.

When Madsen edited *Studies*, and began speaking to the press and writing about his concerns about Mormonism, he had calls and visits from Mormons who said they too did not accept the Book as history; some held high posts in the church, and found great personal value in remaining within the church community, but silently ground their teeth when they heard the historical speeches. They called Madsen to thank him for vocalizing their own feelings on the matter. "There are thousands of people out there who are well-educated, who've taken Anthropology 101, who know that the Americas were not settled just by the Nephites, who came from Jerusalem, but by Indians who came down the Bering Strait, or maybe they went to Monte Verde from the South Seas in Chile. The LDS church doesn't know what to do about this."

One thing the church has done about him: "They've denied me things I've wanted," impeding his research. His most recent request for materials from the church archives was reported by the librarian there to an attorney. "He came back and he was highly embarrassed, and he said, 'They won't let you see them.' So I haven't been back since." The church's action does serve as an effective roadblock to further research. A significant proportion of Madsen's work on the Bear River Massacre stems from those hyper-thorough church records.

So at the meeting with the Shoshone tribal council, faced with this resistance to his presumed religious legacy, Madsen recited the 1873 comment made by Joseph, the Nez Percé leader, who had announced that he did not want any white churches working with his people. "They'll teach us," Joseph said, "to quarrel about God, as the Catholics and Protestants do on the Nez Percé reservation, and at other places. We may quarrel with men sometimes about things on this earth, but we never quarrel about God. We do not want to learn that."

After he explained to the Shoshone his lapsed status with the church, the same big man stood up again. "Oh, let him write his book," he said.

It's OK, then, Madsen says, if awkward, for whites to tell the story of the Shoshone people, since "it's the best you can do. If there are no Indian historians, somebody should do it. I keep hoping that there will be some, and they'll write their own story." Madsen's hope lies in a new generation of young Shoshone people—"especially the women, bless their hearts"—who are getting college degrees.

But when Madsen hopes for future Shoshone historians, he really means Shoshone *academic* historians. For instance, his respect for Newell Hart's book is sincere, but limited. *SourceBook*, Madsen says, is "a wonderful collection. He didn't know how to write history, or interpret it, but boy was he a collector. He collected some wonderful things about the massacre, and I used it in my book."

His evaluation of oral history—that history which nonacademic Shoshone already *have* "written"—is also ambiguous. "I've used some oral history, but they're not trustworthy. They're folk tales that have come down orally, and I've found that some of them just don't add up. They're just like stories that anybody tells." He refers to the legend of the Almo Massacre by way of an example of a folk tale perpetuated by whites. "I wrote an article, and the monument's still there and it's going to stay there forever, probably. They absolutely don't believe what I've said to them, that there's no evidence there. You have to be careful with oral history—particularly with Native Americans," he adds. Why *particularly* with Native Americans? "Well, maybe *not* particularly," he decides. "Whites are just as bad. It gets built in," a story does. Then, like the story of the Almo Massacre, he says, you can't get rid of it once it takes hold in its mysterious way.

But Madsen does rely on the oral history as told by Mae Timbimboo Parry, the Shoshone leader who helped to kick-start the process of developing the national site at the Bear River Massacre field. She got wind, Madsen reminds me, of a new monument being planned at the site, *another* monument by whites to honor the white soldiers. As the granddaughter of Yeager Timbimboo, she was and is the official keeper of the oral tale, and she had had enough of biased white monuments. When she threatened to propose legislation to counter the whites' plans, Idaho Senator James McClure invited the National Park Service to begin their study.

"I think her story is much more accurate than some other oral histories I've heard from the tribes," Madsen says. "I kind of liked that. And she's a direct descendant of Sagwitch," Yeager's father. Madsen reproduced Parry's testimony in full in the appendix of *The Shoshoni Frontier*, but, he says, it wasn't easy to win her cooperation. "I had difficulty with her. She was very independent, doesn't trust white people. I had to work through her son, who was Ombudsman for the state at the time for the Native Americans. I had to sit down with him and say, 'I want to have the Indian story of this, I don't want just my story to be in this. Your mother's is the only one.' So he convinced his mother to let me do it. It is more accurate, and it certainly expresses the hatred these Indians had for Connor and his troops." Madsen has met Parry since then at meetings regarding the Park Service proposals, and their meetings have been cordial.

And he has a great deal of respect for another amateur historian, Allie Hansen, the white Mormon woman from Preston whom Madsen calls "a key person" in getting the monument built. "She's worked all her life for this. She's a wonderful person. She testified in San Francisco," before the Park Service commission. The two have shared concerns about the race issue, which troubles both of them. "She wrote me a letter maybe four years ago, and she said, 'There's one thing I can't understand and maybe you can help me. I've worked much of my life to try to get a national monument erected here, worked with the Northwestern Shoshoni, but they just don't give me any credit for this. I see very little gratitude on their part for what I'm doing for them, and I can't understand it.' So I wrote her a three-page letter, trying to convince myself as well as her, because I run into the same thing."

Part of the tension is racial tension, he agrees; but cultural differences interfere as well. "As I tried to examine this—why is it that they're not grateful to you—and sometimes they're incensed if you do it—I said, 'Well, it's a matter of individualism. They're very individualistic.' I've been with the Shoshone–Bannock at Fort Hall for all these years and it seems to me that there's a new chairman every six months. They're so fractious. And there are different tribes there, too—Northwestern Shoshoni, and the Lemhi Shoshone and the Fort Hall Shoshone, and the Boise–Bruneau Shoshone and the Bannock— so that's part of it. But even within their own groups, they're just very argumentative and they're always fighting each other. And I think it's part of their individualism, their Indian individualism, and I can understand that because I've always been that way myself. The other thing of course is their distrust of whites. They've been cheated over the years by whites and they just don't trust whites. And even if you do something good for them they still don't like it."

Madsen agrees that the act of telling a story is an assertion of power. "I think that's part of it. You're the great 'I am' and they're nothing, they're down here. That's the way it's been for them. And so they resent that."

Some natives also resent the methodology used by white historians, particularly the fascination with body counts. When I ask Madsen if he would revise any of his conclusions in *The Shoshoni Frontier and The Bear River Massacre*, these thirteen years after its publication, Madsen concedes there are some things he would change about his work. "I might deal a little more with the numbers. I was being very conservative when I said 250, but there's information coming out that I think indicates that maybe it was more than 250, maybe you get 280 or even 300. So I might want to emphasize that a little more than I did. If I had to guess right now I'd say 280. Because they were lost in the river and so on." But Madsen does understand native irritation with European Americans who conduct lengthy arguments about how many died. "It's like we're marking up a basketball score. I can understand that they wouldn't like that. This is a terrible way to try to discern how terrible this massacre was, but what other measurement can you use, except the numbers?"

I've been curious about Madsen's biography of Connor, *Glory Hunter*, which may be Madsen's greatest contribution to history. Such may not have been his intention, but the work addresses his own whiteness relative to this tale, explores the motivations of those of his white predecessors who committed these atrocities, and expands this "Native American history" into a European American history from which whites can learn about themselves.

But today he tells me that this biography caused friction on all sides. "I wrote it deliberately. I thought that nobody would ever write it because the Mormons are so opposed to him and hated him so much because he was anti-Mormon—certainly no Mormon historian is ever going to write a biography of him. Who's going to be interested in Connor, for heaven's sake? They remaindered the book, but there's getting to be a sale now that it's becoming known." Madsen wrote it because "I like to be a balanced historian. I said, 'Look, I've written all these books about the Indians. I owe it to myself if to nobody else to look at the other side, and I'm going to do a biography of Connor and I don't care who likes it and doesn't like it. I'm going to see what kind of a guy he was.'"

Some did not like Madsen's conclusion that Connor was a pretty good guy in some ways. "He was certainly a good military man—he made a mistake when he went into mining. He would have been better off if he'd stayed in the military—they offered him a full colonel's position, at a time when even Custer could only get a lieutenant colonel's position—and he turned it down to go into mining, and he was an utter failure as a miner."

But Connor, Madsen says, was a loyal Unionist who thought the Mormons were subversives and traitors. "He had two bad faults: he hated Mormons and he hated Indians," though the former was to change: in 1871 Connor put up Brigham Young's bail when he was threatened with imprisonment by the federal government. But as for the Shoshone, he never repented. "His troops finally killed 375 Indians while he was in control. But he was no different from other military commanders of his day, except he did say, 'I will take no prisoners,' which meant he was just going to wipe them out." Some in the military have objected to his calling Connor a "glory hunter." "Some don't go past the title, and maybe I shouldn't have used that title." And, he adds, "Some Indians have never forgiven me for this. How could I write a biography of the man who mistreated them and killed them and slaughtered them? So they don't care for this part of me. But as a historian I've got to be as fair and judicious and balanced as I can be. That's the only reason I did it. I didn't think it would be successful, but I did it anyway."

Madsen feels strongly that Parry and Hansen, from their different perspectives, are right about the necessity for a monument, and that the Park Service site should be created. Consensus on history can serve to unify people, he suggests, when he recounts the story of the very first meeting about the proposed site, led by Edwin Bearss, then the chief historian of the National Park Service, in August 1989. All interested parties were there: Shoshone leaders from Fort Hall and Brigham City, white historians from Idaho and Utah, landowners and county commissioners—maybe forty people, Madsen recalls. Back then, the incident was still known as a battle. "Ed Bearss started out by saying, 'You want to erect a monument, and the Park Service is interested in doing that, but before I talk to you, I've got to find out how you feel about whether it should be called a battle or a massacre. I'm going to ask for a vote. 'How many of you think it should be called a battle?' No hands. 'How many of you think it should be called a massacre?' Everybody's hands—it was unanimous. Afterward, he said, 'I was dumbfounded. I thought I was going to face a division here—what a relief.' It's been a massacre ever since." From the start, then, while property issues were far from being resolved, there was clear consensus, even from those landowners who would be affected, that the incident was indeed an atrocity by whites against the Northwestern Shoshoni.

Madsen has been consulted by the Park Service on such issues as where exactly the Historic Site should be, and how much acreage should be set aside to tell the story in full; and he has suggested to Dr. Spude that Battle Creek be returned to its original name, Beaver Creek. While he understands the fears of landowners in the area, he hopes Alternative 4 succeeds. "All the other massacre sites have visitor centers and so on. Why not? This is the bloodiest of the ones in the west. I was being very conservative when I came up with the figure of 250 Indians killed. It was more than that, I'm sure, but at least I'm fairly certain about the 250. The other massacres are much less than that. It's been overlooked, ignored, and I just think it should be done."

But Madsen has another reason for feeling strongly about implementing the protection a national designation would assure. "The soldiers were very carefully buried, up here at Fort Douglas. The Indians' bodies were just allowed to lie there on the field." He reminds me of the reports that followed long after the massacre, of skeletons still on the field five months later, five years later. "From my point of view that is a holy place. It ought to be set aside for that reason. It's the last burial—if there was a burial of any kind—for these 250 or more Indians that were killed. They look upon it as a holy place, and for that reason alone it should be remembered and memorialized." Madsen says he has suggested to the Shoshone that they hold a ceremony every year on January 29, and invite the press. "No whites, just you. Be sure you have the TV cameras, and highlight it, and tell them how you feel about this, that this is a sacred place. If you want any kind of memorial, or a national monument, that is the surest way and the fastest way to get it. Leave the whites out of it. You just do it, and tell the story about these bodies that were just strewn on the massacre field."

I ask Madsen to rank in order of importance his reasons, as stated in his book, why the Bear River Massacre continues to go unrecognized by history. He lists as less important the fact that the headquarters for the Washington Territory, which for three more months would still govern present-day southern Idaho, was 700 miles away in Puget Sound. "Were they interested in some little battle that occurred down here? No. Probably didn't even know it happened." Ties for first: "The Mormon Church did not want to highlight this. Because the Mormon leaders in Cache Valley thought they deserved it, the Indians had it coming." The story was not splashed across the pages of the *Deseret News*; Mormon leaders kept mum about it. It was covered at length by the *Bulletin* and the *Union* in San Francisco, home of the soldiers involved, but that was a long way away too. And, "You have to find out what was happening in the Civil War at the time. There was a very important battle around that time." Headlines were claimed by the battle at Fredericksburg, the "Mud March," and Lincoln's staffing problems—"and the Union was in dire straits, they were having a rough time. All of the interest of the news media was what was going on in Virginia, not what's happening out here and some little tribe being destroyed."

Madsen concedes that a possible fourth reason—that U.S. citizens typically avoid any consciousness of Mormon-related history—may also have contributed to the lack of public acknowledgment of the event. "I spent two years in Washington, so I got a little bit of this flavor," he says. "Most gentiles think that the Mormon are like the Amish. Maybe they don't have devil's horns, but they're kind of a clannish people, they have peculiar habits, they still practice polygamy—although they say they don't, they still do—not the Mormons, but branches of the Mormons. So I think they just kind of dismiss it"—dismiss those things, including history, connected to Mormons.

But whatever the reason, Madsen has discovered no response to the massacre from any national figure. President Lincoln had to have known about the incident, since the Overland Mail Route was of great concern to him; the secretary of war certainly knew about it, and Connor earned his brigadier general's commission as a reward for the encounter. But Madsen has found no mention of the incident in Lincoln's papers.

A fifth reason, and the reason Lincoln may not have acknowledged the event, could be because, as Madsen says, "back then, the only good Indian was a dead Indian." Violent racism was almost universal. "Connor was brutal toward the Indians, as I say, but he wasn't the only one. Chivington was, at Sand Creek. Custer was. Nelson Miles was. And not just the generals, or the officers in charge, but the men themselves, and the frontier citizens." Events at Bear River, along with Carson's raids against the Apache, were simply the inauguration of this new era of violence against natives—not an aberration. Madsen notes that Connor was wined and dined and admired briefly in Washington as the great Indian fighter, a title to which he had long aspired.

That sort of racism was manifest also in the Mormon pioneers who settled Cache Valley, but another, more subtle vestige of racism lingers in contemporary church mythology. "The Book of Mormon is very plain, that there were no peoples here in the Americas when the Nephites came. They didn't meet any other peoples, they didn't encroach on other peoples' territory, they didn't war with them because they just weren't there." Dissenting Mormons, such as those who have phoned Madsen in appreciation for his public criticism, now concede that people were present in North America before the Mormons came.

But according to The Book of Mormon, those people were Lamanites. In Madsen's words, "the Nephites were divided in two groups: the good and the bad. The Nephites remained the loyal people of the lord, and the Lamanites were cursed with the dark skin and they were promised that they would become 'white and delightsome'—now it's 'fair and delightsome'—if they would give up their sinful ways and become good." (2 Nephi 30.6 has it as "pure and delightsome.")

Understandably then, there is significant tension between the Shoshone and the Mormons to this day, along with tension between those Shoshone who converted and those who did not. Madsen points out that the Corinne affair of the 1870s severed most ties between the Mormons and the Shoshone, and he launches into a recitation of what happened there.

Corinne, "the gentile capital of Utah," as Madsen has called it, was a town founded by non-Mormon merchants north of Salt Lake, at the end of the Montana Trail and at a junction of the Union Pacific Rail line. It existed for ten years as a rebellious trail town, reminiscent of Dodge City, with saloons and other church-despised service industries, until 1879, when the Union Pacific rerouted the rails away from Corinne. Mormon missionary George Hill was sent to Corinne to convert the nearby Lamanites—Sagwitch's and other bands, who wintered on the Bear River just a few miles from Corinne, and came into town often to trade. Hill successfully baptized hundreds of Shoshone, especially from Sagwitch's band, who then began to farm one summer on the banks of the Bear River. The one thousand "Corinthians" weren't wild about the band's presence in town, and they didn't like them farming nearby, either. Madsen calls this the "big Indian scare." Townspeople called on the troops at Fort Douglas to come up and disband the Indians. Sagwitch's band was driven from the land, and Sagwitch watched the soldiers destroy the crops just as they were ripening for harvest.

"The Shoshone blamed the Mormons for this," Madsen says, for not sticking up for them, for permitting the gentiles to call in the troops. "It's one of the reasons—not the only one—why you have that anti-Mormon sentiment up there right now. The Indians have long memories about such things."

The highly complex racial, religious, and economic relationships between the whites and the Shoshone, and the Mormon and the non-Mormon whites and the Shoshone, and the Mormon and the non-Mormon and the military whites and the Shoshone—it's a maze

Madsen has trouble with at times. He agrees that he feels ambivalence about Brigham Young's role in the massacre. On the one hand he praises Young's feed-don't-fight-them approach to the Shoshone; but still, Madsen recalls, Young never treated with the Indians or compensated them for appropriated land, and he and his people were the primary beneficiaries of the massacre.

Madsen explains the personal ambiguity apparent in his book: "We're captives of our own experience. I come from a family that could take Mormonism or leave it. I had a mother who could say to me, 'You believe that stuff about The Book of Mormon?' And yet she was a loyal member, she worked in the church." His military experience led, he says, without providing details, to his agnosticism. And his first teaching experience was at BYU, the only postdoctoral offer he received that was located in his beloved Rocky Mountains. Back then, he says, it was a small college with a very liberal faculty, "a lot of academic freedom, not like it is today." Even so, he says, "I went there, and after six years I couldn't stand it anymore, and I just quit," right after being named department chair. "I was so independent, and if I couldn't teach the way I wanted to teach I just wouldn't stay there." His independence cost him. Unable to get another academic job in the region after quitting so abruptly, Madsen deployed his carpentry skills and worked as a builder for a decade. He was unable to research and write during this busy period of providing for his growing family.

But in particular, Madsen recalls, the thing that changed his mind about Mormonism was his acquaintance in the 1950s with Wilford Poulson, a psychology professor at BYU. Poulson had researched Joseph Smith's life, including the books Smith had read. He discovered several instances of plagiarism in The Book of Mormon, including the idea that Native Americans descended from the lost tribes of Israel.

As a result of all this intellectual upheaval, Madsen says, "I admire Brigham Young much more than I admire Joseph Smith. I think Joseph Smith was a scoundrel, he was a liar, he was a womanizer. I can't say that to everybody, but he was. He started polygamy, had about forty wives. He was a scamp, a scoundrel—and yet he's the Great Prophet. I admire Brigham Young more because Brigham Young was sincere in his belief. Joseph Smith made the whole thing up. Young was a follower of Smith, he always liked Smith, who had a great charisma. And Smith hornswoggled Brigham Young, and Brigham Young was never hornswoggled by anybody else in his life.

He was a man of granite will, and hard-nosed and determined, but he believed in it. I give him credit for that. He was a very practical man. He was the one that made Mormonism. At the end of Joseph Smith's life, if Brigham Young hadn't taken over, Mormonism would have disappeared like every other little sect. So you have to admire him as an administrator—hard-nosed, certainly, but he created Utah, and the Mormon church. So I like him better for that reason." This is a sentiment that makes it difficult, perhaps, for him to mount an extensive critique of Young's administrative role in the destruction of Shoshone lifeways and peoples.

In analyzing Mormon history, Madsen typically looks at historical incidents and examines the motivations behind them. Non-Mormon historians need to understand, he says, that what drove Mormons, "and particularly Brigham Young," was "the fact that the Kingdom of God is going to overwhelm the United States government and every other government in the world. The Mormon Kingdom of God is going to take over. If you don't recognize this in every incident, you don't know what's going on." Madsen credits another acquaintance, David L. Bigler, as having clarified this in his work, *Forgotten Kingdom.*

And indeed most gentiles do not understand that the Mormon church has been, and remains, deeply committed to its own form of Manifest Destiny—and that it is not in the best interest of the church to expose that commitment. As long as U.S. citizens indulge a vague anti-Mormon bias, and avoid Mormon history, the LDS church has little motivation to disrupt a willful ignoring of its history—notwithstanding the Olympics 2002 banners I ducked in the airport, and the current attempt to solicit international commerce for Salt Lake City. Indeed, many outside journalists covering Salt Lake City scrupulously avoid saying the word *Mormon*, for fear of being accused of "persecution"—which silencing evidently suits the church just fine. So the Mountain Meadows Massacre, the Bear River Massacre—these are secrets that get lost in the general cultural hush about Mormonism.

And in the midst of these many layers of historical silence, another piece of massacre history continues to struggle for recognition. Bigler irritates Madsen (me, too) by insisting on calling the incident a "battle," and by asserting that the rapes of Shoshone women did not happen. "I said, 'Now look, David, you've seen the evidence I have from these Mormon men, who had no motive to say that this happened or didn't happen. They were in favor of what Connor was doing, most of them. But when they saw what had happened they just had to report it.'"

Madsen agrees that a possible motive for the unusually clear documentation of this mass rape was the tension between the soldiers and the Mormon community, particularly regarding sexual behavior. Connor had been very public about his disgust for polygyny, and perhaps the Mormon witnesses had here an opportunity to be equally public with their own disgust—and moral superiority. But Madsen is less able to explain the motivation for the rape itself. "These were not disciplined soldiers," he says. "Connor did his best to discipline them, but they were gold miners." And gender politics in the military, he says, are strained at best. "I spent three years in the infantry," Madsen says, "and look at all the pinups—that's the mildest form of it." It's not just our military, he says, but all armies in the history of the world. "The men reach the point where they don't care. All inhibitions are gone."

Well, all armies in *some* parts of the world, perhaps. Madsen says he has found no documented incidents of Shoshone warriors raping white women, despite frequent fears expressed in diaries and letters. But previous to the Bear River incident, there were a number of white male outlaws who raped Shoshone women. Mountain men were particularly known for taking Shoshone brides; it is unclear how willing these brides were to leave their people.

Madsen can see why the story of the rape has been deleted from the history being presented by the Park Service in their study. "From the pragmatic point of view of trying to get the thing through Congress, it would be better to leave it out. There will be some people who believe in the military, like the old soldiers at Fort Douglas today who refuse to call it a massacre—and there are a lot of old soldiers in Congress. I would leave it out too, maybe. It would just be another disturbing element." In an ideal world, though, "I think it should be covered, of course. I covered it." The story is important because "it adds to the whole feeling that this was brutality, barbarism on the part of the soldiers. Not only did they just kill them and club them to death, including infants, but they raped the women."

In general, however, Madsen feels the Park Service has done "an excellent job. I don't know how they could do it any better. They've been sensitive to the reaction of the landowners, and that's why they've come up with these four proposals." He does understand the concerns of the landowners, especially those who are doing well on the land. "The ones with the smaller units might be willing to sell.

"It's going to be difficult," he says, to remove twenty-eight families for the benefit of 280 million citizens, but he feels that the story of the Bear River Massacre is one that finally must be heard by all U.S. citizens. In his own book, Madsen says, his purpose was to write not only for the Shoshone, but for the Mormons and the non-Mormons, anyone who is interested in massacres of natives, or in western history. "I wanted to persuade everybody that there was a massacre that had been lost to history and forgotten. I wanted everybody to know that."

5

GRIFFIN

The heat is building. It's a warm, damp ride down that sharp hill again, that hill that bottoms out on you when you're doing 65 on US-91.

It's the first I've been back here since the spirits tiptoed across my spine, that night.

I'm early for my interview with Kathy Griffin, the resident who's leading the landowners' opposition to the National Park Service proposal. I haven't been here in daylight before, so I take that right onto Hot Springs Road, nose around a bit, follow the dirt road out along what's now known as Battle Creek. There's no sign to indicate where I am. Just the road, the creek, the pastureland. Some cows grazing. Ahead, I see two guys standing next to their pickup, doing that men-at-work thing. Their arms are set tight across their chests, and they're examining a fence, talking about what to do about it. As I approach, I see a lot of nodding and head shaking going on in this committee of two. *Just do it*, I'm thinking, just to amuse myself—and then they look up at me.

They stare for a while. They decide they don't know me and then they stare harder.

I figure they know why I'm here. I figure they're probably used to this sort of thing.

They keep staring, and even though I offer the requisite pickup-culture wave, there's no smile in the offing. I don't even get back the minimum-requirement nod.

So I figure that's how they feel about this sort of thing.

I figure I've probably seen all they want me to see, so I start to turn the truck around. They watch me do an awkward three-point turn, no power steering in my overheated little pickup, half the size of their own machine, and they watch me kick up some dust driving away. I know this because I watch them in the rearview.

They watch me go for some time.

When I pull into her driveway, I'm surprised to see that Kathy Griffin's charming farmhouse has a for-sale sign dug into the impeccably groomed garden out front. The house rests not on the massacre site, but on the periphery of the "battlefield," along with several other homes (and to protect her privacy, I won't say exactly which one is hers). Behind the houses stretch lush, quiet fields, and a stunning view of the easternmost edge of the Wasatch Range. Inside I see on the coffee table a first-edition copy of Newell Hart's *SourceBook*, his work about the massacre.

As we sit and talk in her cool living room, Griffin's Yorkshire terrier, Midget, pants and fidgets in her lap. She strokes the animal gently, and speaks so quietly that my tape recorder barely registers her voice. I'm again surprised: the outraged woman who led the charge at the Park Service hearing in December 1995 has been supplanted by a patient, modest woman I can barely hear.

Before I have a chance to ask, she insists that the for-sale sign has nothing to do with the Park Service proposal. "That's way down on the list," she says. She and her family have worked their small farm for twenty-seven years, raising alfalfa and barley to feed their herd of ninety-five ewes. Selling out is "not the choice I would make, but there are personal reasons that have pushed us to that. It's been a good place, an excellent place, to raise our family." It was easy here to teach her three children "the value of hard work and seeing a job through to the end." She says it's been hard to explain to people, so she doesn't go into a lot of detail. All she'll say is this: "It's a sad time in your life when you have to make changes you don't want to make."

She doesn't anticipate trouble selling, despite the looming Park Service proposal, but the realtor was concerned when she listed the farm. "I had the study out on the table and that was the first thing he asked." She thinks most buyers believe that even if the proposal is implemented, it won't actually happen for some time. So, "there's been a lot of interest" in her farm.

Born August 26, 1949, Griffin has spent her life in Preston. She works in the Preston Middle School lunchroom during the week, and on Saturdays as a cashier at the Deseret Industries thrift store. Her husband Keith worked at Tri-Millers Packing Company in Hyrum,

Utah, until it closed down in May 1995. Their youngest son is a high school senior, and their two daughters, both graduates of Utah State, work in the northern Utah region. Kerry is employed by the LDS church as an editor at *Ensign*, a monthly magazine.

On her mother's side, Griffin's ancestors go back in Preston to the original settlements. Her parents still live in town. She insists that the Park Service study really hasn't stirred up the town buzz one might expect. "People ask about it," she says. "Of course, they know how I feel about it, from what they've read, but they are sympathetic to us. They don't want to see a lot of huge changes either."

How *does* she feel about it? "I think they should just leave the agricultural area alone, just leave it the way it is. There does need to be a more interpretive sign at the monument site, a road map, a map of the area saying which activity took place where. People who stop here and ask are completely disoriented. They don't know from which direction the soldiers came down the bluffs and forded the river. It needs to be more clear." The site needs better maintenance, too, she adds. Griffin wishes the state would do a better job with mowing the monument area, which she has to pass every day on her way home. "They just don't have the time, is what I've been told."

In their confusion, strangers occasionally knock on her door to ask what happened where. Griffin, who has long taken an interest in the history of the land on which she resides, keeps a basket by her door, full of copies of a map with a brief explanatory note on the bottom. The map shows where the river used to run, behind the spot where her house now stands, and the path the soldiers took past the spot to get to the area across the road, where most of the killing occurred. Her basket also includes copies of a military study done by Utah State University ROTC students, a study examining the effectiveness of the military leadership that day.

The note at the bottom of this map, which Griffin did not herself compose, reads (I've typed it as it's found there):

On a wintry morning January 29, 1863, 40 infantry and 220 cavalry, part of the California volunteers stationed at Camp Douglas, Salt Lake City, Utah, led by Colonel Patrick E. Connor forded the Bear River and attacked a N.W. Shoshone Indian encampment of 75 lodges located along Battle Creek. Almost 400 Indians, accused of marauding mail trains, emigrants, furtrappers, and miners, died in the bloody three-hour battle. The dead included women and children along with Chiefs Bear Hunter, Lehi and San Pitch and their braves. Only a score of Indians escaped. Twenty-two soldiers were killed and another 120 suffered wounds. Indian agent James C. Doty's report to congress called it "the severest and most bloody of any battle with the Indians west of the Mississippi." Historian Hubert H. Bancroft wrote: "Had the savages committed this deed, it would pass into history as a butchery or a massacre."

Griffin guesses that current Park Service estimates of twenty-five visitors a day in the summer are too high. "Maybe ten," she says. "Unless it's Memorial Weekend or something. But it's rarely more than a handful of people who stop." Sometimes, she says, a tour bus stops, and people get off the bus not knowing why they're there. "The looks on their faces say, 'What am I doing here?'" She's seen tourists snapping photos of her neighbor's unusual mailbox—because they're unable to figure out what they should take pictures of. Most of her neighbors, she says, don't share her interest in the history of the site. If more information were available for visitors, she suggests, things might be a bit easier for the people who live there on the site.

Since it rarely attracts significant visitors or attention, Griffin says, the site isn't deserving of the development proposed by the Park Service. "I see other times, on the anniversary of the event—zippo. Or else a small group of people. I don't recall anything this last year happening. And the year before there were a few people—dressed up for the Mountain Man Rendezvous. They came out here and sat for a few minutes like they were waiting for somebody else to come, and left." Over the course of her twenty-seven-year presence on the land, she says, no organized interest in the site was apparent until four or five years ago. "Nothing ever happened on the anniversary date or Memorial Day" until then. "I recognize that people are becoming more aware of it, and the Indian people have come down on Memorial Day to hold memorial services." But "I don't see a lot of activity, just something recently."

Griffin says she *can* imagine a situation in which she would not oppose the project. "Either they leave it the way it is," she says, "or they come in and completely buy the whole area out." She reiterates that she's not necessarily in favor of this latter— "I think it's a pretty drastic step." But she feels that the more modest proposal to take

140 acres and develop "interpretive sites with trails and easements and scenic right-of-ways" would only further complicate life for the residents of the valley. "That's the concern for everybody" living near the site— "the scenic easements and right-of-ways through private property." The result would be too much collision between tourists and residents.

For instance, she says, one of her neighbors has a feedlot, "and this is one of the first things that people will complain about. That's what happens when people move into an agricultural area. They love the scenic beauty and everything out in the country where it's safer and quieter and everything, but yet, then they complain about what's out here in the country, the animals and the flies and things that come with a feedlot, or dairy, or whatever.

"And I realize," she says, "it's a huge thing that happened here historically. It really did. There's a lot of history here and it should be told in a more descriptive way out there. But I don't see the need for a full-fledged museum with a ranger and all that expense."

I ask Griffin what sort of important historical event *would* justify the need for that level of investment. How much more significant would an event have to be before she would agree to a societal investment in its telling? "What makes the difference here?" she says, thinking out loud for a moment. "I'm not sure I have an answer for that."

I also ask how she responds to people who feel that the site should be developed as a courtesy to the Shoshone community, whose ancestors' remains still rest on the site. "I felt like the Indians never knew for years," Griffin says. She points out that she's kept a scrapbook filled with articles pertaining to the site and to the Park Service proposal—a scrapbook she'd like to show me, she says, but she's lent it to a relative. One article tells the story of "this woman who Allie Hansen brought down, a descendant of one of the survivors. She had never been here. She had never even known the history" until a few weeks before coming. "And now if the government's going to do something, they all want a say in the park, which they should. But they want to monitor the park. They want to make some money." Griffin has a problem with that. And the Shoshone are divided too, she says. They're thinking, "'We don't want them to make something off of our tragedy.'"

Like everyone involved, Griffin has her own opinions about what actually happened here, and how those events should be interpreted. "I don't think for an instant anything like that could have happened this day and they'd've got away with it. I don't think either side was heroic. From what I understand, Chief Bear Hunter — there were atrocities committed on either side. He ordered the legs of a five-year-old white girl chopped off, and made her walk on the bloody stumps before she died. That's not a hero. I'm not saying that the white people—certainly they came in. Colonel Connor was mad because he wasn't fighting in the Civil War. Abraham Lincoln sent him out here to watch Brigham Young and take care of the Indians. So he did."

Griffin's grapevine is telling her that the Park Service proposal has been back-burnered at the congressional level. Neighbors who talked to Senator Larry Craig during a visit to the site early in 1998 were told that it was likely that nothing would happen for at least ten years, and possibly not in their lifetimes. But she's not sure. "When they did the landmark status, and then upgraded it to monument status, they figured that would take years and years, and it moved much quicker than that." She also wonders whether the government has the money for this project—although, she says with a slight smile, "of course they do have tons of money that they can spend on really dumb things.

"The feeling I get is the city council and the county commissioners are all thinking it would be a great tourist attraction and bring in dollars. What I don't understand is that there is nothing to hold them in Preston. After they've stopped here, and made their tour, they go on north to Yellowstone or south to Las Vegas or Salt Lake City. They don't stay in the community to spend tourist dollars." If the Park Service bought out the entire area and made the monument into a major site, she agrees, there might be greater reason for tourists to spend time here. A lawyer named Dan Taylor, she says, encouraged the town to think about the possibilities. "He said, 'You people don't know what opportunity you're missing, you could have bed and breakfasts.' I thought, 'Hello, they're not going to allow those things to happen. They want it to be turned back to the natural way it was. They won't allow that kind of development here.'" And Griffin would agree that development on the site should be restricted. "It would spoil it if they did, I think." Griffin says she joked with Taylor that, if he really believed in the local tourism potential, he should start buying up local real estate. "If you want to buy somebody out, here's your opportunity!" she says, and laughs. "You've got to try to keep a sense of humor about things," she adds.

"I've got past the more emotional 'Oh my gosh it's the end of the world' thing." The debate about this proposal has been pretty rough for her, though, she adds.

Although she insists again that local interest in the project has not been active, she concedes that the Preston community is divided over this proposal, but that the division has not affected the community in irreparable ways. "I think it's way down on the list," she says. "The average person on the street, if you asked them, they wouldn't even know what you were talking about. It's not a big concern unless some bigwig comes, and then it brings it up again. Then it dies right back down. I don't see a wholehearted Preston city pushing for this thing, except I do know the merchants think it will bring tourism."

She also concedes that the project was indeed initiated by a well-organized group of Preston citizens, now led by Allie Hansen. Griffin is merely an unofficial spokeswoman for the landowners, who are not organized; they usually talk only at church. "It's a predominantly LDS community, and at church that's where everybody says, 'What's going on? What's happening here?'" Griffin took on the role of spokeswoman because "I felt like things were moving here that we weren't being told about." When the monument committee formed, Griffin says, she asked to be a member, and she did support the original petition to make the site a National Historic Landmark. "It was considered an honor to be involved as part of this landmark status thing, and I wanted to quietly see what was happening, where it was going, because of how it would affect us all. And nobody else did, and I tried to tell them, 'There's going to be more interest here.' I had a feeling that this was going to be a big thing. It could either be really good or really bad."

Apparently, the December 1995 public hearing in Preston was a climactic moment of showdown for this town, coming at the apex of emotions built over a period of years. Friends and relatives sent the stack of supporting materials to Griffin prior to the meeting. She particularly relied on the experience of her brother, David Hansen (no relation to Allie), who now lives in Malibu, California. "He had been through a similar project with the Park Service in Santa Monica," Griffin says. "It was a large area with one person in the middle. It got to be very uncomfortable, and a long drawn-out thing for them. I felt like he had some experience there that could help."

In collecting her papers for the meeting, Griffin says, "I knew I needed to be armed a little bit." She was nervous about speaking in public that night, but more importantly, the personal harshness of the debate troubled her profoundly. "My heart pounded—it pounded so bad it ached for a week after. I was so emotional about it. I thought, 'We have worked all of our lives for what we have. This is our only retirement, so to speak.' I was really emotional.

"There were things that were said that I wish weren't. It could have been a lot better. Of course," she says with a small laugh, "the whole battle could have been handled differently too." She now wishes she'd handled the discussion differently, she says. "I'd like the same point across, but not that emotionally." She says she sensed some animosity between herself and Park Service team leader Catherine Spude, "but afterwards she came up and said some things that smoothed—and I said to her too—we patched over some things.

"But there was one point in the meeting which I didn't care for, when Allie Hansen went over to the sheriff's department and had a police officer come because the meeting was getting out of hand. And her husband afterwards, as we were talking—I said, 'You don't realize what you're doing to our livelihood, what this has done. This thing is snowballing into something that may be bigger than you and I ever dreamed of.' And he said, 'We are going to preserve a part of history whether you like it or not.' I just felt sick." But they're all friends again. Mostly. "We have been throughout the years, but there's a feeling there that'll never be like it once was. And I can see the point. I can see the minorities are really getting a lot of attention. A terrible thing happened here. I just want it to be dealt with fairly."

She feels the landowners have been underinformed as the study process has unfolded. When Senator Craig visited the site, she says, "Allie Hansen was called, and she gave the tour, and we never heard a thing about it until the morning of—and we were at work. We're told after the fact." She and her neighbors also feel that the landowners are being excluded from the discussion of the proposals. "We were all saying, 'What's happening here?' Maybe it was a last-minute visit, but we all felt, 'Here he is, and there he went.'" Craig spoke, she says, with only a few landowners who happened to be on the premises that day.

I tell her that I've heard that Craig plans to hold still more public hearings, to replicate the National Park Service hearings, and ask whether she thinks that will ease her sense that the landowners aren't being heard. She agrees that adequate hearings have already been held. She doesn't feel like going through it again. "But yeah, we'll do it again, however many times it takes." And she'll do it again whether or not she and her husband sell their farm. She will still maintain an interest in the Park Service project, she says. "I've always been interested, and I have kept every article that I've been able to keep from all the local papers. So I plan to keep an interest."

Since it hasn't come up in our conversation, I ask Griffin if she knows about Brigham Madsen's allegations that a mass rape occurred after the killing. She's unaware of it, she tells me, but she's not surprised.

And her lack of surprise surprises me.

It makes sense, she says. "That's true in the case of almost any of them, during the Civil War and when the Mormons were persecuted at Haun's Mill," she says, referring to the massacre and rape of Mormons in Missouri. "The church has chosen not to dwell on that, not to bring that out. I don't know why that has to be a part of war. Unfortunately that is a part of history, conquering another race. Read The Book of Mormon, and that's what happened there too."

(Later, in a letter to me, Griffin would write, "I suppose men would want to justify these acts as part of the total reasons of bringing another nation or country or group of people into submission of their will, by forcing themselves upon their victims in every conceivable way, as to gain complete control over their minds and bodies. I am personally hurt and offended by these acts of men in times of war, as I believe every other woman would be. I would hope that people would learn from the past and all of the scriptures and history we have, that we would some day know enough that we would not have to repeat these same lessons again and again, but be able to work things out more peacefully.")

As a member of a religious people who have themselves been "persecuted," then, Griffin says she is indeed sympathetic to the Shoshone. "I can understand how the Indian people can talk about how their land was taken away from them. It was. I don't want the same thing to happen and hopefully we've reached the point in history that that won't. But there was one mention, when a fellow said that God gave them the land, and they should have it back at prices like 50 cents an acre. And that just made me cold."

But again, if the government wants to buy out the whole place at reasonable prices, that might be OK. One neighbor, she reports, even thinks he's going to make a killing. She shakes her head, and smiles thinking about it. "Greed isn't—" she says but doesn't finish her sentence. A complete buyout, she reiterates, would be preferable to a series of easements. "Could be," she says, that this is a good moment in her neighbors' personal histories for the government to make the purchases. "Our children are grown, our lives have changed dramatically in the last three years. There are some, though, that would have a harder time.

"From what I hear, most of the neighbors say they'd be willing to sell."

6

HANSEN

By the time I visit Allie Hansen in her cottage near Preston's down-town, the weather has settled into a stubborn heat wave. Local mete-orologists have gone to great lengths to explain the bizarre weather. Unusual El Niño spring rains have fueled rainforest-thick vegetation and created honest-to-goodness, recordable humidity in the desert—dewpoints are actually hitting the 50s, even 60s. Temperatures are not falling off at night as desert dwellers are used to. Residents of Pocatello are sleep-deprived. Un-air-conditioned restaurants sit empty. The local news reports on fan inventories, and whenever they tell us a shipment has arrived at Wal-Mart, people line up around the block. I've tried six places with no luck.

Meanwhile, the first casualty of the heat is Tamise's poinsettia, which, until I came along, she'd kept thriving greenly since Christmas. It's now a shriveled brown.

I too am a bit wilted when I drive again through the greenest-ever Cache Valley oasis, head into Preston, and park my truck under a large, cool tree on a residential street that looks more like a country road. Hansen answers my knock quickly, looking fresh and collected, despite the ill health she's told me is plaguing her older age. She set-tles into a green, upholstered rocker and I take the couch across the room, which is darkened to keep out the heat. The tape recorder lies between us on a coffee table, next to copies of Madsen's book and Hart's book, both of which I'll soon discover are copiously marked with yellow highlighter.

Everyone has told me I should talk with Hansen. Her name was the only one to come up repeatedly, unanimously, when I began my research. Park Service officials, congressional staff members, Brigham Madsen—all insisted I darken this door. "She's a gem," one official told me. "She's the one who keeps up on the legislative stuff," Madsen said. "She's done it all."

We begin our conversation with the December 1995 meeting in Preston, because, despite her profound involvement in the project, she did not speak at that meeting. I didn't even know she had been there. She tells me that it had been decided that she should not speak at the Park Service's public hearing—a surprising choice, given her status as the keeper of the massacre story for the local Mormon community. Typically, she says, when federal officials, or Shoshone descendants, or interested European Americans want a tour of the massacre site, they call her. "At that point, I had talked at every meeting, and explained everything at every meeting, and took the part of devil's advocate coming and going at every meeting. I was sick of me." She offers a broad smile to go along with that modesty.

Of course, the hearing, which I now understand to have been a watershed event for the Preston community, did not go as hoped. "I was having a very hard time with it. I was so disappointed in our townspeople for their lack of restraint, their verbal attacking. After the meeting the verbal attacking proceeded to the back of the room, and that's when I got it thoroughly. I left halfway through the meeting. I said to my husband, 'This is getting out of hand.' Now, the Park Service can handle it, but I can't. This is getting me emotionally upset till I want to stand up and say, 'OK you people, this is dumb and stupid, sit down if you can't control yourself.' I didn't want to do that, and I knew I would if I stayed. So I came home for approximately forty-five minutes to an hour, got myself together. When I came back there was a policeman inside the side door." Hansen is aware of the rumor that she's the one who called the police, but it's not true, she says. "I was as surprised to see him there as everyone else, but I'm glad he was there. I know who did call him and that's not important now. The word they got was that the meeting was becoming quite loud, and since the sheriff's office is that close, they asked for an officer to step in, which he did, staying out of sight or just listening."

Hansen, born in August 1932, has a personal investment in this project that goes back a long way. Her great-great-grandparents were among the original settlers of Franklin, she says, sent by Brigham Young in one of his wagons, and they lived in that wagon box through the first winter. Her great-grandparents settled Preston. For twenty years, she and her husband Clair, on a self-employed basis, managed circulation and distribution for the *Deseret News* in their region; since they retired in 1978, Clair now runs his used-car dealership. They have a daughter and four grandchildren in Ogden.

She's always been interested in history, she says, but particularly Preston history. "This is local history, and I was born on the Shoshone Trail straight east of here 12 miles. My sympathies lie both ways. I can see both sides of things. We're looking at it from our century, back onto it, so we're justifying a lot of stuff—Indians and white folks. Now the Indians are pushing things in a different way, white people are pushing things in a different way—neither one is totally correct. So I'm mainly a mediator in all this."

An early interest in Native American history had centered on a self-directed study of the Iroquois presence in New York state. I ask her why she began with the Iroquois, and not her Shoshone neighbors. "The only Indians we ever saw here didn't interest me in the slightest. They were drunken, slovenly—they were the workforce that came here for fieldwork. I never saw an Indian in the productive role of upstanding citizen. So I thought, 'Well, I'll go back another century, and start back in so I can understand a bit better.'"

At some point in her reading about Native American history, Hansen discovered that there was almost nothing in Idaho history books about the Bear River Massacre, an incident she had heard about repeatedly from her own family. She began reading everything she could find—Hart's book, Madsen's book—"and there was so much more to it than my ancestors, my grandparents, had told me.

"I got one side only," she says. Her grandparents had told her "how great a thing it was. So I was prejudicial to start. I didn't know any different." The Northwestern Shoshoni used to camp on her grandfather's ranch, probably for hunting: "we'd find arrowheads and all kinds of stuff there all the time." She recalls a green spot on that ranch, a broad area that tended to grow lushly, as if it had been composted. "That had to be a corral," she says. She has a collection of flint and arrowheads. "I always go first thing before the grass comes, after the rodents have done their digging, because they bring everything up. Then I just find things on top of the ground." Her mother was born in a log cabin on the actual massacre field, in the area where, her research has since taught her, lodges stood on the day of the massacre.

Hansen was disappointed in her ancestors when she discovered a truer story of the massacre in Hart's book. LDS history, she says, refs to the incident as "a rout of the savages—so the prejudicial slang terms for the Indians starts square back when Indians were first discovered on this continent. And they weren't savages in the beginning. They weren't savage with whites until whites betrayed them, though they were savage among themselves, the various tribes. So once I started finding out that there were a lot more sides than the one I'd been hearing, I started digging into it." Her acquaintance with Newell Hart helped, she says, as she could ask questions when she didn't understand something.

Hansen's involvement in the recuperation of Shoshone history began in 1985, when she joined what is now known as the Bear River–Battle Creek Monument Association, started by Ganeale Swainston, who, along with her son, spent a great deal of time in the 1980s presenting slide shows about the massacre to local school groups. Hansen served as the treasurer and as the head of the "Indian Committee," as they called it then, which required her to negotiate with the Shoshone. "This was really my first encounter with an ethnic group, or another race, or anything else. However, my sympathies have always been with Native Americans' plight in certain things."

Hansen's first challenge was to address the cultural differences that impeded her relationship with the Shoshone. "Working with the Indians has been an education I could never have gotten. I learned that they are not the glorified 'Cowboy-and-Indian' Indian. I learned that they are very human, that given the way they have been brought through the centuries culturally, they can hardly be different than they are now. They think differently, traditions are different."

She tells of an instance of cross-cultural miscommunication, when she was in council with the Shoshone. "Their councils get pretty loud, among themselves even. I was there to offer an invitation to a commemoration—I'd been there before, they knew who I was. It got kind of, you know, 'Why are you here?' I was saying, 'We really want you to come and participate.' What I meant was, 'We have a great desire that if you would like to come, to come.' But what I said was, 'I want you to come.' And this Indian lady said, 'Always with you white people, it's always *want want want*.' I, culturally, didn't understand; she, culturally, didn't understand. What happened after that was that they were just talking along being rude—some were and some weren't—some were defending me—and then they'd lapse into Shoshone, which offended me. Which is another ignorance on my part. I didn't understand."

Hansen spent some time with Grant Parry, Mae Timbimboo Parry's husband and a white man who, Hansen says, has been with natives all his life. "I said, 'Can you explain what they're doing? I'm finding it offensive, it feels like I'm on the spot, I don't know what to do, I feel awkward.' He said, 'Let me tell you what's happening. When they go along and they're explaining things, and they're talking, they can only go so far with the English language and then they can't go any further. And the reason they do that is because white man speaks a thousand words to say a hundred things. The Indians might speak ten words to say a hundred things.'" Parry told Hansen that as the natives try to explain themselves to her, "'they'll start out with the story, and that instantly recalls to their minds this and this back through the centuries, so they're getting in a few words a very broad picture that culminates in a very few words. Everything we take an hour explaining is automatically there, because that's the way it's handed down to them. When they lapse into Shoshone, they're not being rude, they're trying to rearrange everything in their language so that they can turn around and explain it to you in yours, so you can understand.'"

When the Monument Association's chairwoman, Ganeale Swainston, fell ill, Hansen took over the committee and became more involved than she had originally intended. Hansen refuses to concede that any "expert" storyteller's knowledge of the Mormon version of the massacre made her a likely candidate for chairwoman. "I'm an organizer, I'm a doer. I had to learn a lot of other things, so that by the time we got to the legislative process" in the pursuit of landmark status for the massacre field, "I knew frontwards and backwards the history."

She first met Mae Timbimboo Parry in 1985. "She came up to one of the meetings. In the beginning she did participate up to a point, and then I think the band didn't want her to participate anymore."

According to Hansen, the controversy had to do with the naming of the site during the legislative process. Hansen's committee was authoring a resolution to request a study that could result in the site being listed as a national landmark; and although the committee agreed that the name of the site should be changed from "battle" to "massacre," in the legal papers the committee was required to use the name by which the site was then known. The legal machinations were lengthy. The committee took their resolution, requesting the study, to the eight counties in Utah and Idaho in which the Northwestern Shoshoni were known to have lived before the massacre; all agreed to the resolution. Then the legislation was written at the state level. That was when relations with the Shoshone broke down.

"The Indians said, 'No way, if you call it a battle.' They sent me some papers saying, 'We'll take you to court if you persist.' I got all kinds of letters like that. We wanted a name change, but to have a study done, which was what we were after, by a federal entity, you have to call these things by what they are then called." Hansen answered the letters she received. "I told them I was really glad to see that they were interested, and I went on to explain. They didn't buy that in any way." There was a series of letters to the editors of Utah papers, which Hansen's committee did not see up in Preston. "So we really didn't know how serious they were about stopping all of this until someone from Utah anonymously sent a copy of a piece in the paper, and a copy of the lawsuit they planned. We hadn't heard a thing. We couldn't figure out why they wouldn't participate—they wouldn't answer."

Hansen contacted Parry, who answered that she couldn't participate because of the pressure being put on her by the band. "They didn't like this and they didn't like that. So I just wrote back and said, 'I'm glad that you're interested enough to take issue with some of these things. Now let me explain. Until we get a study done and verified by the government, that this is an incident of enough importance, we can do nothing. First we have to get the legislation to get the study.'" The People, as Hansen often calls the Shoshone, were still not satisfied. "They still wrote letters to Dr. Charles Odegaard in Seattle," the regional director for the Park Service, "protesting all of this. We talked to Valery Watkins," then regional director for Senator McClure (and later for Senator Craig), "and she talked to the senator, and he talked to Dr. Odegaard, who said, 'This is going to be controversial, I'm getting all these letters from the Indians, and I really don't think I want to handle this at this time.'"

Hansen's committee thought they were doomed, quashed by what they saw as a misunderstanding with the Shoshone. But when Senator McClure returned to Washington, he contacted the Park Service there, and requested that Edwin C. Bearss, the chief historian, look into upgrading the site to landmark. Again, Hansen thought she was doomed. Bearss is a military historian, a Civil War historian, and in the minds of many people who care about recuperating the history of the Bear River Massacre, Civil War military historians are a big part of the problem— not the solution. "I thought, 'Oh please, no!'" she says, laughing again at the memory. "The Civil War was completely inundating the minds of the entire nation, and the territory, at the time the battle-massacre took place." But Bearss surprised her. "He's a marvelous man. He travels the Civil War sites and gives tours," she says in a tone that suggests the professional admiration of one tour giver for another. "Tours that are just like a movie, the way he lays it all out."

Bearss called her to say he planned to visit the Bear River site, and asked her to put a meeting together. She had three weeks' notice.

Hansen's recollection of the discussion at that meeting, in August 1989, differs from Brigham Madsen's recollection. Her recollection is that the women initiated the conversation about the name of the incident. "Mae Parry asked, 'What are you planning on calling this monument?' And Mr. Bearss went on and on about the study. And I asked him, 'Could I interrupt for a moment?' I said, 'This has been a very controversial thing from the very beginning. It's caused trouble between our community and the Shoshone. The media get it all wrong every time, and they pick up on everything negative instead of trying to help us with anything positive.'" As an aside, she tells me, "They're the ones that kept the Indians really going. The *Ogden Standard*, mostly." She returns to her story. "I said, 'I think we've gone far enough in all of these issues these many years, and I know for my entire group, that we all agree it was a massacre, and we would like to have it called the Bear River Massacre National Historic Landmark.' Well, the Indians lit up like sunshine." Mr. Bearss was deeply relieved, she says. "'You have just saved me a lot of trouble,' he said. 'I didn't know how we were going to get around this particular subject.' I said we were advised by people in higher places, who would know about these things, that we were to stay neutral. 'But I think we've remained neutral on the naming of the project as long as we can,' I said. And from that point on, everything just went."

Hansen and Bearss took a tour of the site with Mae and Grant Parry, and Frank, a brother of Mae's. "We walked and talked, and she told the Indian story and I told the other part of the story."

Hansen provided Bearss with copies of Hart's and Madsen's books, and Bearss got back to her quickly. He conceded that it was a massacre, which surprised Hansen, since, she says, "he was very much an army man." Bearss completed an official study, recommending to the Park Service that landmark status be awarded.

At the next Park Service meeting, in January 1990, officials would consider one hundred such recommendations, then eliminate sites until the list was cut to twenty. That list of twenty would then be considered more carefully, and pared to ten.

Hansen and her associates figured they were in for a long winter wait.

But Bearss called Hansen in March to tell her that the Bear River site had fast-tracked its way onto the list of ten. The next meeting would be in San Francisco, in April, just a few weeks later. "'Can you be there?' Bearss said."

Not only was this request again short notice, but it created a financial difficulty for Hansen and her husband. The county had allocated $400 a year to the Monument Association, which was never enough for photocopying and other committee expenses, Hansen says, and she was accustomed to making up the difference out of her own pocket. But a trip to San Francisco was beyond the Hansens's means. They tried to find cheap flights to San Francisco but in the end, Clair agreed to drive if the county would help with expenses. The county agreed to reimburse the Hansens for their car, at 22 cents a mile, and hotel. The rest, "the extras," as Hansen calls them, they covered themselves.

"So I went to San Francisco and spoke before the advisory board, and they were very receptive. They even gave me a standing ovation, which I understand was unheard-of."

What impressed them so much? "That I was a layperson without historical education who took the time and the interest to present a paper worthy, apparently, of a standing ovation. They get very few people who will send someone, or when they do come, they cannot speak elo—"—she cuts herself off—"cannot speak about their subject in a way that was apparently impressive. But I had all the nitty-gritty." Before going she had spoken frequently on the telephone with Dr. Harry Butowski, "a very educated man" who "writes all the criteria for everything. He told me what to do" and sent a tall stack of materials to reference. "You had to have so many points for national interest" which "had to fit this and this and this" to prevent disqualification simply because it was not in the "national interest." "I think they were impressed with my getting this report together that quickly. I had several advisory board members request copies of my report."

Education is clearly a nagging concern for Hansen, who holds a GED, earned fifteen years after high school, and has had no other formal education. She says she's grateful that she didn't know who was on the advisory board before she spoke to them. Before she went home she asked the board's secretary to send her a list of the board members so she would know who they were—they had been introduced only by name. "I would have been very nervous. The chairman was Mr. Meecham, CEO of Pacific Rim Corp.—professional people, and historians, and a whole menagerie of very interesting people: the attorney general of the state of Florida, and the assistant to the attorney general of the United States. I would have been intimidated."

Hansen no longer thinks that she needs a Ph.D. in history to be qualified to speak knowledgeably on her subject. "But in the first three or four years I felt intimidated every time I would meet with a senator, or the governor, or even Brig Madsen in the beginning, because he is the contractual historian for the Sho–Ban tribes. I mean, what can I tell him? So I didn't. I let him tell me. And then, ask, ask, ask, ask, ask."

But one day she did tell him something. "I told him he was wrong. It's been some time now. There was a certain thing he kept pointing to, having to do with the physical site. He would do it every time," she says, and she would grind her teeth. "I'd do it in private. So I said, 'Did you say this and this?' And he said, 'Yeah.' I said, 'Well, I've lived there all my life, my mother was born there, and this is called this.' He said, 'Oh for landsakes!'" She laughs, recollecting Madsen's proclivity for that sort of exclamation. "We've had a lovely relationship since the very beginning," she says. "And he knows so much about all of this. I saw his honorarium at graduation," she adds, referring to the honorary doctorate recently bestowed upon Madsen by the University of Utah.

Hansen has also been known to argue with Jess McCall, the curator of the museum at Fort Douglas, a man "very much military," she says with a laugh. The two "cross swords in a very nice way, every time he comes up with the army and we meet out here." When the curator tells the story, he refers to the "fortifications" supposedly built by the Shoshone—the trenches Porter Rockwell had told Connor to expect at the camp. "I said, 'Now Jess, come here.' We walked up the road. 'Now this is where you're telling that all this was, right?' I said, 'Now when would they have put up fortifications, and for what? If there was anything there, it was a windbreak. But there was nothing there. They had their tepees down around here, this big, deep ravine covered with willows to the point where they just had passages for the people and the horses to get up and down, and they'd hide in the willows and all that—they're not going to go up there, behind fortifications, to try and fire on the army that's up the hill, or the soldiers that are trying to surround them down there.' I said, 'Jess, you'll never convince me of that in a hundred years.'"

Hansen also disputes the hour of the day that historians feel marked the start of the encounter. "It's traditional for the Indian people every morning to get up—their tepee doors are always on the east—and they come out and they always face the sun and do their morning oblations." She points to a map she's pulled out of a box of papers. "The soldiers were here"—on the bluffs—"and they waited until there was enough light that they could see the steam on the horses." Meanwhile, the Shoshone would have been looking east, toward the soldiers. "Well, on January 29, 7:20 is about when you can first see a skyline." The sun rises in the southeast at that time of the year, and she thinks the soldiers may have taken a route different from the one historians aver. Further, "I think it started later than 6:00. I've been out there many years at six, waiting, just trying to see. Some say it began at daylight."

But despite these matters, and even though she was not formally trained, Hansen nonetheless values academic forms of history over other forms. She shares Madsen's suspicion of oral history. "Oral history has to come from memory," she says, "and everybody's memory is faulty. The Indians' memory is colored by the same prejudices as white man's memory." Hansen recalls a time when she discussed this question of oral history with the Shoshone. "I said, 'Now you remember it from your oral history, and yours probably are more accurate because this has been the only method of keeping your genealogies and your stories, whereas the white man has the written language.' No memory is infallible. One story can be told by someone else who heard it from their side of the family, but it'll turn a quarter turn. They're as accurate as people's memories can make them, and from then on it takes digging in and research to try and verify it."

For instance, Hansen feels that the Shoshone recollection of native-settler relations before 1863 is somewhat flawed. "When they start telling these things that happened, they lean just a teeny bit to a prejudicial side. You'll have to excuse how I'm putting this, because it sounds bad, I know, but it's a 'Poor us.' Well it *was* a poor them, we all agree. But it's a *whining* 'Poor us.' They never bring out the depredations they perpetrated on the pioneers, who weren't doing anything but trying to exist. They leave that out all the time. That's what I try to remind them. We all feel bad about what happened here—in fact the last two generations of people probably feel worse than any of the generations before us, about what happened out here. 'But your people,' I tell them, 'did a lot of bad things along the Oregon Trail, which is just north of us here, and along the Overland Mail Route.' The attacks, the massacres that the Indians perpetrated on the white people trying to get to Oregon—they were just passing through. They weren't here to do any harm. These things are never brought out. There are two sides to every story."

Still, despite her extensive knowledge of her "side," Hansen says, "I don't think I'm what you would really call an expert." How much more knowledgeable does one have to be before they're an expert? "I'd probably have to hike right on back to the lack of that diploma on the wall. I do learn well and I do have a good memory and I'm quite a serious person, but I would have to go by what other people say"—and other people say that experts have diplomas.

And are typically men, she agrees. And she agrees that men display their own values when they approach the subject. She notes that anyone researching this matter is referred to her, "because I'm probably more knowledgeable on the complete workings of this subject. Brigham Madsen would know more about the actual because he's talked to the Indians, he's done the research. But he can't get into the feeling and emotion, because that is not where his expertise lies, and that's where I'm dealing with The People. And I deal with the public." Most kids around Preston now know the history. "Over the last five years I've pretty well got everybody in the neighborhood knowledgeable," she says with a laugh. She also deals with historical groups who come through the area, including a group of intermountain west historians. "Now there," she says, "I could have been very much intimidated, because they're all educated, historical people. But they knew practically nothing about it. What made it nice," she says, enjoying the memory, "was that they knew what to ask me." No questions are stupid, Hansen tells the high school students, honors students, and scouts who also visit her for information, but some questions are insightful, provocative inquiries that challenge her own thinking about the incident.

In one area, though, Hansen takes the word of oral history over the word of academic history: the rape. She remains unconvinced by the documents Madsen found. "The Indians say no," she says. "They say the raping and pillaging never happened: 'How can you even think that it would when they just fought a four-hour battle, they just crossed the river, they've got heavy Civil War clothing on, it's twenty below zero, two feet of snow they've trampled through, their hands are frozen.'" Hansen explains that the men had to use their fingers, covered by gloves that came only to the knuckle, to pull bullets, powder, and other supplies from small containers. These were wet and frozen, "hard as rocks," she says. "In the process, they're mutilating themselves, because they can't feel when they do this"—she demonstrates stuffing her fingers into a pocket—"that they're taking off the hide clear to the bone. So when it's over and they receive the word that they're to go among the dead and kill anything that moves, do you think they're going to stop and rape the dead and dying bodies? The Indians say no." She notes that several Franklin citizens who stood on the bluffs and watched, along with Porter Rockwell, never mention a rape in their writings. "They did say they saw them pick up children or babies by the heels and dash them on the ground."

On June 21, 1990, the site was awarded the official status of National Historic Landmark. Bearss called Hansen from Washington after the meeting. "He said there was no question about it, it just went." In late August Bearss asked her to set up a dedication ceremony for October 19. The process had concluded amazingly early. "We were told in the beginning—this was 1985—'It's going to take five to eight years for you to get on a study list.' We dedicated in '90."

Hansen asked for two bronze plaques to be struck, one that the Shoshone could have. This was not standard practice. Hansen called Bearss and said, "With all this we've had to do with the Indians, back and forth, is there no way we can have a second bronze struck that they can put in their office so they have a reminder that this has actually come to pass, and it is in their interest? We didn't do it for us. We actually did it more or less for them, to correct the name."

They made two. "At the dedication we presented it to the chairman of the Shoshone, and they were happy to get it."

Preston citizens may be more knowledgeable about the event now, but as the massacre site project has progressed, she says, townspeople have been but vaguely interested. "I'm always asked, 'How's the Bear River project going?' But people in this area are apathetic. We call our meetings, we publicize it in the paper and on the radio, I send out letters to individuals who absolutely need to be there. We may get a handful of people out of all the people we notify. Because it's been out there, it's been out there all their lives—so what?"

Legislative representatives have also been slow to attend to the project, perhaps because Preston has been divided over this issue, pitting a minority of the landowners against historical preservationists and merchants. After the site was designated a landmark, legislators encouraged Hansen to cool her heels a bit. The next step would be yet another resolution to request a study for an upgrade of the site to a national historic site or reserve. "They said, 'Now give yourself a rest because it's going to take you at least five years to get on the list of a hundred for the study for any upgrade of any kind.' I said, 'Then why wait five years? Let me write my letters now.'"

Hansen appealed to every national historian she had written to for help in attaining landmark status, asking for their support again, this time for a study that could result in the massacre field being declared a National Historic Site. She got letters from renowned academics and curators. "Two years later we're in the top ten in the Denver regional office for a study. I kept letter-writing, and then I got a call from the Denver office saying they'd narrowed the list and 'you are still in the top five.' Six months later, after a little more writing and probing and pushing and carrying on—very gently, because I'm not a hard pusher, but I'm persistent—we were given Number One Priority in the western division. So here we are, from 1990 to 1998, and we are just now supposed to be getting on the top one hundred list for consideration. Well, the study's done, the legislation's being written up. The Park Service told me that from the beginning in 1985, to now, we are fifteen to twenty years ahead of what it could have been." Hansen concedes that this acceleration is due to her own persistence, as she is one of the few members of the original committee still alive, and has been working alone for the past four years, with a helper or two who aids with paperwork.

But it was at this point that the project finally became controversial with white landowners. "If it comes to the next stage, which would be National Historic Site, or Reserve, land will have to mutate for the construction of the small museum, visitor center, Indian memorial. Some landowners are willing to sell, some are not. Those who are not are very adamantly against it. They think it's just going to bring in riffraff, that their privacy's going to be invaded." Hansen knows all these people personally, she says, and has spoken to them many times in an effort to reassure them. "I've said to them, 'If you don't want to sell your property, your property will not be bought. It's willing seller, willing buyer.' 'Well, what if I don't sell?' I said, 'There will probably be a walkway inside of a chain-link fence. Your property will be here, the memorial will be inside the chain-link fence. They will not be wandering your fields.'"

But her assurances have not satisfied her neighbors. "Either they don't want to believe it, or they don't believe it, or they're using that as an excuse for not wanting it." Hansen recalls that Kathy Griffin was with the committee in its early years, but "after it got to be a landmark, that was as much as she wanted. Then she was one of the very loud and very rude persons at the public hearing, with her California brother." As Hansen understands it, David Hansen had a friend on the coast whose property was surrounded by the Park Service. "He said that after the man died they more or less squeezed out whoever else till they obtained the whole thing. So he had her upset thinking that this was what they were going to do out here, even though the Park Service explained over and over, 'If you don't want to sell you will not have to sell.'"

Some Preston citizens think a national historic site could be profitable for the community, but Hansen says she has purposely avoided any involvement with the potential economic boon for which some of her neighbors hold out hope. Park Service employees have told her, she says, "'You people don't know what you have. You not only have your historic site, which you're working on, but you could make this a place of destination, not a pass-through. You have the mountains, streams for fishing, all these lakes around here, all the horseback riding, all the backpacking you do here, the Dutch oven cooking you do here, motocross. You even have big game areas.'" Hansen nods. "We do have big-game hunters who backpack through here. One guy said, 'If this would go, you'd have to build at least two more nice motels, at least two more family restaurants. You're close to Utah State University. People that come from the east will drive 75 miles just like that—to Idaho State University. They want to put their kids in a nice camp area and let them go boating, then get dressed up and go to Salt Lake for the opera. They think nothing of driving 100 miles and back for a nice opera and ballet. Because you're located close to but not in these areas, you would become a destination.'"

Thus, Hansen says, the county commissioners and the Chamber of Commerce is supportive of the project, but she doesn't like to discuss that aspect of the project. "My focus is not in that area at all," she says.

Hers has been to kick-start the legislation necessary to finishing this work—legislation that, as of the date of our talk, is stalled in Idaho Senator Larry Craig's office. She and County Commissioner Brad Smith and the head of the chamber have also traveled to Utah to see Representative Jim Hansen (also no relation). "Utah should be involved," she says, since this is a significant event in Utah history. But the legislation has to come from Idaho.

Hansen is not satisfied with Senator Craig's attention to this matter. "I think he should have shown at least some interest much earlier. His reasoning was that he wanted to wait and see how the people felt about it before he got involved. To me that says, 'I'll wait till after the next election.'" About Craig's plan to hold another meeting so "people can express themselves," Hansen says wryly, "They've only done that for thirteen years."

Senator Craig did request a personal tour of the site late in 1997, for which Hansen was grateful. "It's been a long time in coming. We spent about 2 hours and 15 minutes or so, and he let me know that all of this is sitting in Senate subcommittee right now, waiting for him to get to it and call in Representatives Mike Crapo of Idaho and Hansen of Utah. The legislation is being written, he says—that's all done. He said he wanted to write it all up so he could make certain he was careful about landowner rights, city rights, county rights, Park Service rights. That is what he will present to the public at this meeting. If that's acceptable, he'll take it right through as far as it will go. But in the meantime his people are working on writing this very carefully."

Since that visit, Hansen says, momentum has stopped, due primarily to Senator Craig. "That's the stall," Hansen says. She thinks that if it weren't for Craig, legislation might have already gone to Congress for the preliminary vote. But Hansen is somewhat relieved that things are out of her hands, that all she can do right now is "facilitate" things for the legislators and the Park Service. "My part is basically finished."

Hansen denies the accusation that landowners have been inadequately informed about the process of site development. "They receive phone calls from Greg Rice," Senator Craig's regional director, "especially if there's any controversy. They receive the same letters I receive from the Park Service and the senator." But she does feel that they are not adequately organized. She's told them, "'Don't attack me and call me a "glory hog"—get yourselves organized, get yourselves a spokesman, and get yourselves off your butts. I cannot do it for you. I told you in the beginning that if I find anywhere along this process that you're going either to be taken advantage of, or your land is going to be confiscated against your will, I'll turn every ounce of influence against this program in your favor.' I told them that in the beginning, because I'm not here for that. I'm here to get the history known and to see if this is important enough. Now the government's agreed, they've agreed, everybody's agreed how important it was to the settlement of the West and to the treaties of the tribes—everything happened in 1863 after the massacre. I said, 'You can stop it anywhere along any of these meetings, if you organize and do it. If you don't want it, you won't get it. If you don't represent yourselves, you'll get it and you won't want it. But I can't stop it at that point. Only you can stop it at that point.'"

Hansen tells me that, like Kathy Griffin, she has tons of photocopied material she has prepared for visitors. She gets up from her chair and disappears into a nearby room, dragging a large box from underneath a bed. It contains countless maps and copies of chapters from Hart's and Madsen's books.

As we dig through the box, I ask Hansen how well she and Griffin get along these days. "I'm OK with her, but I don't know how she is with me. I think she has been completely concerned because—part of it is what her brother has fed to her. Part of it is the inborn distrust of all government entities that we're all acquiring, across the country. She should know that I would never do anything that would betray her or anyone else, and I think she's had to learn after an encounter or two, and phoned me about how I'm a 'glory hog' and 'What are you doing this for?' and all that. I hung up on her. I said, 'Kathy, you better re-think this.'" Hansen remains active in her church, and says with a smile that if people there are mad at her, "that's their problem."

Hansen suggests that sexism was part of the landowners' initial failure to respond to the project. "In the beginning we were an ad hoc group of mainly women, and they told us after we finally got the first study under way that they thought we were just a group of ladies who didn't have enough to do. I said, 'Don't let that happen again then, because we're in dead earnest, we're organized, we're not out here playing around.'"

Hansen's goal is a monument that reflects the serious nature of the event that occurred on the site. "How do historians put it? 'It was terrible, it was magnificent.' It was so important to the group of people who were sent here to live, and who did live quite peaceably with them. The fact that it was my family that was born out there before the turn of the century—that has to do with it." And she doesn't feel a sense of family responsibility or accountability for the incident. As a white woman, she says, "I think it's right for me to be telling the white side of the story," because it was her pioneer ancestors who were immediately affected. "Someone needed to see that the history was known, to spur on other people who were interested."

Talking with Hansen, it becomes clear that the "white side of the story" includes more than the "side" that has to do with the Mormon settlers. For instance, the Shoshone have complained about the fact that the army visits the site every January, even though Hansen has explained that it is only a group of ROTC students. "They discuss it: 'Was this the proper thing to do? Would you do this today?' They agree that Major McGarry and maybe even Connor would be in Fort Leavenworth today, but McGarry for sure, because he disobeyed a command. He's the reason fourteen got shot in the beginning, because he was supposed to come down and flank, but got all excited because the Indians were hollering. He ordered them straight forward and got them shot." Hansen has assured the Shoshone that the ROTC students never step on the massacre site. "They walk up the highway, they walk around the canal, they walk down the road, they walk back, they walk up on Cedar Mountain, which is where the flanking move was going, but the Indians were not there."

Hansen also agrees with people such as Newell Hart, who sympathize with those soldiers who were traumatized by the event. She once had a conversation with a tribal council member, who said the Shoshone were offended by that sympathy, and resentful of ROTC presence at the site. "I said, 'Yes, but you've got to realize these young men were under command. They had to do that. In those days, you disobeyed command, you were shot on the field.'" Hansen says she asked if he had ever been in the army, and he told her that he'd been in Vietnam. She asked if he ever did anything he wasn't proud of. He began to cry, which astounded Hansen. "Indian women don't even cry," she says.

The council member (whose name I'm withholding here to protect his privacy) told her that he was "among the troop that was called the 'baby killers.' 'We had to kill everything that moved, regardless of size, age.' I said, 'Then you should understand better than anybody here, that some of these young men who were involved in killing your people, left the army because they couldn't stand it. They wrote in their diaries, they rehearsed it over and over, they told their families over and over. They just couldn't get over it.' I said, 'Not much different, is it? Different times, different people.' And he said yes. And I said, 'Maybe you can help some of the others see that these men didn't come up here with a joyful heart just to rampage. They came up here with the idea of war. They were to rout the Indians, but the manner in which they were commanded to do it was against army regulations.' And Connor was given license to take care of it in any manner he saw fit."

Asked how she feels about Lincoln, who must have provided that license, Hansen says, "Man of the times. I think he could see that there was a problem that could become a very large problem, and he had all he could do to handle the Civil War." The men he had to trust were not worthy of that trust, she says, and abused their authority.

So Hansen appears to be well versed in various "white sides" of the story, but her relationship to the Shoshone story, which she also tells to visitors, is more difficult. She was threatened by natives because of her work on the Bear River Massacre site, at the rededication ceremony in October 1990. "The sheriff does happen to be a good friend of mine, along with being a good sheriff, and he takes so much flak. But he was taking no flak on my behalf that day." The monument area had been roped off for the dedication, but Hansen's car was parked behind the monument so she could have easy access to her car in case her health failed. "They protested that, got real rude about that, and moved the rope and decided they would drive forward. And that's where he stopped it." Someone said, "Well, we have crippled people here too." Hansen and Sheriff Beck arranged for the elders to drive nearby the bandstand, where "they could stay in their cars and still hear. Then others decided they would follow the lead, and finally he had to get angry, and he said, 'If I don't get your cooperation better than you're doing now, then you will be removed from the premises. If you want to handle it this way then we have empty cells in town and if you want to set out the program there'—he finally had to put it that way and then they were fine."

The source of Shoshone resentment of Hansen? "I'm a white woman," she says, "a white woman trying to put forth an Indian program, more or less. Actually, I'm in this whole thing just to get the history of the site known, back into the Idaho history books, back into the Utah history books." I ask her to recall the letter she wrote to Brigham Madsen about what felt to her like a lack of gratitude on the part of the Shoshone. She now feels that neglect was due to "their representation. They have such a mixed emotion and a turmoil within their government all the time." Things are changing; the next generation of young Shoshone interested in the story, Hansen says, seems to be led by Curtis Warner, Parry's great-nephew. Hansen recalls when Warner and his family visited the massacre field with her, following a Park Service meeting in Preston, attended by a group of Shoshone.

At this meeting, Hansen says, a woman told the story of Anzie-chee—and here, in a gesture reminiscent of my talk with Madsen, Hansen reaches for her copy of Hart's book to show me how to spell the name. Anzie-chee's story, as reported by Hart, leaps from the book in highlighted yellow. "She was the mother who had the child. She was wounded twice, and she knew the only way she could manage any kind of escape was to the river." Back then, the river turned toward the creek and ran parallel to it and then came together. "She crossed this area from the Battle Creek ravine, and got into the river to get under the bank. The water, even in January, would have been warmer because of the hot springs. When she got under the bank there were some others of her tribespeople under the bank. And the little girl when she hit the water started to cry, as a two- or three-year-old would, and she knew they were all doomed. The army was right there. So she just pushed her out in the water and let her go. She drowned."

It was Anzie-chee's great-granddaughter who told the story that day. Hansen recalls, "Those of my committee that were there sat there with tears just—"

Hansen shakes her head. Telling the story again, her voice tightens with emotion. "This is the first time I had heard this story other than in the book, and I had been telling this story for more than ten years on tours. And all of a sudden here's Melinda Dunford from Bear Lake, and she's telling it, and we're all sitting there, even the Park Service lady, who's heard this story so many times—"

After the meeting, Hansen took Dunford to the site, along with a member of the Timbimboo family. "We went out and stood at this one spot. And I said, 'Now this is where the main body of the massacre took place, and this is the only place where your great-grandmother could have gotten into the river without being shot by the army.' And she stood there and she looked at that spot, and she looked at that spot. And then she put her head here"—Hansen touches her own breast—"and she just cried. And I did too. It was so moving. She said, 'I have known this story all my life, but I had no conception of how this could have taken place, physically here.' It was just a very reverent, good cry—a sad–good cry."

But the visitors had another request. They wanted Hansen to take them on a tour and tell the story as she knew it. "Now, this right there was a shocker. They said, 'We've been to the monument and that's as far as we've been.' I said it would be my privilege. About sixty or seventy of them came. We started at the monument and took the entire three-hour walk." Hansen gave the Shoshone the option of walking a short distance onto the massacre field, but they didn't want to. "I understood," she says.

"I was being attacked off and on throughout that entire tour: 'What's a white woman like you—what do you care? You don't have any right to do this.' I said, 'I can appreciate where you're coming from. But you invited me to take you and tell you where this happened, so you can understand how the lay of the land was.'" But a woman—"quite inebriated," Hansen says—was persistent. "We stood at the site, and it was as quiet as a church. Of course," she adds, "Indians are quite stoic anyway."

As they walked up toward an A-frame house that sits on the site, "I thought this Indian lady was going to hit me—and this was when Curtis Warner's father came up, called her by name, said something in their language—and then in English, he said, 'This is enough of this. This woman, whether she's a white woman or not, has had the good grace to lead us on a tour today at our request. Now you either restrain yourself or we'll have some of the elders take you off.' So her sister got her and took her off. She was not happy that I was there."

Hansen agrees that it's unfortunate that a white woman is the person most often telling the story. "It's ironic. When they came in January 1990 for the commemoration, they came clear from Albuquerque and all around. It was the beginning of our centennial year here, so I had the ROTC there. And the mountain men were there and they set up rendezvous, so we could see the tents and the things they do. We had regular military from Fort Douglas. We had people representing the pioneers. So what they decided they would do is talk to me and say, 'We don't like what you're doing up there, we don't like the army being there with their tanks.' We had one National Guard chow truck—beans and hardtack and hot chocolate—but only one truck and it was pulled over. 'We're going to protest, we're coming, we're wearing black armbands. And when things get going we're going to protest and slash our bodies and cut our hair and kai-yai.' They came down here to my home to tell me that twice. I was very upset the first time they came. The second time they came, I called Mae, and she said, 'That's what they said in council. I'm very much upset and I don't want them to come.' I had asked her if she would give a brief history and she said she didn't know if she could or not. I said, 'If they're going to boo and hiss and carry on, I don't want you to be subjected to that.'

"So the second time they came I said, 'Listen. It's your privilege to protest. You're given twenty minutes at the podium. Now, I'm expecting three hundred students, from the age of twelve through high school.' I told them the different peoples that were going to be there. I said, 'Now, if this is what you want them to remember about you, you will really impress them, that's for sure. Then what are they going to remember about the commemoration? They're not going to remember the history that I tell, the history that Mae Parry tells, they're going to remember slashing wrists, cutting hair, and kai-yai', which is enough to terrify anybody anyway, if you've ever heard it. But I said, 'That's your privilege.'"

The night before the commemoration, Parry called Hansen and said she had discussed the situation with Friday Tendoy, Bear Hunter's great-grandson and the Shoshone's official song singer, and that they had decided to attend the ceremony as families representing Sagwitch and Bear Hunter. They would perform the sacred eagle feather and arrow ceremony. "I just burst into tears. That was such a relief to think that they would do something nice, not just something ugly. It was just lovely." Tendoy sang, "and then they shot the sacred eagle feather into the air with the arrow which to them is sacred, and it was retrieved by another member of the Tendoy family, who has the official right of retrieval. They presented their Indian flag with the bear claws and different things on it. It was very, very nice. The other people showed up with black armbands, that's all. They kept saying things while Mae was trying to talk, like 'She's a half-breed'—well, she's not.

"The irony is that the people coming from New Mexico and Utah stopped at Mae Parry's house and spent a better part of one afternoon while she had her beautiful things out and told the whole history of everything. They didn't know anything about their own history—they got it from Mae Parry, then came out and protested Mae Parry. I call that ironic."

Nowadays, because of Hansen's poor health, she limits tours to groups of sixth graders and up—those who are serious about understanding the event. But occasionally she talks to elementary-age children about the history of the site. She asks them, "'Where did you go on vacation?' 'We went to Grandma's.' And some of their grandmas are a long ways away. 'And what happened to your yard? Your yard was pretty when you left it and when you came home everything was nice. But what if you came home and there were some people out there, right out in your yard, and they were camped there. And they were digging, and planting things, and using your water—you always used the water out of that little creek, and they're using it, and it was yours, and you don't understand what's happening.' I say, 'The Indians came from their summer gathering of food supplies, and they came back here late in the fall to get their supplies in their wickiup granaries. And here are all these people in their yard. And they built houses there and they're fishing in the water there and they're planting wheat all over.' I say, 'How would you feel? There were all these people, they dressed differently, they didn't talk the same language, they lived in a different kind of a house, and they're on our land.'"

Hansen hopes that becoming conscious of this history will help whites become more conscious of their privilege. She hopes whites will "reflect on the ease of life. The ease of accessibility. The ease in obtaining things, services. Then think of the black people. They are struggling so hard with prejudices on both sides. Then place your American Indian," relative to other American racial groups, "and they are below any other group as far as any of the things mentioned above. Racial prejudice, their ability to obtain goods and medical services, their access to education, their dislocation—continual dislocation, relocation—over the last century and a half." She hopes then that whites will "look inside themselves for the tolerant part. Some of these people, through centuries of habits, have become in some instances very childlike in their inability to trust, and to act on their knowledge. Some white people have no tolerance for this. They see these people as not trying, when in fact in a good many instances they're trying to the best of their ability.

"Tradition plays such a major part—it keeps them tied for fear. They don't fear white man. They fear white man's ways, and traditions that in some instances conflict completely with theirs. They have such a reverence for life and earth and all the elements. They see white man's factories, polluting, looting, burning, killing—animal killing, while they only kill to eat. All these things hold them back, into another place separate from the white man's ability to understand. So we don't have the tolerance for them that we should."

But what do we mean by "tolerance"? Hansen is opposed to what she calls "handouts," and argues that natives should be "educated, to know that they can gain for themselves through the labor of their minds and hands." She refers to the book *Indian Givers*. "Look to the books that teach what they know. So much of our medicines come from their culture. They have the potential if we'll have patience to help them see and trust." Understanding our mutual history will, she says, expedite tolerance, and therefore trust.

Today, she says, Native Americans should be "mainlined" into society. "I don't believe in this nation-within-a-nation with treaty rights and all of this," she says. "I think there should be certain rights they should maintain simply because it's been their right from the beginning of time, like the fishing rights, for a certain period of time. But not for all time." The reservation system isn't working, Hansen says. "There are, of course, certain factions within every reservation for whom it's working out beautifully. But the more educated The People get, the more they can absorb society and the world and still keep their culture." Uneducated natives, she says, are unable to negotiate their presence within two cultures. "They can't make the transition back and forth as the educated Native American can."

Hansen feels that better schools are the key. "But then again, they reject it. It has to come from their people, their educators—and slowly it is coming. We as white people want them to have everything and be able to do everything, and they culturally aren't ready, even now. I would say 60% are not ready, while 40% are being absorbed," are bringing technical training back to the reservations for the improvement of their people. "But they're being fought against too by their own people."

Hansen reports that in 1996, the year after I attended the public hearings, she helped obtain permission for the Shoshone to go on the massacre site and perform ceremony for their dead relatives. "I was not invited," Hansen says, "which was all right. It was their private thing. They had their dedication ceremony, they did whatever they do to bury their dead spirits. They had their prayers and did their songs." Hansen says the Shoshone have seemed more relieved since then. "The spirits of their dead are finally able to find peace after 135 years. That had been such a worry that they would not travel through there at night, because they feel the spirits wander there at night trying to find rest. After the sun went down, the Indians were gone. They couldn't be there. It was a sacred site, but its history was unfinished, so to speak. I hope now that they feel calmness and satisfaction, in the fact that we got to the point where they were given permission from the landowner to be on the site." Hansen clearly feels good about the understanding she now has with the landowner, whose name she will not mention. "I have permission to take out those I think will appreciate the massacre site—otherwise, nobody gets through the fence."

She doesn't get credit for having mediated these many conflicts, she says, which doesn't bother her. "The only thing that bothers me is when they come on television and they interview Mae, and say that for all these years Mae Parry has tried to get—and on and on. My committee should be given credit. She was with us for three meetings in '85 and '86; from that part on we never saw her, she never participated. We didn't get the legislation in till 1989. In fact she was against us for a little while because of the wording. But still she's given credit for the whole thing. I resent that on behalf of my committee, not on behalf of me, because I'm not a glory hunter." Real credit, she says, belongs with Ganeale Swainston, the chairwoman who died of cancer in 1990, before the dedication. "It was her conception."

I point out to Hansen that it has been the work of women that has propelled this project. "We're the ones that get things done," she says, chuckling.

The warm day is waning. It's been a long talk, and we're both tired. I ask Hansen if she has anything to add to our discussion, and she shrugs.

"I've told you the truth, as full as I can remember right now," she says.

She lifts herself from her chair and slowly walks me out to the truck, back into the ovenlike air. We talk about the heat as we go. As I get in the truck, she smiles and says, "You be careful going home now. We'd hate to have to come after you."

I honk and wave and head back down the four country blocks to the steaming main street.

7

PARRY

The heat continues to build. It's record-breaking hot, they say, and Pocatello has now completely sold out of fans, with no hope of getting more. On my way to see Mae Timbimboo Parry, I stop at a Kmart in Ogden and find tons of the things. All varieties: floor, ceiling, rotating, oscillating.

They know how to do air-conditioning down here in the hole that is Salt Lake Valley.

Already sweating, I'm a little concerned about meeting Mae Timbimboo Parry. Brigham Madsen has warned me that she can be very distrustful of whites. Allie Hansen has told me that Parry is a wonderful person, but warns that my experience may depend on what sort of mood I find her in. Hansen advises me to write a letter first, explaining my project, and to call later to make an appointment.

I do this. On the phone, Parry tells me she isn't feeling too well, and that she's not sure she's up to visitors. But she seems reluctantly willing to speak to me anyway, and gives me an appointment. Speaking to visitors about the Bear River Massacre seems to be what she does. She mentions two doctoral students she's seeing that week as well. She's not in the least surprised to hear about my own project. She's used to this sort of thing.

But there's a note of irritation in her voice. I know this could be a challenge, but I lecture myself on the ride down. I remind myself that she sounded welcoming enough on the phone, and remind myself that the two of us may have different styles of speaking. I dust off a basic tenet of journalism from the old days: shut *up*. If *you* fill the silences, I bark at myself, *she* won't. Take it easy, I tell myself. Easy.

And shut up.

When I arrive at her home in a suburb north of Salt Lake City, she's in her kitchen speaking with a man who seems to be a lawyer and who seems to be talking about tribal wills. Parry's husband Grant, an elder gentleman, shows me to a wide living room, and I ask where I should sit. "Anywhere but Mae's chair," he jokes, and points to an upholstered rocker next to a table. A floor lamp shines on a large box strewn with papers and documents that have been sheathed in plastic covers. Parry's husband and I are laughing about where he sits—"Wherever I can find a spot," he says—when Parry comes in.

She's a small woman with a set jaw and a powerful presence despite a slight palsy caused, I've been told, by Parkinson's disease. She doesn't greet me. She just sits down in her chair and begins to hand me documents, talking about what she's handing me as she gives them to me.

This must be what she does with her doctoral students.

Clearly, she has a set routine she's going to want to follow.

On the phone, she had told me she couldn't give me copies of anything, but would let me look at what she had. I thumb through a thick, typed manuscript, the first thing she hands me. It's the story of her people, the Northwestern band of the Shoshone. She explains that she's currently involved in a project organized by the Utah Historical Society, a book to be published by the University of Utah, about the tribes of that state. "Some of the Indian tribes went and hired Ph.D.'s and master's degrees, professors, to write their history from the white man's point of view, and turned that in. The project was supposed to be an oral history from the Indian's point of view and now it's got out of hand. It's getting to the point where it's not an Indian's point of view. I told them I don't want them to change one single word of the things I have written because this is an Indian's point of view. They've been real good about it." (This book would be released in 2000 as *A History of Utah's American Indians,* Forrest S. Cuch, editor; it is distributed by Utah State University Press.)

We talk about whether the state of Utah has been more hospitable to the Shoshone than the state of Idaho. She says that the state of Idaho has been helpful, but that Utah has a Cooperative Council, a group of Native American representatives who meet with the governor regularly to discuss issues of concern to those constituents.

Members of the council are appointed by the governor and approved by the state legislature. "We're the only ones in the whole United States that have this governor-appointed council, where we all know what the other tribes are doing," Parry says.

The doorbell rings. Parry's husband answers it. Parry looks over her shoulder to see who it is: two longtime acquaintances of hers, older women who drove down from the Fort Hall reservation—ten miles north of Pocatello, so they must have been right behind me on the interstate. Parry explains that one of the women has come with questions about her family history. She hands me a sheet of legal paper, with a penciled narrative written in perfect, grade-school cursive. It's everything Parry has heard about this woman's family. She wrote it years ago, she says. Her husband, she explains, is typing all such papers into the computer, but mostly these stories reside in the large treasure box at her feet.

As Parry's husband walks the new visitors to the couch across the room, I comment that Parry must be very interested in history. She nods, saying that all history interests her, all around the world.

The two women settle onto the couch, complaining of the heat and the long drive. And in the moment it takes them to get comfortable—it could be my imagination, but this is what I sense—Parry makes a decision. She will hear my questions before she hears those of the woman who is there to ask about her family.

I'm not happy with continuing before an audience, nor with knowing that I'm now imposing not just on Parry and her husband, but also on these two women. Which means I won't have much time. But I seem to have no choice. Parry has made the choice. Indeed, she has made—or so it feels to me—a selection. She has decided whom to dismiss first.

This rattles me.

Shut up.

I ask Parry what she recalls about how the National Park Service's project to build a monument on the massacre site got started. "Well, I've had a big long fight with them," she says. "I was with that organization when it got started, and then they kept calling it the Battle of Bear River. I told them, 'It's not the Battle of Bear River, it's a *massacre*.' They wouldn't listen." Parry names a woman from Soda Springs who was especially verbal in her opposition to Parry's feelings. "'No,' she said. 'Why don't we compromise and call it The Battle-Slash-Massacre.' I said, 'That's not good enough, it's a massacre, not a battle at all.' I insisted. So one day they were going to have a meeting and I didn't show up, and I told them, 'I'm not coming to this meeting anymore because you people are always running over the Indians. You want your way and I'm not going to get my way, so I'm not coming to your meetings anymore. I quit.' I said, 'I'm going to take it upon myself, and I'm going to start writing to Washington, DC.' I wrote to the senators, congressmen, representatives—Manuel Lujan was secretary of the interior at that time—I wrote to all those people telling them that this committee—I didn't agree with them. It's not a battle. It's a massacre when you kill Indians that were sleeping in their tepees, men, women, and children—getting the children by their braids, swinging them around, slapping them on the ground. I said, 'Is that a battle? They were massacred.'"

Parry says she received a letter from Secretary Lujan saying that they were going to turn the matter over to Edwin Bearss, chief historian of the Park Service. "They had a historian check this out. They said, 'You'll hear from us in a few months.' A little later I got a letter from Edwin Bearss. He said, 'Meet me at Preston.' So we drove over to Preston, and he was there. We took a tour of that whole field: where the soldiers came down, where they were killed, where they camped, the hills the survivors went to after."

I ask Parry when this meeting was, so I can place it among the other accounts of meetings I have heard. The question doesn't interest her. "I've got it written down somewhere," she says vaguely.

"Was it the one in '89?" I press her.

"I have the paperwork on it here somewhere."

Parry returns to her story. "After that, Bearss went back, and later on, he says, 'After having studied this, and having toured the area, I feel like you were right, that it was a massacre.' He said, 'After studying it, we have found out that it's the worst massacre west of the Mississippi, worse than Wounded Knee'—he named several others that we read about. 'But because the Civil War was going on in the South, they paid more attention to those battles, and they didn't care what was going on in the West.'" Bearss informed her that it would have to be an act of Congress to change the name of the event to massacre and the status of the site to landmark. "I said, 'At least once, an Indian won something.' Usually we don't win anything. Usually they try to run over us. I was so upset. I wrote to the Idaho state legislators, besides Utah, and they had to pass a resolution. I was so upset. You know, usually the way you do it is you start down here at the bottom with your council people and then your state legislators, and go up from there. I started from Manuel Lujan and came down." She smiles at the memory. It's a slight smile, and the broadest I'll see from her this day.

I ask Parry how she feels about the folks in Preston who are working for the monument, whether she thinks they deserve some credit for getting things this far. "Right now," she says—and the slight smile is there again—"at my age, I'm just disgusted with everything. I am. The older I get the madder I get." I laugh at this too cheerily while she smiles, again only briefly. "I used to go around to the different schools all over the area—universities and all kinds of clubs, and they wanted to know all about what happened. It got to the point where I just refused to go over and talk to anybody anymore. I decided I'm going to no longer talk about it." She stops herself for a moment, perhaps to reconsider the question. "My own feeling is I think they're trying to do it for themselves. They want the trade, the tourist attraction, and stuff like that. Right now they're saying they're going to invite the Indians to be there and display and stuff, but I doubt it very much—they're looking out for themselves. They're not looking out for us."

I ask Parry if she trusts the Park Service to fully involve the tribe. Parry replies that she knows the staff, that one of her daughters was a secretary for Charles Odegaard. Fred York, she says, has visited her twice, and Catherine Spude has also been here. "They were trying to get me to support that—they wanted me to say something about it. I told Fred, 'I'm so sick and tired of telling about that massacre.'"

I chuckle at this too. We sit quietly for a moment until I ask what it's been like living with the story all this time. "I've lived with it for eighty years almost, and I knew some of those people. I've heard their stories. I guess I just feel like my father. My father says, 'I've written and talked about this massacre for sixty years and I'm not going to tell another story about it. Ask my daughter,' he says. And that was me."

I ask if this is how Parry ended up with the responsibility for telling the story and she says, "No!" in a tone that seems to scold me.

"How did you end up with it?" I ask.

"I don't know," she says. "Maybe I talk too much." We both smile at this, in our different ways. Parry says that her verbosity explains how she ended up writing the story for the Utah book. At a meeting of the Cooperative Council, someone suggested they write a history of Utah, something about the pioneers, a centennial book. "I said, 'Have you forgotten that this is Indian country? Don't the Indians have anything to say about the history of Utah? This is our country. You're leaving us out.' A lot of times I've said I should have kept my mouth shut. Well, then I inherited the job of writing the story. But I didn't have to look for material because I already had it. I have stacks and stacks all over the place."

"Are you glad that the Park Service is trying to do a site there?" I ask.

"Well, I really don't care anymore. And I'm speaking for myself. I'm not speaking for the tribe." She refers me to the band's then-Council President Tony Wongan to ask his opinion—although, she says, "I doubt he's going to know much about it, because he wasn't really raised around the area."

I ask Parry where she thinks the future of the band is headed, and remind her that on the phone, when I mentioned to her that I was acquainted with her nephew Curtis Warner, she told me that young people today don't know the first thing about "how to be an Indian." "That's right," she says, nodding her head. I ask who will take the story after her. "I don't know," she says. "The only reason I wrote these stories is for my grandchildren. I don't care if anyone else sees them or reads them. I'm writing these for my own family. My grandkids, so they'll know where they came from."

I also remind Parry that in my first letter to her, I told her that my intentions are to write my book for the benefit of white people, so white people will know what passed here. "Do you care if white people know about this?" I ask.

"I really don't care anymore, I said." Her tone is impatient.

"You've worked awful hard at it not to care," I say, in as nice a tone as I can manage.

"Yeah. I have things I wrote when I was twelve years old. I've always been interested in history. Not only Indian history, but history all over the country, all over the world. It wasn't hard for me to get these things done."

I ask what Parry thinks of Madsen's version of the history. "Well," she says, "there's a few little mistakes, but I've talked to Brigham and visited with him, and we talked over some of these things before he wrote his book, and every time he writes a book, I get a copy of it." She seems pleased by this latter.

She and I agree that Madsen is an inordinately nice man. "One of the things Madsen says," I say, "is that with the exception of your story, he doesn't really trust the oral histories of other people." I mention that I've heard that there are other versions of the story that conflict in some ways with hers. "You must have some faith in oral history," I say.

"Oh, I do," she agrees. She thinks Madsen is wrong. "Like I said, I have set and listened to some of those old people tell their stories. And Brigham Madsen, not being an Indian, doesn't understand. That's the way we passed our stories on, oral history. We were told it over and over until we just memorized these things. I don't agree with a lot of things that Brigham Madsen says—no matter—You don't understand these things because you're not an Indian!" she exclaims.

"You told him that?" I ask, misunderstanding her—but not really.

"No, I'm telling you!"

I laugh.

She does not.

A short silence ensues. I glance over at the women on the couch to check out their reaction to this. They aren't looking at us. Just sitting there quietly. Fanning the heat away. Resting, maybe. But probably listening intently.

I ask her to explain this thing about young people not knowing what it means to be an Indian. "Well," she says, "like Curtis Warner. He's never lived an Indian life, he's never lived on a reservation, he doesn't know what they ate and how they lived and how they traveled, and all about their superstitions and their marriages—and things like that that *we* know. He was raised in a different atmosphere. His information is coming out of white man's history books. We have the same great-grandpa. I just got through looking at his great-grandpa's writings, letters that he wrote to my grandfather—Frank Warner's letters—that those Warner people don't even know I have. He used to visit my grandpa all the time and spend time with them."

Parry digs through her box and hands me a series of photographs, covered in plastic, of her ancestors. I've seen some of them in Madsen's book, and Hart's book. "I have all kinds of pictures—these people that told the stories. I don't care if anybody else reads them, I'm doing this for my grandkids."

I ask what Parry says to young people like Curt, a young man in his twenties who wants to help the band as best he can. "What can they do to get educated?" I ask.

"I don't know how they feel about it," Parry says, interrupting herself to show me a picture of her grandfather. Then she hands me a yellowed newspaper article, also in plastic, with a picture of herself. The headline proclaims her "Mother of the Year." She tells me she has six children. In 1986, according to the article, the Utah Chapter of the Association of Honorary Mothers bestowed upon her this award.

Another small silence.

I'm struggling to keep any kind of order to my questions, but the notion of "mother of the year" provides something of a segue to a discussion of women's issue—doesn't it? I tell her that I understand that she disagrees with Madsen about whether a rape occurred after the killing. "You know," she says, "that's one thing I have never, never heard my grandfather or some of those people, come along and talk about this. I have never in my life heard them say the soldiers raped the women. Never. I was surprised when I read Madsen's account of that, saying that the women were raped by the soldiers, because that was never mentioned by the Indians. And I don't think it's true. Unless the soldiers that did it reported that—I don't know." She shakes her head. "They'd have to be sick in the head to rape somebody that's dying. I had never in my life heard it. I was surprised when I heard that."

"Then you're not concerned," I say, "about the fact that the Park Service isn't going to cover that."

"Speaking for myself," she answers, "I don't really care."

I'm struggling harder as the silences lengthen. I don't normally have to ask so many questions of an interview subject. "Mrs. Hansen told me," I say, "that the Shoshone performed ceremony on the site in '96."

"Yes," she says, "and a lot of those people that went up there and did this did not even have relatives that were massacred there."

"She was saying that she hopes the Shoshone feel more at peace with that land since the ceremony. Do you think the ceremony helped at all?"

"I don't think it did anything."

"OK."

Silence. Then she speaks again. "I was up there—some honors students a few months ago from the different Utah schools met up there. They wanted me to come there and be the speaker. So I told them, 'OK, this is the last time I'm coming to this area as a speaker, and from now on I'm not going to go back to Preston to that massacre field. I'm never going to step my foot on there and make another speech.' I said, 'This is it. I'm not going to talk about it any-more.' So I don't intend to go back up there. For nothing."

I'm still struggling. I mention that Hansen had told me a story about people who badgered Parry at the rededication ceremony in 1990. "You were going to tell the story," I remind her, "and some Indians had a problem with that?"

"They did," she says. "Well, that was another thing. Good thing it started to rain and stopped everything. They don't know the story. They were all young people. I think there was a lot of jealousy in that, because some of those people, their grandparents came from Fort Washakie, Wyoming, or they came from Nevada, and they really weren't connected with the ones that were there."

Really long silence then.

Shut up, I'm thinking.

"So whatever," Parry says again, and then interrupts herself. "I'm speaking for myself," she says in an urgent tone. "Not the tribe. I'm not going to go up there again for any celebration. I've had enough of them."

I ask how Parry feels about Mrs. Hansen. "She was a nice person," she says. "I get along with Mrs. Hansen very well, but it was some of those others that just—they had their mind made up. The Indians were wrong, they were right. I wasn't going to put up with that. I was just as stubborn as they were."

I ask if white people should be telling the story. "A lot of them do," she answers. "I get a letter almost every week from somebody that says, 'Well, this isn't it, this isn't the way it was.' They're still telling me things from the white man's point of view, not the Indians.'"

I'm having trouble getting my head around that. "People call you up and say you have the story wrong?"

"Call me up all the time and I get letters all the time."

"Saying you have it *wrong*?"

"Yeah. In fact I think I got two letters last week saying, 'The things you're saying are not true.' Well, I don't care what they say."

I ask who's writing the letters. "Just citizens from all over: Pocatello, Preston, in this area. They didn't sit there and listen to these Indians talk. They don't know what they said. I do. I think the reason we had a lot of visitors to our home is because my mother always fed the Indians. Fed them big, nice meals. So we had a lot of visitors. They always stayed and stayed and visited and talked. Indians are like that. They like to tell stories. I was so curious I'd just listen and listen and I'd write a lot of things they said." This was at the Washakie settlement in Utah, she says, the remainder of which, again, has only recently been recognized as a tiny reservation.

Another long silence. "So I would suggest you just go talk to Tony—I call him Tony because I've known him since he was a baby."

"I'll talk to him," I say, but I'm really thinking that I never got an answer to this question of white people telling the Shoshone story. "Do you have a problem with Mrs. Hansen as a white person telling—"

She cuts me off. She's tired of this discussion. "No, I don't pay any attention to it anymore. She's changed her mind since then, you know." I ask what about. "She's found out after inquiring around that the Indians' side of the story was true."

"So that makes it OK with you," I say.

"Like I said, I don't care," she answers. "I don't like to be quoted anymore. I've had too many—gone all over the place—I've taught some classes at the University of Utah—Indian perspectives and stuff like that. And taught classes for the teachers so they could have a better understanding of their Indian students: what to not ask, and what to ask them."

"I'm probably asking all the wrong things," I say, taking the hint, and hoping to get this on the table so we can talk about it.

She doesn't answer.

Really struggling. I ask Parry about her education, and she replies that she went to the LDS business college after she graduated from high school. Last year, she says, her high school sent a letter saying they planned to honor five graduates. "I was one of the five," she says.

I point out that the story seems to have brought her a great deal of opportunity, making it, perhaps, a blessing and a curse.

"Why would you call it a curse?" she asks, again impatient with me.

"You don't seem happy with it," I say with a small laugh.

"I'm not happy with it *now*. It really upsets me, how the Indians have been treated." This last part comes out in that scolding tone again. "They lived here, they were happy here, they traveled and did what they wanted to. All of a sudden white people come along and just shoved them out, kept pushing them and pushing them and taking their things away. Pretty soon we had nothing, not even a place to live, not a place to even spread a blanket. We were kicked around, like a bunch of dogs. I've always been treated fairly. No one's ever treated me badly. If anybody did it's been my own people."

"Why is that?"

"I don't know. You'll have to ask them, not me."

"Well, what do they *say* their problem is?" I ask—but meanwhile I'm wracking my brain for some way to get through to this person. I've tried being extra nice, I've been immensely sympathetic and affirming, nodding my head plum off my shoulders at everything she says. I'm thinking back to Journalism 101—*what else can I try?*

Well, you know, I *might* try being purposefully *aggressive*. *Provocative.*

"Well, they don't tell me what their problem is," she says.

Long silence.

"They just give you a hard time?" I prod.

"Well, they try to give me a hard time, but it goes in one ear and out the other because I know the people."

I tell her that I've seen two versions of her story, one in Hart's book and one in Madsen's, and ask which version she prefers. "No," she says, "because I know both of those men."

Long silence.

As in, REALLY long silence.

I wait for a full twelve painful seconds (I know this because I just counted it on the tape recording as I type this) before I ask if there is anything Parry would like to say to my readers, readers of a book about the difficulty of getting the Park Service project going, that I might not have asked her.

"Not really," she says. "Like I said, those people from the Seattle Park Service have been trying to get me to say something to support it, but I told them at this point I'm just going to keep my mouth shut and not say anything. Let somebody else say something about it. I'm not going to say any more."

"Are you glad they're building it?" I ask.

"I don't care," she says. "To tell you the truth. I really don't. I'm not concerned about it. If they want to build it, let them build it, and if they don't, why, it's fine with me. I'm not going to be around to see it."

OK.

Uncle.

"All right," I say. "I appreciate your time."

"Well, I didn't give you a very good account of what happened," she says.

"Why is that?" I say, amiably.

"I don't know."

"You love to tell stories but you're not telling me any stories."

"I know. Like I said, the older I get the ornerier I get."

I laugh. "I'm young and I'm ornery," I say.

It occurs to me that I forgot to ask her birthdate.

"May 15, 1919," she replies.

I write this down. "So I'm asking you all the wrong questions. What should I be asking you?"

"I don't know what you want," she says in that scolding tone. She's half-smiling again. "I thought you came to ask if I support the thing."

I tell her that I'm interested in the history of trying to make history. I tell her I'm concerned about the fact that most European Americans aren't aware of the story. "What's stopped it from getting out there like Wounded Knee is?" I say.

"Well," she says, "like I said, like the chief historian said, because of the Civil War going on—"

That's it. I decide to try the purposeful aggression thing.

"I don't believe that, Mrs. Parry. Sand Creek was in 1864. It was just a year later."

"I do," she says. "They weren't interested in what was going on out in the West."

"I think something else is happening. I think it has to do with the Mormon church, the relationship between the Mormon church and the rest of the country."

"That's another thing I do not care to discuss is the Mormon church," she says sharply. "I'm a Mormon, my father was a bishop. It's very, very disgusting the things you read in the newspapers every single day—somebody attacking the Mormon church, and I'm not going to discuss religion. I have never believed in discussing religion, or being quoted about—I don't think religion should be brought into this."

"Well," I say, thinking she's misunderstood me, "it's not really about religion so much as the fact that the rest of the country just doesn't want to know what goes on in Mormon territory. They just turn their backs."

Long silence.

Uncle.

"It's just a theory anyway," I say feebly.

I try a different tack. "It's kind of hard that I have to ask you questions," I say, "when what I'd really like to do is just sit and listen to you talk. It seems disrespectful to ask you questions."

"Over the years," she says, "I've been asked thousands of questions."

"Well," I say, "I'm going to leave you to your other guests." Over on the couch, one woman seems now to be asleep, and the other is jotting notes on a stenopad.

What is she writing?

Her face is held still, as if it could be only a grocery list.

Parry mentions someone else she's heard of who's writing the story of the band, someone at Idaho State University. "But I don't know what he knows about our tribe, because he lives on the Fort Hall reservation, and he's a Lemhi Shoshone. He called me a while back—they'll pay so much if you come write your history for Idaho. I turned him down, I didn't want to take that job. So I understand he's over there writing a history. But I don't know what he knows about our tribe, only what he's going to get out of books again."

"So it's hard to get the story right if you don't come from the tribe," I say.

"That's right. Because you'll have to go back to the white man's writings, and they're going to write what they want to, not what the Indians said."

"So maybe it's not important for you if people outside the tribe know about it, or know anything. Maybe it's just not important."

"It isn't really important," she says, "to me. Like I said, I'm doing these things for my grandkids."

"Some people feel that the future of the tribe would be more secure if the story were understood," I say. "Do you agree with that?"

"That's right," she says. "Indians have been misunderstood for centuries, and I don't think it's been right. They have always said things about Indians that weren't quite true, to make themselves look good. We were always the bad people, they were always the ones that were supposed to know everything."

"It's interesting," I say, "that you have a personal interest in history—not just your own but of the world—but you're not concerned with whether the world knows your tribe's history."

"That's right," she says. "I know my tribe's history and I really don't care if anybody else knows about it."

"Do you trust the rest of the world to understand that history?" I ask.

"Like I said, I really don't care what they—I've traveled quite a bit, to reservations all over the country, at conferences in Washington,

DC. If you listen to the Indians, what they say and how they feel and how they're being treated all over—they always have the same feeling that even today we're not being treated fairly. Somebody's always trying to put something over on us, thinking we're not intelligent or able to handle our own affairs. It isn't true, because we do have a lot of very very intelligent people. So I don't know about supporting this project they have at Preston. I'm not going to say anything about it. Whatever they want to do—and I don't think it's going to benefit the Indians."

Since I can't say I disagree with that, I end the long silence that follows by telling Parry that it has been very nice to meet her. She says again that she knows she hasn't said much, and by way of explanation, says that her family has been having health problems that have kept her running to hospitals and worrying over people. She mentions that her mother is 105 and needs a lot of help.

"I know I didn't give you very much information," she says again, "but we've had all these family problems. I hope I'm feeling better next time we talk."

"I hope so, too," I say, "but not for my sake—yours."

She nods. She's not looking at me. I realize then that, except for when she is answering my questions, she always looks away from me, usually at the floor or at her lap.

I tell her again that it's been very nice meeting her.

Then I show myself out. As I go, behind me, I hear Parry speak to her guests. "How ya been?" she says. "You wanted to know about your family?" As I close the door, they are rousing themselves from the couch, and responding—

—but first, complaining about the heat, which hits me like a solid wall as I make my way to the truck for the long ride home.

I've been inside for a grand total of thirty-five minutes.

There in the cab of my truck I push my new fan onto the floor, to get it out of the way.

On the three-hour drive back, the temperature drops 10 degrees when I climb to Malad Pass, climb the hell out of Utah, and drop down into Idaho.

Not long after my talk with Parry, while thumbing through my copy of Newell Hart's book, I come upon his introduction to Parry's tale, which he reprints in his book.

I'd forgotten what he wrote there.

He reminds his readers that Yeager Timbimboo, the boy the soldier couldn't shoot, was spared, it is said, so he would live to tell the tale. His son, Moroni Timbimboo (Mae's father), the first Shoshone to become a Mormon bishop, told the tale after Yeager was gone.

Hart collected the documents gathered in his *SourceBook* through the 1970s. In 1972, as he relates in *SourceBook*, he visited Bishop Timbimboo and his wife, Amy Hootchew Timbimboo, in Plymouth, Utah. The bishop, eighty-four at the time, began to tell his story and then interrupted himself. "He said he was disillusioned after giving history to white people," Hart says. "They only write it up wrong and make money from it; the Indian gets nothing, and then has to read the lies." His wife, then seventy-nine, told Hart that she and the bishop hoped that their daughter would take up the tale. Mae Timbimboo Parry had heard the story, as a child, from her grandfather Yeager's own lips. She had written down the story she heard from him.

After the bishop's passing in 1975, Hart contacted Parry. She agreed to give him her story for *SourceBook*, but Hart reports that writing it down was a painful process for her. He quotes a letter she wrote him: "You will never know how much courage and fortitude it took me to write this account. There were times I had to put the papers away because I could not see for the tears I could not stop from flowing."

Hart says that when he visited Parry, he saw a large box of papers, her collection of historical materials. "There are a number of things that both she and her parents have told me," he says. "I feel, however, that they should be left for her to tell in her own way. I sat staring at her big box of papers . . . the pot at the end of the rainbow . . . and had to keep reminding myself, 'No, no—that is *hers*, it is her story, not *mine*.'

"I felt," he concludes, "as greedy as the invaders of the 1860s."

8

WARNER

I visit Curtis Warner—who calls Mae Parry his "great-aunt" though in European American genealogical terms she's a distant cousin—on yet another in this string of hot days, the day after the death of Tamise's African violet, which, in the end, had proved unsalvageable in this odd heat. Extra water was too much water. Less water was not enough water. Nothing I tried was successful in reducing the distress the poor darkening leaves were suffering. The purple and yellow bloom had closed days ago.

I don't know how I'm going to tell Tamise about her violet; but what I'm really het up about today is that this also happens to be the day after the Pioneer Days Parade in Pocatello. And it's the day after the Aryan Nation stages a much-disputed march through Coeur d'A-lene, in the northern part of the state. These two events may seem un-related, but they take up the entire front page of the Sunday paper that morning, and the juxtaposition leads to jarring conclusions.

Pioneer Days is not, as easterners might think, a time to celebrate the Oregon Trail or some such. It's a reminiscence that runs the entire month of July, to commemorate the arrival of the Mormon settlers in Utah and Idaho. It's an appreciation of hard work and sacrifice, a recitation of the terrible hardships those original pioneers suffered so that subsequent generations of Mormons might enjoy a prosperous, persecution-free existence. "Twenty-fourth of July Day" celebrates the anniversary of Brigham Young's arrival at the mouth of Emigration Canyon ("This is the [right] place!"). These celebrations proceed with no recognition of the Shoshone who were ousted by said emigration; their persecution, sacrifices, and lack of prosperity go unnarrated. So

the existence of Aryan Nation activity in the state, while harshly decried by state leaders, is not quite the anomaly it might seem.

Good fences make good neighbors.

I'm OK, you're OK.

Thus do the northern and southern portions of Idaho, seemingly
so politically disparate, peacefully coexist.

In the late nineteenth century, it's worth noting, Mormons in
Idaho were not permitted to hold office. These days, many state leaders are Mormon.

I use the newspaper to dispose of Tamise's poor violet.

Warner's wife Mallory, then an accountant for a video store chain,
keeps their two-year-old son Tyler at bay so Warner and I can sit at
their kitchen table, under a ceiling fan, in their comfortable new home
on the northeast side of town. We're just a few miles from the border
of the Fort Hall Reservation. They've just moved in, and one of those
clocks that chimes each hour with a different bird call goes off twice
while we're talking. The clock was a gift for Tyler, he explains. Before
him on the table Warner has a copy of the National Park Service study
and a neatly organized, three-ring binder containing papers pertaining
to the band's business, separated by carefully labeled tabs.

I ask him how he feels when he sees coverage of things like Pioneer Days dominating the local broadcast and print media. "I didn't
attend," he says wryly. "I ignore it. I mean, what can we do? It's
something that's gone on for years—we've never had any involvement with it, have never been asked."

Warner was himself baptized in the LDS church, "because it was
the thing to do here. Everybody was. It was a thing you had to do. I
had no idea what I was doing." He was about twelve or thirteen at
the time, he says, and all of his school friends were going to youth
camps and other things that looked like fun. "But I never stepped
foot in a church," he says. His wife's family was LDS, he says, but
they're no longer active. She has resisted the pressure to baptize Tyler,
deciding that that should be his choice when he's older.

We change the subject to the Park Service project. Since Warner
left his job as director of cultural resources for the tribe, and began
working for the U.S. Department of Agriculture as a program techni-
cian, inspecting fields that have been put into fallow with the Conservation Resource Program, he understands the landowners'
objections to the proposed site a bit better, he says. Having spent a lot
of time with white farmers, he's more sympathetic. "I think I'm

grasping their values, their way of life—being worried about it being jeopardized, or having it taken away, something their family passed on for generations. Having that taken away threatens them, and anything that threatens them, they're going to stand up for. I understand their beliefs, but I think there can be some compromise. You know how it is. You mention that the government's going to come in and you automatically have that stereotype that the government's just going to take it and put it all into this national park. 'We're not going to be paid for it, or benefit from it or anything and we ain't going to have no say in it.' So immediately they put up their guard, like what you see in Preston."

Warner feels confident, though, that the alternatives proposed by the Park Service suggest that the government is willing to get some input from both sides to develop a compromise, so that "they understand where we're coming from, and we understand why they're so concerned. And meet in the middle somehow."

I ask Warner if it's really possible to implement this project without somebody getting hurt. "No," he says, "I don't think you can believe something like that." In that case, why do it at all? "Remember," he replies, "I'm in the archaeology part of it. I'm looking at preservation and protection of graves. When I go there and I hear from different people in the area that they've seen skeletal remains— or I see cattle grazing over them, and junk piles and stuff—that is degrading to me, and I would like to see that protected. We don't want to see bones coming out, or people digging wherever they want to dig without first investigating. That's just our belief. And the only way to really do that is to get it under federal ownership. The state doesn't have laws and regulations to protect things like that. They're more for farmers' rights, private owners' rights."

But also, Warner says, "I want the story told. When I was little, I remember my grandfather telling me stories about it, and other people—going to council meetings and other people telling me, 'You know who you are, you know where you're from, you know what happened over there by Preston.'" When Warner's family lived in Montana, his father brought him down to the site to see it. "When I got older I started reading books and really getting into it—I couldn't believe it. Is this true? Did this really happen? And there aren't hardly any books about it. It wasn't taught in school, it wasn't like Wounded Knee, it's not on TBS every weekend. It isn't really publicized. I questioned that—why?"

I ask for Warner's opinion as to why the story isn't common knowledge to people. "It was during the time of the Civil War," he says, "and there wasn't much attention paid by the government or the journalists." Warner visited the National Archives in Washington, DC, and found "very little. You'd see all this Civil War stuff and maybe some stuff in California and then you'd see a little article about a skirmish between Indians and the whites. That was it, and I thought that was interesting. So I started digging into it."

And of course the incident caught his attention for personal reasons. "I wanted to learn about my history. It's interesting to find your grandfather's name in a book, so of course, I wanted to learn more about him. I never met my great-grandfather, and I wanted to learn about what he did."

Warner says that he knows little about his ancestry prior to Sagwitch—"Mae knows the father and mother of Sagwitch," he says—but next in his own family tree is his great-grandfather Frank Timbimboo Warner, two years old at the time of the massacre and later adopted by a Mormon family. Frank Warner converted to Mormonism, became a schoolteacher, and was well-known and admired by whites and Shoshone alike as an intellectual and Native American activist. Warner's grandfather was Wayne Timbimboo Warner; his father is Neal Warner.

He has tons of cousins, he says—not least due to the Shoshone practice of polygyny. "Sagwitch married a number of wives. I've been told he had six, and I've also been told that in different tribes he had married wives and had children, with some of the Western Shoshone. It really needs to be researched." Warner says that the multiple marriages of the nineteenth-century Shoshone differ from Mormon polygyny. "It wasn't meant to have all these wives for status. There was a purpose for it, whether it was survival or to provide for a family, for a certain group of people." He's read several anthropologists on the subject; but then, he says, "you talk to the elders and they don't seem to recall anything about it."

Warner adds that he feels keenly "a responsibility" to tell the story, but he doesn't know why. "Several of the elders have said, 'There's a reason why you're doing this. You didn't just all of a sudden one day wake up and decide you wanted to learn about this. A lot of people in this tribe have no interest. There's a reason. Someone may be watching you or pushing you to do this. Someone wants the story to be told.' That's always pushed me." He sees it as a spiritual matter. "I would like to feel that my ancestors are watching over me, and watching everything I do, and appreciating things I do. I'm doing it for them. I feel this should be told, because we are here today for the things they had to go through. They survived the Bear River Massacre. It's kind of sad to see us now, politically fighting amongst each other, when they went through something like that for the tribe. If they were to watch us now, fighting over money—it's really degrading. I would hope that something like this could unite the tribe, as well as have the rest of the world recognize the Northwestern band of the Shoshoni and what we went through. I think there's a lot of stuff the LDS church needs to—I'd be interested in knowing their side of the story. I think there's a lot of hidden history in there that needs to be told."

And he wants to correct misperceptions about the status of his people. European Americans today have the wrong idea about contemporary natives, Warner says. "People say, 'Yeah, they went through the reservation period and it was a horrible time, starving and everything, but now today look at them. They all have ten acres of land, they all have land—whether they chose to sell it or lease it out was their choice. But at least they had some land personally.' I would love to have some land for my family," Warner says.

Today, he reminds me, the Northwestern band has only 180 acres, the remains of the Washakie settlement set up by the church, unacknowledged as a reservation until 1980. "My dad's dad had some land in Washakie," where Warner's father grew up, "probably only two or three acres. But it was owned by the church and later put into trust." The history of the Washakie settlement is complicated and vague—not least, Warner says, because history books end the Northwestern Shoshoni story with the massacre—but the bottom line is that the Northwestern band was not recognized as a separate tribe (the federal government recognizes separate bands as "tribes") until 1980. It was thought that they did not exist, had been wiped out by the massacre.

He applauds Mae Parry for having worked with the state of Utah for recognition and support, but the state of Idaho still says the tribe doesn't exist. Recently, a member who fished waters included in Northwestern treaty rights was arrested for violating fish and game restrictions. When lawyers argued that the Northwestern Shoshoni have aboriginal treaty rights in those waters, the state of Idaho announced that it does not recognize the Northwestern as a federal tribe, especially since the Northwestern were not given reservation lands. "The state's ready to go all the way," Warner says. "They say, 'You guys are from Utah.' And I find that interesting. Where do they get these borders? I don't understand that. Who cares about these artificial borders that have been put on Idaho and Utah. You cross the border and you're out—you can't come in here? It's ridiculous to me." State recognition is crucial because states are the first level of treaty enforcement. "The Box Elder treaty and the Fort Bridger treaty both recognized our aboriginal territory, and within those aboriginal territories we were permitted to hunt and fish and gather. That was the agreement. And yet I don't know what's happened to it. The state says, 'We don't recognize you, you're not a federally recognized tribe.' I said, 'OK, we're not? That's interesting. Here's my tribal I.D.'"

Other tribes that have land, Warner says, are "building. They're rising. There are still a lot of problems, obviously, still a poverty-stricken people." Warner feels that if the Northwestern Shoshoni had been given reservation land in the nineteenth century, the tribe would have prospered from the opportunity. "But we weren't because the government said, 'These LDS people are taking care of them, why should we have to worry about them?' Especially after the massacre. And I wonder. Why is it that the church felt this need to put us under their wing and show us how to farm? Is it because they felt a responsibility after what took place? And in a way I think they did. But what do we have today? We have 180 acres and that's just because we have a graveyard there. It came from the church, not from the government.

"Before, Washakie was a large area. People lived all the way from Malad down to Tremonton and Brigham City, scattered all over with farms and homesteads. It was parceled out over time." Then earlier in the twentieth century, Warner says, massacre survivors were some of the first Native Americans to establish homesteads and give up their heritage, applying for U.S. citizenship; later in the century, many members intermarried with whites and Chicanos. "The way it was told to me," Warner says, "the problem was that they would still maintain their traditional ways of life. They would still go out hunting, on seasonal trips, and come back two, three months later and find that these white farmers had taken over their land and said these guys had abandoned it." After World War II, when there was less work for young people, a number left the area to find jobs in the city, or at the Hill Air Force Base north of Salt Lake City, near where Mae Parry lives now.

"You'll hear a different story from Mae," Warner says, but his understanding is that the church burned down the supposedly "abandoned" houses. Some of these were the homes of commuters who worked in Brigham City during the week and returned for weekends to see their families. "Story goes that they paid tribal elders five bucks a house, and burned them." Then the church sold the land to white (Mormon) farmers—land the Northwestern Shoshoni thought was theirs, but never had been really, because it had only been held in trust by the church. Parry, Warner says, led the demand for tribal recognition, because there were people with no place to go, and Sagwitch's grave needed protection.

The band is currently researching deeds to farms in the northern Utah area; some attempt may be made to reclaim land that was illegally taken. "We went out and talked to some of the farmers, and some of them didn't know where their grandfathers got the land. A lot of them remembered their dads telling them, 'Yeah that used to be an Indian home over there and we don't know what happened to them.' And now they're farming the land. Well, whose land is it? You go look for the deed and there's no deed on it. But it's just kind of been accepted, and no one's done anything about it."

Warner says his band, whose enrollment fluctuates but tends to total around 450 (about what it was at the moment of the massacre), doesn't have the money to hire big tribal attorneys "to come in and say, 'Look, this is the Northwestern band, this is their aboriginal territory, they demand water rights, fishing and hunting rights, per their treaty agreements'—things that we need—and establish a reservation." Some people want to live on a reservation, he says, and some people don't, but the choice should be available. "There are a lot of tribal members that need that source of income and housing," he says. He'd like to see the band buy land around the Washakie area, for schools, housing, hotels, truck stops, other services. Southeastern Idaho boasts one of the busiest Powerball lottery-ticket outlets in the country, frequented as it is by buyers visiting from lottery-prohibitive Utah, and Warner thinks a casino might be profitable in northern Utah.

"Maybe we would have a casino, start building stuff up ourselves, start making a name for the tribe. It's the only way we can do that, because we have such a small tribe, and very little money." The band currently has a tribal council with monthly meetings, and an office staff in southeastern Idaho, most of which is funded by grants through the Bureau of Indian Affairs, the band's only source of income (a new office has since opened in northern Utah as well). Warner's former position, for instance, was financed by a natural resource grant, which paid for an officer to provide hunting and fishing tags, and to develop cultural preservation projects. For now, health care is contracted through the Shoshone–Bannock facilities in Fort Hall, but the Sho–Ban Council would prefer to work solely for their own members. The Northwestern Shoshoni are at risk of losing that source of health care.

The band's future is insecure without land, Warner says, "because that seems to be the precedent in Indian Country. You've got to have land. We want to be able to learn our history, have powwows, sun dances, but you really need more land. We're small, but if you provide these services, people will move back from all around, helping out where they can.

"The Bear River Massacre site," he concludes, "if it were put into national park status, would definitely help us. We have to be careful and there are things we will have to approach as we go, but other tribes who have some sort of national park have benefited from it. People from all over the world come to these places—tourists, books, movies—these are things the tribe can benefit from." He agrees that the Lakota, who have the best-known site at Wounded Knee, still struggle as a nation despite the presence of the site, but he feels that the cases are different. "We're a small tribe and most of us were not waiting around for handouts. Most of us have had to learn to survive and haven't had any government money to help out. Everybody has their own life and their own job. We're more interested in just telling the story, and I think that from the start, if we watched, if we didn't let someone come in and take over the story—we need to watch carefully everything that happens.

"We want it in the tribe's hands," he says, referring to the proposed park. "That was the thing from the start—some of the tribal members wanted total control. They felt the government shouldn't be involved." He notes that one of the proposed alternatives would leave Franklin County in charge of the site. "We didn't want that. We've seen that the only real way is federal acquisition of the site. We have a government-to-government relationship with the federal government. That works out better than the state or local level. In a lot of legislation, whether it be cultural preservation or cultural resource management laws, states are always worse to deal with. They're always fighting regulation of states' rights." The federal government, he says, has a trust responsibility to the tribes—a paternalistic obligation to care for the descendants of natives the United States has dispossessed. The desire for a trust relationship can be difficult to reconcile with the desire for sovereignty, but in this case Warner feels that honoring the treaties will support sovereignty. "I feel we should continue that trust responsibility, and if it requires them to help us out with establishing this park, then that's what should happen."

A project such as this one could serve to unify factions within the band; and if that happened, members might feel they had more reason to remain enrolled, and involved in self-government. "I've seen quite a few people that just wanted out. There was nothing here for them. They were sick of the bickering and the fighting and they could go somewhere else to another tribe and have more benefits with them. There is so much this tribe could benefit from, if we can get over our own bickering and our own family feuds."

Warner himself felt forced to quit his post with the band, an unfortunate decision not least because the flexible, half-time hours permitted him to continue to work on his anthropology degree. On this day, he is still a few courses shy of graduation and plans eventually to study for a master's. But his paychecks were inconsistent, which was difficult for a college student with a family. There have been a few "government shutdowns," he says wryly, when funding was pulled and the entire operation ground to a halt. He often worked to prepare a proposal only to have the council fail to take action to implement it. The band continues to call him with consulting projects. "In a way it's sad," he says. "I love doing it, and I love talking to people and learning history, meeting more of the tribal members and getting to know them. I just can't deal with the political stress. It wasn't worth it. My hope is that they'll get things resolved." Or maybe, he says, if the Park Service opened a cultural resource center at the massacre site, he could serve there with other members.

We talk about the possible causes of the community fracture Warner so regrets. He acknowledges that perhaps an unusually high number of Northwestern Shoshoni assimilated—abandoned traditional ways for European American ways—because there was no economic support, no reservation on which to build the unified community necessary for the perpetuation of lifeways. Warner suspects that there may be hidden problems with the nineteenth-century conversion of many survivors to the LDS religion, problems he can only guess at. The influence of the Mormon church may have hastened that assimilation process; today, the band is often split politically between members devoted to the church and those who question its influence on council decisions. Often his projects get caught in the crossfire between the two factions. On the council, he says, before a recent election, "three members over here were against the other three members over here. And why was that? Well, you had three Timbimboos over here, and you had three other ones from the other side. Three of them from Utah and three of them from Idaho. There was never consensus on anything." He'd spend weeks on a grant he thought could benefit the band, and then need a resolution from the council. "Well, these guys aren't voting. They're upset about something. Or they never met. It was pointless. There was always this bickering. So no tribal resolutions got passed, nothing got done."

The factions are the result of a vast history. "If you go over here to Fort Hall, and you meet some of the members that have lived on the reservation all their life—completely different beliefs. But those around Salt Lake City where the Timbimboos live, they're kind of in the white world. They've done things with white people, trust white people. You go over here," he says, waving his thumb to the north, toward Fort Hall, "and they don't. Not at all. These people remain traditional, still living their ways—not *traditional* ways, but still attend sun dances, sweats every weekend—whereas these other people go to church every weekend, and that's their new religion."

Warner struggles with his own questions about religion, feeling like he's halfway between two worlds. He thinks maybe he should be doing sun dances, since he feels more comfortable with the older ways, and doesn't think his religion should be confined to a church. "But I'm fearful of going in there," he says. "It's like, 'You're not enough Indian. You can't do that.' I get a lot of that." Consequently, he says, he makes things up for himself as he goes along. "It's kind of a learning experience."

This not-enough-Indian problem has also affected his ability to work on the Park Service project. "When you start talking about the massacre, to people, to tribal elders, it's a touchy issue. There are a lot of strong emotions about it still, and it comes out. Some people didn't even want to talk to me. They said, 'You're a Timbimboo, aren't you?' 'Yeah.' 'You're related to Mae, aren't you?' 'Yeah, and I'm probably related to you, too. What does it matter?' I'm amazed at some of the people—we are so small that we're probably all related, somewhere down the line. And yet, it's 'I'm not going to talk to you about that. You already know it all. All you're going to believe is your family's story.'" Actually, Warner says, he accepts the Parry story as being the one his family knows, but believes there are other stories equally valid.

Then too, there's a language barrier. Warner has been studying Shoshone, he says, but "I don't speak Shoshone fluently enough. I can understand it, but I can't speak it as well. 'Don't talk to me unless you can speak in your native tongue.' So I'm trying all these things and I get shot down."

This fracture, Warner agrees, reflects the still-lingering impact of the Indian Reorganization Act of the 1930s, which required tribal governments to organize as majority-rule, elected "democracies." Perhaps contemporary Shoshone haven't adapted easily to the imposition of more rigid, European American concepts of government, in which a 51% majority can possess 100% of the power, while a 49% minority gets 0%.

But this fracture also reflects remnants of traditional Shoshone lifeways, when people would follow the leader of the choice, moving to follow a different leader later if they no longer approved of the first. "There were," Warner says, "within the Northwestern band, several bands. Originally, Sagwitch's people were around the Promontory area. Bear Hunter's people were from the Brigham City–Tremonton area. Pocatello's people were up in Grouse Creek, near the City of Rocks. There were some that were over in the Cache Valley area, and some up here in the Portneuf Valley area. That was just a way to survive. It wasn't like you had to stay here."

He's thought about this a lot, he says, as he's struggled to understand where the intracultural differences come from. "I can pick out certain tribal members. As soon as you go and meet them they're always angry, really violent. Why is that? If you go back and look, certain bands were more war parties, or they went with other tribes that were." Sagwitch didn't believe in violence, Warner says.

Money is always a hot issue on the council. For instance, Warner says, when NAGPRA (the Native American Graves Protection and Repatriation Act) was passed, it was not accompanied by a federal appropriation to finance the return of remains now required by law. "Museums and other federal agencies were given money to conduct inventories, but the tribes were never given a dime. There are a number of grants tribes can get, but grants aren't steady funding—it might not be there in ten years. It might be, but it might not. Until the tribe is self-sufficient—but how can we do that unless we have land?" The economic base is lacking, he says.

History is another hot issue. A lot of the differences, he says, "have to do with jealousy. There's Bear Hunter's family and his descendants, and then there's Sagwitch's family, and then there's the ones in between." These latter, he says, are descendants of Sanpitch and others, but the Bear Hunter and Sagwitch families dominate tribal politics. Some of the tension revolves around academic history, particularly the way European American historical methods have intruded into band relationships. "Bear Hunter's descendants say Sagwitch was never there. He wasn't a chief. And I agree. I don't think he was a chief, and I don't think Bear Hunter was a chief. I don't think there were chiefs. That's just another label. A white guy comes in with a piece of paper and says, 'Who's the leader here?' A chief back then wasn't someone that signed papers. It was just a person they followed. 'Hey, he knows where the best hunting is. We're going to follow Sagwitch. He knows where the elk are.' He was just somebody that people followed and looked up to. People on Bear Hunter's side get upset that Sagwitch has this recognition now. When they see his story being told, then they've got a story. 'That wasn't the way it was. Sagwitch wasn't there.'

"But the fact of it is, I told every one of them, 'If you guys want to be a Mae Parry, I can get plenty of people that would be willing to come and talk to you and take down everything you say.'" There is no storyteller for the Bear Hunter family, and consequently the story hasn't been heard much outside the tribe, he says. Warner worries that an attempt to recuperate that "side" of the story could backfire on the tribe. "We're going to have tribal members within tribal members publishing information saying, 'Sagwitch wasn't nothing, the whole Bear River Massacre story was a crock.' It's going to look bad for us."

And often, money and history seem to be inexorably linked. "They feel we're getting all this money. 'You're going to get rich off this stuff,'" Bear Hunter's descendants have said. Since the Park Service made its proposal, some of the Bannock now say their people were present that day. "They want a piece of that pie," Warner says.

Parry, he asserts, fell into the role of primary storyteller because—ironically—she had many things written down. "It's a lot easier for someone to talk to her because she has it all. She knows what you want to know, she knows what questions you're going to ask." Warner is a bit concerned about Parry's certainty regarding her story. "She might even argue that there is no other story, that this is the way it happened. I don't agree with that."

A multi-band approach to the story might be useful, but the relationship between the Northwestern band and the much larger Shoshone–Bannock reservation is "not good," Warner says, which could explain why there's so little about the massacre in the Sho–Ban Museum. The Lemhis and Shoshone–Bannock interact well, he says, but the Northwestern cousins tend to be ostracized some. "I don't know what it is. There are certain people at Fort Hall who won't talk to me because they know I'm a Northwestern. One woman looked at me once and said, 'You know why I don't talk to you?' I said, 'No.' She said, 'Because your tribe's a sellout. You guys sold all your land and just let the government take over.' I said, 'I think you don't know anything about our tribe.' I said, 'We had no choice. We didn't sell anything. If we did sell something, I would have something. I don't know where you got that.'"

So the proposed park has several purposes, he says. "Not just to tell everybody the story of what happened, but to bring out a lot of things that should be out. Our tribal elders are dying every day. The more they die the more those stories are gone. It needs to be somehow recorded, put down—whatever. Books and everything are great, but I'd really like it if tribal members could go to the massacre field, have ceremonies, do what we need to do, take our children there, explain our history. Just like anybody else. If we had the money to do it, I know we'd do it in a heartbeat."

Warner isn't sure who will tell the Sagwitch story after Mae. "I would hope a number of people do," he says. He thinks that keeping the story with one person has drawbacks, and he would prefer to see a collection of stories providing multiple perspectives of the event. When oral culture flourished, this was how it operated. "Every family's going to have a different story of what took place, and over time things are going to change, and you're going to put it your own way and glorify your family over others. Of course you're going to do that. But I think there are things in the stories that are the same, and if we work together somehow—you'd have a whole other story, with whole other heroes."

He would like to be involved in the telling of the story. "I'll continue to do this, I'll continue to do whatever I can to help the tribe—not just for the tribe but for myself, and my family—that's Mae's whole thing. She's not trying to benefit herself. She's thinking of her family. She's thinking, 'Hey this stuff needs to be told. I want my grandkids to know this so their grandkids can know.' This is her only way."

I ask him how he responds to Parry's lament that young people today don't know what it is to be an Indian—an interesting complaint in light of his own assertion that the Salt Lake Shoshone, including Parry, live in a "white" world. "You have to remember," Warner says, "Mae's a very highly spoken person; people look up to her." He shakes his head. "I get that—'You're not Indian, you don't know Indian.' What is Indian? That's the thing I question. What is Indian? What's the difference? Nothing can ever change. I was born by my dad, he was born by his dad, I have Indian blood, I can't get rid of it, that's the way I am. I'm willing to learn. I know I don't practice traditional ways. I'm willing to learn about them.

"Are you Indian because you're darker?" he continues. "My dad's dark, he looks Indian." Warner reminds me what he told me three years earlier: that while he was in the service, his father wouldn't talk much about being native, until twelve or thirteen years ago when he moved back to the area. Neal Warner now works for the band, which makes him feel proud to be a Native American. He ran the most recent tribal election. "Is he Indian? Do you call him Indian?"

It strikes me that Warner never talks about his mother. "That's because the whole history is on my dad's side." His mother, he says, is Polish; his parents live nearby. But he identifies more with his father's background. "My mom said that to me one time, and it made me feel bad. 'You're doing all this history on your dad's side of the family, but you don't know anything about mine.' I said, 'You know, that's true, I should start looking into that.'" Warner says he'll probably end up spending his life researching the two very disparate cultures that make up his family background. He doesn't find his mother's history less compelling, he says, but given the career he's chosen—anthropology and archaeology—his father's side ties in more with his primary academic interests.

But he does not want to approach these interests in an exclusively academic way. "A lot of the tribal elders deal with oral history, and what they've been told. And I've always been very careful, because I've seen a lot of professors that walked up with big brains and said, 'Hey, I know everything about your tribe.'" Warner's status as an anthropology student makes him even more suspect in the eyes of some of his cousins. "'You're a college kid,' first of all, so 'you know everything, why do you need me to tell you anything. You're not going to listen to me.' I was careful about it, but a lot of people just did not want to talk to me, were upset from the very first, didn't know me, didn't want to talk to me. I tried everything. Some people I got in arguments with. It was sad for me. I was trying everything to help the tribe and I got these people yelling at me that don't even know me."

Warner isn't concerned about the preponderance of white folks who seem to be telling the story on behalf of the Shoshone because he is counting on the Park Service to live up to its agreement to involve Shoshone oral historians. "The whole thing was to provide funding to train tribal members to take oral history." Part of his job was to teach band members to take the stories of those who would not talk to Warner himself. "I pictured it in my head—all these oral histories from different families. That's what I wanted, because then everybody in the tribe could be happy." Anybody who felt their story wasn't being heard could come down and be recorded or transcribed. He also imagines a cultural center at the site where, at certain times, different tribal elders would come to tell their story to visitors.

"We did not want this as a white, Madsen-type of book, something published. We're willing to incorporate academics and what they've been told—they have the expertise." But Warner wants to include a variety of types of expertise in this process. "It's always amazing to me. In anthropology, I learn about all these great anthropologists with all these theories and we're supposed to follow these theories. Why? Well, they decided this should be conducted this way and this is why these people do this. So everybody takes a piece of each book and cites information. So to me, you aren't even telling a story, you're just gathering information off other people's books. Where's the truth in it? Did you go talk to people?

"I have seen some good Indian books that just tell oral stories that have been written." Books are useful, Warner says, but need to be seen as just one part of a wider truth-telling mechanism. "I've talked to some members of the Shoshone–Bannocks and they don't like anything in books, don't believe anything. And some members of our tribe say, 'Yeah, get all the books you can, let's get the information about it. We're learning about our history too.' But then we take it, pick through it, get what we want out of it, what we feel is true.

"That's how I took Madsen's book. It wasn't a great source of information I needed." Warner acknowledges that when last we spoke, he felt differently about Madsen's book; but he was just beginning to study the history then. "You look at someone like Madsen who's published all these books, and he's written something about you and your family—and I'd heard Mae's story, and I read Madsen and thought, 'Hey, it's all here!'" But then Warner took anthropology classes that taught him something about how perspectives can differ. "I don't think Madsen's even talked to anybody else. He never approached anybody besides people that had already been recognized, like Mae Parry.

"After I started talking to more tribal elders and learning more that way, instead of just academically, out of a book, one tribal elder told me, 'You can read all the books you want, but you're not going to learn anything. You think all your knowledge is up here'"— Warner points to his head—"'but it's out there.'" He's pointing out his sliding doors now, at the patio. "'All your people. That's where your knowledge comes from. It doesn't come from your books. You listen to your people.' And that's what I did, but I use both." Still, oral history, Warner says, is "the most important part."

Even when memory is flawed, Warner says, even when stories conflict, oral histories are still useful, because accuracy, he says, is not his primary concern. "If this is something that you have held deeply in your heart, in your family, about what you were told, there's got to be some reason you remember this." He repeats his idea that similarities can be located among the different stories. "If anything, people romanticize a story, and that's normal. I don't think you should ever degrade somebody that has been willing to tell you something that's been in their family for generations. Madsen would take Mae's story and say, 'Well, this is what this person said,' and then reevaluate it. That's degrading. That's when we get into trouble." He's also concerned about academic control of cultural materials. Photographs of band members are stored at Utah State University; "we want to at least get copies."

Warner agrees that having whites like Madsen, Allie Hansen—and me—telling the massacre story is a problem for some Shoshone, but says that, often, having anyone tell the story is a controversial act. Many people in the band, he says, want the story told, because they believe as he does that getting the truth out will benefit the people. But then, he says, some members refuse to speak with researchers. "In a lot of ways they're scared. Of criticism. Afraid maybe they're not intelligent enough—stuff like that. It really does scare them." He recalls an appointment he made for three elders to speak before a historical society. Only one showed. "They all wanted to do it, and they were all excited about it, and all of sudden they just didn't show up. The one that showed had a hard time, getting in front of these old white people who wanted to hear about it. They were fascinated by it, and after she learned that these people really do want to learn, then she opened up and told everything. She cried when she told it. People were really sympathetic. I wish I could get everybody to realize that, that these people want to learn about it, but they bitch and moan: 'Nothing's being told, just the Mae Parry side.' I say, 'Well, come out and tell them.' That's why I'm inviting them to these functions."

I ask Warner about the rapes. Does he agree with Parry, or with Madsen? Does he think they happened?

He does. "I think so. I think there were a lot of things that happened after that massacre that are really sad. That's where I think the anger comes out—a lot of tribal members told that part of the story, not just the killing." Warner first read about the rape in Madsen's book, and then asked elders. "Mostly it was women that knew about it, particularly one that knew about it. Maybe there's a reason for that." He spoke with three women who say they heard their mothers talk about it. "It's unwritten history—not just the rapes or a lot of disgusting things that went on afterwards, from bashing in heads to body parts being cut off. These California Volunteers were brutal. You get a group of men that went that far, in that time, and wanted to be somewhere other than where they were, and then someone like Connor—evil people."

Warner has read, in Hart's book, the stories of the veterans who suffered all their lives from the memory of that incident. "You're ordered to do something, but you have different people with different personalities. Some of them hated Indians, some of them had that belief that they're not human, they're just like animals. So you kill them, you beat them, you have no human emotions for them. And some probably had that in the back of their heads, 'We're killing these children, these babies, these women.'"

For this reason, Warner says, oral histories from the white settlers, witnesses, should also be included. "Where are their stories?" Warner asks. "I'd like to know that."

When I ask if Warner is concerned about the Park Service's exclusion of the rape story, he corrects me irritably. "Everybody's thinking that the Park Service is going to tell the story. They're going to bring in their own anthropologists and they're going to say, 'Let's take Mae's story and put this on a nice big board and have some signs over here and we'll take some people on tours.' No. No. That isn't the way and we had that understanding. And it will be that understanding—it won't be like that." With Shoshone involvement in the park, Warner feels confident that the "hidden" stories, such as the rape, will get told. "My understanding was that there will be oral histories, and anthropologists to help. I've worked with anthropologists and been traveling, I've learned to take what I want, instead of them always coming in and taking what they want. You see several of these anthropologists or archaeologists who come in and seem really interested and want all this stuff—but there's always a goal, a single goal that they want. And we're left with nothing. We didn't benefit from it."

For now, he feels, the band has to use the Park Service as the only means of establishing the site. But the original understanding was that "we have the rights here, and we're going to be the one telling the story, not the Park Service. We understand that there's going to be a lot of involvement from the Park Service, of course. But in the end the tribe's going to have the say on what happens, what goes there, what needs to go here." Whether the Shoshone have to share control with, for instance, the Pioneer Days committee—well, that's a bridge they'll have to cross, but "when it arises we're going to have to say no, we're going to be the sole player here. We want to run this place." If it's organized in any other way, "we'd probably protest out in front of it, that we're not involved in this. They came to council and they said, 'We want you guys to tell the stories, we'd love to see you have tribal members working there, have oral histories told on a regular basis, having functions, having ceremonies.' That's what we'd like to see."

But sole player? Warner softens his position. "I think there's got to be a federal government overseeing it. But you've got to have a tribal member in there at all times, an elder." Warner mentions another massacre site run by the Park Service but staffed by natives who guide tours of the site. "I feel that the public would rather see a member of the tribe answering questions and taking them out and showing them what happened, rather than a Park Service person."

That bridge yet to be crossed may be a good distance away. Warner joins Parry and Hansen in reporting that he hasn't heard a thing about the status of the proposal for almost two years. Via the Internet, he keeps an eye on the agenda of the relevant congressional subcommittee, but the matter has not been scheduled so far. "Now we're in a situation," he says, "where we really need someone up there in DC pushing this thing forward, talking to representatives." Senator Larry Craig, he says, has a reputation for supporting farmers' rights. "So it should be interesting."

Craig's stall is unfortunate, given the need to recapture history. There was a time, Warner says, when the Northwestern band was the envy of other tribes. People would come down from Fort Hall, he says, and see the farms around Washakie, and how the church was helping people out, how everyone had homes and work. "A lot of tribes looked up to us. And what did we get? In the end, nothing."

As he talks, Warner points out that his concern about providing some land—land, which can be "a way of life and well-being," a place where "you can do whatever you want on it, build a home, pass it on to your children, a way of saying you're here"—this sentiment, he realizes, "is probably the way the farmers feel," the ones in Preston who would be dislocated by the proposed historic site in Preston.

"I just want us to be recognized," Warner says—by European Americans *and* Native Americans. He speaks of going to Native American conferences, wearing a name tag marked with his enrollment as a Northwestern Shoshoni. Other natives see this and ask if he's from Alaska. "They say, 'Oh yeah, Shoshone–Bannock.' I always ask, 'Have you heard of the Bear River Massacre?' 'No.' Of course. I do that just to see." Getting that story out, he feels, is the only way—particularly without land on which to build a presence—to draw attention to their survival. "If this comes out, you'll see members of our tribe uniting, some who don't even know about it, that have maybe heard bits and pieces about it." Warner has cousins, he says, "with maybe a sixteenth or an eighth Indian in them, who don't even know. They have a right to that history. It's been hidden, suppressed. If you grow up in the white world, like I have, you don't hear about it, so why should you be interested in it? Unless you're told, like I was. Then it becomes your problem, your history, and you want to know and you have a right to know."

If the Park Service builds Alternative 4, "they'll know. That's what our tribe needs. We have nothing to look forward to. You go to every council meeting and see the same people there. You see somebody you've never seen before, and you find out who he is, or who she is, and they've finally decided to come—and there's no reason for them to come. They don't want to listen to fighting and bickering. If there were some major event, it would bring people back together, more and more people that could help in a lot of ways. I'd like to see everybody unite, and hopefully something good will come out of it."

9

POLITICS

CRAIG (1998)

So, after years of a highly unusual acceleration through procedures, the proposal to establish a National Historic Site on the Bear River Massacre field has crawled to a stop, stalled since February 1996 in the office of Senator Larry Craig (R-Idaho). As of July 1998, Senator Craig's office seems to be sending mixed signals, with the landowners feeling, as Kathy Griffin noted, that the proposal has been "put on a back burner" and unlikely to succeed "in our lifetimes"; while Allie Hansen's Monument Committee has the impression that things are moving slowly, but still moving.

Who can propose the legislation to establish a National Historic Site on the field of the Bear River Massacre? Holly Bundock, of the National Park Service, reports that any member of Congress may do so. However, she continues, "whether such legislation gets heard before the House committee if it's not sponsored by the representative of the district is another question." Precedent has it that there is a "will" of the House Authorizing Committee, she says, "to not address any legislation on land management that the local congressperson does not support."

In effect, then, the legislation must be sponsored by Idaho's congressional delegation.

A conversation on June 29, 1998, with Greg Rice, Senator Craig's Pocatello-area regional director, revealed that although the senator has had, since early 1996, the Franklin County commissioners' recommendation to commence the process of declaring the area a historic site, legislation is still not being written. Craig toured the site, as both Griffin and Hansen report, in January 1998. Now, Rice adds, "the senator is planning a hearing for public input, late this summer or early this fall." Following the hearing, "we would put something together." Asked why the senator feels the need to repeat the National Park Service's hearings, Rice says, "We need to gather our own information and base the legislation on that."

CRAIG (2002)

As we go to press, local community members report that no hearings have been held by Senator Craig. Will Hart, spokesman for Senator Craig, confirms in November 2002 that no hearings are in the immediate offing. "It's in the hands of the stakeholders," Hart says, "who can't agree on what the designation should be. There has to be an agreement on the ground before we can proceed with legislation. Senator Craig believes in the collaborative process," he adds, "but also believes Congress should not mandate legislation in the face of no agreement."

These stakeholders among whom the senator would have to find consensus include the National Park Service, the local community, the local church, the local group which originally requested that a historic site be established, and the state.

Asked if the senator would have to have 100% agreement from all parties, Hart replies, "We would seek the best compromise. This means we need people sitting down and working things out. That progress has been stilted."

The agenda for the 108th Congress has not yet been established, he says, but "we will look at it again. We would look to see if we can facilitate the sides coming together for an agreement."

CRAPO (2002)

Senator Mike Crapo (R-Idaho) could also introduce the legislation, but he too seems unlikely to do so. Communications Director Susan Wheeler released this statement from Senator Crapo's office on November 18, 2002: "Regarding the Bear River Massacre and Senator Crapo's plans, at this point we don't have any. There was no agreement from county, state, federal, or tribal folks on what to do, so no decision was ever made. As long as local disagreement exists as to how best to proceed with the area, Senator Crapo believes that Congress should not mandate to local communities how to commemorate the site."

SMITH (1998)

Is there vast disagreement among the "stakeholders" that are "on the ground"?

In July 1998, Franklin County Commissioner Brad Smith reports that he is "very supportive" of some plan that would fall, he says, "about halfway between Alternatives 3 and 4." Regarding Senator Craig's apparent caution, he says that he "can't think that this issue would do anything but be a strong boost" to Craig politically, and doesn't think supporting the project would entail much of a political risk.

Smith concedes that the issue does ignite controversy among some Idaho citizens, but says his constituency is not as divided as outsiders, and Senator Craig, might expect. "A few landowners have concerns," he says. "Some are emotional, some are realistic. But most express a willingness to participate. They just want to be assured that this thing will happen the way we say it will. That's natural."

"Dollars could be an issue" in Craig's reluctance to proceed, he says. "We're not asking for new dollars, and the Park Service is supportive" of the prospect of reallocating their internal funds to the development of a Bear River site. Still, "it's difficult to think they're going to come up with the full amount" of several millions to achieve Alternative 3 or 4.

Smith acknowledges that dollars were an issue in his county's support for the project. "I'd be a fool to say it wasn't," he says. If the National Park Service spends the proposed $11 million or $14 million to build the site, "that will be a strong boost to our local economy, and continuing activities there will continue to provide a boost." He recalls the preparation for the 2002 Olympics in Salt Lake City; the hope is that tourism will receive a shot in the arm all up and down the Wasatch Front. "Here," he says, "tourism is a nonconsumptive resource," and notes that the Bear River Massacre is only one of many historical events that occurred in his county, all of which, taken together, might someday be attractive to tourists.

Smith remains hopeful that Craig will support the measure. "This is our chance to bring several cultures together," Smith says, "an opportunity to bring diverse peoples together and to see how far we have come" in our interracial relationships. The project would "bring recognition to Craig's home state. The massacre resulted in the largest number of lives lost in a Native American–related event. That was a major event, and this is an opportunity, a chance to do our part to preserve history and represent this tragedy."

Bear River, he says, "has been swept under the rug." The National Park Service proposal serves as "a sign of the fact that we can learn. We as Americans can learn from it—we have learned." This piece of history, once regained, he says, is not something we can now retreat from. "We can only go forward."

DAVIS (2002)

Conspicuously absent from Will Hart's list of "stakeholders" is the Shoshone band most greatly impacted by this story. In a November 2002 conversation, Gwen Davis, now the elected head of the Tribal Council of the Northwestern band of Shoshone, says the proposal to memorialize the Bear River Massacre field has been "a long time coming. Recognition needs to be made. We have been patient and hopeful." Davis understands that some landowners have resisted the National Park Service's proposal. "People are afraid we are rushing in to take things over," she says, "but that's not how we do business."

As to which National Park Service alternative the tribe supports, Davis is reluctant to speak for the tribe as a whole. "We hope it's done in such a way as to represent our needs," which needs are being defined by Patty Timbimboo Madsen (no relation to Brigham D. Madsen). Madsen is the current tribal resources manager, the position once held by Curtis Warner (who is now active in the tribe's housing program, which subsidizes housing for members who need it). Davis defers to Madsen, saying "the tribe would support her views."

Madsen's primary concern is the protection of the land on which remains lie. Her preference is for Alternative 4, as long as no building occurs directly on the massacre field, and as long as the field itself is returned to the control of the Shoshone.

Madsen also says the tribe has been approached by Preston residents supportive of some sort of monument at the massacre field. A member of the Preston Chamber of Commerce asked if the tribe could do something themselves, without the National Park Service. When two parcels of land recently came up for sale, the landowners invited the tribe to make offers, and the band considered purchasing them. But one nineteen-acre parcel had an asking price of $49,000. "We don't have that kind of money, and it's not our intention to make money off the site," so there's no way to make that sort of money in the future.

Hence the National Park Service's proposal is the only likely means of protecting the site. When asked if she would support the proposal if the land were controlled by the federal government, rather than the tribe (as the National Park Service proposes), she replies that "the Park Service has been more understanding of our feelings with regard to this site. We could work with them.

"This is a place of history," she says, "but for the tribe it is also a place of hurt."

POLITICS

As of this writing, then, most parties actually have reached agreement about the National Park Service's proposal to establish a National Historic Site. Local government, the Shoshone tribal council, and Allie Hansen's original group all agree that some version of the National Park Service's Alternative 4 would be best for the site itself and for the surrounding constituencies.

After several years of asking, I am aware of no objections lodged by either the LDS church or the state of Idaho. I can also report unofficially that the majority of the affected landowners in the area would agree to a willing-seller acquisition of the land.

So we must conclude that this legislation is being blocked by Senator Craig and Senator Crapo's fear of a small but vocal minority of affected landowners.

As a resident (as of this writing) of Colorado, I can attest that a similarly small group of landowners loudly protested the establishment of a National Historic Site on the field of the Sand Creek Massacre. That legislation, however, was sponsored and passed in 2000.

As Patty Madsen put it, "You have different representation down in Colorado."

Yes, we do. Senator Ben Nighthorse-Campbell (R-Colorado) is the first Native American ever elected to the Senate.

PART III

CONCLUSIONS WITHOUT ENDS

A book, apparently there is a book—I want to make the book of looking for this book—the book of everything that has happened, of everything that will happen.
    —Bhanu Kapil Rider, *The Vertical Interrogation of Strangers*

The prejudice against color, of which we hear so much, is no stronger than that against sex. It is produced by the same cause, and manifested very much in the same way. The Negro's skin and the woman's sex are both prima facie evidence that they were intended to be in subjection to the white Saxon man.
    —Elizabeth Cady Stanton, Speech to the New York Legislature,
                                                    February 18, 1860

They say a woman puts the whole of her letter in the post-script.
    —Helen Hunt Jackson, Letter to Henry Teller, May 16, 1883

10

TEN DIGRESSIONS ON WHAT'S WRONG:

A POSTSCRIPT

DIGRESSION THE FIRST

Beginnings, middles, ends.

The narrative impulse to "end" a historic tale has the effect of "ending" any responsibility concerning that event.

This work is more about process than about ends.

For instance, a writer writes for the same reason a reader reads: to learn. To change. To change her mind.

It's 2003 now. In 1999, Joe and I moved to Boulder County, Colorado, where he's taken a tenure-track job teaching poetry at the university. I'm teaching adjunct: freshman courses in women's literature and "ethnic" "American" literatures.

It's been eight years since my pickup dropped down that precipice, and the dancing spirits screamed along my spine.

I did learn something, something life-altering, in the eight years it's taken me to write this book.

At first, I struggled with the question of Who Has The Right To The Stories. The Shoshone have rarely been grateful to Brigham Madsen and Allie Hansen for Telling Their Story. I don't expect gratitude myself, and, in the early going, often wondered whether I should be writing this book.

Jane Tompkins, in her influential 1986 essay "'Indians': Textualism, Morality, and the Problem of History," wrote of her research that, "while I started out to learn about Indians, I ended up preoccupied with a problem of my own" (102).

This comment haunted me for a long time. Yes, I thought—I'm thinking about My Problems, not Their Problems.

That's bad, right?

I walked around feeling guilty. And you know how leftists love to feel guilty.

After all, I wanted to HELP, right??

Then I learned something. While engaged in the struggle of Whose Story Is It? I learned why this white, middle-class, feminist woman has maintained an interest in Native American studies since her teens.

I have maintained that involvement because the white woman who speaks against the subordination of people of color is rewarded, in some circles at least, with a fair amount of social acceptance.

At the same time, the white woman who speaks against the subordination of women is disdained in almost all circles.

Try it, you white, middle-class, feminist women out there. Go to a party attended by all your left-leaning friends. Sit at the lovely table with a glass of red wine in your hand. Wave your glass about and talk about the terrible things this country has done to Native Americans. See what sort of response you get.

Next time, wave your glass about and talk about the terrible things that happen to women of all colors, in every country. See what sort of response you get.

I figure women of color aren't free to raise questions of either race or gender. Who's pursuing class issues? White men, usually. Sexuality? White men and women, often of the upper classes. The occasional exception proves the rule (or fool).

Go ahead. Experiment.

It's 2003 now—more water under the bridge. The Salt Lake City Olympics were a success, but in late 1998 there emerged a foul-up regarding how city leaders effected that triumph. The mainstream media rarely mention that most of the overzealous Olympic Committee members were also esteemed LDS church members. As I listen to the Public Radio reports, it's all sounding a bit familiar to me. The church a little too gung-ho at first, a little too willing to outdo all competitors on their own terms; they don't do anything that hasn't been done by other cities, but they do it to some nth degree, and then are dutifully penitent when caught. Eventually.

In 2000, one lovely Saturday just after we relocate west, Colorado Public Radio announces a story on the horrific slaughter of three hundred Shoshone in southern Idaho.

"After the news."

To my knowledge, National Public Radio's story is the first national broadcast about this atrocity.

It's January 29, 2000. The 137th anniversary of the massacre.

I'm thinking, Great—this is finally going to break now. People are finally going to pay attention. After all, media junkies will tell you that NPR often serves as a feeder mechanism for mainstream broadcast journalism, telling CBS's producers what's worth covering.

Joe and I hang next to the radio, listening greedily. The voices of old friends fill the room.

The story contains not one mention of the rape that followed the massacre.

Afterward, magazine editors continue to reject my queries regarding articles on the subject.

Then, 2001. One typically sunny Tuesday in late-summer Colorado, Public Radio reports that a commercial jetliner has hit the World Trade Center.

We all stop listening to the radio, stare endlessly at horrible video footage.

In the months that follow, there is much talk about what to do with the site now that it has become the final resting place for the remains of more than one thousand people. Some say that whatever structure replaces "Ground Zero" (which, at the tip of Manhattan, is some of the most valuable real estate in the world) must at the very least be "reverent." Some relatives of those lost call the area "sacred," and demand that a monument to their memory be built, rather than another monument to commercialism.

It doesn't seem likely they'll get what they want, since the Port Authorities of New York and New Jersey have only so much control over the developer who owns the lease for several more decades.

But some of my atheist friends go public with their aversion to the word *sacred*. Indeed, 911 has been an absorbing event for atheists: when a "Holy War" is declared anywhere, we tend to get a bit self-righteous. In particular, President George W. Bush's earliest public response to the event, which included a recitation of Psalm 23, drew big groans from my crowd. If fundamentalist Islamists have declared jihad on you, it doesn't make much sense to shout back bible verses.

So I understand that atheists are a bit cranky at the moment. But I'm willing to secularize my definition of *sacred* to mean "cherished," if—*if*—I can get everyone to understand that the Bear River Massacre field is just as cherishable as Ground Zero.

And oh yeah—*if* we'll all promise to remember the rape too.

And thus must the reader beware.

In writing this book, you see, I have chosen to privilege written, white, academic (male) history over oral, native (female) history. I have chosen to dispute Mae Timbimboo Parry's assertion that the rape that followed the Bear River Massacre couldn't have happened. Once again, a European American intellectual dismisses the word of a Shoshone American leader.

And we are both women.

Separated by color, history, education, religion, age, health, and perhaps class.

Two women, miles apart.

You understand why I'm in an awkward position. Any good leftist worth her salt would balk at my assertion that Parry is wrong, and I am right.

Parry and Allie Hansen agree that the rape that followed the Bear River Massacre *couldn't* have happened, because they just can't imagine it.

But according to Susan Brownmiller, who wrote the book, so to speak, on rape—1975's *Against Our Will: Men, Women, and Rape*—Brigham Madsen has it pretty much right when he says that rape among men in the military is just part of the scene. And Kathy Griffin has it right when she avers that rape is about control, about the victors "forcing themselves in every conceivable way." Brownmiller writes:

> War provides men with the perfect psychologic backdrop to give vent to their contempt for women. The very maleness of the military—the brute power of weaponry exclusive to their hands, the spiritual bonding of men at arms, the manly discipline of orders given and orders obeyed, the simple logic of the hierarchical command—confirms for men what they long suspect, that women are peripheral, irrelevant to the world that counts, passive spectators to the action in the center ring.
>
> Men who rape in war are ordinary Joes, made unordinary by entry into the most exclusive male-only club in the world. Victory in arms brings group power undreamed of in civilian life. Power for

men alone. The unreal situation of a world without women becomes the prime reality. To take a life looms more important than to *make* a life, and the gun in the hand is power. The sickness of warfare feeds on itself. A certain number of soldiers must prove their newly won superiority—prove it to a woman, to themselves, to other men. In the name of victory and the power of the gun, war provides men with a tacit license to rape. In the act and in the excuse, rape in war reveals the male psyche in its boldest form, without the veneer of "chivalry" or civilization. (32–33)

It is important also to realize that rape is not just license; it is also a highly effective military tool. Brownmiller continues: "When a victorious army rapes, the sheer intoxication of the triumph is only part of the act. After the fact, the rape may be viewed as part of a recognizable pattern of national terror and subjugation. . . . [R]ape in warfare has a military effect as well as an impulse. And the effect is indubitably one of intimidation and demoralization for the victims' side" (37).

Specifically, the civilian population is intimidated. Recall: Most of the survivors of the Bear River Massacre were women and children. Connor's men took the band's horses. On foot, the women, Sagwitch, and other survivors were able to move only a short distance away from the field in the hours immediately following the horrors of January 29, 1863. When they gathered, the Shoshone had to make a decision about how, and where, to proceed. Had these women chosen to return to the Cache Valley with their children, they very likely *might* have been rejoined by Sagwitch and his remaining warriors; this larger group *might* have been (re)joined by Pocatello's more militarily aggressive band of agitators; and the Mormons and Union-affiliated troops *might* have had to fight for the Cache Valley all over again.

Mormon witnesses report that Shoshone women refused to take refuge in town for fear of encountering Connor's men.

Indeed, the rape that followed the massacre was a necessary guarantor that this most valuable Cache Valley real estate had been thoroughly cleared of those who disputed European American claim to the property.

It is also worth noting that the National Park Service's decision, in 1995, *not* to include the story of the rape in the historic site materials occurred in the same historical moment as the decision, by the Bosnia War Crimes Tribunal, to prosecute rape—for the first time—as an international war crime. Prosecutors have documented the use in Yugoslavia of rape as a tool most effective for, among other goals, herding civilian populations from place to place—freeing territory.

Jane Tompkins has written that when a historian looks back, that which is invisible in her own time is also invisible in that look back.

Rape as a military tool is only beginning to come into our cultural focus.

For instance, here is something you have probably forgotten, in the midst of our recent efforts to build a monument to the "Great Generation": from 1942 to 1947, 971 American soldiers were convicted, by U.S. Army courts-martial, of rape.

Our public discussions of rape often address the faux question of why so many women are reluctant to admit to having been raped, so the perpetrators might be prosecuted. But since rape is still viewed as a shameful sexual act, rather than as a militaristic tool of manipulation, we might much better ask this: When we do know a rape occurred, why do we know it?

"An aggressor nation rarely admits to rape," Brownmiller writes (37). Typically, mass rape is not reported unless the reporting benefits the teller in some way—for instance, as propaganda designed to incite a unified, nationalistic anger toward opponents; or, as evidence, to remove a man from power. In Vietnam, the U.S. military floated rumors of rape as part of their "psychological warfare" campaign. Often, women have been pressured to tell stories they would prefer not to make public, stories they perceive as shameful, so that those stories could be used against a person or a group in power (on a far less violent scale, think of Monica Lewinski, whose relationship with President Bill Clinton was exposed without her consent, by a partisan opposition). The real beneficiaries of the telling of those "truths" are not the rape victims, but the men struggling for power.

When no such political reasons exist for the telling, women's tales of rape are often silenced, ignored.

What political purpose, then, motivated the telling of the rape of the Shoshone?

I would speculate that the motivation for documenting the rape at Bear River finds its source in tensions regarding sexual behavior. If Connor was going to blast Mormons for polygyny, then Mormons were going to take note of the rape committed by Connor's soldiers. The memory of Haun's Mill was only two decades old. The Mormons of 1863 Utah knew better than most the military effectiveness of such brutality.

And if accusing Connor's troops might, by some chance, get Connor off their backs in Salt Lake—well, all the better, then.

The rape of Native American women by European American invaders is poorly documented. According to Brownmiller, narratives similar to those recited by abolitionists, to document the rape of African slaves, were not taken down on behalf of natives. Not much more is known about the rape of white women by natives. White men spoke frequently about the rape of white women, often to excuse their own violent "retaliations," but white women were silent on the matter. Narratives of abducted white women were edited for chastity; it is unclear, when a captive says she "lived as Indian wife," whether we should understand that as sexual coercion. Brownmiller suggests we consider each narrative separately, according to the length of captivity. Most historians concede that in actuality, and excluding captivity situations, natives raped white women far less frequently than whites raped native women. This is not to say that rape did not occur in some indigenous cultures. Margaret Mead's research on Plains cultures uncovered remembered histories of rape, perpetrated by "young men" who "regarded rape as a great adventure," upon "bad" women, defined as divorced women lacking male protection, or argumentative women (qtd. in Brownmiller 285).

We do know that perceived threats against white women were used to incite violence against natives, and perceived threats against native women were used to incite violence against whites. For instance, the scalps of white women were used to taunt Major McGarry into a rage, prompting the blunder that killed fourteen of the soldiers who died that day. And recall how, after the Dakota War, the innocent Chaska was "accidentally" killed in the mass hangings, an "accident" likely caused by local rage at his friendship with a white woman, Sarah Wakefield.

So: We do know that white women were used against natives, and native women were used against whites.

How would it be *possible* to use women of one race against another, if we did not *first* define women as property, and define female sexuality as a thing to be controlled, a thing of shame?

As an occasional HELPER, I have often wondered whether my HELP is a thing that gets used this way, as Wakefield's HELP was used.

Of course it is the concept of HELP that most requires revision.

We whites often pretend that when we HELP people of color, this has nothing to do with us.

I understand why Allie Hansen said, We did this primarily for Them.

But still. As if We did not do this in the first place.

When the dominating attack the dominated, whose history is the history of domination?

Women's History, another cultural phenomenon, is (in an important sense) not about women. It's about the male-generated system that persists in dominating women. Is this not, therefore, Men's History?

You may find this book, the one you now hold, on the bookstore shelf marked "Native American History." But in truth it is the story of what European America did *to* Native America.

Is it not, then, Our History? Not Theirs?

Do we not need then—instead—to HELP *ourselves* operate more responsibly in this world?

Indigenist activist and intellectual Ward Churchill has contributed perhaps the most eloquent, and concise, explanation for why it is necessary that we remember our Bear River Massacre.

And the rape that followed it.

"My Lai," he writes, "that hideous symbol of the American 'effort' in Southeast Asia, can *only* be understood through comprehension that it had happened before at Sand Creek. The reason of My Lai rests solidly in the forgetting of Sand Creek" (*Son* 504).

Like many who have dedicated their lives to native rights and native history, Churchill is apparently unaware of the Bear River Massacre, or he would have pointed out that Sand Creek happened because Bear River was itself immediately forgotten.

Not that this is his fault. James Welch, in his book *Killing Custer*, also locates the root of this evil in Sand Creek. Many of us, despite the best of recuperative intentions, do not know about the Bear River Massacre.

Sexual assault and mutilation were a part of My Lai. And Sand Creek. And Bear River.

Thus we might conclude that when we forget rape, that forgetting will be the seed if its happening again.

"The crossroads of racism and sexism," Brownmiller concludes, "had to be a violent meeting place. There is no use pretending it doesn't exist" (255).

Again: The intersection of sexism and racism was bound to be a violent place.

In what way does my difference with Mae Parry constitute such an intersection?

As a white woman HELPER, shouldn't I simply defer to her?

DIGRESSION THE SECOND

One October 1998 day, back from the summer's research in Pocatello, I'm in the library, looking up a name I've seen referenced occasionally in works such as Peter Matthiessen's *In the Spirit of Crazy Horse*, but have never seen discussed at any length.

Grabbing one moldy, crumbly tome at random, I consult the introduction and discover immediately that this white woman writer was extremely well-known in her day, and vastly influential in the field of what was known as "Indian reform."

I load up my book bag and check out the entire shelf.

("Pardon all these words about myself," Helen Hunt Jackson once wrote [Mathes, *Letters* 136].)

Allie Hansen is simply the latest in a long tradition of white women who have concerned themselves with their race's—the dominating race's—treatment of other peoples. And I'm just another in a long line of women writers. The book considered by many to be the first novel written in English, *Oroonoko, or The Royal Slave: A True History*, was published in 1688 by the Englishwoman Aphra Behn: spy, playwright, bawdy poetess, and the first recognized professional woman writer in English. Her novel describes the cruel murder of an aristocratic, European-featured African in the West Indies. Although this work ostensibly concerns class more than it does race or gender, it seems clear that, right out of the gate, white women writers of English used the novel to explore social power dynamics, particularly in a romantic context.

In the eighteenth century, the U.S. Founding Fathers begat, among other things, a mulish inability to address the evil of slavery. In the nineteenth century, abolition was, to no small degree, of white-woman born, finding tenacious support in grassroots organizations of upper-class women. Ultimately, our first organized feminist movement was born of the abolition movement, when this latter refused to apply equal fervor to suffrage for black men *and* for all women. Nineteenth-century feminists were effectively divided and conquered by the question of which oppression was primary: that based on race, or that based on gender. Elizabeth Cady Stanton believed that all means of oppression must be fought together, or none would be truly conquered.

Her face does not adorn a dollar coin.

That of her partner in activism, the more compromising Susan B. Anthony, once did.

Harriet Beecher Stowe was thirty-nine (just a bit younger than me) when she began to write *Uncle Tom's Cabin, or, Life among the Lowly*, inspired by her outrage at The Compromise of 1850 (which permitted Utah to be a slave territory), and the inability of her male leaders to end slavery. Her initial vision for the novel was the image of Uncle Tom's death: his fervent prayer for his torturers while being flogged. Intending a short novel, Stowe wrote on and on in serial form, her editor growing anxious about the length (as later critics would decry the lack of revision), and writing, she said, intoxicated by the influence of God. Like Behn, Stowe takes a romantic view of the murder—a martyrdom—of the leader of a people less "educated" than her readers would be; and chewed up the scenery a bit to extract that audience's sympathy; even as she determined to present a "realistic" picture of the horrors of slavery (which she had never witnessed herself). Stowe was not a declared feminist; but, despite complaints about the literary worthiness of her novel, literary critics note that, among American woman writers, only Stowe has so thoroughly fueled a national cause. President Lincoln greeted her in 1863—the year of the Bear River Massacre—as "the little lady who made this big war." Interestingly, in her novel, white male characters are frequently morally inferior to white women, who are the instigators of much of the pro-black action of the plot. In this book, male and female slaves, and white women, are the only people who care about justice.

Thanks to recuperative work by Valerie Sherer Mathes and the University of Oklahoma Press, a trip to the library reveals that another "little lady" wrote to fuel a cause. But her cause never caught on quite so strongly.

Please pardon a long story.

Helen Maria Hunt Jackson (née Fiske) was born October 14, 1830, in Amherst, Massachusetts, the daughter of Nathan Welby Fiske, a professor of moral philosophy and metaphysics, and his wife,

Deborah Vinal. Both died by the time Jackson was seventeen; the professor died while on a trip to the Holy Land. She married Edward Bissel Hunt, a West Point engineer, who drowned in 1863 (again, the year of the Bear River Massacre) in the submarine he had designed for the Union. Jackson's first son had died shortly after birth; her second died in 1865. In need of money, but unencumbered by domestic obligations, she determined to become a writer. She published poetry, fiction, and articles in such journals as *Atlantic Monthly*, *Nation*, *Christian Union*, and *Scribner's*, becoming well esteemed in literary society. Ralph Waldo Emerson dubbed her the "greatest American woman poet" (qtd. in Mathes, *Legacy* 22), and carried one of her poems in his notebook. (Emerson and I differ on this point, and I will not recommend Jackson's poetry, except as it illuminates her life.) She enjoyed some commercial success with romantic novels, but her later marriage to William Sharpless Jackson, a wealthy Colorado Springs banker, permitted her to write without concern for marketability.

To most of today's literary scholars, Jackson is known primarily as a close friend of Emily Dickinson's. Jackson was the only renowned poet of the age to recognize the quality of Dickinson's work. The two attended the same school but did not become friends until Jackson's reputation was established; they met only a few times, but corresponded often, and Jackson's encouragement was much cherished by Dickinson, whose letters reveal a crushing disappointment at Jackson's premature death in 1885.

Jackson often left Colorado for long visits to Boston and New York, and in 1879 she attended an unusual gathering. The Ponca Indians of South Dakota, through a bureaucratic error, had seen their 96,000-acre reservation subsumed in 1868 by the Lakota (Great Sioux) reservation, resulting in attacks on the Poncas by the Lakota. In 1876 Congress decided to relocate the Poncas, purportedly for their safety, though Ponca leader Standing Bear protested the move. One hundred sixty Poncas died of malaria or other diseases as a result of this removal. In late 1877, President Rutherford B. Hayes denied Standing Bear's request: return them to their reservation (the Lakota had agreed to peace), or relocate them again to the Nebraska reservation held by their relatives, the Omaha.

On January 2, 1879, Standing Bear lifted the body of his own dead son and began a defiant ten-week march to the Omaha reservation to bury his child. He and a small band of followers were given land by Omaha leader Joseph LaFlesche. General George Crook ordered the arrest of Standing Bear and his followers, but was critical of the federal policy requiring their return. He conferred with *Omaha Herald* assistant editor Thomas Henry Tibbles, who persuaded attorneys John L. Webster and Andrew Jackson Poppleton to draw up a writ of habeas corpus preventing the Poncas' return. *Standing Bear v. Crook*, a formative civil rights case decided by Nebraska District Court Judge Elmer S. Dundy, declared natives to be legal "persons" with the right to sue for a writ of habeas corpus. The *Standing Bear* decision meant that, in peacetime, natives could no longer be detained or removed without their consent.

Thus freed, the Poncas agreed to accompany Tibbles on a tour of eastern cities to raise money and support to sue for the restoration of lost lands and the legal status of Native Americans. Through interpreter Susette LaFlesche, Joseph's daughter, Standing Bear related his story at a reception attended by Massachusetts Governor Thomas Talbot, Massachusetts Senator Henry L. Dawes, Henry Wadsworth Longfellow, Oliver Wendell Holmes—and Helen Hunt Jackson.

Standing Bear's tour marks the start of an early pro-Indian fervor experienced by elite, white America, detailed by Mathes in *Helen Hunt Jackson and Her Indian Reform Legacy*. That year, 1879, saw the founding of the Boston Indian Citizenship Committee and the Women's National Indian Association (the more influential, and male, Indian Rights Association would not organize until 1882). Some former abolitionists embraced the new cause of Native Americans, but—unsurprisingly, given the profit to be taken from native lands out west—most did not.

Jackson became, she said, "what I have said a thousand times was the most odious thing in life,—'a woman with a hobby'" (*Letters* 84). Her conversion is particularly unusual since she had not been given to "hobbies" during earlier political movements, and was known neither as abolitionist nor suffragist. In fact, Jackson had been critical of early feminist rhetoric, and had also largely ignored a debate raging near her own Colorado home, where citizens were attempting to remove the White River Ute so their reservation could be mined. Why natives, why natives at the age of forty-nine, and why the Poncas? It may be that financial independence made such a controversial commitment possible; it may also be that Standing Bear's personal tale contained the rhetoric of emotion, more appealing to her than the impersonal rhetoric of political debate. Jackson would activate equally effectively using both discourses, but like Behn and Stowe before her, may ultimately have found the former most compelling; indeed, it was certainly more acceptable for a woman. Ultimately, the discourse of emotion would be her greatest legacy as a writer.

As a woman whose writing was published only when suffered by male editors and publishers, Jackson was limited at first to an intense flurry of letters to the editor, particularly to the *New York Tribune*; and to begging editors to write editorials themselves (Rebecca Harding Davis was one who complied). Via letters, Jackson staged a public dispute with Secretary of the Interior Carl Schurz over his policies regarding the Poncas, and later the White River Ute. The debate, reprinted in several newspapers in early 1880, sparked a national discussion. She quarreled in another series of letters with William N. Byers, founder of the *Rocky Mountain News* and regional apologist for Colonel John Chivington's Sand Creek Massacre. (Like many of her day and ours, Jackson was apparently unaware of the Bear River Massacre and of Connor's consultation with Chivington.) Jackson quoted directly, and devastatingly, from transcripts of the investigations of that massacre and mutilation. Jackson's letters, collected by Mathes, are a piercing study of the rhetoric of public persuasion, particularly of the author's favorite and most effective device, the rhetorical question.

Jackson's personal letters provide clues to the public's reception of a female activist in 1879. Jackson was quickly labeled a "sentimentalist"—by no less a critic than her own abolitionist husband, who chastised her for "berating" Secretary Schurz, and insisted she "keep cool" (*Letters* 63). Stung, Jackson penned a pained answer to her dear Will: "A woman does not need to be a statesman," she wrote, "to know that it is base to break promises—to oppress the helpless—!—" (*Letters* 62). The sentimentalist label must have tortured her, not least because she was herself attracted to the cause by Standing Bear's use of that very rhetoric; she had earlier told Will, "I can hardly tell you the praise I am getting for the manly method in which I have stated things—the quiet tone—the repression" (*Letters* 50). Senator Dawes also scolded her; she answered, "I quite agree with you that even the shadow of suspicion of what is technically known as 'lobbying' should not rest on a woman. . . . But would it not be possible for me, in a quiet and unnoticeable way—(now at the Capitol)—to make opportunities of reading a few statistics—a few facts, to men whom it is worthwhile to convert?" (*Letters* 150).

Jackson's letters reveal the complexity of her personal racial constructions, and those of her time. "The thing I can't understand," she wrote to abolitionist Moncure Daniel Conway, "is that all you who so loved the Negro, & worked for him, should not have been ever since, just as hard at work for the Indian, who is on the whole much more cruelly oppressed; . . . he is far worse off than the average slave ever was—and is a higher nobler creature" (*Letters* 135). This attitude, not uncommon among elite activists in the postbellum era, confirms June Namias's observation that, since natives possessed land the Europeans wanted, natives were a full-fledged "conflict partner"—an Other crucial to U.S. development. Consequently, some whites expressed a preference for the cause of "noble" natives.

Like Stowe, Jackson felt herself mystically drawn to the native cause—"*led*," "*impelled*," "in the hands of powers & events I could neither resist nor understand" (*Letters* 49). In 1880 this possession led her to spend seven feverish months researching and writing *A Century of Dishonor*, a history of treaties broken with the Delaware, Cheyenne, Nez Percé, Sioux, Ponca, Winnebago, and Cherokee ("that is as many as people will stand" [*Letters* 123]). A later chapter also details "Massacres by Whites." The University of Oklahoma edition restores the entire appendix (a postscript that measures one-third of the original volume), including Jackson's correspondences with Schurz and Byers, and Jackson's report to Congress on the status of Mission Indians (of which more in a minute).

A Century of Dishonor was published in 1881, but did not sell well. At her own expense, Jackson sent a copy to each member of Congress. The book garnered several reviews, good and bad, provoking a public discussion which, she said, may have done more for the cause than had the book. Although the work was often maligned by historians, and by politicians such as Theodore Roosevelt (who called it "thoroughly untrustworthy" and "capable of doing great harm," since it was oft quoted by "a large class of amiable but maudlin fanatics" [qtd. in Senier 213n]), historian Allan Nevins would grudgingly concede in 1941 that Jackson's research had never been refuted.

Jackson first visited California to write about the Mission Indians for *Century Magazine*. There she found a situation more politically and racially complicated. Mission Indians were so-named because Spain had gathered them on lands held by Franciscan priests, where they became religious neophytes, learning farming while providing labor for the missions. In 1833 Mexico secularized the Spanish missions, leaving many natives dependent on the elite ranchers who took over the lands but who later, with California statehood, were themselves at pains to prove ownership of their property to a U.S. government that strove to take land from Mexicans. In 1851 Congress rejected several treaties made with Mission Indians who gave up lands in exchange for reservations. White land theft via "survey errors," "purchase," litigation—and murder—was common. By the 1870s, California native populations had fallen to about 20% of their 1840s level.

Her first visit to the Mission Indians ignited another flurry of letters to government officials, leading to Jackson's appointment as a special agent to investigate their plight. Because she finally had official sanction, her letters to federal officials would now result in action. At government expense, she returned to California in early 1883; to cover extra personal expenses she contracted to write several articles for the *New York Independent*. Still, she suffered from a sense of powerlessness. "Don't," she wrote to reservation teacher Mary Sheriff, "if you can help it, let any of them think I can '*help*' them. It breaks my heart. Do try to make them understand that all I can do, is to *tell* about them" (*Letters* 253).

She and partner Abbot Kinney, a young reformer, managed more than that at times, helping to save some lands, and helping Indian Agent S. S. Lawson to resign. This latter because, once again, Jackson embroiled herself in a brawl of letters, complaining over Lawson's head—perhaps unfairly, Mathes says—about the agent's failure to respond to the natives' plight. Jackson and Lawson quarreled over a Temecula Day School teacher named Arthur Golsh, who had impregnated a native girl; he was also, Jackson believed, involved in a theft of Indian land. Lawson consulted with Golsh, who complained that he was having a terrible time fending off the advances of young native girls, and that he was innocent of land theft. Lawson fired Golsh, but protested to Hiram Price, commissioner of Indian Affairs, that Jackson had "assumed the prerogative of the Agent" (qtd. in *Legacy* 66), and that he hoped never again to work with another female commissioner. Local papers referred to her as a "busy body" (qtd. in *Letters* 287n).

Jackson's report was filed in July. Her recommendations included the removal of white trespassers; the patenting of reservations for twenty-five years, to be allotted individually at government discretion; the repurchase of some lands; the hiring of a law firm to restore other lands; annual inspections of villages; a fund for the aged and sick; and more schools. Commissioner Price wrote a bill based on these recommendations and distributed her report to Congress; in

July 1884 the bill, supported by reformers, passed the Senate but failed in the House.

Late in 1883, with her official duties completed to disappointing results, Jackson turned her attention to a novel about the Mission Indians. Having failed to influence the public using the "manly" rhetoric of debate, she hoped that the more "romantic" novel form would win the personal sympathy she herself had felt on hearing Standing Bear. "If I can do one-hundredth part for the Indians that Mrs. Stowe did for the Negro," she wrote, "I will be thankful" (*Letters* 307). "The success of it—if it succeeds—will be that I do not even suggest any Indian history,—till the interest is so aroused in the heroine—and hero—that people will not lay the book down" (*Letters* 314). *Ramona* was written, again feverishly, in three months.

As a work of imagination, *Ramona* is more compelling than *Uncle Tom's Cabin*; Jackson's understanding of racial and class constructs is more complicated and less stereotyped than Stowe's, though these subtleties were lost on most readers of the day (and remain lost today on Avon's editors, if we may judge by the bodice-ripping portrait that adorns their 1984 reissue; the New American Library edition is more staid in presentation). The beautiful, blue-eyed Ramona is half Scots–Irish and half Mission Indian, but passes for aristocratic Spanish in her adoptive home. Her guardian, Señora Moreno, easily keeps Ramona's native heritage a secret. Alessandro, Ramona's lover, is royalty, the son of a Temecula leader who is fighting to keep his people's lands. The Moreno ranch employs working-class Mexicans who look down on Alessandro's migrant band, hired temporarily to do the shearing, but we're also told that the skin of Ramona's aristocratic brother is the same color as Alessandro's ("light") native skin. And Señora Moreno is herself losing lands to the avaricious whites flooding California, though not by the more brutal methods employed against Alessandro's kin. Thus the lovers aren't doomed by perceived racial difference, but by class—and by native history. Aside from a lower-economic-class white woman outraged by the atrocities against Alessandro's people, the only whites in the novel are offstage thieves—horrible, lower-class invaders—and Alessandro's murderers. Yes, like Behn and Stowe, Jackson martyrs her hero to spark maximum sympathy. In this case the homicide is based on a true story: the murder of a native by a white man who, during Jackson's visit to California, was quickly acquitted of justifiable homicide.

Serialized in the *Christian Union* in May 1884 and published as a book in November 1884, *Ramona* would again disappoint its author, this time because it succeeded as a page-turning romance—too well. To Jackson's chagrin, most reviews largely ignored the "Indian history." Ultimately, the impact of *Ramona* would be felt more as a love story than as a polemic. The book sold very well: 7,000 copies within the first three months and 15,000 within ten months.

Historians often draw a direct line between the publication of *Ramona* in 1884, and the passage of the Dawes Severalty Act in 1887, crediting Jackson—which is to say, discrediting her—as having been responsible for allotment. (Matthiessen's *In the Spirit of Crazy Horse* contains one such critique of her legacy.) The Dawes Act, which destroyed reservation holdings by reallocating those lands to individual natives, was supported by the Indian reformers of that era who predicted—too correctly—that allotment would prove a crucial assimilation tool. Mathes's *Legacy* summarizes the white elite's belief that assimilation via private property, education, and Protestantism would rescue natives from extinction.

Siobhan Senier has argued that Jackson's oeuvre is too ambiguous to allow us to dub Jackson "the little lady who made the Dawes Act." Jackson, whom Mathes calls a "renegade," was neither religious nor anti-Catholic, and was only peripherally associated with reform groups. She did argue at times for allotment, but a review of her letters reveals that she also advocated (as she did in California) for the protection of reservations, with the hope that economic independence would preserve native culture. Indeed, in 1881 *The Nation* criticized *A Century of Dishonor* for failing to support severalty.

And although *Ramona* contains several picturesque scenes of domestic tranquility (every time Ramona and Alessandro are ousted from a home, Alessandro builds Ramona another house, and she relishes housekeeping), the book's primary focus was, as Jackson herself insisted, the destruction of a people caused by the theft of their lands. It was Jackson's unpopular contention that *white settlers were the problem*, not the natives. (Senier believes as well that another event went further to galvanize Indian reform than did the publication of *Ramona*: the Supreme Court's decision, also in 1884, in *Elk v. Wilkins*, that Indians were not citizens under the 14th Amendment.) Jackson's challenge in *Ramona* was to walk a line between those two great nineteenth-century literary divides, realism and romanticism. As Senier reminds us, the book's very appeal was its reliance on fact.

(Sam Temple, the real-life murderer whose act so inflamed Jackson, toured World Fairs as the "real" murderer of "Alessandro.") One might even argue that the novel's great act of radicalism was the collapse of the masculine genre, realism, into the feminine genre, romance—all in the cause of cross-racial cultural critique.

About which, Senier feels, Jackson did not do quite enough. Jackson's position as a "cultural tourist" (Senier 72), and as someone who enfranchised herself by "infiltrating" patriarchy to HELP anOther, resulted in an excess of individualism in her thinking. Senier writes, "In [Jackson's] formulation, human contact and community lead to empathy, which will lead to social change and activism. However, the basis for *collective* action is less clear" (58).

Ramona's popular reception remains intact: it has undergone more than three hundred printings; the story continues to be staged annually as a pageant in Ramona, California; and several film versions have been produced in Hollywood. More sadly, its reception by intellectuals remains intact. Most of the scholars doing work today on writers such as Harriet Beecher Stowe and Rebecca Harding Davis continue to ignore *Ramona* and its artistic/political achievements, judging, perhaps, Avon's book by its cover.

In March 1884, Jackson wrote, "Some day I shall write a long story without a purpose.—not a weapon,— . . . but this one, is not *for myself*" (*Letters* 318). In June, Jackson fell down the steps in her Colorado Springs home and broke her leg. It was never to heal. In March 1885 she wrote Will from California that she knew she was dying, that she was ready to go, that she regretted the time her writing had taken from their marriage, and that he should marry her niece, Helen Fiske Banfield (which he did). She died on August 12, 1885, in Colorado Springs, apparently of cancer, and was buried there. She was not yet fifty-five. That year, *A Century of Dishonor* was removed from print while *Ramona* sold thousands of copies. Six years after her death, in January 1891, the Act for the Relief of the Mission Indians in the State of California, based on Jackson's report, finally became law.

In Ramona, California, Jackson is known not as the woman responsible for severalty, but as the woman responsible for the twenty-six reservations that continue to exist in southern California.

The scribbling-white-woman-busybody tradition continued beyond Jackson: novelist Mary Austin would publish in 1903 *The Land of Little Rain*, about the lands and people of the Shoshone southwest;

anthropologist Alice Cunningham Fletcher would collaborate with Francis LaFlesche in 1911 on *The Omaha Tribe*; and Theodora Kroeber would publish in 1964 *Ishi: Last of His Tribe*, about the Diggers— a Shoshone group—of eastern California. . . .

Wait. Alice Cunningham Fletcher.

Alice Cunningham Fletcher, also enraptured by Standing Bear's talk, felt herself moved to become an ethnologist.

Fletcher initially opposed allotment, but after Jackson's death grabbed the reins of the bandwagon and rode them hard. Also appointed a special agent by the commissioner of Indian Affairs, she sold off Omaha land by the hectare, in defiance of the Omahas— whom she called her "children" (qtd. in Senier 63)—who opposed the decimation of their lands. She even went so far as to abandon treaties with the tribes. In 1897, when she visited the Omahas and found them destitute, she never so much as apologized. She also treated Francis LaFlesche as a research assistant, and when he asked to be credited equally for their work, Fletcher resisted, causing an argument between Francis and his sister Susette that, according to Senier, resulted in a permanent breach.

White women HELPing to divide.

Enrapture. Diaries of women missionaries, who went west to save native souls, are peppered with evangelical fervor. This I understand. But the same sort of fervor (different goal) was also expressed by the women who went west as field matrons, establishing houses and schools where native girls and young women could be conscripted to learn the European domestic arts. These HELPers not only spread sexist divisions of labor to native cultures, but also HELPed, by their actions, reinforce same in their own culture.

I assume that today's white women HELPers do not want to be Fletchers or field matrons. Where do we find our precursors, then?

Eerie echoes exist between Helen Hunt Jackson and Allie Hansen. The enrapture thing, for instance: this idea that these women were somehow "called" to this work of "telling," remembering. And not *for themselves*.

I feel called to it myself, by those spiny dancers I told you about. By the coincidence of my acquaintance with Curtis Warner. By the coincidence of having lived near the site. By the availability of Tamise

Van Pelt's apartment, just when I was looking for a book project. By the urgency that follows encounters with the not-told.

What's up with these near-religious conversions?

For instance, I have never felt "spiritually," mystically, "called" to activate on behalf of the environment or women—my two earliest causes (in that life-order). These were "natural," somehow obviously *necessary*, concerns of mine—matters that affect me directly, immediately, personally.

I do feel that the potent "coincidences" I experienced as this story unfolded for me—these coincidences are not to be ignored.

I do feel that the spinal tap dancers are not to be ignored.

But I wonder about the presumed spirituality we find in the commitment to "tell" stories that at first seem to be about, and for, Others. That which is about Them is not natural to Us. So I wonder whether the lack of "natural"-ness we find in that Other's cause contributes to a sense of spiritual authority, of a summons issued from Above. Beyond. From forces above and beyond Us and Them.

That is to say, Jackson, Hansen, and I, by virtue of our white skin (and middle- and upper-class status), could have lived our lives without once thinking about any massacre of natives, and nothing in our lives would have changed. Given current we/they divisions, we are *permitted* to ignore them, so they do not affect Us unless we allow them to affect Us. And so they are not natural to Us.

That which is not natural must be spiritual.

Plus, I have to return to Siobhan Senier's concern about Helen Hunt Jackson's expressed individualism. What happens when the socially "dispossessed" (women) become "possessed" by a social reform fervor (the urge to HELP)? If we re-possess ourselves within the context of patriarchy, by fighting *not for ourselves*, then possession leads to enfranchisement leads to ownership. Within patriarchy, we own this protest.

But said protest, which provides us with individual power, does not lead to collective action. Nor cross-racial anything.

But wait. It's *not* about *ourselves*?

DIGRESSION THE THIRD

"All I can do, is to *tell* about them," Jackson said.

Jackson meant that telling to spark sentimentality, empathy, and, consequently, activism in support of the cause of natives. Michelle

Burnham has pointed out that sentimental novels are moving because they foster identification with the hero or heroine, which identification (I am virtuous like Ramona) fuels a sense of community (a we-ness), which itself often establishes a sense of nationhood (we Americans are virtuous like Ramona). This identification is predicated on an obstacle (someone is trying to crush we virtuous Americans), which is itself predicated on difference (that someone is not we). I admire *Ramona* not least because Jackson complicates this difference (there are so many factions in the novel that the bad guys seem to be everyone but Allesandro's people); still, to achieve sympathy, she relies on our identification with the virtuous Ramona—an identification that, as Burnham has it, "offer[s] the consoling illusion of a community based on resemblance." We find that resemblance particularly reassuring "during periods of crisis in national cohesion" (68), but it obscures our responsibility for genocidal programs. One such period of crisis and obscurantism would be the Indian Reform movement of which Jackson was a part.

Burnham points out that another genre relies on this nationalistic identification process: the captivity narrative, that earliest illustration of the intersection between race and gender, of the unholy relation between white women and native men.

In his short story "Captivity," Spokane/Coeur d'Alene writer Sherman Alexie examines that relation, directing his rebuttal to the first and best known of these narratives, that published by Mary Rowlandson in 1682. *The Sovereignty and Goodness of God: Being a Narrative of the Captivity and Restoration of Mrs. Rowlandson* details the Puritan rectitude that sustained Rowlandson through the three months of constant relocation and starvation she shared with the Narraganset, when she and her children were held captive during Metacom's War in Massachusetts in 1676. The work documents her friendship with her captor, Quinnapin, whom she called "master"; she called his three wives her "mistresses," and construed herself as servant to them.

Rowlandson, whose husband was a leader of high standing in Massachusetts, also relates that a sore hostility prevailed between herself and one of Quinnapin's wives, the famous "squaw sachem," Weetamoo. Weetamoo was a powerful military leader of the Wampanoag, and enjoyed a greater social standing than did Quinnapin. Rowlandson and Weetamoo became bitter rivals, and most of the physical abuse Rowlandson suffered came at the hands of Weetamoo.

Most historians have ignored this fascinating dynamic between two powerful women, preferring to focus on the more specious questions of sexual conduct. When Rowlandson was released, rumors persisted that she had "lived as wife" with the Nashaway Micmuc the English called One-eyed John, and it was in the hope of quieting those devastating rumors—and in so doing, preserving her family's social and economic standing—that she was compelled to compose her story of twenty "removals" (relocations). Toward the end of her narrative, she protests—too much, given that the protest is apropos of nothing at that point in the story, or even in the paragraph—that nothing had happened:

> *I have been in the midst of those roaring Lyons, and Salvage* [sic] *Bears, that feared neither God, nor Man, nor the Devil, by night and day, alone and in company: sleeping all sorts together, and yet not one of them ever offered me the least abuse of unchastity to me, in word or action. Though some are ready to say, I speak it for my own credit; But I speak it in the presence of God, and to His glory.* (107)

The insistent italics are entirely hers—or her original publisher's. Perhaps the most salient phrase here is this one: "some are ready to say, I speak it for my own credit." Clearly, she had been accused, or had reason to fear accusation, as well as social punishment. Or, her publisher knew that teasing out these suspicions would sell books.

Alexie begins his frequently anthologized short story with an epigraph, evidently a "quote" from Rowlandson's narrative: "*He (my captor) gave me a biscuit, which I put in my pocket, and not daring to eat it, buried it under a log, fearing he had put something in it to make me love him*" (342).

Alexie's fiction romanticizes Mary Rowlandson's "love" for her captor, "the Indian man who has haunted your waking for 300 years" (344), thereby extrapolating, we may conclude, a romanticization of the relations between white women and native men over these few centuries. The story mentions frequently the work of naming, remembering, and forgetting. "I remember your name, Mary Rowlandson. I think of you now, how necessary you have become" (342).

"How much longer can we forgive each other?" Alexie's story asks (343). "It's too late, Mary Rowlandson, for us to sit together and dig up the past you buried under a log, salvage whatever else you had left behind. What do you want?" (344). The narrator's cousins "don't need you, will never search for you in the ash after your house has burned to the ground one more time. It's over" (344).

In the story, another white character, a white boy visiting the reservation one summer, is fictionalized unromantically, treated in fact as white male captives actually were treated during the early conflicts. Which is to say, he is beaten, tortured, and forced to run a gauntlet of contemporary sorts, a masculine competition among equals. "I was the first to stop laughing when the white boy started digging into dirt, shit, the past, looking for somewhere to hide. We did not make him any promises. He was all we had left" (344).

It is not the white *boy*, but the white *woman* who arouses the narrator's more visceral anxieties, haunts the waking of the young native male, inspires his gender-specific anger, the anger of failed romance. Alexie treats Rowlandson as if her fear was of "love," neglecting to acknowledge that "love" could be code for "rape"; and neglecting to acknowledge that, at the very least, she had every reason to fear loss of status back home. He suggests that Rowlandson is guilty of refusing to requite the narrator's mythic fascination with white women.

But here's another nagging problem. I don't know where Alexie got his epigraph, but it's not to be found in the second edition. I assume that he's using one of the many altered versions of Rowlandson's narrative one can discover on library bookshelves, in which event we can forgive Alexie his imprecision. Editors of later editions were in a hurry to exploit the American public's fascination with captivity narratives—those early national(ist) best-sellers—which were received in their day and beyond as adventure fantasies. (*Sovereignty* is one of very few pieces of English-language literature by women that has remained in print for hundreds of years.) In the days before copyright, each subsequent edition bore the mark of its new promoter's attempts to titillate his buying public. Neither the manuscript nor the first edition of Rowlandson's narrative exists, and scholars of early American and women's literatures rely on the extant second edition as that being closest to Rowlandson's actual composition.

"The best weapons are the stories and every time the story is told, something changes," Alexie writes in this same piece (343).

In their day, captivity narratives by white women, altered in their tellings by white male profiteers, were both hugely popular and highly political, performing at least two cultural functions intended by those male editors. First, their primary political purpose, as June Namias has illustrated, was to make westward emigration permissible, by inflaming the populace against natives. The young United States faced a tricky rhetorical challenge: white women had to be taught to withstand the traumas of what for some was unwanted dislocation; had to be conscripted in the conflicts with natives; and had to be taught all of same without being encouraged to turn the direction of their rifles 180 degrees—at the white patriarchs who were most responsible for race and sex discrimination.

Captivity narratives, after defining race relations in these combative terms, served secondly to prescribe gender roles, regardless of race. In his narrative of the captivity of Mary Jemison, first published in 1824, James Seaver wrote:

> One thing respecting the Indian woman is worthy of attention, and perhaps of imitation, although it is now a days considered beneath the dignity of ladies, especially those who are the most refined; and that is, they are under a becoming subjection to their husbands. It is a rule, inculcated in all the Indian tribes, and practised throughout their generations, that a squaw shall not walk before her Indian, nor pretend to take the lead in his business. And for this reason we never can see a party on the march to or from hunting and the like, in which the squaws are not directly in the rear of their partners. (157)

Many white women narrators understood how their stories of captivity would be used. As Brownmiller has indicated, some women did not want their stories told, even when those stories were horrible, knowing that those stories would be used against natives with whom they sympathized—and against the women themselves. The stories were told anyway, when it suited the political needs of white officials to tell them.

Captivity narratives do, however, boast an unintended, and doubtless undesired, achievement: they teach cross-cultural collaboration. Mary Jemison, who was captured near my own hometown in central Pennsylvania in the late eighteenth century, was one of several women who chose to remain with their adopted peoples even when their release had been approved. Despite James Seaver's intrusive editing, and the fictional enhancement of Jemison's story by a series of male (re)publishers, Jemison's warmth for her adopted Seneca people is clear. Publishers were especially unable to conceal wealth she ultimately accumulated as a landowner, and the esteemed leadership position Jemison won among the Seneca—a position unavailable to her in European America.

Indeed, the details of her adaptation to Seneca lifeways serve as a workbook on how two very different peoples can come together and accommodate one another. Even those white women (and white men) who did not remain with their captors tell stories of survival, stories that provide instruction in cross-cultural merging.

Necessarily then, as Vine Deloria, Jr. has pointed out, these survival stories provide information about a possible alternative to the genocidal policy European invaders chose to pursue with natives. Michelle Burnham affirms that, even in the case of a text such as Rowlandson's, which is particularly antinative, the facts of Rowlandson's captivity as she relates them belie the prejudices Rowlandson expresses. The narrative implicitly "critiques the assumption that readers can identify only with figures whose culture, race, or nationality resembles their own" (52).

So, while white women have been used to HELP effect this genocidal policy, by HELPING to inflame rage against "rapists"—have HELPED to effect a genocide from which we white women have benefited—white women have also served as primary explorers, among whites, of alternative relations between races—relations of accommodation and adaptation, rather than genocide.

The story of one HELPer is particularly painful. Please permit me a retelling. When the Dakota conflict of 1862 was over, and Sarah Wakefield was released from her captivity, and more than one thousand Dakota men were imprisoned and charged with what today would be called "trumped-up" war crimes—charged, in effect, with having made war in the first place—when Wakefield protested that Chaska, her protector, could not have been present at the atrocity of which he was accused—well, the more she protested, the more (Wakefield suspected) the powers that be felt she protested too much. So when Chaska was "accidentally" hung, his mother blamed Wakefield, for being unable to HELP.

The two women, one red, one white, never spoke again.

Was Wakefield naive to insist on telling the story? What would I have done in Wakefield's place? I suffer, as you know, from this storytelling impulse. From this drive to get the record as complete as possible.

Damn.

As I think about myself and my predecessors—of the Sarah Wakefields, the Mary Jemisons, the Helen Hunt Jacksons, the white women who have concerned themselves with Native American issues—the white women who have HELPED—and those who have NOT HELPED—I begin to suspect that indeed, white women *have* HELPED a *bit*.

We/they have HELPED to address all interdependent dominatings together. Many white women have acted as bridge figures, a term usually reserved in Native American studies for natives who operated between the cultures, translating each back to the other. Male "Tonto characters" are and were frequently criticized as people with fraught loyalties, facing admiration and revilement on both sides. Bridge figures are frequently used *against* the marginalized peoples they hope to bridge *to*.

Squanto serves as an archetypal bridge figure, legendary as the native who taught the Puritan Pilgrims how to farm, saving them from starvation. As a child, Squanto had been taken (perhaps against his will) to labor in England in the early years of the seventeenth century, thus learning English. There he was seized by a British slave trader, with other North American natives, and sold into slavery in Spain. He escaped and made his way back to New England, only to find that his entire village was lost to European disease. He found a new and familiar community among the Mayflower emigrants, and remained to HELP them.

Given European restrictions regarding the role of women in society, female bridge figures face an even more fraught arena of appreciation. Speculation continues as to whether Sakakawea slept with William Clark, of Lewis and Clark fame. (I use the spelling of her name that closely resembles the Shoshone phonemes.) While Squanto's motivations seem clear (he had lost his people), historians still fret over Sakakawea's—even though she too had lost her people.

Sakakawea had been taken from the Lemhi Shoshone when she was around the age of ten and made a slave by the Hidatsa, who then sold her to the French trapper Charbonneau when she was about fourteen; she was pregnant when, at age sixteen, Charbonneau contracted himself as an "interpreter" to Lewis and Clark. Sakakawea would do most of the interpreting; would perform heroic feats like leaping into treacherous waters to save valuable equipment; would provide food when the entourage was in danger of starving; would guide the "voyage of discovery" through familiar Shoshone territory; would give birth to her son without the aid of any other women; and would negotiate safe-passage permissions with many native leaders, including—in a stunning accident—a Shoshone leader who would turn out to be her brother, Cameahwait.

Historians have often asked why Sakakawea, upon (re)discovering her brother, did not leave the expedition for the presumed safety of her brother's village. Historians also never fail to point out that while Meriwether Lewis treated the girl coldly—until she had saved his ass so many times that he had no choice but to grudgingly admire her—William Clark treated her affectionately. In his journals he called her "Janey," and gratefully catalogued the special gifts of food and ornament she bestowed upon him. Anthropologists like Clara Sue Kidwell claim that Sakakawea had little choice but to stay with the expedition, since as "a captive and the wife of a white man, she no longer had a place within the structure of her own tribe" (qtd. in McCall 46).

Why do historians continue to find disputatious Sakakawea's decision to remain with Lewis and Clark, while Squanto's return to his New England comrades raises nary an eyebrow? Surely both Sakakawea and Squanto were subject to conflicted loyalties, yet Squanto's go unremarked (along with his male status); while Sakakawea's loyalty—to Clark in particular, and to the expedition in general—continues to provoke controversy. As it is customarily rendered, though, Sakakawea's decision seems to stem from a rather "womanly" set of virtues—particularly, the virtue of muted sexuality. We can wonder, for instance, whether she had sex with Clark; but as to whether she acted of her own free will in staying with the expedition—well, surely, as a woman, she must have more mysterious motivations (among which, sex with Clark). By ascribing to her a conventionally feminine agency—which agency is understood as encumbered by her status as a woman—Sakakawea can be made to serve as a stand-in for any representative virtue—or vice.

Indeed, when white feminists fashioned Sakakawea into a fin-de-siècle "symbol of the strong, accomplished woman," as historian Laura McCall reports (42), it was her nationalistic contribution we wished to memorialize. As an adventuress, she was the equal of Lewis and Clark in exploring this great land (etc.). It was not Sakakawea's acting of her own free will that we recalled when commissioning statues all over the country. And when some late-twentieth-century white feminists reframed their assessment of Sakakawea as complicit in her own people's genocide, it was again not her freedom of choice we recuperated.

I mean, surely we would not put on the head of a coin the face of a woman who fully exercised all of her freedoms.

Too, Kidwell correctly asserts that when questioning Sakakawea's decisions, we must remember that she would have "acted from motives that were determined by [her] own culture," not ours (qtd. in McCall 50). What is it about our culture that has compelled white feminists like me to have so vitiated Sakakawea's agency? European American gender constructs are likely at play here. Kidwell also writes that "Indian women were the first important mediators of meaning between the cultures of the two worlds" (qtd. in McCall 50). So Squanto's freedom to mediate goes unchallenged historically, but Sakakawea's remain suspect. And her motivations must have been—sex.

The same can be said for white women bridge figures.

What happens when a white woman works as a bridge figure?

History gives us two models. We have the Sarah Wakefields, who risked their social standing to protest the treatment of natives. This model is largely forgotten. Recall your grade school education, and name one such legendary figure your teacher told you about.

The second model is the white, female captive. Now these we sometimes remember.

And you'll recall that both Sarah Wakefield and Mary Rowlandson—both HELPER and NOT-HELPER—were accused by their contemporaries of having had sex with native men.

DIGRESSION THE FOURTH

We live today in an era of attempted remembering.

During the summer of 1998—the summer of her husband's sex scandal—Hillary Rodham Clinton took a tour similar to mine. She traveled from historic site to historic site, arguing for the preservation of landmarks. In particular, she stood for a photo opportunity at the site of the (apparently crumbling) Thomas Edison edifice.

Given the political clime of that moment, we may conclude that support for historical preservation must be a fairly safe political "opportunity" for vulnerable political figures such as now-Senator Clinton, who won approval in this country only after having been "victimized" in 1998 by her philandering husband. In our culture, the only sort of female protest we will listen to is the protest of the victim. And then, we listen to her only when she isn't expressing that protest angrily, when she isn't (heavens!) implicating *us* in her complaint.

We may also conclude that some histories are safer than others. Apparently no one disagrees that Thomas Edison's legacy must be preserved.

Inaccurate though some of that legacy may be. In 1951, a British film premiered entitled *The Magic Box*. Directed by John Boulting and starring Robert Donat, this four-star film tells the story of William Friese-Greene, the "real" inventor of movies, who struggled financially throughout his life not least because credit for inventing movies accrued to others, particularly Edison. Well, the Brits have their inventors, the French theirs, the Danes theirs, the United States ours, and so forth. All are appropriately territorial appropriations.

Point is, these days a good bit of the remembering occurring in popular culture can be found in movie theaters. In fact, Natalie Zemon Davis, former president of the American Historical Association, told the *New York Observer* in December 2002 that academia should encourage this medium of remembering. "I think," she says, "that for historians at least, making films—and not just documentaries, but historical fiction—could be a wonderfully creative way of thinking about history" (see McGeveran and Traister). Herself the screenwriter of 1983's *Le Retour de Martin Guerre*, Davis argues this primarily to address the increasing difficulty of getting an academic book published, and an academic career established—but that's a problem for another day.

We've seen how well pulp novels and roadside historical sites are educating the U.S. populace. How well is (semiacademic) Hollywood doing? *Schindler's List. Amistad. Buffalo Soldiers. Tuskegee Airmen. Beloved. Rosewood.*

Rosewood.
I had to watch *Rosewood* twice.
This 1997 film purports to tell the true story of the destruction of the black community of Rosewood, Florida, in the first days of 1923,

a devastation sown by one white woman's false accusation of an assault against her by a black man.

Immediately we know, then, that here is another story at that same crossroads, that violent intersection between racism and sexism.

As the credits roll, however, we quickly see that this film is about men. We know this because the first five cast members are men. We see that we have a male producer (Jon Peters), writer (Gregory Poirier), and director (John Singleton).

The film begins with Sylvester Carrier (Don Cheadle), a black music teacher, playing his piano; but cuts to the image of white Mr. Wright (Jon Voight), roughly fucking a young black woman, whom we soon learn is Sylvester's cousin Jewel. Jewel does not appear to be enjoying the sex. We learn that Mr. Wright is in the back of the store he owns—along with plenty of other property—in the heart of this black town; that Jewel works for him there; and that he's getting rich by overcharging his black customers and refusing to serve those who don't play along with his white man's monopoly.

I will digress here to mention an odd moment of little import to the plot. The next scene shows the murdering bigot Duke Purdy (Bruce McGill) out hunting boar. He's teaching his son Emmett to be a murdering bigot too. "You'll be a man soon," Duke tells Emmett. "I'll get you there." Emmett doesn't want to take the shot, so Duke kills the boar. Duke lectures his son in nonstandard English (thus identifying him as lower in class than the black piano teacher): "The Seminole say you only supposed to kill what you eat." It is strange that the film's only acknowledgment that both whites and blacks profit in Florida on stolen Seminole land—should come from the mouth of a survivalist, a white separatist who has borrowed his personal notion of masculine identity from some stereotypical, mythic notion of "noble native."

White Sheriff Walker (Michael Rooker) comes by to let us know that a black man has escaped from prison and is on the loose.

Cut to the Taylor house, in the nearby white town of Sumner. Young James (Loren Dean) wants to have sex with his wife Fanny (Catherine Kellner, *way* down in the cast list), but she shrugs him off not least because black Aunt Sarah (Esther Rolle) is working in the next room and can hear everything they're doing. James slaps his wife and leaves.

Next we are treated to scenes intended to let us know that black Rosewood is financially secure, is "doing better" than white-trash Sumner, with black men fully employed in lumberyards (owned by whites). When a black World War I vet named Mr. Mann (Ving Rhames) happens through, he's encouraged to remain in this haven, the likes of which, he admits, he has never encountered. Plus, James Bradley has five acres of Rosewood land to sell. Everyone assumes Mr. Wright will win the bidding at the next day's auction. Mr. Wright, who points out that he too is a veteran of the Spanish-American War, is surprised to discover that Mr. Mann has money, and intends to bid on the same five acres of land Mr. Wright wants.

So this will be a film about Mr. Wright and Mr. Mann, who are competing to control five acres of land in the economic-boom center of Rosewood. While the women in the story negotiate various demands for sex or subservience—or sexual subservience.

At New Year's Eve dinner, Sylvester tells his family that he paid a visit to some white men who had whistled at Scrappie (Elise Neal), soon to become Mr. Mann's romantic interest. "I don't mess with your people, and I don't want you messing with mine," he tells the white men.

Sylvester's concerns seem to have less to do with the "messings" than with the "yours" and "mines." Thus are the women of one race (as we've said) used against another, exploited *as* property in the racial, economic conflict *over* property. I'll say it again: If we didn't in the first place define women of all races as property, this comment would not resonate as it does with the film's focus on land ownership.

Thirty minutes into the film, on New Year's Day, the plot thickens. Aunt Sarah is outside the Taylor house, working with Philomena, another of the Carrier clan. She hears sexual activity inside. The camera shows someone (again roughly) fucking Fanny (again, Fanny's having no fun here). As the man finishes and begins to dress, Fanny accuses him of "double-timing" her. The camera finally reveals that the man is not her husband—and that he's white. Fanny presses her charge and the man responds by beating her, badly. Aunt Sarah and Philomena hear it all, do nothing to help, and also see the man emerge from the house.

Let's set aside for a moment the utter illogic of any woman begging to remain in the company of such a lousy lay.

Aunt Sarah and Philomena do nothing to help. These are not simply three women, then; these are two women of one race/class and one woman of another race/class ("yours" and "mine").

From there, the film follows three plot lines at once: the auction of Bradley's land, Fanny's accusation, and the journey of Fanny's "lover" (Robert Patrick), who goes to Sam Carter, Rosewood's black blacksmith, for help in getting out of town.

At the auction, Mr. Mann offends the whites by bidding up the price of Mr. Wright's land.

Back at Fanny's, Aunt Sarah watches as the bruised white woman comes out of her house and begins to scream for help. "A nigger done it!" she wails, a "stranger." We are left to conclude that she's doing this because she can think of no other way to explain to her husband the severe injury to her entire body. Aunt Sarah shushes Philomena and remains silent. The auction is interrupted when the deputy arrives to report Fanny's accusation. The men again employ some rather limited logic and decide that the prison escapee must have done this; there is some suspicion that Mr. Mann might be this escapee.

Sheriff Walker delicately asks Fanny if the man raped her. She responds with horror. "I sure wasn't raped," she insists. "Just got beat."

Yes, *anything* but face the shame of having been raped. Obviously, Fanny is willing to humiliate herself only so far.

A mob forms quickly, led by Duke Purdy and never adequately controlled by Sheriff Walker, and the dogs lead right to Sam Carter—and to another logic leap, that Sam must have helped the escapee get away. The dialogue frequently alludes to miscegenation while the first innocent black man is hung. A beaten Sam Carter says to Duke, "You can kill me but you can't eat me. You ain't no Seminole." For this bizarre insult, Duke shoots him dead. Meanwhile, Mr. Wright refuses to sell bullets to Sylvester; in return, Sylvester yanks Jewel out of the store, indicating that he well knows what's been going on between them.

From which we conclude that he would have left her there if only Mr. Wright had sold him the damn bullets.

At home, Fanny is finally getting the loving attention of which she's clearly been deprived—the only such attention she receives in the whole film—from James. Uncomfortable with the concern, she says, "I'm just a woman." What this non sequitur means the filmmakers do not tell us. When James tells her Sam Carter's been killed, she begins, horrified, to tell him the truth. But neighbor women knock at the door bringing still more affection, and she silences herself.

That night at church, Aunt Sarah tells the black community that she saw a white man leave the Taylor house. There is some discussion about whether she should have told the sheriff this immediately, but she insists that they would have killed her. Indeed, the next day, when the mob comes to the Carrier house, Sylvester gets his gun and a standoff begins. Aunt Sarah goes out and tells them about the white man—and she's shot dead as soon as the word "white" leaves her lips.

The massacre starts then in earnest, and goes on for days. We see men and women hung, homes and businesses burned, the Ku Klux Klan on horseback, women and children on the run through swamps, mass graves. Mr. Wright is disgusted, but doesn't stop the white mob from taking ammunition out of his store. When the sheriff promises to pay him back, it becomes clear that Wright takes profit from both sides of the conflict.

From there, it's the story of two old war heroes: Mr. Wright bonds with Mr. Mann, who left town to save himself, then returned, and will henceforth manage several times to escape being killed. Mr. Mann's vastly superior military prowess makes him the hero of the film. Mr. Wright, accused by the mob of being a "nigger lover," is finally convinced—by his new wife—to hide some of the black customers who made him rich in the first place. In the film's climax, he uses his social status as a rich white man (which status, unlike violent prowess, is not romanticized in the film as heroism) to arrange for a train to pick up the women and children who are hiding in the swamp. Mr. Mann leads the women and children to the meeting point.

Meanwhile, in another odd aside for this film, Mrs. Wright lets us know that she has right along felt like a guest in her new home, with little say about what goes on there. Finally, in her husband's absence, she picks up a gun and stands off the mob that has come to capture the people she convinced her husband to hide. When her stepsons tell their father what she did, this act becomes her acceptance into the family.

We can't help but wonder why she didn't take similar good aim at her ass of a husband. And we can only hope that her sex life will now be better than Jewel's. Or Fanny's.

The women and children escape on the train in a final shoot-out; we're given to understand that Sylvester and Mr. Mann survive as well.

The incompetent white sheriff convinces James—belatedly—of the inevitable truth.

Thus righteously justified, James goes home and beats his wife.

Duke Purdy's son Emmett decides to leave home. "I hate you," he tells his rotten bigot father. "You ain't no man."

The final scene is of a smoking Rosewood, over which an end card tells us that in 1993, the Florida legislation at last granted reparations to the Rosewood families. "The success of the case was due largely to the sworn testimony of several SURVIVORS . . . and to the deposition of one WHITE citizen who testified on behalf of the victims. The official death toll of the Rosewood massacre, according to the state of Florida, is eight . . . two WHITE and six BLACK. The survivors, a handful of whom are still alive today, place the number anywhere between 40 and 150, nearly all of them AFRICAN AMERICAN."

In my *Rand McNally Road Atlas*, neither Sumner nor Rosewood is visible on the Florida state map.

That's a lot of detail about a film, I know.

But this film really makes me sweat.

What the male filmmakers don't seem to recognize here is that *the action of their film begins and ends with the beating of a woman.*

Said beaten woman is then demonized as being the Eve, the cause of the massacre, the cause of the loss of Rosewood's paradise. The NOT-HELPER. Indeed, even for a feminist like me, Fanny's final beating is an effective catharsis, the final poetic justice of the film.

And it's a bit of an unfair catharsis, if we believe Susan Brownmiller: "[T]he black man's fortune was inextricably and historically linked to the white woman's reputation for chastity, a terrifying imbroglio that the black man and the white woman neither created nor controlled" (221).

The film, which is (trust me on this) proimbroglio, promilitary, and (under certain conditions) proviolence, does not question the underlying notion that women's bodies are male property; that heterosexual practice has exclusively to do with forceful, penile penetration; that female sexuality, and choice of mate, must on the one hand be controlled, and must on the other hand be avenged when "violated." The film seems unaware that Sylvester does not protest Mr. Wright's sexual exploitation of Jewel until a competitive military situation develops between them. It does not note that even Mrs. Wright, the richest woman in Rosewood, has no power over what goes on in her house, including Mr. Wright's sexual activity, which she cannot and does not challenge. The film seems vaguely aware of the ways in which racial constructs are used to perpetuate constructions of gender: "I'm just a woman," Fanny says; "You ain't no man," Emmett says. And it seems vaguely aware that, at bottom, race and gender constructs serve primarily to perpetuate white monopolies: Mr. Mann might never have been noticed in that town, and subsequently threatened in any way, had he not offended the whites by attempting to buy

that land away from Mr. Wright. But the filmmakers, however enlightened they may be, are unable to wade through this morass of
complication, and in the end give us an antiwoman, probullet, prope-
nis work of racial incitement.

In this way, our cultural moment of remembering moves forward
in baby steps. John Singleton helps us remember the racial and economic conflict of Rosewood (I had never heard of the event prior to
his film).

Baby step.

Perhaps fifty years from now, three screenwriters, a black woman
and a white woman and a Seminole woman, will write a more complete story of Rosewood.

They'll write about how the Seminole were removed, and how
white and black women were used against each other by white and
black men on the battlefield of property dispute.

An economic conflict that wouldn't even be possible if the Seminole hadn't been "removed."

Of course it is the concept of HELP that most requires revision.
Some have pointed out that the problem with bleeding-heart liberalism
is that our blood spill is rarely attended by accountability. Grief does
not always lead to activism. Guilt does not lead to the sort of change
that would threaten the socioeconomic position of the guilty. Grief
rarely results in a willingness to accept personal responsibility. "I didn't
do it, my ancestors did!" my students often wail. OK. But I continue to
profit from what my ancestors did. Am I willing to return that profit?

Perhaps left-leaning folks like me who think they want to HELP
should put themselves through a bit of a self-test.

Am I willing to do everything I can to contribute to an emerging
situation of mutual parity?

Let's consider again the work of Ward Churchill. Churchill has
written that progressive whites, who are otherwise HELPful, get a bit
"queasy" when he makes proposals—such as the restoration to natives of one-third of the land in the forty-eight states, most of it west
of the Mississippi—that would lead to real sovereignty for natives.

You'll recall that Curtis Warner argues for the necessity of land.
In our capitalist society, property equals parity.

White progressives who want to HELP natives are often stymied
by the realization that many native radicals want nothing to do with

Marxism or feminism. Ward Churchill has written that "indigenous spokespersons such as Russell Means . . . view marxism not as a potential revolutionary transformation of world capitalism, but as a *continuation* of all of capitalism's worst vices 'in [quoting Means] a more efficient form'" (*Son* 467). Instead, Churchill writes, "We must continue to pursue our traditional vision of a humanity *within* rather than *upon* the natural order" (*Son* 479). Churchill's intent is to:

> arrive at new sets of relationships between peoples that effectively put an end to the era of international domination. The need is to gradually replace the existing world order with one that is predicated on collaboration and cooperation between nations. . . . A concomitant of this disassembly is the inculcation of voluntary, consensual interdependence between formerly dominated and dominating nations, and a redefinition of the word "nation" itself to conform to its original meaning: bodies of people bound together by their bioregional and other natural cultural affinities. (*Son* 532)

Voluntary, consensual, interdependent use of resources.

Further, "If we are to be about turning power relations around between people, and between groups of people, we must also be about turning around the relationship between people and the rest of the natural order" (*Son* 535).

Turning around the power relation between the dominating and the dominated.

I would interject that this binary, this apparent pairing of only two choices—dominating or dominated—is insufficient to chart the complexity of those who are both dominating and dominated. Then all three. Then shades of all three. *Et cetera.*

But OK. Turning power relations around. Let's.

DIGRESSION THE FIFTH

When white women HELP, we are often unaware of our implicit insistence upon our own privilege. That we feel we are *able* to HELP, that we have the ability to, say, VOLUNTEER, is due to the privilege of whiteness—that (varying) access we do have to the top of the power scheme.

I shudder when I recall Stowe's alternate title for *Uncle Tom's Cabin*.

Life among the Lowly.

To paraphrase Howard Zinn, How certain are we that what we HELP is inferior?

American Indian Movement (AIM) activist Mary Crow Dog told Richard Erdoes, for their 1990 book *Lakota Woman*, the story of her participation in 1973's second siege of Wounded Knee. You may remember Mary Crow Dog as the woman who famously gave birth to her baby right in the middle of that standoff, refusing to leave her comrades-in-arms. "Most of the New York women who had supported us had been feminists," Crow Dog reports. "On some points I had disagreed with them. To me, women's lib was mainly a white, upper-middle-class affair of little use to a reservation Indian woman. With all their good intentions some had patronized me, even used me as an exotic conversation piece at their fancy parties" (244).

I have no doubt that this is true.

Perhaps I'm even doing that myself, here.

I have myself been guilty of a thing I call "political codependency," empowering myself by being so HELPful to a people "in need," thus helping myself to feel indispensable—as well as not in need of help myself.

As noted, white women are susceptible to a tendency to interact with others this way not least because our place within patriarchy is tenuous. When white women HELP nonwhites, we cement our status as representatives of whiteness.

This is how we know that racial oppression and gender oppression are inextricably linked. When she turns on C-SPAN, it takes only a minute for a little girl (of any color) to see that she won't be running this town anytime soon. She can only HELP now as she is able, as she is permitted—and this ability will differ from race to race and from class to class.

Political codependency is a problem not just for those we HELP but also for ourselves. Psychologists will tell you that codependents often distract themselves from their own problems when they focus on the problems of others.

So who's been in charge of women's rights while we white women have dabbled in native rights?

Which brings us to the story of Joanna LeDeaux.

I know. It's another long story.

Last one, I promise.

On June 26, 1975, *a day that shall live in infamy*, LeDeaux, white, young, probably middle class, lived on the Pine Ridge Reservation of South Dakota, serving as an aide to the Wounded Knee Defense Committee. The committee had been set up to provide legal support for members of the American Indian Movement who had been arrested for participation in the 1973 occupation of Wounded Knee.

I won't rehash for you every detail of the day of the "ResMurs" (or "Reservation Murders," the FBI's name for the case that resulted in the political imprisonment of Leonard Peltier), but the story of Joanna LeDeaux is one you probably don't recall. After FBI Special Agents Ronald Williams and Jack R. Coler set out that morning with a warrant to arrest Jimmy Eagle for the incredibly pressing crime of having stolen a pair of cowboy boots from a white poker buddy; after the agents followed Mr. X and his passenger in their pickup truck onto the Jumping Bull compound—west of Wounded Knee, just south of Oglala; after (who shot first?) gunfire was exchanged; after Mr. X shot and killed Special Agents Williams and Coler, execution style; after Mr. X and his passenger left the area so their load of explosives wouldn't be ignited by gunfire (yes, explosives—Pine Ridge was a war zone then); after Leonard Peltier, Bob Robideau, Dino Butler, and others ran down from their camp and began exchanging fire with other agents from some elevated distance away; after most of the women and children in the compound had begun to leave the area; after a large force of (somehow, mysteriously) nearby law enforcement officials had begun to descend on the compound from all directions; and *just* after Peltier, Robideau, and Butler approached the agents' cars, surveyed the scene, listened to the radios and heard what kind of force was coming down on them; and *just* after Peltier began to help organize what would ultimately be a miraculous escape from a vast FBI dragnet—

—in the middle of one of the most violent, chaotic moments in contemporary U.S. law enforcement history—

—young, white Joanna LeDeaux walks down the ridge at the edge of the Jumping Bull compound—

—*to HELP*.

She had convinced the FBI to let her go in, hoping to negotiate a cease-fire, arrange for any necessary medical help, and give the women and children a chance to leave safely.

(Reading this again in Peter Matthiessen's *In the Spirit of Crazy Horse*, I'm thinking, *Bizarre.*

(I'm thinking, *Joanna, Joanna, Joanna. What the hell were you thinking?*)

But the women—those who wanted to leave—and children were already gone. The gunfire had already ceased. The agents were dead, so Peltier had no leverage with which to negotiate. He had already waited too long to get the hell out of there.

An hour later, LeDeaux left.

This strange incident began when LeDeaux had just happened to be driving her station wagon near the shoot-out and she was stopped by FBI Agent David Price, who tried to commandeer her vehicle because his own engine had overheated in his rush to the scene. He told her about the gunfire at the Jumping Bulls's house and she drove him to the area, insisting that he would have to get out before they arrived, so that she wouldn't be seen HELPING the FBI by driving him there. (*Joanna!*) According to the FBI, who watched her every move through rifle scopes, she drove her wagon to June Little's house; walked the short distance into the compound; talked briefly with three or four native men; vanished into the cabins; and walked toward the bluff from which the bodies of the agents could be seen in the flat below. Then she drove out, met BIA Superintendent Kendall Cummings, and told him that no negotiations were going to happen. Cummings said she was "frustrated and crying," and wouldn't discuss it further. She left before the FBI thought to ask her what she had seen.

This was because, when she left, the FBI and the BIA were distracted by a brief argument about who would get to be field marshal for the assault storm on the compound—the next logical step, as far as the G-men were concerned.

Not to mention the fact that, shortly after Joanna left, the FBI trained their weapons on the camp and hollered, "This is the FBI!" In response to which two young AIM men began to run for cover, firing one warning shot as they ran; at which point the feds fired off a bunch of guns at once, instantly ending the life of Joe Killsright Stuntz.

That "ResMur" has never been investigated.

Two days later, the FBI went looking for LeDeaux. Belatedly they realized that she was, after all, the first official to visit the compound following the murders; doubtless she could serve as a witness for the prosecution of *someone*. In the ensuing weeks, the FBI discovered that she and Leonard had been romantically involved in recent months, a discovery that implicated her as a possible accessory to what the FBI was now trying to prove had been an ambush of their agents. Angie Long Visitor, the Jumping Bulls's granddaughter, and her husband Ivis, had spoken to the FBI in the early days about what they knew; but when it became clear to the Lakota community that it was actually the FBI that was trying to ambush AIM, everyone clammed up tight. The first grand jury had to be dismissed for lack of witnesses. A second was convened, and the Long Visitors and Joanna LeDeaux, who was by then pregnant, were imprisoned for contempt. Because she would not testify, LeDeaux spent eight months in federal prison in San Pedro, California, delivering her baby there. Prison authorities refused to let her nurse her baby; public outrage led to her release.

What did the AIM warriors think of LeDeaux's HELP?

Peltier and Robideau saw "that white woman" (qtd. in Matthiessen 433) walking down the hill from where they were standing near the agents' bodies. Robideau told Matthiessen, "I seen Leonard get angry. Leonard don't get excited too often, but when he does, you can see it from a long way off" (550). Peltier told Matthiessen that he was "feeling crazy" at that moment. "I felt we were all dead. . . . [T]here were still women and children up there in June's cabin. . . . So I was running back and forth, making sure that everybody was moving out; we knew what was coming. And all of a sudden I look up and see this *white* woman! . . . *Shock!* Where in hell did *she* come from!" (550).

Peltier agrees he "got pretty excited—I did. I couldn't take it in— what was she *doing* there? Here was this white woman up there on the hill screaming, Stop! Stop! Stop *what*? What the hell's she talking about? I mean, this was a while after they were killed. Joe [Killsright] was back up there, and I hollered to him, Get her *out* of there!" (550).

Robideau says that LeDeaux asked if anyone needed medical attention, and that Peltier told her no—"kind of rough, you know" (550). Then she wanted to go down the hill to tend to the agents. "She started to insist, and he got mad, yelling, Nobody down there needs medical assistance, because they're all dead! What we need here now is ammunition!" (551). Dino Butler told Matthiessen, "Leonard was angry that she was in there in the first place; I guess he figured that this white woman was the last thing we needed at a time like that" (551). Robideau then took LeDeaux to a cabin where he thought Nilak Butler and her children might still be, but they didn't find them. He adds that he tried to explain that he, Peltier and Butler, whom LeDeaux had seen standing by the agents' cars, guns in hand, had not killed the agents; then he encouraged her to leave, since there was nothing she could do.

"Some of them Oglala women," Robideau concludes, "didn't like her so much—there was some kind of a personality problem—but she never said one word to the feds about who she had seen in there, or what, even though she spent eight months in jail" (551).

Joanna LeDeaux was indeed the first official to visit the compound after the agents were killed, but her story is an aside in Matthiessen's massive, indispensable study of "the FBI's war on the American Indian Movement"; he interviews damn near *everyone* who knew *anything* about the case—but not Joanna. Although the story of Peltier's *anger* at her presence receives rather lengthy attention (550–551), the story of her actual appearance does not appear in the book in any sort of cohesive summary. I have pieced it together from various mentions throughout the book. In fact, I did not, I must admit, notice her story myself until a recent third read. Peltier's book, *Prison Writings*, and Michael Apted's documentary, *Incident at Oglala*, mention her not at all. In truth, she is a troublesome historical detail; she progresses the plot not a whit, had zero impact on the outcome of the "incident." Matthiessen never asks the immediate and plaguing question that pops up for any woman who can count to nine: *Who is the father of her child?*

Joanna, Joanna. What were we thinking?

I can't help but ask. What bothered Peltier the most: that LeDeaux was *white* or that she was a *woman*? Matthiessen's italics, which we assume reflect Peltier's tone, suggest an easy answer: *white*. There were native women, including Jean Bordeaux and Nilak Butler, among the fugitives as they ran from the camp. But we could speculate that Peltier might have seen a white *man* as the *second* to "last thing" he needed that day; presumably a white *man* could have, say, handled a rifle, or been of some other practical use.

So the truth is that the problem is indivisible: LeDeaux was white *and* woman.

When I related LeDeaux's story to a group of feminist colleagues, they clucked their tongues and wondered *why*. An elder African American historian recalled her own work in the Civil Rights movement, these many years ago, and how much the black women activists hated the white women activists. "They always seemed to be sleeping with our men. Why is that?" A Native American sociologist nodded and said the men the white women chose to sleep with often amazed her. She mentioned the name of a renowned male AIM member. "What did they see in him? He's not good-looking, and we don't even think he's Indian."

When I mentioned my political codependency theory, they all nodded in unison. "Men of color and white women," one colleague said—"it seems like a natural alliance. They unify to fight the white man."

"But the men of color," another answered, "see it as a one-way street. The white woman is there to help him get at the white man. But does he see that he should be helping the white woman?"

Again in unison, all shook their heads sadly.

DIGRESSION THE SIXTH

Repeating: The intersection of sexism and racism was bound to be a violent place.

Ward Churchill writes:

> Very often in my writings and lectures, I have identified myself as being "indigenist" in outlook. By this, I mean that I am one who not only takes the rights of indigenous peoples as the highest priority of my political life, but who draws on the traditions—the bodies of knowledge and corresponding codes of value—evolved over many thousands of years by native peoples the world over. This is the basis on which I not only advance critiques of, but conceptualize alternatives to, the present social, political, economic, and philosophical status quo. In turn, this gives shape not only to the sorts of goals and objectives I pursue, but the kinds of strategy and tactics I advocate, the variety of struggles I tend to support, the nature of the alliances I'm inclined to enter into, and so on. (*Son* 512)

Churchill goes on to say that indigenism "cannot be associated with the legacy of the 'Hang Around the Fort' Indians [elsewhere also 'Vichy Indians'], broken, disempowered, and intimidated by their conquerors, the sell-outs who undermined the integrity of their own culture, appointed by the United States to sign away their peoples' homelands in exchange for trinkets, sugar and alcohol. . . ." Instead, "indigenism stands in diametrical opposition to the totality of what might be termed 'Eurocentric business as usual'" (*Son* 512).

Further, "the beginning point for any indigenist endeavor in the United States centers, logically enough, in efforts to restore direct

Indian control over the huge portion of the continental United States that was plainly never ceded by native nations" (*Son* 519).

Again, this is what Curtis Warner is saying. Give us the land.

But, my white students often say, We conquered Them. They lost the land, and that's just How It Goes when you *Conquer* someone. (More on this in a bit.)

Churchill:

> The unqualified acknowledgment of the right of the colonized to total separation ("secession") by the colonizer is the necessary point of departure for any exercise of self-determination. Decolonization means the colonized can then exercise the right in whole or in part, as they see fit, in accordance with their own customs and traditions and their own appreciation of their needs. They decide for themselves what degree of autonomy they wish to enjoy, and thus the nature of their political and economic relationships, not only with their former colonizers, but with all other nations as well. (*Son*, 531).

I feel that I do understand Churchill's point—not least because I am a woman. And further, as Gloria Steinem would have it, because I am not a blind woman. (I forget where I heard her say this: There are two kinds of women: feminist and blind.)

Permit me to borrow Churchill's words.

I have identified myself as being "feminist" in outlook. By this, I mean that I am one who not only takes the rights of women as the highest priority of my political life, but who draws on the traditions—the bodies of knowledge and corresponding codes of value—evolved over many thousands of years by women the world over. This is the basis on which I not only advance critiques of, but conceptualize alternatives to, the present social, political, economic, and philosophical status quo. In turn, this gives shape not only to the sorts of goals and objectives I pursue, but the kinds of strategy and tactics I advocate, the variety of struggles I tend to support, the nature of the alliances I'm inclined to enter into, and so on.

Feminism cannot be associated with the legacy of the "Hang Around the House" women, broken, disempowered, and intimidated by their conquerors, the sell-outs who undermined the integrity of their own sex, appointed by states the world over to sign away their bodies in exchange for trinkets, sugar and alcohol. Instead, feminism stands in diametrical opposition to the totality of what might be termed "male governance business as usual."

The beginning point for any feminist endeavor in the United States centers, logically enough, in efforts to restore direct female control over the huge portion of bodies that were plainly never ceded by women.

The unqualified acknowledgment of the right of women to total separation ("secession") by the colonizer is the necessary point of departure for any exercise of self-determination. Decolonization means women can exercise the right in whole or in part, as they see fit, in accordance with their own customs and traditions and their own appreciation of their needs. They decide for themselves what degree of autonomy they wish to enjoy, and thus the nature of their political and economic relationships, not only with their colonizers, but with all other peoples as well.

Churchill might not like my doing that. (I don't entirely like it myself, as it's too second wave—but more on this later.)

I suspect he might not like it because he also points out that "making things like class inequity and sexism the preeminent focus of progressive action in North America inevitably perpetuates the internal colonial structure of the United States" (*Son* 521).

I will assume that there is some truth in this assertion. Many feminists have asserted that women have been especially complicit in their own subordination, their own dominating—for instance, by blaming Hang-Around-the-House women.

For women to subvert patriarchy, they would have to subvert— patriarchy. Hierarchy. And many middle-class and upper-class white heterosexual women wish to protect the minimal privileges available to them.

So I'm willing to assume that attention to sexism, half-assed as it usually is in this country, *does* help divert attention from the larger interdependencies of many subordinations. Many dominatings.

I would concede that to Churchill, whose writings I have much admired. But he seems unwilling to concede to me that gender-specific dominating is just as important as race-specific dominating.

For Churchill also claims that "[t]here is no indication whatsoever that a restoration of indigenous sovereignty in Indian Country would foster class stratification anywhere, least of all in Indian Country" (*Son* 522). Similarly, he asks, "Would sexism be perpetuated?" He suggests not. "Women in most traditional native societies not only enjoyed political, social, and economic parity with men, they often held a preponderance of power in one or more of these spheres" (*Son* 522). Ditto homophobia.

And so here we part ways.

I assume there is almost no truth to his *implication* that neither sexism nor elitism exists in Indian Country; I must say implication because, in an odd rhetorical dodge, he speaks first of the future ("Would . . . ?") and then of the past ("held"), but not of the present. Is sexism currently being perpetuated in native social organizations?

As a white feminist I have a hard time imagining not.

At any rate, for some reason Churchill has assumed an either-or situation for social rebellion: either we fight for gender/class equality, or native rights. I understand that he believes that the theft of North America from natives was the foundation of this country, and so must be addressed by leftists foundationally.

But as Elizabeth Cady Stanton would have it, sexism and racism find their roots in the same problem. From this we conclude that they must share the same long-term solution.

AIM activist Mary Crow Dog was, as noted, none too fond of white feminists:

> At one time, a white volunteer nurse berated us for doing the slave work while the men got all the glory. We were betraying the cause of womankind, was the way she put it. We told her that her kind of women's lib was a white, middle-class thing, and that at this critical stage we had other priorities. Once our men had gotten their rights and their balls back, we might start arguing with them about who should do the dishes. But not before. (131)

She goes on: "I disagreed with [feminists] on their notions of abortion and contraception. Like many other Native American women, particularly those who had been in AIM, I had an urge to procreate, as if driven by a feeling that I, personally, had to make up for the genocide suffered by our people in the past" (244).

When I read this, all I am able to hear is the process of yet another uterus being co-opted for purposes of the state.

Since the uterus *is* the most political of all organs.

And it *is* the lot of uterine peoples to do the dishes.

I try to see this question from Crow Dog's perspective. I squint my eyes real hard. But I just can't do it.

Perhaps part of the problem (as Siobhan Senier suggested regarding Helen Hunt Jackson) is that I am born of a culture that favors individual life, liberty, and the pursuit of happiness; and Crow Dog is born of a culture that favors community life, liberty, and the pursuit of happiness.

Does my inability to see her uterus as community property disqualify me to activate on behalf of natives?

Perhaps it does.

Wanting to check myself, I post an e-mail to the Women's Studies List, a community of (then) fifteen hundred scholars (teachers and students) of women's studies around the globe. Do you know, I ask, of any Native American scholarship on feminism?

The responses are as expected: not many, and mostly Paula Gunn Allen's anthology *Spider Woman's Granddaughter*, a collection of writings by and about native women.

Not exactly hard-core feminist theory. Not the profoundly difficult work of continental theorists like Julia Kristeva, Luce Irigaray, etc. (Not to favor these latter.)

A day or so later, I download my e-mail and discover an indignant post from a Native Canadian woman who insists that there is no such thing as Native American feminism. That if you practice traditional native religion, you have no need of feminism, since woman is a powerful and revered part of this belief system.

I ask her if I might quote her in this discussion, and she tells me not to use her name, since she would not want her individual opinion misconstrued as the opinion of her native nation.

(Where have I heard that before?)

Our conversation takes some enlightening (for me) turns. Eventually I ask her whether she thinks it's true that women in today's native communities are not subordinated to men.

She replies in the affirmative.

Really? They're *not*?

DIGRESSION THE SEVENTH

Lorelei Deora Means, a founder of Women of All Red Nations (WARN), once commented, "We are American Indian women, in that order" (qtd. in Meranto 3). Native scholar Oneida J. Meranto reports that it is "typical" of native women that, "rather than con-front the inequality of today they revel in the equality of the past" (12n). Meranto points out that although WARN was "an indigenous women's organization, it was . . . colonization that they were fight-ing, not gender inequality" (3).

Meanwhile, white feminists like me have two problems with na-tive activists: their assertions that contemporary inequality is irrele-vant; and their assertions that there was no inequality in the past. (I'll critique the concept of "in/equality" shortly.)

No inequality?

None?

It is frequently difficult for white, middle-class feminists like me to wrap their heads around that. Most preinvasion native nations promoted few women to formal leadership positions; and a sex-specific division of labor made women responsible for crafting tools, clothing, ornament, and shelter; gathering, cultivating, preparing and storing food; healing; and raising children.

Plus, you know, how come it's always *women* who are sacrificed to accompany a leader like the Shoshone's Walker to his great reward? That's "equality"?

Well, it might be empowerment. Writing in 1995 in *Women and Power in Native North America* (Laura F. Klein and Lillian A. Ack-erman, eds.), Daniel Maltz and JoAllyn Archambault present a model for evaluating power, which they think proves that native women did enjoy a preinvasion equality of sorts. They attribute the model to a 1967 essay by Ernestine Friedl, which was then further developed by Susan Harding in 1975. It goes like this: to assess the level of social power attending a group, you must measure:

1. apparent power as determined by ideology and formal institutions,
2. real power as determined by indirect influence, and
3. the limitations on different types of power based on the structural re-lationships between different power domains. (234)

By this model, European American women fare rather poorly:

1. given that the Eve myth (in its many guises) blames us for the fall of "man"; our social systems define us as property; our bodily activities are regulated at every turn; our constructs of "person" are divided into two vast differences—masculine and feminine; our language works against our ability to define ourselves ("c" is for . . . ?); and

our religious, commercial, governmental and formal-educational institutions refuse our offers of nonmasculinist leadership (what would
that look like?)—

2. and given that our real influence, even today, lies within the spheres
of domesticity, the nuclear family, and the immediately local community (women are often the workers at the lowest—and on election
day the most crucial—ranks of the two-party system)—

3. but given that domesticity, the nuclear family, and the local community are vastly devalued compared to institutions of religion, commerce, government, and formal education—and that, even in the
family, middle- and upper-class women are not permitted to make
the major decisions about how to allocate the family's assets (at best,
we middle-class chicks get to supervise a limited budget—and then
get abused when we forbid going beyond it)—

—given all this, I conclude that white women have limited apparent
power, and some real influence, but their contributions to domestic
survival are far less valued than those contributions usually attributed
to men.

But by this model, preinvasion native women were not powerless:

1. given that religious mythology was often prowoman; property was
rarely construed as a personal matter; bodily activities were far less
regulated; constructs of the "person" were far less gendered (or
raced); divisions of labor were less strict (a woman sometimes
hunted, a man sometimes prepared food); and some nations offered
women veto power over male officials—

2. and given women's active influence within the spheres of domesticity, the extended family (which *was* the community), and tribal governance (which *was* the community)—

3. and given that domesticity, the family, the community and the tribe
were in many nations the same unit; and that religion, commerce,
and government were often closely connected, and closely connected
to the community, so that there was little difference in the valuation
of those spheres; and that women's influence on the decisions made
by male officials was in some cases (the Iroquois nation, for instance)
fully acknowledged, institutionalized, and even codified (written
down)—

—given all this, I conclude that native women had significant apparent
power, including real influence, not least because their contributions to
social survival were valued similarly to those attributed to men.

In other words, yes, there was a sex-specific division of labor, as exists in European culture. The difference is that the division did not necessarily result in hierarchical notions of whose work was more valuable.

Maltz and Archambault point out that native men and women existed in a relation of complementarity and reciprocity—and thus our white, second-wave-feminist insistence on "equality" (I know, more on this soon) falls flat with natives. White feminists also confuse authority with autonomy. While it is true that the acknowledged and encouraged ability to influence the decision of a male leader is not the same thing as complete *authority* over that decision, *autonomy*, as defined within a community-culture context, is nonetheless still possible. There are many paths, it would seem, to autonomy, which to white feminists means (roughly speaking) the power to define one's own condition. Autonomy will of course be viewed differently by members of individualistic cultures, such as European Americans, and by members of community cultures, such as Asian and Native Americans. So it is difficult for white (individualist) feminists to comprehend an autonomy whose goal is the freedom to do what's good for the community (since what's good for the community *is* good for the individual). Historians admit that the women of matrilineal and matrilocal nations had more real power than did others. But even in the context of patrilineal groups, women in community cultures all over the globe have fared more equitably than have women in competitive cultures.

But what of native women today? Scholars like Meranto believe that the European invasion brought to North America, along with smallpox and other diseases, an epidemic of sexism. Not only did white men and women (field matrons!) impose European gender constructs and discrimination on native women and men, but native men quickly found that they would be rewarded by their white male oppressors for embracing those gender discriminations.

And *that* is the minimal privilege available to *men of color*—and it's an asset they've worked to protect. See also white women: men of color, by oppressing women of *all* colors, gain enfranchisement within male-ness—within the patriarchy.

Meranto agrees that "the disempowerment of Indian women corresponds with colonial domination" (3), and that the tribal governments imposed by the Indian Reorganization Act of 1934 have "transformed indigenous male attitudes toward women, and continued the process imperialism began by consolidating patriarchal and racist gender values into tribal structures" (3). Reorganization "indoctrinat[ed] Indian men into the all-male administrative machinery" (3) supported by the BIA, which machinery "secured economic rights for men while eroding rights for women" (4). Just as damaging were the "paternalistic Christian religions and white educational systems that focused on domesticating women" (4). All of these institutions worked together to destroy the gender reciprocity of preinvasion native nations, making native men "the indigenous elite" (8) and forcing native women to underground their petticoat politics, as their influence—that is, *real power*—was disparagingly termed by nineteenth-century white males (when you can't immediately stop women from having power, *name* the exercise of that power something *nasty*—bitch!—then watch the power dissipate).

Recollecting: In his reminiscences of Shoshone business council meetings, Brigham Madsen notes that while the men sat in the big chairs looking down, the women did the work of the community.

Thanks to colonization, then, Indian country is a far cry from being the sexism-free land Churchill implies it is. Meranto reports that the two-thirds of Indian women who live off reservations "face the realities of sexism, racism and colonization off the reservation, and sexism and colonization when they return to the reservation" (13). Although these are two differently functioning systems, she says, "manifestations of sexism and violence . . . should not . . . be trivialized . . . even though the larger issue of tribal sovereignty reigns" (13).

Meranto confirms that native women who activate today on behalf of women's issues are caught in the race-versus-gender crossfire. On the one hand, they're often accused of being "white-washed women libbers," guilty of "undermining their Indian heritage" by being "selfish, self-centered and not being of that group" (2). But, she says, "there is little to suggest that with decolonization, native women would once again become empowered" (3). Furthermore, Churchill and other members of the intellectual "indigenous elite" criticize Marxism and feminism, Meranto writes, as "Eurocentric paradigms. . . . In reality, the campaign against feminism and Marxism has been done at the expense of forming any critical analysis of gender socialization within Indian communities" (12).

At the same time, however, white feminists, Meranto agrees, need to understand that "Indian women's sense of priorities is radically, and irrevocably different from those espoused by the mainstream women's movement. First of all, Indian women were not integrated into the economic structure as were African, Asian and Latin women"; therefore, native women are faced with "different types and levels of subjugation and oppression" (12). The difference is that "most of the inequality of Indian women is rooted in federal government policies and events," like allotment and reorganization.

Meranto argues that the race-versus-gender dispute would be put to rest if all parties understood that when native women work for gender equity, tribal sovereignty is strengthened—even when native feminists work outside of the tribe to effect that change. As an example, she cites the work of Canadian women on behalf of the Tobique Reserve in New Brunswick. Although the Tobique were not, during preinvasion days, a patrilineal group, with tribal membership conferring from father to son, Canadian legislation had made it so. Tobique women who "married out" were no longer Tobique. When disenfranchised Tobique women asked the United Nations in 1977 to intervene, to help Tobique women end legislated sex discrimination, Tobique leaders fought the activists, claiming that the women were threatening tribal sovereignty. But, Meranto says, "[a]s a result of the women's work Indian Affairs of Canada allowed Indian people to decide their membership rather than [have] that decision made from the top-down as it historically had been done" (15). Tobique feminists, then, won that authority back for the *entire* tribe.

To strengthen sovereignty *and* strengthen women, Meranto says, "American Indian women must develop a feminism that specifically addresses sexism, racism and colonization; a theory that is built on politics of self-determination rather than politics of inclusion. That is to say, women of *all* colors must pay special attention to their particular patterns of subjugation, for within these patterns lie the various shapes of their resistance" (16).

DIGRESSION THE EIGHTH

Permit me now—newly enlightened by generous colleagues—to return to the matter of what I will call "genocidal rape."

In the United States, for the past three decades, public discussion of rape has tended to see sexual violence as being strictly a matter of gender, unrelated to race and class. But America's conversation about rape actually began with race.

Maria Bevacqua's book *Rape on the Public Agenda: Feminism and the Politics of Sexual Assault* teaches us that at the same historical moment when Helen Hunt Jackson decried the treatment of natives, African American women began to argue that racial and sexual violence were connected. (What follows is my synthesis of numerous insights provided in Bevacqua's important work; readers are advised to consult it directly for a thorough account.)

In 1892, seven years after Jackson's death, Ida B. Wells became the first woman in the United States to argue that rape is part of a systemic abuse of women. Lucy Stone, Elizabeth Cady Stanton, Susan B. Anthony, Victoria Woodhull, and others had thirty years earlier, and at various instances, protested the personal tragedy of what we now call "marital rape." But, Bevacqua reports that "Wells articulated . . . a *political* understanding of sexual assault" (21; emphasis added). Her research into the lynchings of black men (and some black women) in the postbellum South led her to observe that the alleged rape of white women was the most common excuse for these murders. While rape had occurred in some instances, in the majority of cases rape had neither been charged nor proven; and white men raped black women much more often than vice versa.

Wells showed also that the late-nineteenth-century rapes of black women by white men were an extension of the hyper-patriarchal social organization of slavery. Feminists writing more recently have also concluded that the "Jezebel" image of a "lustful and lewd" black woman (Bevacqua 23) may have been a cross-cultural mistake made by European men who, on their sojourns to Africa, interpreted partial nudity as promiscuity; for these and other reasons, Bevacqua says, the late nineteenth century saw "the myth of black women's promiscuity firmly established" (23), which mythology provided an excuse to tolerate the rapes of black women by black men, as well.

Gerda Lerner and other scholars have concluded that during and after Reconstruction, rape provided white men with an effective tool for controlling black citizens. Rape instilled fear in black women and men alike, even as it served as justification for more white violence should black communities attempt to retaliate. Consequently, Bevacqua writes, "black women possessed an understanding of rape as connected to racism, sexism, and economic oppression" (24).

Wells correctly predicted that the lynchings would stop when white women had had enough of the sexism (i.e., "chivalry") on which these murders were predicated. Bevacqua details the efforts of the Association of Southern Women for the Prevention of Lynching, founded in 1930 "in part to resist the insult of white men's supposed chivalrous attitudes toward white women" (25). Unfortunately, when southern women managed to initiate a discussion of lynching, rape—lynching's "corollary issue," as Bevacqua puts it (115)—did not follow lynching to the table. Perhaps this is partly why the Wellsian definition of rape—as one component in a superstructure of patriarchal oppression—would be forgotten in the earliest days of second wave feminism.

The connection would prove easy to forget. A study by Helen Bendict found that the coverage of rape cases in newspapers and magazines from 1900 to 1950 was limited almost entirely to reportage about alleged rapes that resulted in lynchings, or interracial rapes for which black men were charged in the legal system. During the 1950s, coverage of interracial rape usually addressed false charges by white women against black men, "virtually blam[ing]," Bevacqua says, "white women for black men's disenfranchisement" (122).

In 1948, Ruth Herschberger first wrote that "rape is a form of violence involving the personal humiliation of the victim" (qtd. in Bevacqua 26). By 1970 an antirape ideology was forming around such Wellsian notions as "the personal is political" (first formulated in these terms by Carol Hanisch in 1970); and, as Bevacqua summarizes it, an understanding of "male dominance as a total system," with rape considered "a political problem that functions to keep women subordinate to men." A popular antirape poster of the day contained the slogan, "Disarm rapists: Smash sexism" (31).

But the connection between racial oppression and sexual oppression would continue to linger beneath the surface as the antirape movement developed in the United States. When Susan Brownmiller began working with antirape groups, she too thought rape was a myth. She told Bevacqua in 1996 that "the typical liberal-left position" of those days held that "rape was a false accusation by a white woman against a black man down south" (32).

As Bevacqua details it, publications such as Eldridge Cleaver's 1968 *Soul on Ice* further complicated that early discussion of rape (see also the late 1960s poetry and plays of LeRoi Jones [Amiri Baraka]). The civil rights revolutionary admitted to "an antagonistic, ruthless attitude toward white women," and to having made a conscious decision to "become a rapist" by way of expressing his fury at the oppression of blacks. He began, he says, by "practicing on black girls in the ghetto," and later "crossed the tracks and sought out white prey."

Rape, he explains, "was an insurrectionary act. It delighted me that I was defying and trampling upon the white man's law, upon his system of values, and that I was defiling his women." This latter achievement was particularly "satisfying" to him since he was "very resentful over the historical fact of how the white man has used the black woman. I felt I was getting revenge" (qtd. in Bevacqua 45).

Although he does say that, by the time he wrote *Soul,* he had come to think better of such strategies, few readers heard that renunciation. The vast popularity of Cleaver's book accomplished several things, few of them productive. Some white male leftists failed to understand the gender issues at stake in his prorape thesis, and embraced the hyper-masculinist sentiment as validation of the propenile "sexual liberation." Some white feminists responded as if their greatest fears had been validated: men of color *were* targeting them for brutality. Some African American feminists said that the rapes of black women were, again, being lost in the black male/white woman paradigm. Indeed, Cleaver's decision to "practice" his personal antiracist revolution first on *black women* indicates clearly that he took racism to be a far more pressing concern than sexism.

(Cleaver would convert to Mormonism in the 1980s, before his death in 1998.)

This atmosphere was the setting for Brownmiller's nascent research. Her first task was to delineate the myths surrounding rape—many of them racial. Through her work, Brownmiller learned that rape charges were *not* always false, and that rape happened to all kinds of women, serving patriarchy by constraining female sexuality and autonomy—by keeping all women in fear.

In moving perhaps too far beyond race-specific myths, Brownmiller's landmark work *Against Our Will* has been criticized for its failure to address race matters. Her thesis stumbles, Alison Edwards writes, on a strategy that posited women's liberation as "isolated from the fight against all other forms of oppression" (qtd. in Bevacqua 233n). Susan Griffin has also criticized Brownmiller for insisting that rape is about violence, not sex; it's not a question of being *either,* Griffin argues, but instead *both,* inseparable.

A 1970s radical movement that took as its battle cry "Sisterhood Is Powerful" was inclined, then, to neglect the relevant differences between, say, black sisters and white sisters. Some movement historians insist that women of color *were* active in antirape work—the first woman to direct a rape crisis center, for instance, was Nkenge

Toure—and activists like Loretta Ross told Bevacqua that "they were frequently accused of not being feminist enough for the mostly white feminist community and not being black enough for the black community" (79). But other historians report that women of color did not respond to white antirape activism. Angela Davis wrote in 1990 that the antirape movement neglected to interrogate the history of rape charges against black men, and failed to "develop an analysis of rape that acknowledged the social conditions that foster sexual violence as well as the centrality of racism in determining those social conditions" (qtd. in Bevacqua 39).

Further, Davis argued, women of color worried that a successful antirape movement would disproportionately imperil men of color, who are more frequently convicted of rape even though most (non-militaristic) rape is *intra*racial. Indeed, as Bevacqua reports, feminists led by Ruth Bader Ginsburg went to the Supreme Court in 1977 to argue that using the death penalty in rape convictions was cruel and unusual punishment; they did so primarily out of fear that the death penalty would make it harder to get convictions in rape cases. But when they did so, they argued—opportunistically, one might say—that the harshest rape sentences went unfairly to black men.

Today, antirape legislation owes part of its existence to race matters. In 1970, the majority of U.S. citizens knew little about rape as a social issue, and concerned themselves almost not at all with its prevention. By 1980, antirape legislation had been written and passed, self-defense classes were commonplace, rape crisis centers had been founded in most large cities, and public discussion of rape was widespread. Bevacqua credits the network created by the women's movement with the lightning-fast acceptance of this feminist concern. But it is also true, she says, that the antirape movement happened to collide historically with the law-and-order agenda introduced by conservatives in the late 1960s. In the context of a civil rights uprising occasionally accompanied by violence, it wasn't difficult to convince middle-class whites that a "crime wave" had begun, and that their personal safety was at risk—even though most violent crime remains, again, intraracial. "White fright" was fueled so successfully that by the 1990s, even liberals had to take up the "tough-on-crime" banner. Antirape activists forged an uneasy alliance with law-and-order proponents like Senator Charles Mathias (R-Maryland), who sponsored a 1974 bill to establish the National Center for the Prevention and Control of Rape.

Since 1973, much antirape legislation has been sponsored or cosponsored by Republican anticrime legislators, even though the justifications for Republican involvement have often been paternalistic, rather than profeminist. Rape activists have not suffered this happily, and have often been forced to compromise their radical agenda to get pro-victim legislation passed. For instance, some government agencies have refused to cooperate with rape crisis centers unless the centers require victims to participate in prosecutions—a choice one would *think* we could all agree should be left to each individual *victim*.

And as we saw with the Fifteenth and Nineteenth Amendments, an alliance that exploits one oppression (in this case racial oppression) to benefit another (sexual oppression) is bound to be fraught. In the 1990s, Bevacqua reports, the alliance with tough-on-crime legislators was shaken by the Violence Against Women Act. The bill was written and sponsored by Senator Joseph Biden (D-Delaware); addressed domestic violence and rape; and brought sexual violence under the umbrella of civil rights law by allowing civil suits against rapists who, a victim might argue, were "gender-motivated" to rape. The most radical of the sexual violence laws, it took four years to pass and was vilified by the conservative right, as well as by the American Civil Liberties Union, which protested that it is impossible to tell whether, when a woman is battered or raped, said violence is the result of gender discrimination. (The Supreme Court would ultimately strike down the act.)

All of which has taught us, here in (or after?) the third wave of feminism, that we need to smash more than sexism in order to disarm rapists.

If civil rights legislators, and U.S. citizens, were to understand race oppression, gender oppression, economic oppression, and oppression of gays and lesbians as interrelated, interdependent manifestations of a patriarchal superstructure, one Civil Rights Act would have been enough, and marginalized groups would not now be reduced to competing with each other to benefit separate constituencies.

And the superstructure would be that much closer to history.

DIGRESSION THE NINTH

I don't like the term *third-wave feminism*. The basic tenets of the third wave—that the exploitation and control of race–gender–class–sexuality—the four winds—are interconnected, interreliant, are not four separate winds but one careening killer cyclone—and that none will be conquered so long as any one remains spinning—this sentiment has been a part of feminism, in some fashion, right along. The tenets of third-wave feminism have been easy to ignore right along, because our leaders codified and institutionalized a divide-and-conquer strategy—kept the Fifteenth Amendment (suffrage for men of color) separate from the Nineteenth (suffrage for all women)—thus forcing men of color, women of color, white women, gays, the working classes, and the disabled (etc.) to fight each other for the improvement of their own status—and to fight each alone for the improvement of their own status relative to white, upper-class heterosexual men—*not* to fight for some *alternative* social structure that might be more complementary than competitive.

Which brings us back to those futile struggles for "equality." Why settle for an "equal" piece of an *oppressive* pie, when, together, we might achieve a whole new kind of American Pie? This is how divisiveness perpetuates the status quo, and such divisiveness will remain until, again, we all understand a forgotten history. Gerda Lerner, in her 1986 classic, *The Creation of Patriarchy*, argues that the exploitation and control of race–gender–class–sexuality—the four winds—were born (slowly, over perhaps three millennia) at the same moment, approximately five thousand years ago. The development of the concept of private property, and the shift to an agricultural economy, required the attendant development of a pool of peoples, controllable by emerging landowners—required bodies whose labor could be exploited to the profit of the landowner. "Women themselves became a resource, acquired by men much as the land was acquired by men," Lerner writes (212). The commodification of women—making of women a thing that could be bought and sold, with a bride price attached—"may very well represent the first accumulation of private property" (213). And once acquired, women's sexuality had to be controlled, by chastity and compulsive heterosexuality, to secure the property interests of the owners: the fathers, brothers, and husbands of the priced, the owned.

She further asserts that landowners first "practiced" enslavement on the women and children whose familial bodies were immediately available for control (86). "By experimenting with the enslavement of women and children," Lerner writes, "men learned to understand that all human beings have the potential for tolerating enslavement, and they developed the techniques and forms of enslavement which would enable them to make of their absolute dominance a social institution" (81). In the early days of slavery, in all known societies, captured women were enslaved while captured men were killed:

> It was only after men had learned how to enslave the women of groups who could be defined as strangers, that they learned how to enslave men of these groups and, later, subordinates within their own society.
>
> Thus, the enslavement of women, combining both racism and sexism, preceded the formation of classes and class oppression. (213)

Racism and sexism, for Lerner, need to be addressed as if they are *The Twin Relics of Barbarism.* But whether we agree that gender and race oppression are the foundation from which other oppressions arise, we must understand genocide as being irrevocably linked to genocidal rape. Neither makes much sense without an understanding of the other.

Or, as Lerner puts it, "patriarchy as a system is historical: it has a beginning in history. If that is so, it can be ended by historical process" (6).

DIGRESSION THE LAST

Beginnings, middles, ends.

All I can do, is to *tell* about them.

And so we return finally to the focal question of this book: How must history change? For instance, should a National Historic Site be built on the Bear River Massacre field? And if it should, should we include the story of the rape that followed the murders?

In October 2000, Congress voted in support of a National Historic Site to be built on the field of the Sand Creek Massacre, here in Colorado.

As noted, the trajectory of the fight to establish the Sand Creek Massacre site followed closely that of the fight to establish a Bear River Massacre site: grassroots activation; support from nearby Arapaho and Cheyenne peoples; a National Park Service study; disinformation spread by white opponents, resulting in white fright that land was being "taken" and "given back"; and limited discussion of the sexual mutilation that punctuated the murders.

Why Sand Creek and not its predecessor, Bear River? Also as noted, Senator Ben Nighthorse-Campbell was committed to the legislation.

His party colleague, Senator Larry Craig, shares no such commitment.

This is what history is? (Identity) Politics?

Perhaps I should tell you something about My Perfect Historical World: there can be no "final say."

In his 1914 poem "Mowing," Robert Frost writes, "The fact is the sweetest dream that labor knows."

Desperately seeking facts, I pick up Bernard Grun's translation and expansion of Werner Stein's *Kulturfahrplan*, the massive *Timetables of History*. My father gave me the 1991 third edition for Christmas some years back. It follows the general outlines of the founding of the United States. For instance, 1619: "First Negro slaves in N. America arrive in Virginia."

The year 1637 has a strange mention of the most horrific massacre in U.S. history: "Destruction of Pequod Fort, Conn." From this entry the reader is unable to conclude that about five hundred (?) Pequot were killed in the Mystic Massacre by colonists led by Major John Mason. Nor of course that survivors were enslaved.

This cryptic entry is odd not least because of this later item: "1650: Beginning of extermination of N. Amer. Indian."

OK, so it's off by thirteen years.

1683 reads, "Peace treaty between William Penn and N. American Indians."

Really? *All* of the N. American Indians?

1862 contains no mention of the Dakota War. 1863 contains no mention of the Bear River Massacre. 1864 reads, "Massacre of the Cheyenne and Arapahoe Indians at Sand Creek, Colo." Sitting Bull's birth date (1837) is noted, but nothing else. No mention of Crazy Horse. Oddly, the Wounded Knee Massacre is not recorded, but the Second Siege at Wounded Knee, in 1973, is reported ("Militant Amer. Indians occupy the S. Dakota hamlet of Wounded Knee for 70 days"). No mention of the ResMurs or Leonard Peltier.

As for the LDS church, 1830 notes the founding of Mormonism, 1846 reports the exodus from Nauvoo, 1847 the founding of Salt Lake City, and 1885 the split between polygynists and monogamists.

And of course the history of women of all colors and creeds is largely absent.

Grun does not reflect the whole body of academic history, but this level of confusion and inconsistent selection does reflect the average

U.S. citizen's understanding of "timetables." And here my friend, the Canadian poet Barbara Schott, steps in to translate *kulturfarhplan* for me. *Kultur* means (of course) "culture"; *fahr* means "to drive"; *plan* means (again, of course), "plan," specifically a time plan; a German train station, Barbara says, posts a *fahrplan*, or schedule.

So a kulturfahrplan, which Grun translates as "timetable of history," is a schedule of the culture—and as we have seen, history sometimes arrives late on the cultural platform. Howard Zinn's work, *A People's History of the United States: 1492–Present*, confirms the arbitrary nature of the scheduling. "History is the memory of states," he writes, quoting Henry Kissinger. But "[n]ations are not communities and never have been. The history of any country, presented as the history of a family, conceals fierce conflicts of interest . . . between conquerors and conquered, masters and slaves, capitalists and workers, dominators and dominated in race and sex" (9–10). Narratives told "from the viewpoint of . . . leaders . . . , ignoring the millions who suffered from those statesmen's policies" are subject to a nationalist "distortion" Zinn describes as "ideological" (8).

So history is political as hell.

This is not a fresh observation. In the 1980s and 1990s, the primary battlefields for our Culture Wars were Literary Studies and History. And why not? It makes sense that as we begin to reevaluate ourselves, we take a hard look at the stories we tell as well as the language we use to tell them. (Which is not to say that the sciences, for instance, could not benefit from a similar bout of navel gazing.)

As Leslie Marmon Silko wrote in *Ceremony*, stories are "all we have to fight off illness and death":

> So they try to destroy the stories
> let the stories be confused or forgotten.
> They would like that
> they would be happy
> Because we would be defenseless then. (2)

In more academic terms, June Namias agrees: "The more we know about our early migrations and the meeting of people along the cultural boundaries that made up the earliest frontiers, the better chance we have to know the origins of our hopes and fears and perhaps deal with each other more humanely" (xv).

Indeed, the controllers of our culture work damn hard to control our narratives. So in an age of cultural reflection, we begin there.

Now "we," as a culture, have only to respond to the results of that reflection. An initial result has been the sense so many of us share that something is wrong with history. For instance, I return to Siobhan Senier's concern: How does simply telling a story result in collective action?

What's wrong with history? Please indulge a language worker's take.

Patricia Nelson Limerick's landmark 1987 book *The Legacy of Conquest: The Unbroken Past of the American West* illustrates how academic territoriality and competition led to those categorizations and oversimplifications that are the "burdens" of history. She and others sought a new era of history making, one inclusive of "multiple points of view" (39). This was a good thing, but we could perhaps not anticipate then that many of the newly included voices would assimilate—would tell new stories, but in old ways. As Oneida Meranto has suggested, inclusion is not always about self-definition. That is, History opened its doors to previously excluded members, but expected those new members to accommodate History's ways; historical discourse did not change significantly. Nowadays, it's Old History, bogged down by New Categories. "Identity," however "hybridized" by more theoretical inquiry, persists as the basis upon which new research will be conducted: Historian A will work on the History of A, a history of (say) marginalized peoples; but since the History of A is (politically) motivated by the identification of these peoples as such, Historian A need not account for the History of B. (Or, A ≠ B). What Limerick and others had hoped for was complication of the political, cultural, etc.; but the New Categories have resulted instead in New Simplifications. The African American History guy still isn't working with the Gay History guy, etc., and both still use the same Old Discourse.

(Discipline-wise, of course, I pitch stones from a glass porch: literary studies has fared no better.)

Even with the advent of the New Historicism—a development abetted by us litcritters, and ethnographers, anthropologists, and linguists—and the substitution of more self-reflexive narrative accounts for the "objectively" grand metanarratives of the past, History persists as a set of specialized and subspecialized language practices. And these practices are still executed by a highly individualized Expert. "Nothing is better suited to lead to a repetition of the past," writes Hayden White in 1982, "than a study of it that is either reverential or convincingly objective in the way that conventional historical studies tend to be" (82). It becomes incumbent upon us to imagine a corresponding discourse and work to institute it. Such a discourse might take fuller stock of the teller of historical tales—that subjective subject position with which historians such as White have often been preoccupied.

Which is to say, the making of history begins and ends with the historian.

Here's one thing that concerns me: reading their works, we have no way of divining the personal biases of most historians, especially those employing traditional historical rhetoric. Consider Brigham D. Madsen and David L. Bigler for a moment. Both take great pains in their works to avoid editorializing. Bigler is especially careful to qualify all assertions about the veracity of The Book of Mormon ("An essential Mormon scripture, *The Book of Mormon*, is the **professed** record of a God-fearing man named Lehi. . . . The history of these two peoples, prior to about 421 A.D., was **allegedly** preserved on gold plates" [64; **boldface** emphasis added]). Author biographies generally provide little illumination of possible conflicts of interest. So readers are left to wonder whether the objectivity claimed in such careful diction does indeed exist.

And as we have seen, there's much in a name. Poor Brigham Madsen's first name plagues his credibility; it is too bad that historical conventions don't permit him to say something like, "Cut me a break, folks, I've lapsed!" With Bigler, the problem continues, though only for those who've read widely in Mormon history. For instance, is he related to Henry Bigler, the Mormon Battalion vet who built Sutter's mill? Or is he related to Jacob Bigler, bishop of Nephi, who helped fan the Reformation flames in 1856 and was later indicted for his role in the Mountain Meadows Massacre?

But having named a given perspective, does it necessarily follow that we know anything more about the bias of the individual? I continue to be apprehensive about my own biases, by the fact that I must dispute Mae Timbimboo Parry's assertion that the rape did not happen—not least since the dictates of identity politics have it that it's not "my" story to expose anyway.

Perhaps you will find this interesting: I attempted to apply for a summer travel grant from the National Endowment for the Humanities to support the research necessary for this book. But I could not find three academic historians willing to write a letter in support of this work. I could not find *one*. Why? I am not a historian. Consequently, it was felt, this would not be history. Also, I am not Native American. Consequently, it was felt, this would not be Native American History.

I also could not find three literary studies folks to write, either. This isn't textual analysis. It's history.

Well, OK, they may have had other reasons—I concede this. But I did find Tamise Van Pelt's apartment. A white-chick community-supported antidisciplinary research grant.

What I learned from writing this book: Their story *is* (in an important sense) My story. My people did it, not Theirs.

Unlike Allie Hansen and Helen Hunt Jackson, I don't tell this story *for them*. Assuming that I can accept the foundational premise that there *is* a *them*, well then, I tell this story *for us*.

Of course I have the right to tell the story of the Bear River Massacre and Rape. It's my story too. If white women authors of various captivity narratives can help recapture the narratives of the violent encounters between European Americans and natives, of course we should.

But—but—we must take vigilant care that we don't also recapture our own history of prejudice and oversight.

Meranto's critique of the politics of inclusion (as at times disruptive of simple self-definition) is affirmed in the extremely complicated case of the Bear River Massacre and Rape. Let's consider: Allie Hansen feels a lack of gratitude from the Northwestern Shoshoni *for whom* she has labored to tell their story. So does Brigham Madsen.

But let's look at this: As a man, and as an educated man, Madsen could build an academic career on this story. He could be appointed tribal historian; he held that official position which Jackson found to be much more effective than the role of sidelined storyteller. Hansen can build no such career; her work has cost her income, not supplemented it. As a member of the merchant-middle class, uneducated formally, she hasn't Madsen's social clout.

Meanwhile, across town, Kathy Griffin activates as another white woman. She would like to have the story more fully told for visitors, but not so fully as to cost other whites their income from that land. What are the differences between her and Hansen? Within the caste system of Preston, Idaho, Hansen ranks more highly. She has more clout in the community as a whole. As an autodidact, she has pursued her intellectual leanings further than has Griffin, not least because she has had the leisure time and the class-specific motivation to do so.

And yet, in the face of these vast divisions of class and ideology, these two women manage to live in the same small town, participating in the same small religious community—and get along.

Three Mormon women: Allie Hansen, Kathy Griffin—and Mae Parry.—Held together by a finely knitted lace of alliances and fissures—

Four Mormon people: Allie Hansen, Kathy Griffin, Mae Parry—and Brigham Madsen. Together, a community of various knowledges, various trainings, various educations, various leanings.

Five Mormon people: Allie Hansen, Kathy Griffin, Mae Parry, Brigham Madsen—and Curtis Warner. Add Curtis's small son Tyler, and you see the future. Or, you see *a* future.

All five feel called to tell a story. (Is Tyler also to be called?) One story, five stories, myriad stories and agenda. Together, these stories become miraculously complex.

Allie Hansen and Kathy Griffin both insist that there are "two sides" to this story.

Would it were that simple.

Meanwhile, everyone I talked to at the Park Service, about the work to develop the historic site at the Bear River Massacre field, advised me to talk with Allie Hansen. Allie Hansen, Allie Hansen. Catherine Spude did refer me to Curtis Warner. But no one mentioned Kathy Griffin. No one mentioned Mae Parry.

No one suggested I contact Madsen. I was impelled to contact him out of my own academic-class prerogative: Me Ph.D., you Ph.D.

Thus does history's recent politics of inclusion collapse at the entryway. "Inclusion" still suggests a finite product, an enclosed "place" where "all" will be welcomed—a commodified "pie" that can be "equally" divided, rather than a structural process by which we recognize difference as well as similarity.

Do we have a vocabulary for that recognition, for that process?

But is it just about vocabulary? In her book *Looking White People in the Eye,* Sherene Razack urges an academic politics of accountability, and refutes Helen Hunt Jackson's assumption (once mine as well) that we may find justice simply by knowing more about each other. "[W]e need to direct our efforts to the conditions of communication and knowledge production that prevail, calculating not only who can speak and how they are likely to be heard but also how we know what we know and the interest we protect through our knowing" (qtd. in Senier 27).

Would our society accept an intellectual community whose primary concern would be to inquire into "the interest we protect through our knowing"?

Not without a new way of understanding bias and self-interest—the interest of the individual historian as well as that of the wider culture.

Then too, there's the heart/mind divide that rules academic history. Allie Hansen is dead right about women being the keepers of emotional history. Indeed, what choice have we had? Jackson discovered quickly that women, even white, upper-class, heterosexual women, were not permitted to "lobby" a story, to "berate" their officials. (What has changed?) Jackson and Hansen both win personal admirers with their persistence and dedication; but it is easier for a white male, for a Madsen, to profit professionally—publicly—though still at great personal cost (race traitor! religious heretic!). Jackson immediately found that women profit far more from telling a personal, emotional story: "manly" tones for women are, even today, viewed with suspicion (cf. references to "feminazis"). Meanwhile, gender expectations cut both ways: my students read Madsen's book and complain of its lack of emotion. Apparently, "manly" talk is also "boring!" Even though Madsen's prose is lovely, lilting, containing the faintest drop of disparaging self-deprecation, you can tell, he's reining himself in, choking the hold, gripping his biases (only he knows for sure what they are—doesn't he?), going only as far as he thinks he can get away with—which isn't very far—

Would it be possible to make a history that contains the manly facts, the "statistical record" as we perceive it for the moment—*and* the emotional, the personal? Would it be possible to make a history that contains all five stories, in five different ways of telling them, with the full presence of all five narrators?

With a politics of (complex) self-definition and accountability, would it be possible also to seek a politics of syncretism? When two cultures meet, efflorescence—dramatic changes in *both* discrete cultures—is usually the result. Historians have documented the more obvious changes that manifested in native culture; but have downplayed the many changes, catalogued by Jack Weatherford in *Indian Givers: How the Indians of the Americas Transformed the World*, that manifested in European culture. What the United States has most stubbornly resisted is syncretism: the development of a third culture that blends the two.

In the United States, according to Allie Hansen, natives must change; natives must be educated. Not "us." To this day we refuse to concede: *white settlers are the problem.*

When I talked with Mae Timbimboo Parry on the phone before visiting with her, she told me that the name "Timbimboo" translates in English to "people who write on rocks."

Write how?

We must continue to examine the linguistic issues at play here—the competing "discourse practices," or ways we talk to one another—to consider the limits on what can be said, as well as new possibilities of articulation. I am myself a culprit: look at the language I employed in part 1 of this book, my attempt to lay out the broad historical landscape of the Bear River Massacre and Rape. Without even thinking about it, I fell quickly into the stylistics common to the disciplines we call "anthropology," "geology," "history." Notice the distant tone, as if I have nothing to do with what I'm writing about—and as if that distance somehow mitigates my subjectivity and guarantees my "objectivity." Notice the certainty with which I write about things 140 years old, and 140 million years old, as if I really know what I'm talking about. Notice the many passive verbs: "Meat could be had from groundhog. . . ." "Sagebrush was woven. . . ." "The chastity of a number of women was defiled by force; some of them were strapped to benches and repeatedly ravished. . . ."

Permit me to linger on this latter. Julia Penelope has pointed out, in *Speaking Freely*, a 1990 study of the gendered nature of language, that rape is almost always described using passive voice. "Jane was raped." Who raped Jane? Who bears responsibility? It is mighty rare indeed to hear, "John raped Jane." At best we might say, "Jane was raped by John." And that syntax has an important impact: we may hear then that John was the culprit, but since we say so in passive voice, it seems as if Jane is the subject of the verb *was raped*, as if *Jane* is the responsible agent here. As in, *Jane got herself raped.* It's subtle, but unmistakable.

Your high school English teacher may have encouraged you to avoid passive phrases like "Mistakes were made." And yet they dominate our public discourse, especially in reference to sensitive issues.

Accuracy. Passive verbs do not facilitate accuracy, which nonetheless is the obsession of European American historians like Madsen and Hansen. Accuracy, we white academics believe, can be found in books. Madsen and Hansen leap up regularly to consult books to provide accuracy in reporting. Meanwhile, when I ask Mae Parry for the date of the meeting about calling the "battle" a "massacre," she shares none of my journalistic impulses to provide accuracy. I press her for the accurate date and she responds as if I am a nuisance. And clearly I am. What is the use of knowing the exact date the damn incident was renamed? The salient point is that there was a great deal of conflict over its naming. The salient point is that we renamed the incident appallingly recently, long after we knew better. The salient point is that naming is the most powerful tool a culture has for controlling opinion and information. Who the hell cares what day it happened?

Missing also in my discussion of orality, among other complexities: "the" story, from the perspective of Bear Hunter's descendants. "Expertise," another concept that greatly concerns Allie Hansen and Curtis Warner—"expertise" is needed for gathering oral tales. I am not "expert" in oral collection, and I leave that work to those who are, hoping that this book will establish the need for collecting narratives by Bear Hunter's descendants, as well as narratives about the rape. But when I—and Hansen and Warner—express anxiety about expertise—who has it, how to get it—we're dealing with a white notion. A European American academic idea that knowledge is something that can be boxed and bagged, like potatoes in the produce section of your grocery—bought, carted home. *Owned.* Manipulated. Used against others to control opinion and information. ("You can't say that—you're not an expert!") Our worship of expertise contradicts Warner's other idea, his vision of the story as something to which all contribute. Of story as *community* property. Community *process.*

Scholarly citation practices are a great example of this problem. Most narratives like this one, which aspire to interest scholars while remaining accessible to fellow citizens—narratives such as Matthiessen's *In the Spirit of Crazy Horse*, James Welch's *Killing Custer*, and Fergus Bordewich's *Killing the White Man's Indian*—are spared the academic rigmarole of footnoting. In fairness, allow me to note that these works were all published by trade presses. Note also: these are all male authors. In *The Legacy of Conquest*, Patricia Nelson Limerick uses footnotes; it too was published by a trade press. I struggled with whether to spare you said footnotes. As Paul Metcalf has written apropos of his poetic-historical work (yes, another male, I know, and the great-grandson of Herman Melville to boot): "I was, and am, averse to attaching little burrs at the bottom of each page, referring to notes at the back; this would have broken the flow, the rhythms" (see Metcalf "Author's Note").

For me, these burrs do worse than that. They suggest a formality of discourse, an expertise which all along I have been attempting to subvert; most important, they imply an *accuracy* I cannot abide. "If you don't believe me," a footnote suggests, "look it up! I have to be right!" How are footnotes used in academic circles? Occasionally, they serve the actual purpose of referring the interested to other sources of information. But all too often, they are used as weapons of intellectual combat. The writer is required to support each and every assertion with said burr; at which point the opponent runs to the library to check each and every source, disallowing them as unauthoritative if the slightest glitch—an erroneous date, page number, etc.—rears its ugly . . . foot. Your expert is no good! the opponent cries. You misquoted your source! You're misapplying theory! Your shoes don't fit! Please note: I was advised to use footnotes by colleagues who reminded me that, *as a woman*, I am more likely to be subjected to such a round of footnote fire.

(I already agree, so you needn't chide me, that my use of MLA parenthetical citation is not much better. I compromised, I know—on the other hand, I'm publishing with a university press. It would seem that these categories—trade/university, male/female—mean everything.)

The same thing happens with bibliographies, which are scoured by opponents for absences. You did not read X. You missed the discussion of Y. You stole the wording of Z and forgot to cite her. Translation: My box of knowledge ammunition is bigger than yours. You're outgunned. Outmanned.

If I burr-up and participate in that game, how can I undermine its racist/sexist/elitist system of rewarding the individual competitor? Mayn't I enact a new concept of "knowledge," one that emphasizes process rather than history-as-widget? "Error" as a notion can only be paramount if I view expertise as product. What if I just *assume* that error is part of my *contribution* to this process, and invite other *contributions*, by knowledge workers who begin by *accepting the spirit* of my contribution, then work to add to, not detract from, our mutual process of community understanding?

Now, I don't mean to suggest that I won't eschew error, or that all dialogue about research is bad, or that we should not complain, for instance, about that study that "proved" lesbians typically have short index fingers. But I do mean to suggest that "collegiality," the notion that scholars work together to develop a community consensus on, say, how to treat cancer, is often a combative (as opposed to contested) arena that cares little about the community it pretends to serve. Scholarship is more frequently an individual industry of autonomously conceived agents modeled on the competitive marketplace, rather than on the common good.

Then too, there is the question of selection. In a culture addicted to three-act movies and pulp-novel page turners, historians and nonfiction writers often borrow novelistic (and cinematic) devices to keep their reading publics entertained. Unfortunately, the novels from which they steal devices are those written in traditional form (beginning, middle, happy ever after). It's hard to blame them: publishing conglomerates have all but eliminated the distribution of avant-garde fiction; most readers, including most fiction writers, don't know (or don't want to know) that alternative fiction exists and has existed in various forms for three hundred years (see Sterne, Melville, Woolf, Joyce, Stein, Barnes, Federman, Sukenick, Katz, Field, Mullen, Kapil Rider—to name a very few—and see also the emerging web of media writing).

Which is not to say that historical narratives are thoroughly chronological. Actually, historians rarely present things "in order"; they skip all over, grouping related events (itself a selection process) and relegating the less important (again, selected) to one of two verb tenses: past ("had earlier . . .") and future ("would later . . .").

As in (as with the novel *Idaho!*), *Something had just happened there. . . .*

And the choice of traditional story structure is a selection too. For instance, ending the history of the Northwestern Shoshoni at the massacre erases the tribe's current struggle for recognition, which then erases our nation's obligation to support them, or provide them with land, or whatever they decide they need to recuperate themselves.

Certainly immediate judicial attention should be paid to the question
of what happened to the lands around Malad sixty years ago.

In sum: The literary forms history has borrowed from "the
novel" (as if there is only one heteroglossic kind) are poor enactments
of who we are and where our responsibilities lie. We need a different
kind of New History.

I'm naive, I know, but I was shocked to hear that a man sits in an
office in Washington, DC, and decides whether a historical event will
be called a battle or a massacre. I was shocked to hear that historical
documents, like the one penned by Sergeant William Beach, and
found at an estate sale in 1997, are considered private property. Are
owned by their finders. Are traded for other documents more valuable to the finder, or for cash, or can be kept hidden from the community if the owner so chooses. I was shocked to hear that
institutional and governmental entities have the ability and the right
to keep certain people—people they don't like—away from historical
documents they don't want them to see. I was shocked that the sorts
of programmatic tactics used to keep me from teaching radical literatures are also used to keep lapsed members like Brigham Madsen
out of the church archives so crucial to his work—which work is crucial to us all. I was shocked to discover that on behalf of the citizens
of this country, the National Park Service can decide what our history
is going to be, but also that they can prepare to, after all this time, *finally make history in Preston, Idaho*, and that one man—*one man in
the Senate*—can stop them.

OK, four men, since any of Idaho's congressional representatives
could submit the legislation (Senator Craig is the senior member and
clearly stepped forward to remove the heat from the other three).

Or, OK, the people of one state, since they elected these guys to
represent them.

Shocked, shocked I tell you.

This is one of the drawbacks of capitalist–democratic realities.
History—expertise—access to information—history—is something
that can be owned. By an individual, a group, an institution. Indeed,
as the Shoshone observe regarding the National Park Service proposal, history is profitable. History equals tourism equals cash.

I am not a historian. This book, as I've said, is primarily a "tertiary" work—I get most of my information from other people (mostly
white men) who have studied primary works (European American

documents) and presented their conclusions in secondary works based on those primary works.

I am not a historian. I am a novelist. Worse (wince), a postmodern novelist, with one book of experimental prose to my credit (forthcoming) which most novelists will refuse to call fiction. Any historian can tell you we postmodern writers are the devil in blue jeans. As Tim Woods has written, "Postmodern fiction reveals the past as always ideologically and discursively constructed" (56). As a language worker, and like the New Historicists, I see history—the aggregate of secondary and tertiary works—as itself a narrative subject to literary analysis. And as a feminist writer, I practice interdisciplinarity, utilizing the products of (as reflected in part 1) anthropologists, archaeologists, behaviorists, geologists, historians, linguists, sociologists.

My interest lies in the effects these products—stories—have on peoples. On us.

I hope to reassure Siobhan Senier: When we tell new stories in new, subversive terms—terms disruptive to oppressive systems—that *is* a collective (if symbolic) action. To enable our collective accountability, we need a history fully accountable to us—to how it is made *for* us. Of course, we each have a hand in this making: materially, personally, institutionally, culturally. Not a history that encourages passivity from an individual reader, but one that requires our participation. A history that is a flip book (and this idea I steal from the poet Laura Mullen): inert unless the reader picks it up—and actively directs it. Seen in this light, *this* book is but a baby step toward such (useful) child's play.

I am not a historian, and I am not an "Indian reformer." It is not my sense that Helen Hunt Jackson was, either; it does not seem that her primary endeavor was the reforming of *Indians*. Her concern was the reform of United States *policy* toward natives. Her concern was the relationship between her race and the native race. That is, "our" treatment of "them," or as Elizabeth Cady Stanton might have said, "our" treatment of "us"—since we do, let's face it, treat the *Ourselves* precisely as we treat the *Thems*. Ida B. Wells and Virginia Woolf taught us this, too: any form of dominating across the continent is a trial run for another form of dominating down the hall, behind closed doors.

And vice versa.

We also need historians trained in the subversive art of hearing silence, detecting the not-said. Darlene Clark Hine has written about a "culture of dissemblance" pervading female slave narratives (qtd. in Senier 24); and Henry Louis Gates, Jr. has applied to African American literatures the analogy of "masking" common in African traditions. On the one hand, a subordinated culture wants the powerful culture to know something about them, by way of asserting legitimacy—but on the other hand, giving away that information is to give away power to the already powerful.

Does Mae Parry "dissemble" when she says the rape could not have happened? Not consciously. Does the National Park Service "dissemble" when they decline to include Madsen's evidence about the rape? *Very consciously.* With good intentions, yet no less unfortunately, in my view. But that which the feminist me hears in Parry's story as cultural denial—well, it might not be that exactly. Why lay claim to yet another horror, another suffering, when this one can be relegated to mere speculation? Genocide has an undeniable result: bones are ultimately unearthed (to be horded by the descendants of the conquerors, perhaps, or sold in a black market). And why should I recuperate that which leaves behind but the skeleton of a conflict so remote from my own (sense of) heritage?

Because it didn't happen just to "your people." If "you" are "we."

Since that is the last great frontier of categorization: you/me.

Because, with the postmodern collapse of category, it happened/is happening to me too.

Or, if you prefer your homilies in subtler, nineteenth-century trappings, here is Walt Whitman, the final line from "Song of Myself" (1855):

"I stop somewhere waiting for you."

And yet we must acknowledge, no "we" can ever be all-encompassing, not to the point of eradicating all difference. If it happened to me, it happened in a different way. Very different.

In a 1998 interview with *CBS Sunday Morning*, Sherman Alexie said that he is both "Native" and "American"—both.

Lorelei Deora Means, a founder of WARN, insists that "we are American Indian women, in that order," but if she considers herself "Indian" *before* "woman," surely she does *not* consider herself "American" *before* "Indian" (?).

From this, we see how complicated this question of "order" *is.* Which oppressive system *is* "first" in "order"? A nationalist, post–911 "America" that denies the existence of "hyphenated peoples"? A sexist and racist "American" society that circumscribes a subset of sexist "Indian" society?

Clearly, the various oppressive systems are intertwined.

How Alexie mixes these two—and Means mixes these three—since inevitably they must be mixed, what with all the conquering that's been going on here—how they mix these is entirely up to them.

It's not just a question of assimilating or not assimilating. "Communitism" is a term coined by Jace Weaver, who combined "community" and "activism" to assert "a proactive commitment to Native community, including the wider community" (qtd. in Senier 16). This idea is possibly more radical than traditionalism, which yearns, perhaps impossibly, to reestablish a preinvasion lifeway. The strength of indigenous cultures has always been the capacity to adapt useful aspects of other lifeways into the practices of the moment—by which we don't have to mean assimilation. Carol Batker has written that native women journalists of the early twentieth century may have utilized dominant language practices, but they did so as part of "a complex negotiation between Native and non-Native practices that suggests cultural dynamism rather than cultural loss as a paradigm for assimilation" (qtd. in Senier 19).

Cultural dynamism. The part of "me" that is not "them" begs out of this discussion. How native nations decide to resolve the inherent conflicts between traditionalists and modernizers; and between the desire for sovereignty, and dependence on the U.S. government's trust obligation—is up to them.

What "we" (whites, blacks, yellows, browns, greens—in short, non-reds) need to do: seek ways to support those (life)ways. Get the hell *out* of the lifeway(s).

Thus, accountable, dynamic, self-determination. However that self is defined *by* that self.

To *my* "we," I have to ask: Cultural dynamism—a two-way (twenty-way) street? Might "we" have something to learn as well? Adaptations to perform?

Take the test put before you by Curtis Warner and Ward Churchill: Am I willing to give the land back to the people we conquered?

My own answer, I regret to say, is, Well, some of it. Which I'm sure does not satisfy Warner and Churchill. What does that make me?

While we're on the subject: "conquer"?
Naming is vitally important to our understanding of relations.

In their 1999 book *Tribes, Treaties, and Constitutional Tribulations*, Vine Deloria, Jr. and David E. Wilkins argue that the United States did not conquer native nations. Instead, they established and enjoyed a largely peaceful treaty relation with most of the peoples they encountered here.

Now, this may sound like the semantic splitting of hairs, but Deloria and Wilkins have a good point. So many U.S. citizens justify the encroachment on native sovereignty by arguing that *we conquered them*, and to the victor go the spoils.

But we have a treaty arrangement, which followed military struggle, with both Canada and Mexico, and our contemporary popular lexicon does not *tend* (yes, there are exceptions with regard to Mexico) to describe these nations as "conquered" by us. We do not regularly question the location of our borders with these nations. We squabble with them over immigration, we spat about such things as water rights, and we do work to assimilate them to our lifeways; but it has not occurred to us of late to try to manipulate them legally in order to confiscate more of their land or natural resources.

Deloria and Wilkins point out that (at least) two things threaten the sovereignty of native nations: the fact that their borders are surrounded on all sides by a predatory and far more powerful nation; and the fact that the citizens of that predatory nation routinely dismiss, in their discourse, the existence of that treated sovereignty in the first place.

History must choose its terms carefully, lest a lack of care result in a difference that degrades and endangers us.

And since we are not perptually assured of that care, we realize that we need a new kind of *reader* of history, one with the fortitude to consider the *terms* of the history she is given.

Among other things, we readers of history need a renewed patience. For instance, if you have read this far (a big *if* indeed) you probably best understand the terms of this different kind of investment: the active, critical, perhaps even frustrated reading required to get this damn book to pay off for you.

The punch line, I know, has been some time in coming. For which I do not apologize, even as I appreciate your hanging in there with me.

History must choose its terms carefully, lest a lack of care result in a difference that degrades and endangers us.

There is only one major assertion, one major vision, that Parry, Hansen, Madsen, Griffin and Warner all hold in common:

A national, cultural acceptance of the story of the Bear River Massacre will have the result of unifying the many, disparate peoples affected by this story.

Which is to say, collective action leading from the cultural acceptance of the story of the Bear River Massacre and Rape could lead to . . . redemption.

Can history really do that? Words? Networks?

As the people who live in Preston can tell you, history is place. In capitalism, place is property.

And as Curtis Warner and Ward Churchill would have it, property is parity. So, they say, the acquisition of equitable property results in the acquisition of equitable history.

Repeating: Timbimboo means "people who write on rocks." And I do find myself tempted to applaud this sort of monumentalizing.

But I support Gerda Lerner's assertion that the oppression of sexed and raced peoples was born of private property. I would go on to argue that part of what is wrong with history is—public property.

The National Park Service is a government agency that organizes our nationalist impulse to write on rocks. Once it is set in stone, then, we privilege those rock texts over our continuing community learning. In this way, place—public property—becomes part of the systemic impulse that would perpetuate oppression.

Remember the Almo Massacre!

Most of the historical monuments that exist in the United States are really monuments to our refusal to hear. Our refusal to be held accountable, to change.

Which is to say that, years after "we" (as a society) learned from Lerner that racism and sexism are the same killer storm, and years after we learned from Brownmiller that the intersection of racism and sexism is a violent meeting place—and around the same time that we decide to prosecute rape as a war crime—despite all this learning and at that same moment, we *still* propose to build yet another monument to a rigid, archaic prevarication: that rape has not been the inexorable partner of genocide.

We propose to take the private property, make it public property, and write upon this property the lie that *began* with property.

I'm not sure Churchill and Warner are right when they suggest that land equals parity. Equals sovereignty.

It *does*, I see, but only in the context of this capitalist society that values individuals and groups according to their landed assets.

Do Warner and Churchill really want to buttress that context by participating in it? Isn't there a still wider revolution to be fought here? Does writing on rocks—by a nation or by a people—detour our truth tours?

What can history do?

All I can do, is to *tell* about them, Helen Hunt Jackson writes.

Every time the story is told, something changes, Sherman Alexie writes.

Jackson's friend Ralph Waldo Emerson writes, "Speak what you think now in hard words and to-morrow speak what to-morrow thinks in hard words again, though it contradict every thing you said to-day" (981).

In 1985 Madsen felt he had evidence of 50 bodies left bleeding in the river, making the total dead 250; now he feels it was 80. This was plus some women. We've added a drowned child. Tomorrow it will be—?

History is not always in a place, or in the rocks. As Heraclitus said of life, history may be a river. It is a current of learning, of flux, of tides and floods and drought.

We happen to be cursed with interesting times. We live in a moment in the United States that is marked by a flood of learning, a flood of learning about learning, an uprooting of the stubborn verities we still call Departments of "English" and "History." Goes for the sciences too.

But even with all this learning, history still gathers its forces one raindrop at a time. History is for the babies, the children, the ones we were not forced to drown, who must learn not to drown, and how not to be drowned.

"Oblige me by not beginning," Gertrude Stein wrote. "Also by not ending" (*History* 185).

History begins and ends with the historian, and historians are the products of a culture that fails to acknowledge (among other things) the fact that process is an ongoing part of *any* product, and that the process is never complete.

If you have read this far, you know that this narrator of history "has issues." Yes. I am an easterner invading, once again, the West. I once and briefly lived in a Radical-Infested City. I am a feminist, a half-baked socialist, an atheist with little patience for religious groups that exploit the bodies of women. I am the westerner's worst nightmare: an easterner with an opinion.

Worse still, a white woman with a hobby. A busybody, variously "manly" and "sentimental."

This busybody language worker believes that it is now our duty not simply to build a better monument, but to see the monumental as the etymology of the word would suggest: as being a *monstrum*—from the Latin for "a divine omen or warning" (Ayto 353). Perhaps as a warning that our work is never done, that we must always revisit the place of that work.

There is no beginning, middle, or end to the Bear River Massacre and Rape. There is only today's effort to understand, to pursue the consciousness necessary for not repeating it. To pursue syncretism: the new "us." Where "us" is "them."

Melinda Dunford sees the place where her grandmother let her baby go, the place where her grandmother pushed her howling toddler out into a current of ice and blood. Dunford has heard her grandmother's story her whole life. But she has never seen the place. She is shown this place by a white woman, Allie Hansen.

She sees.

She puts her head on Hansen's breast, and two women cry.

I see. I see a *them*, for a brief moment.

Curtis Warner's father used to drive him to the Cache Valley from Montana. "This is the place."

Curtis saw.

Someday Curtis and Mallory Warner will bring Tyler here.

And Tyler will see. A *we*.

Will we see the we of them?

If you have read this far, I ask you: Will we monumentalize the Bear River Massacre *and* Rape? Will we build a National Historic Site, set a painful history in stone, and rest content that our work is done? Or will we build the site and tell it all in the river, let it flow, and—in the end that can never be an end—let tomorrow speak what tomorrow thinks?

AFTERWORD

As Arthur Schlesinger, Jr. recently put it (do we *really* need to know exactly where?), History is an argument without end—that's why it's so much fun. I learned this lesson from Mae Timbimboo Parry and Curtis Warner, who are distrustful of academia's tendency to squabble over the trees, while willfully neglecting the forest.

I do, however, accept full responsibility for failures in a good-faith intention to present What We (Now) (Think We) Know. Thus, an afterword on my methodology:

In chapter 2, the descriptions of the public hearings held in Preston and Fort Hall by the National Park Service in December 1995 are gleaned from notes taken at those events. My memories of experiences at Idaho State University are aided by journals, letters, and e-mails written at the time. Consequently, speeches and events represented in that chapter should be considered approximate transcriptions, rendered to the best of my ability; hence the absence of quotation marks.

The descriptions of historical sites in chapter 3 are based on my access to these sites during July 1998.

The five interviews in chapters 4 through 8 were all conducted during that same July. All of the interviews were tape-recorded. In composing most of these chapters, I again took the liberty of editing the natural repetitions expected in conversation; at times to regroup what was said along the lines of like subject matter; and occasionally, and only when doing so would not affect the spirit of the speech, to alter the syntax of the speeches to ease the work of the reader. Two of the interviews, however, I have presented in near entirety. In the case of Mae Timbimboo Parry, I have transcribed our conversation as a whole, and in its original order, so that the reader may judge my own responsibility for the awkwardness of that encounter. Also, I realized only after the fact that during my interview with Curtis Warner, I spoke much more frequently and freely than I typically do when interviewing. This may be attributed to the fact that we have known each other for some years; but it is also true (I must concede) that he was once my student, a relation that perhaps empowers me to interrupt and challenge him more frequently than I would, or should, have done with an interviewee. In composing that interview, I include for the reader some hint of my intervention in that conversation.

The conversations relayed in chapter 9 are re-created from e-mails, voice mails, and notes taken during telephone calls made in July 1998 and November 2002. I have represented these utterances as accurately as possible.

By raising the problem of the language practices typical of that discipline we call history, I have tried to account for a little-known, yet nonetheless pivotal, event in U.S. history. Theoretical problems are bound to surface once the telling *and* the teller are deemed vital to the tale, and I refer readers interested in pursuing this line of inquiry to the work of the New Historicists (see, e.g., Veeser, White); recent work in cultural, ethnic, and postcolonial studies, and cultural politics (see, e.g., Chow, Saldívar, Spivak, Tal); studies in cultural ethnography (see, e.g., Clifford and Marcus); and more imaginative approaches to historical, biographical and sociocultural incident (see, e.g., Alexie, Anzaldúa, Cha, Erdrich, Hogan, Howe, Kingston, Metcalf, Olson, Ortiz, Ridge, Rothenberg, Silko, Sukenick).

Any errors of comprehension or perception in the foregoing are, again, mine.

WORKS CITED AND CONSULTED

This list includes works cited in this book, as well as works I have encountered over the years that have helped shape my thinking about the issues I have addressed in this book. (For a more extensive bibliography of Native American literature, see Ruoff's invaluable compilation.)

Alexander, M. Jacqui, and Chandra Talpade Mohanty, eds. *Feminist Genealogies, Colonial Legacies, Democratic Futures.* New York: Routledge, 1997.

Alexie, Sherman. "Captivity." *Postmodern American Fiction.* Ed. Paula Geyh et al. New York: Norton, 1998. 342–45.

Allen, Paula Gunn, ed. *Spider Woman's Granddaughters: Traditional Tales and Contemporary Writing by Native American Women.* New York: Fawcett Columbine, 1989.

———. *Studies in American Indian Literature.* New York: MLA, 1983.

Allred, Janice. *God the Mother and Other Theological Essays.* Salt Lake City: Signature, 1997.

Alt, David D., and Donald W. Hyndman. *Roadside Geology of Idaho.* Missoula: Mountain P, 1989.

Anderson, Gary Clayton, and Alan R. Woolworth, eds. *Through Dakota Eyes: Narrative Accounts of the Minnesota Indian War of 1862.* St. Paul: Minnesota Historical Society, 1988.

Anzaldúa, Gloria. *Borderlands/La Frontera: The New Mestiza.* San Francisco: Aunt Lute, 1987.

Austin, Mary. *The Land of Little Rain.* New York: Houghton, 1903.

Ayto, John. *Dictionary of Word Origins.* New York: Arcade, 1990.

Bagley, Will. *Blood of the Prophets: Brigham Young and the Massacre at Mountain Meadows.* Norman: U Oklahoma P, 2002.

Bagley, Will, and Harold Schindler. *West from Fort Bridger: The Pioneering of the Immigrant Trails across Utah, 1846–1850.* Logan: Utah State UP, 1994.

Barry, Kathleen. *Susan B. Anthony: A Biography of a Singular Feminist.* New York: New York UP, 1988.

Barthes, Roland. *Mythologies*. Trans. Annette Lavers. New York: Hill, 1983.

Bartholomew, Rebecca, and Leonard J. Arrington. *Rescue of the 1856 Handcart Companies*. Rev. ed. Charles Redd Monographs in Western History Series No.11. Provo: Brigham Young U/Signature, 1993.

Beckett, Samuel. *The Unnameable*. New York: Grove, 1958.

Behn, Aphra. *Oroonoko, The Rover, and Other Works*. Ed. Janet Todd. New York: Penguin, 1992.

Belenky, Mary Field et al., eds. *Women's Ways of Knowing: The Development of Self, Voice, and Mind*. New York: Harper, 1986.

Bernstein, Charles. *A Poetics*. Cambridge: Harvard UP, 1992.

Bevacqua, Maria. *Rape on the Public Agenda: Feminism and the Politics of Sexual Assault*. Boston: Northeastern UP, 2000.

Bigler, David L. *Forgotten Kingdom: The Mormon Theocracy in the American West, 1847–1896*. Vol. 2 of *Kingdom in the West: The Mormons and the American Frontier*. Spokane: Clark, 1998.

Bird, Isabella L. *A Lady's Life in the Rocky Mountains*. Norman: U Oklahoma P, 1960.

Bloom, Howard. *The American Religion: The Emergence of the Post-Christian Nation*. New York: Simon, 1992.

Bolz, Diane M. "Rediscovering an Idaho Photographer." *Smithsonian* 26.11 (1996): 86–89.

Bordewich, Fergus M. *Killing the White Man's Indians: Reinventing Native Americans at the End of the Twentieth Century*. New York: Doubleday, 1996.

Bowling for Columbine. Written and dir. by Michael Moore. United Artists, Alliance Atlantis, and Dog Eat Dog Films, 2002.

Brafford, C. J., and Laine Thom. *Dancing Colors: Paths of Native American Women*. San Francisco: Chronicle, 1993.

Bringhurst, Newell G. "The Mormons and Slavery: A Closer Look." *Pacific Historical Review* 50.3 (1981): 329–38.

Brooks, Juanita. *The Mountain Meadows Massacre*. Norman: U of Oklahoma P, 1991.

Brown, Dee. *Bury My Heart at Wounded Knee: An Indian History of the American West*. New York: Holt, 1970.

Brownmiller, Susan. *Against Our Will: Men, Women, and Rape*. New York: Fawcett Columbine, 1975.

Buck, Claire, ed. *The Bloomsbury Guide to Women's Literature*. New York: Prentice, 1992.

Burnham, Michelle. "Between England and America: Captivity, Sympathy, and the Sentimental Novel." *Cultural Institutions of the Novel*. Ed. Deidre Lynch and William B. Warner. Durham: Duke UP, 1996. 47–72.

Buscombe, Edward, ed. *The BFI Companion to the Western*. New York: Atheneum, 1988.

Cameron, Deborah. *Feminism and Liguistic Theory*. 2nd ed. London: Macmillan, 1992.

Carley, Kenneth. *The Sioux Uprising of 1862*. St. Paul: Minnesota Historical Society, 1976.

Carter, Lyndia McDowell. "The Mormon Handcart Companies." *Overland Journal* 13.1 (1995): 2–18.

Certeau, Michel de. *The Practice of Everyday Life*. Berkeley: U California P, 1984.

Cha, Theresa Hak Young. *Dictée*. 1982. Berkeley: Third Woman P, 1995.

Chambers-Schiller, Lee Virginia. *Liberty, a Better Husband: Single Women in America: The Generations of 1780–1840*. New Haven: Yale UP, 1984.

Chow, Rey. *Ethics after Idealism: Theory, Culture, Ethnicity, Reading*. Bloomington: Indiana UP, 1998.

Christensen, Scott R. *Sagwitch: Shoshone Chieftain, Mormon Elder, 1822–1887*. Logan: Utah State UP, 1999.

Churchill, Ward. *Fantasies of the Master Race: Literature, Cinema, and the Colonization of American Indians*. San Francisco: City Lights, 1998.

———. *From a Native Son: Selected Essays on Indigenism, 1985–1995*. Boston: South End P, 1996.

Cleaver, Eldridge. *Soul on Ice*. With an introduction by Maxwell Geismar. New York: McGraw, 1968.

Clifford, James, and George E. Marcus, eds. *Writing Culture: The Poetics and Politics of Ethnography*. Berkeley: U of California P, 1986.

Coleman, Ronald G. "Utah's Black Pioneers: 1847–1869." *Umoja: A Scholarly Journal of Black Studies* 2.2 (1979): 95–110.

Collins, Patricia Hill. *Black Feminist Thought: Knowledge, Consciousness, and the Politics of Empowerment*. New York: Routledge, 1991.

Convis, Charles L. *Native Women: True Tales of the Old West*. Carson City: Pioneer P, 1996.

Crow Dog, Mary, and Richard Erdoes. *Lakota Woman*. New York: Grove Weidenfeld, 1990.

Crum, Beverly, and Jon P. Dayley. *Western Shoshoni Grammar*. Occasional Papers and Monographs in Cultural Anthropology and Linguistics. Vol. 1. Boise: Boise State U, 1993.

Cuch, Forrest S., ed. *A History of Utah's American Indians*. Salt Lake City: Utah State Division of Indian Affairs/Utah State UP, 2000.

Davis, Rebecca Harding. *Life in the Iron Mills*. Ed. Cecelia Tichi. Boston: Bedford, 1998.

Deloria, Philip J. *Playing Indian*. New Haven: Yale UP, 1998.

Deloria, Vine, Jr. *Custer Died for Your Sins: An Indian Manifesto*. New York: Avon, 1969.

———. *Of Utmost Good Faith*. San Francisco: Straight Arrow, 1971.

Deloria, Vine, Jr., and David E. Wilkins. *Tribes, Treaties, and Constitutional Tribulations*. Austin: U of Texas P, 1999.

Denton, Sally. *American Massacre: The Tragedy at Mountain Meadows, September 1857*. New York: Knopf, 2003.

Derig, Betty. *A Roadside History of Idaho*. Missoula: Mountain P, 1996.

Derrida, Jacques. *Dissemination*. Trans. Barbara Johnson. London: Athlone P., 1981.

Dorn, Edward. *The Shoshoneans: The People of the Basin-Plateau*. New York: Morrow, 1966.

Doubiago, Sharon. *Hard Country*. Albuquerque: West End P, 1999.

Douglas, Christopher. "'You Have Unleashed a Horde of Barbarians!': Fighting Indians, Playing Games, Forming Disciplines." *Postmodern Culture* 13.1 (2002). 4 Dec. 2002. <http://muse.jhu.edu/journals/pmc/v013/13.1douglas.html>.

Eicher, David J. *The Longest Night: A Military History of the Civil War.* New York: Simon, 2001.

Emerson, Ralph Waldo. "Self-Reliance." *American Literature: Tradition and Innovation.* Vol. 2. Ed. Harrison T. Meserole, Walter Sutton, and Brom Weber. Lexington: Heath, 1974. 976–94.

Emoff, Ron, and David Henderson, eds. *Mementos, Artifacts, and Hallucinations from the Ethnographer's Tent.* New York: Routledge, 2002.

Epstein, Jason E. *Book Business: Publishing Past, Present, and Future.* New York: Norton, 2001.

Erdoes, Richard, and Alfonzo Ortiz, eds. *American Indian Myths and Legends.* New York: Pantheon, 1984.

Erdrich, Louise. *Love Medicine.* New York: Bantam, 1984.

Estrich, Susan. *Real Rape.* Cambridge: Harvard UP, 1987.

Etienne, Mona, and Eleanor Peacock, eds. *Women and Colonization: Anthropological Perspectives.* New York: Praeger, 1980.

Faragher, John Mack. *Men and Women on the Overland Trail.* New Haven: Yale UP, 1979.

Fausto-Sterling, Anne. *Sexing the Body: Gender Politics and the Construction of Sexuality.* New York: Basic, 2000.

Federman, Raymond. *Critifiction: Postmodern Essays.* Albany: State U of New York P, 1993.

Feyerabend, Paul. *Against Method: Outline of an Anarchistic Theory of Knowledge.* London: Verso, 1978.

Fletcher, Alice Cunningham, with Francis LaFlesche. *The Omaha Tribe.* 1911. New York: Johnson Reprint, 1970.

Foster, Hal. *The Anti-Aesthetic.* Port Townsend: Bay P, 1983.

Foucault, Michel. *The Archaeology of Knowledge and the Discourse on Language.* Trans. A. M. Sheridan Smith. New York: Pantheon, 1972.

———. *Discipline and Punish: The Birth of the Prison.* Trans. Alan Sheridan. New York: Vintage, 1977.

Frazier, Ian. *On the Rez.* New York: Farrar, 1999.

Friends of the Native Americans of Northern Utah, The. *Bear River Massacre.* 2 Feb. 2002. <http://www.genealogical-institute.com/bear_river_massacre.htm>.

Frost, Robert. "Mowing." *Robert Frost's Poems.* With an introduction and commentary by Louis Untermeyer. New York: Washington Square, 1971. 91.

Fukuyama, Francis. *The End of History and the Last Man.* New York: Free P, 1992.

Fuller, George W. *A History of the Pacific Northwest.* New York: Knopf, 1931.

Gates, Henry Louis, Jr. *The Signifying Monkey: A Theory of African-American Literary Criticism.* New York: Oxford UP, 1989.

Gellhorn, Martha. *The Face of War.* New York: Atlantic Monthly P, 1988.

Godfrey, Kenneth W. et al., eds. *Women's Voices: An Untold History of the Latter-day Saints, 1830–1900.* Salt Lake City: Deseret, 1982.

Gouldner, Alvin. *The Future of Intellectuals and the Rise of the New Class.* New York: Seabury P, 1979.

Grafton, Anthony. *The Footnote: A Curious History.* Rev. ed. Cambridge: Harvard UP, 1997.

Greenblatt, Stephen. "Racial Memory and Literary History." *PMLA* 116.1 (2001): 48–63.

Griffin, Susan. *Rape: The Politics of Consciousness*. San Francisco: Harper, 1986.

Griffith, Elizabeth. *In Her Own Right: The Life of Elizabeth Cady Stanton*. New York: Oxford UP, 1984.

Grun, Bernard. *The Timetables of History*. 3rd ed. New York: Simon, 1991.

Gutman, Roy, and David Rieff, eds. *Crimes of War: What the Public Should Know*. New York: Norton, 1999.

Hart, Newell. *The Bear River Massacre: Being a complete SourceBook and Story-Book of the Genocidal Action Against the Shoshones in 1863—and of Gen. P. E. Connor and how he related to and dealt with Indians and Mormons on the Western Frontier*. Preston: Cache Valley Newsletter, 1982.

Hartmann, Betsy. *Reproductive Rights and Wrongs: The Global Politics of Population Control*. Boston: South End P, 1995.

Hedrick, Joan D. *Harriet Beecher Stowe: A Life*. New York: Oxford UP, 1994.

Heinerman, John, and Anson Shupe. *The Mormon Corporate Empire*. Boston: Beacon P, 1985.

Hejinian, Lyn. *The Language of Inquiry*. Berkeley: U of California P, 2000.

Heywood, Leslie, and Jennifer Drake. *Third Wave Agenda: Being Feminist, Doing Feminism*. Minneapolis: U of Minnesota P, 1997.

Hill, Donna. *Joseph Smith: The First Mormon*. Salt Lake City: Signature, 1989.

Hill, George W. *Vocabulary of the Shoshone Language*. 1877. Pocatallo: Little Red Hen, 1986.

Hobgood, Mary. *Dismantling Privilege: An Ethics of Accountability*. Cleveland: Pilgrim, 2000.

Hogan, Linda. *Mean Spirit*. New York: Ivy, 1990.

Hoig, Stan. *The Sand Creek Massacre*. Norman: U of Oklahoma P, 1961.

hooks, bell. *Talking Back: Thinking Feminist, Thinking Black*. Boston: South End P, 1989.

Howe, Susan. *My Emily Dickinson*. Berkeley: North Atlantic Books, 1985.

Humm, Maggie, ed. *Modern Feminisms: Political, Literary, Cultural*. New York: Columbia UP, 1992.

Hunter Gray (né John R. Salter, Jr.). *Agitator at Large: Native Rights, Worker Rights, Civil Rights, Civil Liberties—And a Better World over the Mountain Yonder*. 15 Oct. 2000. <http://www.hunterbear.org>.

Huntington, Samuel P. *The Soldier and the State: The Theory and Politics of Civil-Military Relations*. New York: Vintage, 1957.

Hutcheon, Linda. *A Poetics of Postmodernism*. New York: Routledge, 1988.

Ignatiev, Noel, and John Garvey, eds. *Race Traitor*. New York: Routledge, 1996.

Incident at Oglala. Dir. Michael Apted. Narr. by Robert Redford. Carolco International N.V. and Spanish Fork, 1992.

Irigaray, Luce. *This Sex Which Is Not One*. Trans. Catherine Porter, with Carolyn Burke. Ithaca: Cornell UP, 1985.

Jackson, Helen Hunt. *A Century of Dishonor: The Early Crusade for Indian Reform*. 1881. Norman: U Oklahoma P, 1995.

———. *A Century of Dishonor: A Sketch of the United States' Dealings with Some of the Indian Tribes*. Ed. Andrew F. Rolle. New York: Harper, 1965.

———. *Poems.* New York: Arno P, 1972.

———. *Ramona: A Story.* New York: NAL/Dutton (Signet), 1988.

Jeffrey, Julie Roy. *Frontier Women: The Trans-Mississippi West, 1840–1880.* New York: Hill, 1979.

Keller, Robert H., and Michael F. Turek. *American Indians and National Parks.* Tucson: U of Arizona P, 1998.

Kenner, Hugh. *The Pound Era.* Berkeley: U of California P, 1973.

Kimball, Stanley B. *Historic Sites and Markers along the Mormon and Other Great Western Trails.* Urbana: U of Illinois P, 1988.

Kingston, Maxine Hong. *Hawai'i One Summer.* Honolulu: U of Hawai'i P, 1998.

Klein, Laura F., and Lillian A. Ackerman. *Women and Power in Native North America.* Norman: Oklahoma UP, 1995.

Kleinberg, S. J. *Women in the United States: 1830–1945.* New Brunswick: Rutgers UP, 1999.

Knack, Martha C. *Life Is with People: Household Organization of the Contemporary Southern Paiute Indians.* Anthropological Papers No. 19. Socorro, NM: Ballena P, 1980.

Knight, Hal, and Dr. Stanley B. Kimball. *111 Days to Zion: The Day-by-Day Trek of the Mormon Pioneers.* Salt Lake City: Big Moon Traders, 1997.

Kristeva, Julia. *Desire in Language: A Semiotic Approach to Literature.* Ed. Leon S. Roudiez. Trans. Thomas Gora, Alice Jardine, and Leon S. Roudiez. New York: Columbia UP, 1980.

Kroeber, Theodora. *Ishi: Last of His Tribe.* Drawings by Ruth Robbins. Berkeley: Parnassus P, 1964.

Laake, Deborah. *Secret Ceremonies: A Mormon Woman's Intimate Diary of Marriage and Beyond.* New York: Morrow, 1993.

Leacock, Eleanor. *Myths of Male Dominance.* New York: Monthly Review P, 1981.

Leonard, Elizabeth D. *Yankee Women: Gender Battles in the Civil War.* New York: Norton, 1994.

Leonard Peltier Defense Committee. 16 Oct. 2000. <http: www.lpsg-co.org>.

Lerner, Gerda, ed. *Black Women in White America: A Documentary History.* New York: Random, 1972.

———. *The Creation of Patriarchy.* New York: Oxford UP, 1986.

———. *The Grimke Sisters from South Carolina: Rebels against Slavery.* Boston: Houghton, 1967.

LeSueur, Stephen C. *The 1838 Mormon War in Missouri.* Columbia: U of Missouri P, 1987.

Lévi-Strauss, Claude. *Structural Anthropology.* Trans. C. Jacobsen and B. G. Schoef. 1967. Chicago: U of Chicago P, 1983.

Limerick, Patricia Nelson. *The Legacy of Conquest: The Unbroken Past of the American West.* New York: Norton, 1987.

———. *Something in the Soil: Legacies and Reckonings in the New West.* New York: Norton, 2000.

Limerick, Patricia Nelson, and Drex Brooks. *Sweet Medicine: Sites of Indian Massacres, Battlefields, and Treaties.* Albuquerque: U of New Mexico P, 1995.

Loewen, James W. *Lies My Teacher Told Me: Everything Your American History Textbook Got Wrong.* New York: New P, 1995.

Madigan, Tim. *The Burning: Massacre, Destruction, and the Tulsa Race Riot of 1921*. New York: Dunne /St. Martin's P, 2001.

Madsen, Brigham D. *Against the Grain: Memoirs of a Western Historian*. Salt Lake City: Signature, 1998.

———. *Glory Hunter: A Biography of Patrick Edward Connor*. Salt Lake City: U of Utah P, 1990.

———. *The Northern Shoshoni*. Caldwell, ID: Caxton, 1980.

———. *The Shoshoni Frontier and the Bear River Massacre*. Salt Lake City: U of Utah P, 1985.

Magic Box, The. Screenplay by Ray Allister and Eric Ambler. Dir. John Boulding. Prod. Ronald Neame. Perf. Robert Donat, Margaret Johnson, Maria Schell, Renée Asherson, Richard Attenborough. British Lion Films/Mayer–Kingsley, 1951.

Mathes, Valerie Sherer. *Helen Hunt Jackson and Her Indian Reform Legacy*. Norman: U of Oklahoma P, 1997.

———. *The Indian Reform Letters of Helen Hunt Jackson, 1879-1885*. Norman: U of Oklahoma P, 1998.

Matthiessen, Peter. *In the Spirit of Crazy Horse*. New York: Penguin, 1992.

May, Antoinette. *The Annotated Ramona*. San Carlos, CA: Worldwide/Tetra, 1989.

McCall, Laura F. "Sacagawea: A Historical Enigma." *Ordinary Women, Extraordinary Lives: Women in American History*. Ed. Kriste Lindenmeyer. Wilmington: Scholarly Resources, 2000. 39–54.

McGeveran, Tom, and Rebecca Traister. "The Groves of Academe." *New York Observer*, 6 Jan, 2003: 1+. <http://www.observer.com/>.

McKnickle, D'Arcy. *The Surrounded*. Albuquerque: U of New Mexico P, 1936.

Menzies, Gavin. *1421: The Year China Discovered America*. New York: Morrow, 2003.

Meranto, Oneida J. "From Buckskin to Calico and Back Again: An Historical Interpretation of American Indian Feminism." Unpublished paper presented at the Front Range Feminist Scholars Colloquium, Denver, 20 October 2000.

Metcalf, Paul. *Collected Works*. 3 vols. Minneapolis: Coffee House P, 1996–97.

Mies, Maria. *Patriarchy as Accumulation on a World Scale: Women in the International Division of Labour*. London: Zed, 1986.

"Mormon Index." *Sunstone: Mormon Experience, Scholarship, Issues, and Art* (June 1998) 21:2.

Morrison, Toni. *Playing in the Dark: Whiteness and the Literary Imagination*. Cambridge: Harvard UP, 1992.

Mullen, Laura. *The Tales of Horror*. Berkeley: Kelsey St. P, 1999.

Muscio, Inga. *Cunt: A Declaration of Independence*. Seattle: Seal, 1998.

Namias, June. *White Captives: Gender and Ethnicity on the American Frontier*. Chapel Hill: U of North Carolina P, 1993.

Nichols, David A. *Lincoln and the Indians: Civil War Policy and Politics*. Columbia: U of Missouri P, 1978.

Olsen, Tillie. *Silences*. New York: Dell, 1978.

Olson, Charles. *Call Me Ishmael*. San Francisco: City Lights, 1947.

Ortiz, Simon. *From Sand Creek*. New York: Thunder's Mouth P, 1981.

Ostling, Richard N., and Joan K. Ostling. *Mormon America: The Power and the Promise*. San Francisco: Harper, 1999.

Patterson, Richard. *Butch Cassidy: A Biography.* Lincoln: U of Nebraska P, 1998.

Peltier, Leonard. *Prison Writings: My Life Is My Sun Dance.* Ed. Harvey Arden. New York: St. Martin's Griffin, 1999.

Penelope, Julia. *Speaking Freely: Unlearning the Lies of the Fathers' Tongues.* New York: Pergamon, 1990.

Perdue, Theda, ed. *Sifters: Native American Women's Lives.* Oxford: Oxford UP, 2001.

Peters, Virginia Bergman. *Women of the Earth Lodges.* North Haven, CT: Archon, 1995.

Postman, Neil, and Charles Weingartner. *Teaching as a Subversive Activity.* New York: Delta, 1969.

Powell, Allan Kent, ed. *Utah Historical Encyclopedia.* Salt Lake City: U of Utah P, 1994.

Razack, Sherene H. *Looking White People in the Eye: Gender, Race, and Culture in Courtrooms and Classrooms.* Toronto: U of Toronto P, 1998.

Remini, Robert V. *Andrew Jackson and His Indian Wars.* New York: Viking, 2001.

Reynolds, David S. *Walt Whitman's America: A Cultural Biography.* New York: Knopf, 1995.

Rich, Adrienne. *Of Woman Born: Motherhood As Experience and Institution.* New York: Norton, 1986.

———. *On Lies, Secrets, and Silence.* New York: Norton, 1979.

Rider, Bhanu Kapil. *The Vertical Interrogation of Strangers.* Berkeley: Kelsey St. P, 2001.

Ridge, John Rollin [Cheesquatalawny; Yellow Bird]. *The Life and Adventures of Joaquín Murieta, the Celebrated California Bandit.* 1854. Introd. Joseph Henry Jackson. Norman: U of Oklahoma P, 1977.

Rister, Carl Coke. *Comanche Bondage: Dr. John Charles Beale's Settlement of La Villa de Dolores on Las Moras Creek in Southern Texas of the 1830's with an Annotated Reprint of Sarah Ann Horn's Narrative of Her Captivity Among the Comanches.* Lincoln: U of Nebraska P, 1989.

Roberts, Chris. *Powwow Country.* Helena: American and World Geographic, 1992.

Rosewood. Screenplay by Gregory Poirier. Dir. John Singleton. Prod. Jon Peters. Perf. Ving Rhames, Jon Voight, Don Cheadle, Michael Rooker, Bruce McGill, and Esther Rolle. Warner Bros., 1997.

Rothenberg, Jerome, ed. *Technicians of the Sacred: A Range of Poetries from Africa, America, Asia, Europe, and Oceania.* 1968. 2nd. ed. Berkeley: U of California P, 1985.

Rothenberg, Paula S. *White Privilege: Essential Readings on the Other Side of Racism.* New York: Worth, 2002.

Rowlandson, Mary. *The Sovereignty and Goodness of God. With Related Documents.* Ed. Neal Salisbury. Boston: Bedford, 1997.

Ruoff, A. Lavonne Brown. *American Indian Literatures: An Introduction, Bibliographic Review, and Selected Bibliography.* New York: MLA, 1990.

Russ, Joanna. *How to Suppress Women's Writing.* Austin: U of Texas P, 1983.

Russell, Don. "How Many Indians Were Killed? White Man versus Red Man: The Facts and the Legend." *American West* 10.4 (1973): 42–47, 61–63.

Saldívar, José David. *Border Matters: Remapping American Cultural Studies.* Berkeley: U of California P, 1997.

Salter, John R., Jr. *Jackson, Mississippi.* Malabar, FL: Krieger, 1987.

Sanders, Edward. *America: A History in Verse*. Vol. 1, *1900–1939*. Santa Rosa, CA: Black Sparrow, 2000.

———. *America: A History in Verse*. Vol. 2, *1940–1961*. Santa Rosa, CA: Black Sparrow, 2000.

Sartwell, Crispin. *End of Story: Toward an Annihilation of Language and History*. Albany: State U of New York P, 2000.

Saussure, Ferdinand de. *Course in General Linguistics*. Trans. Roy Harris. LaSalle: Open Court, 1994.

Schiffrin, André. *The Business of Books*. New York: Verso, 2000.

Schindler, Harold. "The Bear River Massacre: New Historical Evidence." *Utah Historical Quarterly* 67.4 (1999): 300–08.

Schissel, Lillian. *Women's Diaries of the Westward Journey*. Ed. Gerda Lerner. New York: Schocken, 1982.

Seaver, James E. *The Life of Mrs. Mary Jemison*. New York: Corinth, 1961.

Sedgwick, Catherine Maria. *Hope Leslie; or, Early Times in the Massachusetts*. 1827. New York: Penguin, 1998.

Senier, Siobhan. *Voices of American Indian Assimilation and Resistance: Helen Hunt Jackson, Sarah Winnemucca, and Victoria Howard*. Norman: U of Oklahoma P, 2001.

Serres, Michel, with Bruno Latour. *Conversations on Science, Culture, and Time*. Trans. Roxanne Lapidus. Ann Arbor: U of Michigan P, 1995.

Sheler, Jeffrey. L. "The Church of Latter-day Saints Grows by Leaps and Bounds." *U.S. News and World Report*, 13 Nov. 2000: 59–65.

Shields, Steven L., "The Latter Day Saint Churches." *America's Alternative Religions*. Ed. Timothy Miller. Albany: State U of New York P, 1995. 47–59.

Silko, Leslie Marmon. *The Almanac of the Dead*. New York: Penguin, 1991.

———. *Ceremony*. New York: Penguin, 1977.

Silliman, Ron. *The New Sentence*. New York: Roof, 1989.

SLC Punk. Written and dir. by James Merendino. Perf. Matthew Lillard, Michael Goorjian, Annabeth Gish, Jennifer Lien, Christopher McDonald, Devon Sawa, Jason Segel, Summer Phoenix. Sony Pictures, 1999.

Smith, Joseph. *The Testimony of the Prophet Joseph Smith*. The Church of Jesus Christ of Latter-day Saints. 1 Nov. 2002. <http//:scriptures.lds.org/bm/jsphsmth>.

Smith, Sidonie. *Subjectivity, Identity, and the Body: Autobiographical Practices in the Twentieth Century*. Bloomington: Indian UP, 1993.

Spence, Mark David. *Dispossessing the Wilderness: Indian Removal and the Making of the National Parks*. New York: Oxford UP, 1999.

Spender, Dale. *Man Made Language*. 2nd ed. New York: Pandora, 1985.

———. *Mothers of the Novel*. London: Pandora, 1986.

Spivak, Gayatri Chakravorty. *A Critique of Postcolonial Reason: Toward a History of the Vanishing Present*. Cambridge: Harvard UP, 1999.

Stauffer, John. *The Black Hearts of Men: Radical Abolitionists and the Transformation of Race*. Cambridge: Harvard UP, 2002.

Stegner, Wallace. *Mormon Country*. New York: Bonanza, 1942.

Stein, Gertrude. *The Geographical History of America*. Baltimore: Johns Hopkins UP, 1936.

————. *How to Write.* 1931. Los Angeles: Sun and Moon, 1995.

Steinem, Gloria. *Moving beyond Words.* New York: Simon, 1994.

Stowe, Harriet Beecher. *Uncle Tom's Cabin, or, Life among the Lowly.* Ed. Ann Douglas. New York: Penguin, 1981.

Sukenick, Ronald. *In Form: Digressions on the Act of Fiction.* Carbondale: Southern Illinois UP, 1985.

————. *Mosaic Man.* Normal: FC2, 1999.

————. *Narralogues: Truth in Fiction.* Albany: State U of New York P, 2000.

Svaldi, David. *Sand Creek and the Rhetoric of Extermination: A Case Study in Indian–White Relations.* Lanham: UP of America, 1989.

Tal, Kali. *Worlds of Hurt: Reading the Literatures of Trauma.* Cambridge: Cambridge UP, 1996.

Tannen, Deborah. *You Just Don't Understand: Men and Women in Conversation.* New York: Ballantine, 1990.

Tedlock, Dennis. *The Spoken Word and the Work of Interpretation.* Conduct and Communication Ser. Philadelphia: U of Pennsylvania P, 1983.

Tompkins, Jane. "'Indians': Textualism, Morality, and the Problem of History." *Critical Inquiry* 13.1 (1986): 101–18.

Townley, John M. *The Overland Stage: A History and Guidebook.* Reno: Jamison Station P, 1994.

United States Department of the Interior, National Park Service. *Draft Special Resource Study and Environmental Assessment: Bear River Massacre Site.* Denver: Denver Service Center, 1995.

————. *Final Special Resource Study and Environmental Assessment: Bear River Massacre Site.* Denver: Denver Service Center, 1996.

United States Geological Services. "Columbia Plateau." 3 Jan. 2003. <http://vulcan. wr.usgs.gov/Volcanoes/ColumbiaPlateau/framework.html>.

Unruh, John David. *The Plains Across: The Overland Emigrants and the Trans-Mississippi West, 1840–1860.* Urbana: U of Illinois P, 1979.

Van Wagoner, Richard S. *Mormon Polygamy: A History.* Salt Lake City: Signature, 1989.

Veeser, H. Aram, ed. *The New Historicism.* New York: Routledge, 1989.

Vizenor, Gerald. *The Heirs of Columbus.* Hanover: UP of New England, 1991.

Volosinov, V. N. *Marxism and the Philosophy of Language.* Trans. Ladislav Matejka and I. R. Titunik. Cambridge: Harvard UP, 1973.

Wakefield, Sarah F. *Six Weeks in the Sioux Teepees: A Narrative of Indian Captivity.* Ed. June Namias. Norman: U of Oklahoma P, 1997.

Walker, Alice. *In Search of Our Mothers' Gardens.* New York: Harcourt, 1983.

————. *Living by the Word.* New York: Harcourt, 1988.

Walker, Deward E., Jr. *Indians of Idaho.* Moscow: U of Idaho P, 1978.

Watt, G. D., and J. V. Long, eds. *Journal of Discourses Delivered by Brigham Young, His Two Counsellors, the Twelve Apostles, and Others.* Vol. 10. London: Wells, 1865.

Watten, Barrett. *Bad History.* Berkeley: Atelos, 1998

Weatherford, Jack. *Indian Givers: How the Indians of the Americas Transformed the World.* New York: Fawcett Columbine, 1988.

Weaver, Jace. *That the People Might Live: Native American Literatures and Native American Community.* New York: Oxford UP, 1997.

Welch, James, with Paul Stekler. *Killing Custer: The Battle of the Little Bighorn and the Fate of the Plains Indians.* New York: Penguin, 1994.

Wells, Merle W. *Anti-Mormonism in Idaho, 1872–92.* Provo: Brigham Young UP, 1978.

Wheeler, Ross G. "Craters of the Moon: A Novel." Diss. Binghamton U, 1992.

White, Hayden. *The Content of the Form: Narrative Discourse and Historical Representation.* Baltimore: Johns Hopkins UP, 1987.

Whitman, Walt. "Song of Myself." *Leaves of Grass.* Ed. Harold W. Blodgett and Sculley Bradley. Comprehensive Reader's Ed. New York: Norton, 1973. 28–89.

Williams, Linda. *Playing the Race Card: Melodramas of Black and White from Uncle Tom to O. J. Simpson.* Princeton: Princeton UP, 2001.

Wilson, Gilbert L. *Waheenee: An Indian Girl's Story Told by Herself to Gilbert Wilson.* Lincoln: U of Nebraska P, 1981.

Winnemucca (Hopkins), Sarah. *Life among the Paiutes: Their Wrongs and Claims.* 1883. Reno: U of Nevada P, 1993.

Woods, Tim. *Beginning Postmodernism.* Manchester: Manchester UP, 1999.

Zinn, Howard. *A People's History of the United States: 1492–Present.* Rev. ed. New York: Harper, 1995.

INDEX